Economic Performance

Contributions to Economics

Albrecht Ritschl
Prices and Production
- Elements of a System - Theoretic Perspective -
1989. 159pp. Softcover DM 59,-
ISBN 3-7908-0429-0

Arnulf Grübler
The Rise and Fall of Infrastructures
- Dynamics of Evolution and Technological Change in Transport -
1990. 305pp. Softcover DM 85,-
ISBN 3-7908-0479-7

Peter R. Haiss
Cultural Influences on Strategic Planning
1990. 188pp. Softcover DM 65,-
ISBN 3-7908-0481-9

Manfred Kremer/Marion Weber (Eds.)
Transforming Economic Systems: The Case of Poland
1992. 179pp. Softcover DM 69,-
ISBN 3-7908-91415-3

Marcel F. van Marion
Liberal Trade and Japan
1993. 298pp. Softcover DM 90,-
ISBN 3-7908-0699-4

Michael Carlberg
Open Economy Dynamics
1993. 203 pp. Softcover DM 75,-
ISBN 3-7908-0708-7

Hans Schneeweiß/
Klaus F. Zimmermann (Eds.)
Studies in Applied Econometrics
1993. 238 pp. Softcover DM 85,-
ISBN 3-7908-0716-8

Gerhard Gehrig/Wladyslaw Welfe (Eds.)
Economies in Transition
1993. 292 pp. Softcover DM 90,-
ISBN 3-7908-0721-4

Alfred Franz/Carsten Stahmer (Eds)
Approaches to Environmental Accounting
1993. 542 pp. Softcover DM 178,-
ISBN 3-7908-0719-2

János Gács / Georg Winckler (Eds.)
International Trade and Restructuring in Eastern Europe
1994. 343 pp. Softcover DM 98,-
ISBN 3-7908-0759-1

Christoph M. Schneider
Research and Development Management: From the Soviet Union to Russia
1994. 253 pp. Softcover DM 85,-
ISBN 3-7908-0757-5

Valeria De Bonis
Stabilization Policy in an Exchange Rate Union
1994. 172 pp. Softcover DM 75,-
ISBN 3-7908-0789-3

Bernhard Böhm
Lionello F. Punzo (Eds.)

Economic Performance

A Look at Austria and Italy

With 83 Figures

Springer-Verlag Berlin Heidelberg GmbH

Series Editor
Werner A. Müller
Peter Schuster

Editors
Dr. Bernhard Böhm
University of Technology, Vienna
Institute of Econometrics, Operations Research
and Systems Theory
Argentinierstraße 8/119
A-1040 Vienna, Austria

Professor Lionello F. Punzo
University of Siena
Department of Political Economy
Piazza S. Francesco 7
I-53100 Siena, Italy

Printed with the financial support of the Österreichische Forschungsgemeinschaft, Vienna.

ISBN 978-3-7908-0811-7 ISBN 978-3-642-51170-7 (eBook)
DOI 10.1007/978-3-642-51170-7

Die Deutsche Bibliothek - CIP-Einheitsaufnahme
Economic performance: a look at Austria and Italy / Bernhard Böhm; Lionello F. Punzo (ed.). - Heidelberg: Physica-Verl., 1994
(Contributions to economics)

NE: Böhm, Bernhard [Hrsg.]

Ursprünglich erschienen bei Physica-Verlag Heidelberg 1994.

88/2202-5 4 3 2 1 0 – Printed on acid-free paper

Contents

Balance of Payments Problems

IV. Cross Country Mobility Issues

V. Macroeconomic Theory

Introduction

Bernhard Böhm[1] and Lionello F. Punzo[2]

[1]University of Technology, Vienna
[2]University of Siena

The unifying theme of all contributions in this volume is the comparison of the economic performance of two close neighbouring European countries, Italy and Austria. This comparison reflects on a variety of structural aspects, broadly defined, as they surfaced in a host of dynamic processes that took place in a period of dramatic changes in the overall economic environments. The contributions by Austrian as well as Italian researchers intend to analyse and interpret the observed historical facts from an overall, macro or aggregate economic level, but also in more detail, with a close look at structural issues and specific problem areas: the monetary sector, the balance of payments, the industrial sectors, and the labour markets. The changing economic structure of these two countries poses challenges from the perspective of economic methodology and the conduct of economic policy. Both aspects are covered in the volume.

Different relative sizes, degrees of international openness and of integration in Europe are alone important sources of differences in economic behaviours and corresponding policies. One needs only to add the differences in political history and traditions of social decision making, and recall that Austria and Italy are neighbours, with a fair number of similar problems, not the least the fact of sharing a future in a unified Europe, and the motivation for a joint research project emerges clearly. This has produced the papers published in this volume. Most of them "narrate a one country story". This "parallel architecture" of exposition seems to be appropriate for analyses either based on a macroeconomic outlook, or directed to focus on specific problems, like those of the balance of payments, monetary sectors, labour markets issues and the like. Strongly comparative evaluations, on the other hand, are offered, whenever an essay addressed issues bearing on a typical European perspective as, for instance, when the effects are discussed of co-ordinated policy measures devised for the promotion of innovation, or else the structural dynamics of industrial sectors in the two countries are contrasted. Given the large built-in complementarity between these two kinds of essays, and the duality offered by the two scenarios they deploy, the Mesoeconomics of sectors and industries and the Macroeconomics scenario, the reader will hopefully find sufficient material to form an opinion about the difference in national approaches to assess economic problems and in methods of attacking them.

Basically, all the research results presented in this volume can be to advantage, theoretically located and understood against one or another of the theoretical directions that have emerged in the more recent macroeconomic literature on growth and development. In fact, in an effort to rationalise the rapid sequence of often "new" events of the seventies and eighties, the relevant literature has tried a number of different directions, which can, however, be collected under two general headings, or "approaches". If one is characterised as exogenistic, by contrast its alternative is endogenistic.

It is fair to say that for most of the time span covered by the research reported hereafter, the exogenistic approach has been dominating. Its explanation of the dynamics of (basically all the developed economies in) the seventies is founded on their necessity to (passively) adjust to the swarms of domestic and/or external shocks that hit them at irregular time intervals. The analytic/interpretative model associated with this view, is characteristically expressed in terms of an aggregate macroeconomic structure, a feature which is partly inherited from the growth accounting literature on international comparisons of economic performances, but is shared with New Classical Macroeconomics. With the latter, the approach shares also the notion of a natural tendency of the economic system to rest on an isolated equilibrium (generically, a trend) which is robust, hence stable, to all random disturbances or shocks. Deviations from it are seen as the temporary shortcomings of stochastic disturbances.

Towards the middle of the eighties an alternative approach begins articulating itself in parallel to the still then dominant stochastic macro-modelling. To put differences in an extremist fashion, such "alternative" focuses upon the endogenous characteristics of a regional, national, or sectoral system (its design, the interplay between political and economic institutions on technical change and its relationship with the production structure, and the like). It privileges explanations of differences in performance across regions, countries, sectors and of the varieties of patterns of economic development that is based on internal mechanisms and induced dynamic processes. In place of the traditional macroeconomic, aggregative analysis of income and productivity, new work was started in this vein also in a more disaggregate (sometimes "micro", but on the whole more often in a sectoral, or "meso") analytical framework.

The version of the latter approach most popular in academic circles these days is associated with endogenous growth theory, which retains a formal aggregate setting together with the focus on equilibrium behaviours typical of the new classical macroeconomics. In such a framework, an exploration is proposed of the implications of increasing returns to scale linked with accumulation of capital productivity effects. The paper by Hanappi included in this collection supplies an example of a model for comparative simulation where the latter effect is emphasised. Endogenous growth theory makes a creative use of traditional tools and must be credited the ability of going beyond "mere" disequilibrium or adjustment dynamics. Its standard version, however, seems unable to account for that behavioural diversification within a given system, which appears to accompany the cumulation of positive feedback effects and increasing returns. Thus, it goes little beyond the boundaries of classical disequilibrium analysis, or it stops just where the analysis of structural dynamics begins.

A comparison of Austria and Italy suggests that the interpretative model based on the notion of an adjustment dynamics induced by exogenous shocks can be less useful than otherwise expected. At any rate, it is not the unique explanation. The same set of shocks, in fact, has hit the two economies during the two decades covered by this research project, but they definitely appear to have caused different dynamic reactions and long run "adjustments" at the structural levels in the two systems. A remarkable differentiation within each of the two economies and between them, emerges as a feature of their recent economic developments. And it is practically impossible to separate the share of such phenomena to be attributed to exogenous shocks, and that resulting from what can be called country's own specification of fundamentals. The papers by Seidel, Signorelli and Vercelli, and to some extent also the one by Breuss and Schebeck help to gain this insight. At the same time, the relevance of the unfolding of dynamic responses makes one recognise the loss of perspective and information which is the cost associated with abandoning altogether the disaggregate multidimensional framework for a purely aggregated one. The importance of geographical and sectoral diversity emerges as the manifestation of capabilities of re-organisation that an economy can and will fully exploit in bad economic times. This lies at the basis of its performance and therefore motivates the search for an complementary, disaggregate framework to reformulate the endogenistic approach. In the overall lesson drawn below, the two viewpoints must supplement each other and they are both represented in this volume.

Times of severe shocks, like the seventies and a large part of the eighties, are thus ideal laboratories to test for endogenous dynamics at a structural level. The role for the workings of "adjustment" or reactive behaviours in the actual dynamics of a given economic system therefore is not denied. These, however, represent steps in the discontinuous evolution of the fundamental structure. Testing for an endogenous interpretation means testing for the relevance of the interplay between system internal laws and the environment from which a variety of stimuli is received. Research based on a comparison of different countries over a common time interval is the best setting for a reconsideration of the actual economic dynamics from the point of view of the structural (in)stability therein reflected, bridging the gap between disequilibrium dynamics and the analysis of structural change.

The contributions to this volume have been grouped into five sections. The first part, *Macroeconomic Scenario*, presents the essential macroeconomic phenomena and fundamental economic policy positions of Austria and Italy. H. Seidel offers a view of the "Economic Miracle" that Austria experienced in a survey of its macroeconomic performance, the special features of its economic policy and its expected future problems. The Italian counterpart is provided by the paper of M. Signorelli and A. Vercelli who focus on the sources of instability typical of advanced industrial countries and apply their insights to the development of the Italian economy. European perspectives are the common ground for future development of both economies. F. Breuss and F. Schebeck provide a synthetic view of both countries in relation to their European future and give estimates of the potential economic gains from participating in a completed internal European market.

The second section is devoted to the discussion of *Structural Dynamics and Industrial Policy*. In our own contribution we attempt to propose a new approach to deal with structural change, and experiment with time series of the two countries. Starting from questions raised above and using system theoretic concepts we develop an empirically relevant classification of the dynamic morphology which is then applied to temporal, sectoral, and regional dimensions of the two countries. The paper by Hanappi, as mentioned before, investigates endogenous technical change in simulation models from an aggregate point of view. In a third contribution to this section, H. Leo comments evidence about the technological position of Austria and complements our study with respect to Austrian industrial policy prospects.

A Perspective on Monetary Policy and the Balance of Payments is given in the third part of this book. One group of papers is devoted to issues related with the central bank policy, both in the international as well as in the domestic sphere. The two essays of M. de Cecco are concerned with the evolution of the European monetary arrangements. While the first paper centres on the discussion of the features of the European System of Central Banks, the second contemplates the prospects of the European Monetary Union in view of recent political events. E. Hochreiter reports on the Austrian experience of independence of its central bank and the way monetary policy is conducted. These papers provoke a set of reflections by F. Farina which expand on the effects of the German unification on the co-operation between central banks during the process towards the European Monetary Union. The balance of payments subsection contains two papers, each on one country, which pinpoint the relevant factors determining structure and evolution of the country's balance of payments. For Italy, C. Bianchi addresses the problem of determining the relevant external constraint with reference to a theoretical framework and contrasts the theoretical implications with performance actually observed. D. Proske attempts to show, by complementing a decomposed absorption approach with an elasticity approach, that weak domestic demand in Austria was mainly responsible for the improved performance of its current account in the eighties. Differences in the relative position of the two countries in Europe will be apparent from reading these papers, thus shedding some light on problems that will likely be associated in the future with an intensified integration.

A separate section on *Cross Country Mobility Issues* points at recent hot problems of labour markets. In Italy the traditional dualistic tendencies are considered responsible for the determination of labour supply trends. The contribution of G. Baffi and P. Piacentini presents an exercise in extrapolating labour supply trends to the turn of the millennium and draws implications for future developments and consequences on "dualism". In a small, internationally exposed economy like Austria, the recent wave of immigration hitting Western Europe since the fall of the "iron curtain" has raised concern about earnings and employment levels for the resident population. K. Pichelmann and M. Schamschule report on a simulation study of the effects for the Austrian economy of a rapid increase in foreign labour supply. Institutional and legal conditions for foreign employment are reviewed and the quantitative impact of the labour supply shock assessed.

A final section on *Macroeconomic Theory* brings us back to themes mentioned at the beginning of this introduction. Contrasting with the other dominantly empirical papers in this volume, H. Frisch and F. X. Hof have engaged in a theoretical examination of the effects of shocks on a model economy. Their analysis is a relevant addition to this volume, contributing to the theoretical understanding of inflationary shocks of imported materials under alternative institutional wage setting behaviours. (The paper is reprinted here from *Economic Notes* with permission as their research has been provoking stimulus during the implementation of this joint research project.)

We have, finally, to thank the Consiglio Nazionale delle Ricerche in Rome for financial support of the Italian colleagues (Contracts nos. 87.01206.10 and 88.03105.10) and the workshop held in Siena. We are grateful to the Österreichische Postsparkasse and the Institute for Advanced Studies in Vienna for supporting a workshop in Vienna, and the Österreichische Forschungsgemeinschaft for financially supporting this publication. The editors have also to thank Mr. Abdur Rahman and Mrs. Anna Luptacik for their editorial assistance, and have to acknowledge generous help from a number of referees who have contributed to make this volume possible.

I. Macroeconomic Scenario

The "Economic Miracle" of Austria

Hans Seidel

Institute for Advanced Studies (1984-1991) and
Austrian Institute for Economic Research

Introduction

The following overview of the Austrian economy is organised in three sections:

- part one presents the stylised facts of macro-economic performance;
- part two describes some specific features of economic policy;
- part three sketches a few economic problems which Austria has to face in the future.

The study covers the last four decades, starting from the beginning of the 50s.[1] At that time the Austrian economy had returned to - what might be called - "normal peace-time" conditions. The Marshall-Plan was terminated, productivity had surpassed pre-war level, and post-war inflation was brought under control.

1 Macro-economic performance

1.1 Economic growth

Convergence

Modern growth theory focuses on the question whether and how fast poor countries are able to catch up with rich ones[2]. The empirical evidence is mixed. Considering both developed and developing countries growth rates do not seem to be systematically (negatively) correlated with the level of GDP per head (measured at purchasing power

---

1 It would be tempting to include the reconstruction period proper, since economist nowadays are rather sceptical about the effects of the Marshall-Plan for the economic reconstruction of Europe (see e.g. Eichengreen/Uzan,1992). This, however, cannot be achieved in a short paper.

2 In the last couple of years a few articles on the "empirics of economic growth" were published. This paper relies heavily on Barro/Sala-i-Martin (1992)

parities). There are, however, clear cases of convergence. Japan and some NIC in South-East-Asia are notable examples for countries with strong catch-up effects. In the post-war Europe countries with heavy war damages (especially West Germany) regained (or nearly regained) its previous position. Between the early 50s and 1990 the gap in per capita income between the USA and a group of European countries (Germany, France, Italy, Finland, Norway) was reduced at a rate of 3% p.a. Austria belongs to this group; its rate of conversion (3,3% p.a.) was even slightly higher.

In 1950 Austria was economically a laggard. Its GDP per head at PPP reached only two thirds of that of the OECD countries as whole and less than 40% of that of the USA. The people and the economic policy makers in Austria did not put up with this state of affairs[3]. Getting as productive as the advanced countries in Europe became a widely accepted slogan. Many economic policy measures (e.g. investment promotion) were designed to achieve this goal. The Council of Economic and Social Affairs pleaded for growth strategies even in the middle of the 80s when concern for the environment was mushrooming. Social peace (there are practically no strikes in Austria) could be maintained, because the representatives of business and labour felt that it is wiser to cooperate in order to increase productivity rather than to fight over the distribution of income.

At the beginning of the 90s the gap vis-à-vis the OECD area was approximately closed. Compared with OECD Europe GDP per head at PPP ($1990) was 15% higher. If Austria joins the EU it will be a net contributor.

Table 1: GDP per head at purchasing power parities ($-1990)

	Germany	OECD total Austria=100	OECD Europe
1950	118,00	154,00	119,00
1960	127,73	119,95	94,23
1970	122,38	117,17	92,47
1980	111,43	103,29	86,69
1990	110,28	103,60	85,00

3 Experts from Eastern Europe countries often doubt that the catch-up of the Western European countries after World War II can be repeated by the countries formerly under commmunist rule under the present circumstances. To counteract the wave of pessimism appears to be a major task of a program for transition.

Middle rank

Austria now belongs to a fairly broad group with a medium position on the income scale of the industrialised world. Within the range of plus or minus 5% of the Austrian level fall 10 European countries. The ranking within this group depends on the cyclical position, on statistical procedures (e.g. the coverage of illegal transactions, the selection of goods and their weights in purchasing power comparisons) and on other factors not relevant for the stage of economic development.

Varying growth differentials

The growth differentials between Austria and the group of OECD countries were not always positive. Periods of strong relative growth (the 50s, beginning of the 70s and end of the 80s) were followed by periods of sluggish growth (most of the 60s, middle of the 80s). It goes without reasoning that the catch-up process in the 50s mainly reflects the successful reconstruction of the economy after World War II (In this decade the economy of West-Germany grew even faster, partly because its stabilisation crisis was already in the late 40s). The Austrian "economic miracle", however, was not contained to the reconstruction period proper. It continued later on, albeit on a much slower and somewhat uneven pace. What made the Austrian growth record persistent, has not yet been analysed thoroughly. Anecdotal evidence suggests that three, not necessarily exclusive factors were especially relevant:

- European economic integration
- the rate of investment
- structural adjustment

European integration

European economic integration started in the wake of World War II with the gradual dismantling of import barriers under the surveillance of the OEEC (while discriminating against the superior competition of producers from the USA). Therefore, reconstruction after World War II started with the vision of a large European market. Economic growth in Austria for a long time was led by exports. This was especially important for a small country which could only exploit economies of scale by exporting a large part of its production (and which had suffered severely from the economic disintegration in the Danube region in the interwar period).

Chart 1: Growth differential Austria/OECD-Europe

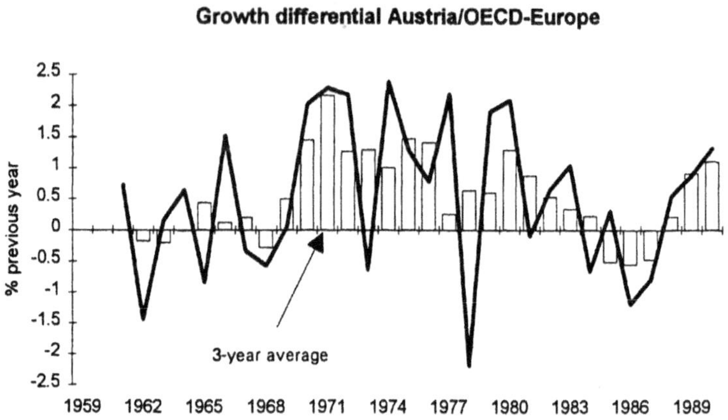

In the 60s, the establishment of the Common Market - in which Austria for political reasons could not participate - gradually discriminated domestic producers on its main external market. This was especially detrimental since at that time Austrian exports consisted to a large part of basic products with high shipment costs, such as timber, paper, magnesite, iron and steel. It was not until 1972 that the Free Trade Treaty with the EC removed the trade barriers for industrial products. Austria then got approximately (with the exception of origin rules) the same access to the EC market as member countries.[4]

High rate of investment

The Austrian economy used to be a hefty investor. The rate of gross investment rose continuously in the post-war period to a peak of 29% in 1972. Since the labour force remained approximately constant, capital per worker increased rapidly. The marginal productivity of capital was high (as indicted by the inverse of the incremental capital-output ratio.) Technical progress to a large part was brought about by buying up-to-date machinery from abroad and by foreign direct investment.

4 F.Breuss (1992,p.23) estimated the dynamic effects of EC on the Austrian growth rate at minus 0,12% p.a. in 1960/72 and plus 0,24% p.a. in 1973/91.

Chart 2: Marginal productivity of capital and the rate of investment

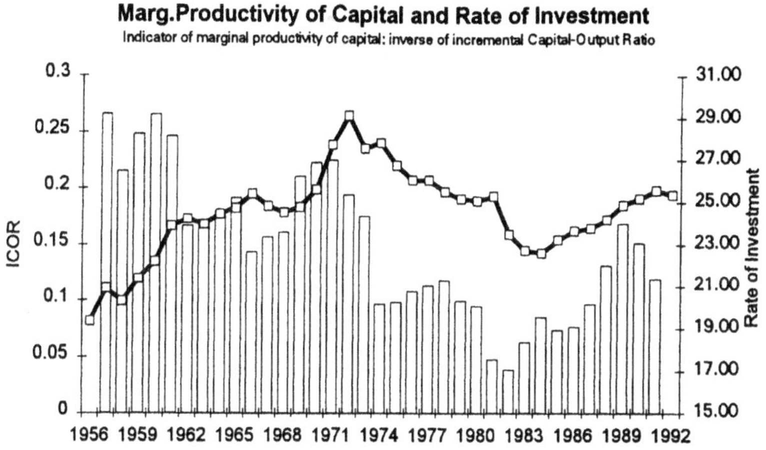

After 1973 the rate of investment declined to an average of 25%, but it has remained above the European level. Since private savings continued to flow at an almost constant rate, budgets deficits of the Federal Government filled (at least statistically) the saving/investment gap. At the same time the marginal productivity of capital diminished, probably somewhat faster than in the OECD area as a whole. Various factors contributed to the decline. In the 70s capital was substituted for energy. In the 80s a growing part of investment was devoted to environmental protection. The stock of productive capital was less fully used than before 1973. Finally, some experts claim that the Austrian economy invests too much in physical capital and too little in human capital. Austria spends less for R&D than other developed small countries. Given the present high level of income it is not sufficient to apply the existing techniques. Austria should search more actively for product and process innovations.

Structural adjustments

The structure of the economy cannot (or for social reasons is not allowed to) adjust smoothly to changing conditions at home and abroad. During adjustment periods economic growth falters, after successful "supply side" measures the economy is booming again. Most of the 60s can be identified as an adjustment period. The product mix had to be shifted from the needs of the reconstruction period to those of a "normal" growing economy, the highly protected industry had to face increasing foreign competition at the home market, and - as was already mentioned - the establishment of the Common Market discriminated Austrian exports on its main foreign markets. In a similar way the 80s may be labelled as an adjustment period. In the 70s - as some critics put it - structural deficiencies were swamped by demand management. The most prominent example provided the nationalised industries. They postponed necessary adjustments in the 70s, and, consequently, had to undergo a major restructuring in the 80s - with limited success as we know at present.

Nationalised industries

At this point a few words about state ownership seems to be appropriate. In Austria already at the beginning of the century most "public utilities" such as railways, urban traffic facilities, gas, water and electricity providing companies were owned by the communities, the provinces and the central government. Industry was private until the end of World War II (socialisation plans after World War I were not carried out). It was not before 1946 when nationalisation of industrial firms with a share of 20 -25% in total industry was enacted. From that point on Austria was the country with the highest share of public ownership in the business sector among the OECD countries.

Nationalisation in 1946 at that time was regarded as a pragmatic solution of ownership problems. The firms concerned, as a consequence of war and post-war events, were left without private owners. At that time a global "take-over" by the State seemed to offer a convenient way out. Privatisation techniques which have become familiar recently in the countries formerly under communist rule, were not discussed or were politically unacceptable. Economic reconstruction after World War II was exclusively financed by retained profits, bank credits and ERP counterpart funds. The bond market was developed much later, and the stock market is still underdeveloped.

The nationalised industries which mainly produce basic products such as iron and steel, aluminium and petroleum as well as some investment goods were quite successful in the decades of unprecedented growth after World War II. Their problems started in the 70s when economic growth (and therefore the demand for basis products) faltered. The nationalised firms were not permitted to dismiss workers in loss making plants until suitable new job opportunities were created. When subsidies soared in the first half of the 80s industrial policy had to be changed fundamentally. For some time the reconstruction of the nationalised industries seemed to be successful. However, in the recession 1993 big losses occurred again.

1.2 Price stability

The Austrians were not always as much concerned about inflation as their German neighbours. That is amply demonstrated by the fact that, at present, one DM (Deutsch Mark) buys seven AS (Austrian Schilling), whereas in 1945 one Mark was converted to one Schilling. Most of the devaluation of the AS in terms of DM occurred in the post-war period.

The post-war inflation was stopped at the end of 1951, nearly 4 years later than in West-Germany. From hindsight, and considering the experiences of Latin American countries and of Eastern European countries with anti-inflationary policies later on, the Austrian price-stabilisation program was well designed (a mixture of cost stabilisation and demand constrains) and well timed (at the end of the Korea boom). It achieved its goal with only a temporary setback of production and employment (of about one year). In contrast to stabilisation outcomes elsewhere, the Austrian economy was not trapped in a "bad expectational equilibrium" (economists at that time did not even know that such a thing exists). After 1952 the price level was not absolute stable. A creeping inflation repeatedly provoked anti-inflationary steps. In 1957 the Price-Wage-Commission (see p.26) was set up, because it was felt that institutional changes were necessary in order to contain cost pressures. However, until the end of the 60s the average rate of inflation remained moderate (3½% p.a.) and in line with the overall inflation rate of the OECD area.

The shocks of the seventies

In the first half of the seventies a series of shocks upset the world economy: the end of Bretton-Woods system, the hausse in the markets for raw materials, the economic consequences of the Vietnam war, the breakdown of traditional wage behaviour, and last not least the first oil price shock. National policy makers were faced with the difficult decision whether they should accommodate the shocks or lean against the wind. The industrial world became divided in countries with soft currencies and those with hard currencies. Domestic inflation followed more or less the exchange rate regime although in some cases for prolonged periods exchange rates over- or undershooted purchasing power parities. In the whole OECD area the average rate of inflation accelerated from 3,5% in the 60s to 9,4% in the 70s; the standard deviation (17 OECD countries) widened from 1 %-points to 3%-points.

Table 2: Price inflation (consumer prices; % change p.a.)

	Austria	OECD total	OECD-Europe	Standard deviation*)
1960/70	3,58	3,50	3,93	1,01
1970/80	6,29	9,37	11,03	3,03
1980/90	3,51	5,67	7,63	3,88

*) 17 OECD countries

In the early seventies it was an open question if Austria could qualify for the group of countries with low inflation rates and appreciating exchange rates. The effective devaluation of the AS in 1969 and the hausse in raw materials led to imported inflation while the upsurge of demand accelerated the pass-through in the domestic economy. A period of relatively high and accelerating inflation began which reached its climax in 1974 as a result of OPEC I. The inflation at the consumer price level jumped from 3,5% in 1969 to 9,4% in 1974, the average wage increased from 8,0% to 13,4%. Especially disturbing was the fact that in Austria consumer prices rose much faster than in West-Germany[5].

Stabilisation through a hard currency

The roots for containing inflation were laid by the exchange rate policy. Since the beginning of the 70s until 1977 the effective rate of the AS increased both in nominal and in real terms. To put it very simple and somewhat provocative: Austria opted externally for a hard currency, but for quite some time tolerated internally a soft currency. Even taking into account that in 1970 Austria was in a comfortable external position, this process has to be stopped or even reversed. It was essential for the success of this unconventional strategy that the trade unions accept the lead of the exchange rate and adjust their wage claims accordingly.

[5] Another gap between inflation rates in Austria and in Germany, although on a much smaller scale, developed at the beginning of the 80ies when West-Germany tighened its fiscal policy.

Chart 3: Inflation in West-Germany and in Austria

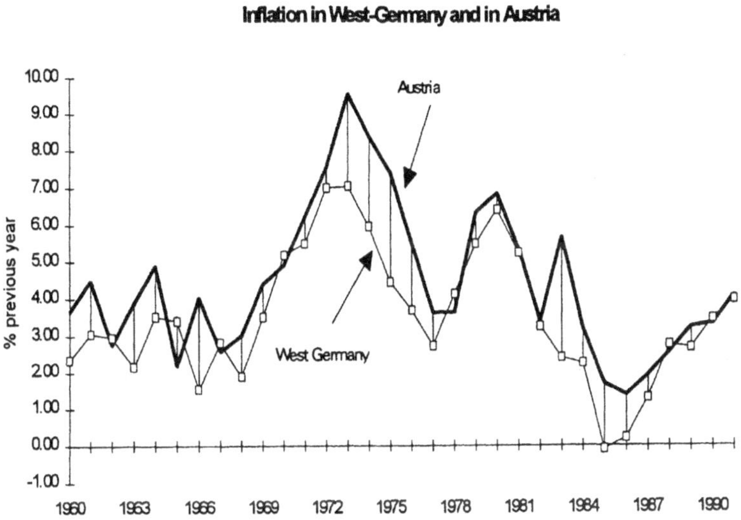

Wage moderation

This condition was met in the second half of the seventies. Between 1974 and 1979 nominal and real rates of wage increases fell from 13,4% to 5,6%, and from 4,0% to 1,7% respectively. According to standard wage equations Austria exhibited a high degree of both real and nominal wage flexibility. (This point will be elaborated further in the policy chapter below).

The anti inflationary stance of economic policy (including the behaviour of the trade unions) brought the rate of inflation back to 3½% (average 1980/90), the rate prevailing in the sixties. The shocks of the seventies, therefore, had no permanent effect on the monetary regime in Austria. Price and cost developments also became better in line with exchange rate movements. Unit labour costs of manufacturing industry expressed in a common currency declined since their peak in 1977 by one quarter. Cost and price disparities, however, were allowed to persist or even to become larger in the sheltered sector of the economy.

1.3 External equilibrium

Balance of payments crisis

Since the beginning of the 50s the Austrian economy did not run into serious balance of payment problems requiring immediate shock treatment such as an enforced devaluation or rocketing interest rates. That may be partly explained by inherent properties of small countries. Such countries know that there is a "need" to export and therefore have learned to accommodate to changing word market conditions. Since their currencies are not used as international reserve media, they are less subject to speculative shocks. In this context it has also to be mentioned that the Austrian monetary authorities were rather slow in relaxing foreign exchange restrictions. IMF convertibility was not introduced before 1963. Restrictions on capital movements were only gradually reduced during the seventies. Full liberalisation of capital transactions was only attained at the beginning of the 90s.

Periods of current account deficits

Although major balance of payments shocks could be avoided, minor adjustments were periodically necessary. In the middle of the 60s the balance of payment on current account ran into deficits, mainly for the reason which caused the slowdown of economic growth: structural deficiencies in the Austrian industry, the opening up of the domestic market, the outsider position vis-à-vis the Common Market. In the 70s the "Austro-Keynesian" policy mix (see below) strained the external balance. In both cases corrective actions were taken on behalf of the monetary and fiscal authorities, before the situation got out of control and shock treatment became unavoidable.

Exchange rate philosophies

Generally speaking, the Austrian exchange rate policy has not be used for what it originally was devised, namely to correct "structural" balance of payments disequilibria ex post. Roughly speaking, in the 50s and 60s parity changes were mainly motivated by growth considerations. In 1953, when the stabilisation crisis lasted longer than expected, a devaluation (unification of the multiple exchange rates) was used as a Keynesian demand stimulating device (as an alternative to public works). The same purpose had the decision in fall 1969, not to follow the DM-appreciation.

Chart 4: Exchange rates (based on AS)

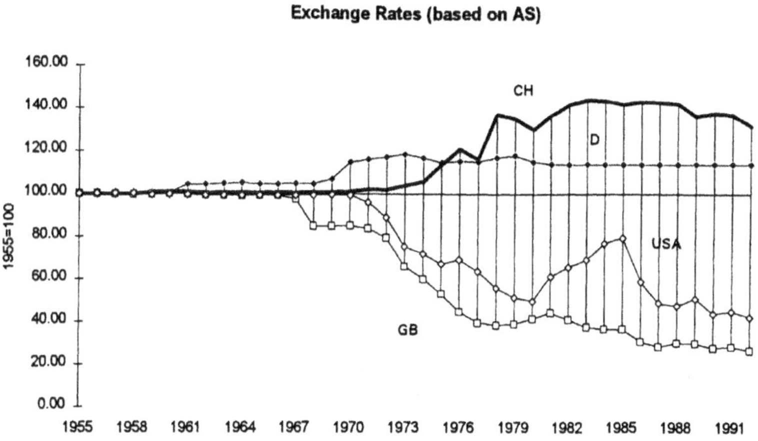

Nominal anchor

In the 70s - as was already mentioned - the exchange rate was used as an anti-inflationary weapon. That decision had far-reaching consequences, and it was met with a lot of criticism. It therefore seems appropriate to elaborate this point further. The so-called "hard currency option", as the pegging of the AS to the DM was named, developed gradually. Three stages can be distinguished: In 1971, when the Bretton-Woods-parities were realigned, the AS was clearly a candidate for an appreciation (remember: the AS did not follow the DM appreciation of 1969). Phase 2 began with the regime of flexible exchange rates. In that period the Austrian authorities, after experimenting with a basket of stable currencies, choose the DM as standard. They sticked to that decision although since the beginning of the 70s prices and wages had risen faster than in West-Germany and although the external balance had deteriorated between 1975 and 1979 considerably. In that period the exchange rate policy acted against the conventional wisdom to redress structural imbalances as soon as possible. Respectable institutions advised Austria to devaluate the AS.

In the 70s the exchange rate was used as an instrument of short term macroeconomic stabilisation within the paradigm of mainstream Keynesianism, although with an unusual emphasis on containing cost pressures. The DM-AS-relation was allowed to fluctuate within limits and was occasionally changed purposely. In phase 3, from the beginning of the eighties, the AS was strictly tied to the DM. The exchange rate became a fixed anchor rather than a flexible tool. The long term advantages of fixing the AS in terms of the DM were regarded more important than possible short-run inconveniences. With phase 3 economic policy in Austria shifted from "Austro-Keynesianism" to "Austro-Monetarism". Defending the DM parity and urging other fields of economic policy to live up to the requirements of a hard currency became the core of monetary policy.

Chart 5: The external account

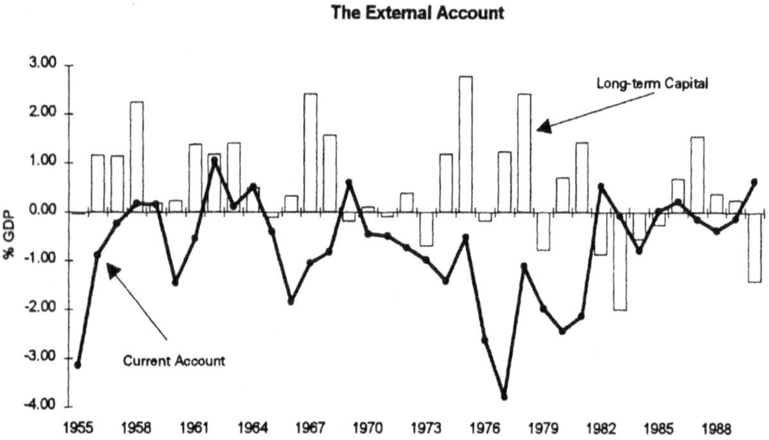

Credibility

As a matter of fact, it took some time until the hard-currency option of the Austrian Central Bank became internationally credible. Both short- and long- term interest rates for most of the 80s were approximately 1 % higher than in Germany[6]. Apart from taxation (a withholding tax was introduced, then cancelled, and later reintroduced), there was one reason, why expectations did not adjust earlier: the so called fundamentals for a long period were less solid than in Germany. In Austria consumer

6 See: A.Wörgötter (1992).

prices continued to rise faster than in Germany, although the inflation differential was modest; the deficit in the Federal budget was higher than in Germany; and the balance of payments on current account could be kept approximately in equilibrium whereas Germany had a persistent large surplus in its external account, supporting the expectation of a further appreciation of the DM. In the last years, however, the fundamentals converged. The reunification of Germany weakened its external position and strengthened the AS. The interest rate differentials became negligible, and the Austrian monetary authorities gained some room for manoeuvre.

Small, open economy

In the period under review the Austrian economy was transformed from a small economy with some trade to a "small open economy". Increased openness characterises especially the markets for goods and services. The share of exports of goods and services in GDP rose from 21% in 1955 to 44 % in recent years. The export of services proved to be more dynamic than the export of goods. Tourism expanded until 1992 although the natural capacity of many tourist resorts appears to be exhausted.

The structure of foreign trade became more competitive and less complimentary. The share of manufactured goods rose continuously, while food, raw materials and energy became less important. In 1992 38% of exports and 40% of imports were machinery and equipment compared to 13% and 5% in 1955. The share of foreign trade in GDP has been levelling off in the last decade. The stimulating effect of the Free Trade Agreement with the EC was exhausted. On a world-wide scale non-tariff trade barriers have been mounting. Foreign trade might enjoy a new boost, when the EC will be enlarged and the economies in transition will get off the ground.

From the factors of production labour is not very mobile, although immigration from Eastern Europe becomes difficult to control (see below). As far as capital is concerned, Austria has been a capital importing country for a long period. The net inflow of long-term capital, however, was modest (less then 1% of GDP p.a.). The removal of capital controls had minor effects on the balance of capital transactions, but did inflate its gross volume. Direct investment in Austria by foreigners have declined (especially in manufacturing) while Austrian firms have increased their investments abroad (especially in the former communist countries of Central Europe).

The growing openness of the economy, especially the volatility of international capital flows has reduced the scope for macro-economic strategies. The shift in economic policy since the beginning of the 80s (see the policy chapter below) can be largely explained by external constraints rather than by ideological reasons.

1.4 Employment

Unemployment low in the seventies

Economic policy in Austria always ranked full employment very high. Nevertheless ambitious employment targets could be achieved only temporarily. The rate of unemployment exhibits - apart from short term cyclical swings - a distinct U-shape. It exceeded 5% in the second half of the 50s, declined in the following years gradually and reached its minimum with 1,3% in 1973, at the eve of OPEC I. Until 1980 it could be kept at the very low level of 2%. This was regarded as a major success of the specific stance of economic policy at that time. However, the success was only transitory. Since the beginning of the eighties the rate of unemployment rose almost continuously to 6% in 1992. And it is bound to increase further during the ongoing recession. Nevertheless, unemployment in Austria still is much lower than in the European Community (especially if differences in definition are taken into account).

Hysteresis

While the relatively high rate in the 50s can be easily explained by the structural imbalances of the reconstruction period, the rising trend of unemployment of the eighties is still a puzzle. The explanation that the "natural" rate of unemployment has risen, cannot be accepted without a solid micro-economic foundation. To be sure, some hidden unemployment which has been accumulating during the 70s was transformed into open unemployment. But that affected the time path rather than the level of unemployment. There is hysteresis in the sense that unemployment once accepted (or became unavoidable) had a tendency to persist. Contrary to the 70s, wages did not respond to the higher unemployment rates. At the same time the Beveridge-curve shifted significantly outward without clear signs of a mismatch between the structure of supply and demand. (For some years both the rate of unemployment and the rate of vacancies rose.) One is tempted to conclude that unemployment rates are hard to compare not only between countries but also between different regimes in the labour market in one country.

Chart 6: The Austrian Beveridge curve

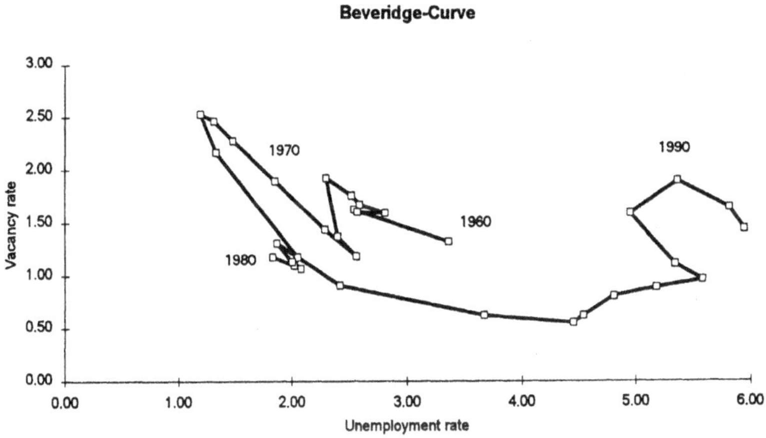

Demographic conditions

Labour market conditions were shaped by many forces. On the supply side, of course, demographic factors played a major role. Over the last decades population has grown only modestly (at a rate of 1/3 % p.a.). A baby boom in the in the late 50s and in the 60s let the number of persons in working age increase with a time lag of about 15 years. Since the 70s, however, birth rates fell well below reproduction levels provoking very pessimistic demographic forecasts for the decades after the turn of the century. These perspectives, however, had to be changed recently. The removal of the iron curtain caused a wave of immigration from Eastern Europe well above the socio-economic absorption capacity in the short run. "Population management" rather than "population decline" seem to be the challenge of the future.

Declining volume of work

The share of the labour force in the population in working age was declining over the whole period. Higher participation rates of women were more than compensated by longer education and early retirements. The actual retirement age fell below 60 both for men and women. Nevertheless, since the beginning of the 70s the labour force kept growing although at a very moderate rate (half a percentage per annum). That was - especially in the 70s when normal working time was reduced from 45 to 40 hours per week - not enough to compensate the reduction of working hours. Labour input expressed in working hours are at present 20 % lower than in the 50s. (That figure refers to labour input measured in hours worked and not in "efficiency" units, which include the labour augmenting effect of technical progress.)

Foreign workers

Since the end of the 60s foreign labour has been used to overcome structural imbalances of the labour market and to smooth cyclical swings. The share of guest workers rose from 1% of the dependent workforce in the mid-sixties to 8,7% in 1973. In the following years, when the supply of domestic labour became more elastic and the demand for labour was faltering, the share of foreign workers was gradually reduced to 5,1% in 1985. On the other hand the share of Austrians working abroad (mainly in Germany and in Switzerland) remained relatively stable (around 3,5% of the domestic labour force). Until the end of the 80s the inflow of foreign labour was strictly regulated. These controls became ineffective in the last years. After the systemic change in Central and Eastern Europe foreign workers swamped the domestic labour market. Their share increased to 9% (official figure) in 1992, at a time when unemployment was rising.

On the demand side the slowdown of economic growth since OPEC reduced employment opportunities. The repercussions on the labour market, however, were damped by various factors. In the 70s the labour market was very tight and "hire and fire" procedures were regarded as socially undesirable. Employment to a certain degree was decoupled from short term economic fluctuations. Firms kept (or were induced to keep) their workforce even when profitable employment opportunities were lacking. In the 80s the labour market became less tight and the market participants developed a more individualistic behaviour. Employment again reacted with short lags to fluctuations in economic activity. Labour saving technical economic progress, however, was smaller than in the sixties. Much less growth was "needed" to keep employment from shrinking. According to simple employment functions (regression of employment on production and production changes) in the eighties a permanent growth rate of 1,4% kept the level of employment stable, compared with 4,7 % in the sixties.

Chart 7: Unemployment and foreign workers

2 Economic policy

Economic policy in Austria by and large followed international trends. In the decades after World War II Keynesian "mainstream" economics was gradually transferred to Austria, although demand management did not seem appropriate given the supply constraints of the reconstruction period[7]. With the normalisation of economic life, after post-war inflation was checked and production well above pre-war levels, demand management and incomes policy, two pillars of Keynesian economics, were used to steer the economy on an even path. Incomes policy was based on the institution of socialpartnership and was more successful than similar attempts elsewhere.

[7] However, it might be argued that the constant fear of a recession prevented the policy makers to introduce restrictive monetary/fiscal measures and to continue wartime controls. The transition to a market economy - according to the now prevailing doctrine - was unnecessary slow.

It was widely thought that the unexpected favourable development in the post-war decades was to no small degree the result of an "activist" stabilisation policy mixed with growth enhancing structural policies. Everybody was convinced that the Keynesian medicine would work if eventually the unlikely event of a serious recession would occur. The success tempted policy makers and economists who were in high esteem at that period to strife for more ambitious goals, such as fine-tuning or growth strategies with quantitative targets.

In the seventies Keynesianism was put to a test and largely failed. The Austrians sticked longer to a full employment strategy and developed a special brand of Keynesianism called "Austro-Keynesianism". Later on, as everywhere, although with a considerable time lag, economic policy focused on supply-side adjustments rather than on demand management. Creating a stable framework was thought to achieve better results than an attempt to steer the economy by an activist policy.

Two specific features of Austrian economic policy are especially worth of mentioning:

- the continuous socialpartnership and
- the temporary "Austro-Keynesianism" in the seventies.

2.1 Socialpartnership

The Austrian system of socialpartnership or "neo-corporatism" can be characterised by the following features:

- Business, labour and farmers have set up interest group organisations with a high degree of centralisation and representation partly based on mandatory membership.
- The socialpartners can reach a consensus on many important issues.
- If the social-partners agree on an vital matter, government and parliament usually accept the compromise and take the necessary legal steps.

Price-wage policy

The socialpartners are active in the field of price-wage policy which to a large part fall in their own competence. And they try to influence other economic policy matters for which legally other institutions (government, central bank, parliament) are responsible. In 1957 they set up a Commission for Prices and Wages in order to restrain price and wage pressures on a voluntary basis. The principal idea was a social contract of the following kind: The trade unions are strong enough to push through any wage claims. They are, however, prepared to subject their claims to economic reasoning if they can get something in return. The control of non-wage income is a crucial element in all types of incomes policy. The Austrian socialpartners tried to solve this problem by asking firms in a market dominating position to submit intended price increases to the Commission for approval. The Commission has no legal basis. Nevertheless, the entrepreneurs in the Austrian environment could not neglect socio-political factors in their price behaviour. (The usual argument that the Commission distorts the allocation of resources is not well taken, because price strategies in monopolistic markets violate the optimality conditions anyhow.) Which influence the Commission on prices and wages really had, is hard to assess. Very likely the price-wage policy supported a "price-fix, quantity -flexible" regime. In many cases price increases could be postponed and (or) moderated.

General economic policy

Economic policy matters for which other institutions are responsible are influenced by the socialpartners via different channels. The Chambers are entitled to comment any new legal acts before they are submitted to parliament. Representatives of business, labour and agriculture are represented in all advisory boards dealing with economic and social matters. Independent of institutional arrangements: if the presidents of the big interest group representations agree on specific recommendations, government and parliament are under substantial pressure to accept and implement these recommendations.

Advisory council

In the sixties the socialpartners dominated the political decision making process to a degree that legal experts considered unconstitutional. In 1963 - shortly after the foundation of the German "Sachverständigenrat" -they established a Council for Social and Economic Affairs. While the German advisory council was established by law and its members are independent experts (mostly university professors), the Austrian counterpart was based on a decision of the socialpartners and is composed of experts from their own ranks.

Since the 60s the political power of the socialpartners has been gradually declining. As in other European countries a tendency from neo-corporatism toward a classical parliamentary system could be observed. The loss of influence has political, social and economic reasons such as the decline of the large political parties, the shift in the social structure towards employees, the growing importance of non-economic goals like environmental protection and the increasing openness of the economy which reduces the scope for a national price-wage-policy.

Nevertheless the socialpartners are still important although no longer dominating. The presidents of the big interest group organisations still are able to agree on economic matters of top priority. For instance, they recommended the Austrian Government to apply for EU-membership before the government made up its mind.

2.2 Austro-Keynesianism

Generally speaking, countries with strong neo-corparatist elements were better equipped to absorb the shocks of the turbulent 70s. This was especially true for Austria. In this period the Austrian economy performed well compared with most other industrialised countries. Economic growth was higher than in the OECD-area and inflation could be kept well below average. And what seemed most important, given the priorities of domestic economic policy: until the beginning of the 80s the rate of unemployment did not exceed 2%.

Economic policy makers and some experts in Austria claimed that the above average macro-economic performance of the Austrian economy, was at least partly the result of an economic strategy labelled "Austro-Keynesianism"[8]. In a narrow sense this term describes a specific mix of macroeconomic instruments. In a wider sense it includes the whole set of conditions connected with decision making processes based on co-operation and on consensus rather than on competition of the large groups of the society.

Stabilisation strategy

Some key elements of this policy have already been described. What remains to be done, is to explain how they fit into a comprehensive strategy. The economic policy

---

[8] A survey gives the discussion of representative authors about "Austro-Keynesianismus" in "Wirtschaftspolitische Blätter" 1982.

mix applied was based on a simple (Keynesian) interpretation of the oil price shocks. The dramatic price increase of an input of general use appeared both as cost-push inflation and as demand deflation. In order to cope with both problems two different set of instruments were applied. Inflation was to be contained by a restrictive incomes policy supported by the so-called hard currency policy (by tying the AS to the DM). At the same time an expansionary budgetary policy supplemented by an accommodating monetary policy should fill the demand gap caused by the oil price shock until structural changes (energy saving, promotion of exports to OPEC) could become effective. Gaining time for an orderly adjustment was a declared goal of economic policy.

Wage moderation

Some of the risks of this strategy - albeit not all of them - were well known. Pertaining to price-wage-policy one could doubt whether prices and wages, even under the rein of socialpartnership, were so sticky that over the medium term quantity movements could be separated from price changes. Actually, these concerns were not justified. It is true that inflation differentials to West-Germany were negatively correlated with growth differentials (see chart). But that just means that incomes policy must not be overstrained. The main goal was achieved. The rate of inflation as well as nominal and real wage increases could be reduced dramatically within a few years, and that at a level of unemployment of 2%. This is acknowledged even by those experts who otherwise are rather sceptical about the wisdom of the Austrian experiment.

Some experts[9] give the credit for the dramatic anti inflationary process to the exchange rate policy. They claim that the hard currency option was so credible (at least for the actors in the markets for labour and goods) that price and wage moderation followed more or less automatically. But one cannot reject the hypothesis that historically unique non-economic events (such as the close ties between the government and the trade unions and the strength of some of the top political leaders) played a major role.

External account in deficit

Another candidate for troubles was the external account. Textbook economics teaches that a small country which tries to stimulate domestic demand is liable to run into

---

9 See e.g. Hochreiter/Winckler(1992).

balance of payments difficulties. As a matter of fact, between 1975 and 1977 the current balance deteriorated at an alarming pace. Critics commented that Austria's economic policy demonstrated that it could boost demand, but foreign firms rather than domestic ones were the beneficiaries. Although some deficit in the current account was part of the scenario, consolidating efforts were necessary in order to maintain the hard currency option. The shift toward an external-account-conscious policy meant that not much scope was left for demand management.

Chart 8: Nominal wage increases and the rate of unemployment

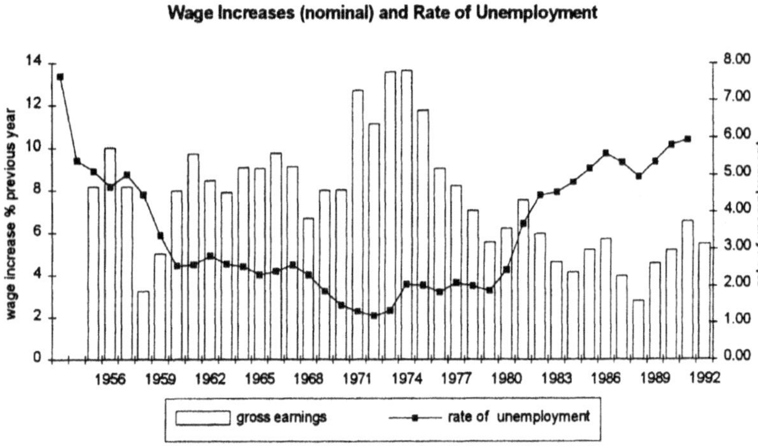

"Dive-through" strategy

The strategy chosen later on was called a "dive-through"-strategy. It might have succeeded if the world economy would have returned to its old growth path. Unfortunately, this was not the case. When at the end of the 70s a second oil price shock hit the word economy and world economic policy under the leadership of the IMF decided not to finance the emerging gap in the international flows of payments, the Austrian government tried to apply the same medicine as in 1975. Under the given constraints the expansionary thrust could only be weak and it did not prevent domestic demand to shrink considerably. Unemployment could only be kept at a low level by temporary measures such as early retirements and hoarding labour in the nationalised industries.

The end of Austro-Keynesianism

It was evident that the stance of economic policy in Austria had to be changed sooner or later. Micro-and macroeconomic adjustments which were delayed in the seventies became necessary. At the micro-level the nationalised industries were running high deficits and needed reconstruction. At the macro-level the budget deficits became unsustainable.

Structural adjustment

The shift from Austro-Keynesianism to a conservative policy emphasising structural adjustments and a stable framework was launched gradually. When the socialist party lost its absolute majority the old policy mix was discontinued without a firm commitment to a new strategy. It was not until 1987 when the two large political parties formed a coalition government that clear economic priorities were set, such as consolidation of the federal budget in predetermined steps over a period of 5 years, a supply-side reform of direct taxes and a reconstruction of the nationalised industries.

These goals could be achieved to a certain extent. The net deficit in the federal budget was cut from 5,1% of GDP to less than 3% in 1992. It became dynamically stable in the sense that no further deficit reduction was required in order to stabilise the national debt in relation to GDP. The primary balance was already in surplus. The national industries were slimmed and reorganised. They were supposed to act like private firms. As a group they made again profits. However, both achievements were to no small degree the result of the unexpected boom at the end of the eighties and the beginning of the nineties. The recession which started in late 1992 inflated the budget deficits again although lower interest rates alleviated the burden of the national debt. The national industries made losses again. Since the government now is not prepared to bail out the ailing firms, further privatisation steps are necessary. The nationalised industries as an important group of the Austrian manufacturing industry will cease to exist although the government will keep the majority of shares in some important firms.

3 New external environment

The new Europe

The economic environment of Austria has been changing for some time and will continue to change in the future. Austria has applied for EU membership and faces the challenges of the systemic change in the former communist countries in Central and

Eastern Europe. In principle and in a longer term perspective, both factors are likely to stimulate economic growth[10]. However, painful adjustments are bound to occur in the short and medium run.

Chart 9: Federal budget deficit

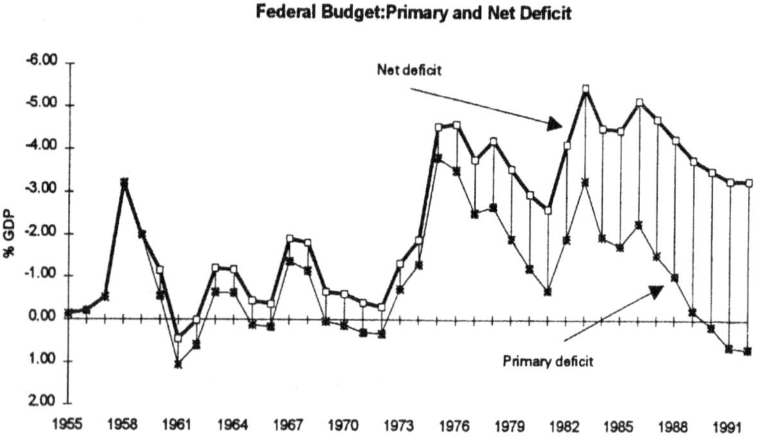

The Austrian economy is already highly integrated with the Common Market. Trade with the EU accounts of two thirds of external trade. 80% of the tourists visiting Austria are citizens of the EU. Time series analysis show that the domestic economy is strongly affected by events in the EU. Europe-wide (global) shocks play a much larger role than local (national) shocks. The pegging of the Austrian Schilling to the DM over a long period has been a strong integrating force. The requirements for a European Monetary Union are better fulfilled than in most EU member countries.

Inefficient sheltered sectors

Nevertheless, adjustment problems do exist. While the exposed sector of the economy had to bear the brunt of the hard currency policy and therefore is used to fierce competition from abroad (and undoubtedly will benefit from the removal of non-tariff

---

10 Breuss/Schebeck(1989) estimated that EU-membership will over a period of 6 years increase real GDP by 3,5% and employment by 1,9%, while lowering prices by 5,2%.

barriers), the sheltered sector partly regulated by agreements of the socialpartners will face competition unknown up to now. Agriculture and food processing is one important example, public procurements is another one. Furthermore, in view of the overboarding transit traffic a compromise between environment protection and free access to markets will have to be found.

The systemic change in the countries formerly under communist rule (CEEC and NIS) provides the Austrian economy with a location advantage. It will bring the socio-economic distances more in line with the geographical distances. Close economic interactions are now possible with an area which 80 years ago belonged to the "common market" of the Austrian-Hungarian monarchy. It certainly would be unrealistic to assume that the former division of labour (and of economic power) will be restored. But many opportunities for profitable business were opened up. The majority of Austrian industrialists expects to benefit from the liberal economic and political system in the former Communist countries. The firms in the western parts of Austria hope to enlarge their markets, the firms in the eastern part expect to benefit mainly from an elastic and cheap supply of labour.

Austrian firms were quick to exploit the new opportunities. They established many joint ventures mainly in Hungary, Poland and in the Czech Republic, exports to this area are flourishing. Some experts claim that the unexpected vigorous economic growth at the beginning of the 90s was the result of the opening up of the countries formerly under communist regime, although probably the indirect effects of the German reunification were more important.

Problems for low wage industries

However, the dismantling of the iron curtain was not just a blessing for Austria. The transition strategy chosen provoked a severe recession in the former communist countries and led to equilibrium exchange rates which overshot the purchasing power parities by a big margin. In a fairly wide range of products (iron & steel, some building materials, agricultural products) the supply from the East is much cheaper than that from Western competitors. If the present price relations will persist, some industry branches not only in Austria but in many Western Europe countries will operate at negative value added and will go bankrupt unless the government bails them out. The areas near the former iron curtain which belong to the less developed parts of Austria will benefit from the socio-economic interactions across the border, but may loose their low-wage industries to the economies in transitions where labour is much cheaper.

Literature

Abele, H., Novotny, E., Schleicher, St., Winckler, G. (eds.) (1982): *Handbuch der österreichischen Wirtschaftspolitik*, Wien, Manz.

Androsch, H., Haschek, H. (1987): *Austria. Past and Present*, Vienna.

Arndt, Sven (ed.) (1982): *The Political Economy of Austria*, American Enterprise Institute, Washington D.C.

Barro, J.Robert, Sala-i-Martin, X. (1992): Convergence. *Journal of Political Economy*. Vol.100. No.2. p.223-251.

Breuss, F., Schebeck, F. (1989): Die Vollendung des EG-Binnenmarktes. Gesamtwirtschaftliche Auswirkungen für Österreich. *WIFO-Gutachten*, Vienna.

Butschek, F. (1985): *Die österreichische Wirtschaft im 20.Jahrhundert*, Vienna.

Eichengreen, B., Uzan, M. (1992): The Marshall Plan: economic effects and implications for Eastern Europe and the former USSR. *Economic Policy*, No14.p.13-75. April.

Hochreiter, E., Winckler, G. (1992): Signalling a Hand Currency Strategy: The Case of Austria. *OENB Working Papers*, No.10. Vienna.

Maddison, Agnus (1987): Growth and Slowdown in advanced capitalist economies: techniques of quantitative assessment. *Journal of Economic Literature*, June. p.649-698.

Seidel, Hans (1985):Der österreichische Weg der Inflationsbekämpfung. In: *Schriften des Vereins für Sozialpolitik*, NF. B157: "Nationale Wege der Inflationsbekämpfung". Berlin.

Weber, Wilhelm (ed.) (1961): *Österreichs Wirtschaftsstruktur, gestern- heute-morgen*. Berlin.

Wirtschaftspolitische Blätter (1982): Discussion "Austro-Keynesianismus" with contributions (among others) by H.Seidel, K.Sochor, E.Streissler, G.Tichy.

Wörgötter, Andreas (1992): Das östereichisch-deutsche Zinsdifferential und der österreichische Kapitalverkehrssaldo. In: *Schriftenreihe Volkswirtschaft der P.S.K.* No.12. Vienna.

Structural Changes in the Post-War Italian Economy

Marcello Signorelli*
Alessandro Vercelli*

University of Siena

1 Introduction[1]

The aim of the present paper is to analyse some of the fundamental characteristics underlying the process of structural change which has taken place in Italy from the post-war years to the present day. Although in the 1950s and 1960s such changes followed a relatively coherent and steady path, in accordance with the existing technological and institutional paradigm[2], the 1970s witnessed an abrupt change in structural development. In the 1980s, failure to provide thorough and coherent answers to the need of a deep structural change, which had its roots in the previous decade, contributed to the rise of both dynamic and structural instability phenomena, which now characterise the early 1990s.

The problem of channelling structural change towards a sustainable direction must be tackled if the consequences of "spontaneous" evolution - which may turn out to be thoroughly undesirable - are to be avoided. This should foster the re-shaping of the technological and institutional paradigm, which once again will lead the economic system towards "sustainable growth", in accordance with the country's need for more efficient institutions and better living standards.

Such issues are dealt with in the present paper according to the following outline.

---

* Though the paper was jointly worked out by the authors, Alessandro Vercelli takes responsability mainly for the second section and Marcello Signorelli takes responsability mainly for the third section.

[1] This paper is based on previous work of the authors: Vercelli (1986a; 1986b; 1989) and Signorelli (1990; 1992).

[2] This may be defined as *ad hoc* combination of Fordism and Keynesism, which allowed the system to make full use of the opportunities of development made available by the new technologies through large centralised organisations: large firms and Keynesian welfare state (Vercelli, 1986b).

In the first part of the paper the main sources of instability and the relevant forms of regulation are presented according to a heuristic scheme of a qualitative type. The second part focuses on the sources of both dynamic and structural instability which have characterised the Italian economy, with reference to the labour, commodity, financial and monetary markets, which will be examined in this order.

2 Instability and regulation

First of all, the fundamental links among the main sources of instability typical of advanced industrial economies are presented, in the format of a qualitative heuristic model.

2.1 The fundamental sources of instability

In the present paper three principal sources of dynamic instability[3] are analysed:

a) labour and wage instability, concerning the labour market and industrial relations;

b) macroeconomic instability, concerning the links between production of goods and accumulation of the productive capital stock; these links characterise the market for goods (both consumer and investment goods are considered);

c) monetary and financial instability, concerning the links between amounts and prices of assets and liabilities in the monetary and financial market.

Although closely related, these three forms of instability maintain substantial (albeit partial and temporary) autonomy. Therefore, in principle, each form of instability is controlled and regulated by different institutions, which are basically as follows:

a) trade unions and other institutions, dealing with the regulation of industrial relations;

b) government and non-government institutions, dealing with the regulation of industrial, technological and budgetary policies;

c) Central Bank and other institutions dealing with the regulation of monetary and financial policies.

---

[3] The term "sources of instability" indicates those articulations of the economic system affected by serious and persistent imbalances. When these phenomena become too serious and/or too persistent, a structural change is unavoidable. Thus, dynamic "sources of instability" are also sources of structural instability. As to the distinction between dynamic and structural instability, see Vercelli (1991).

Figure 1 illustrates the heuristic scheme used in the present analysis and shows its fundamental variables and their mutual links

Figure 1: Forms of instability and regulation

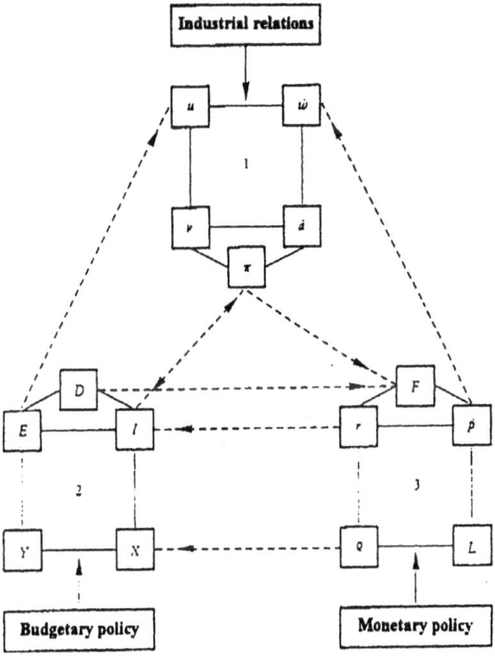

Legend:

1 = Wage and occupational instability
2 = Growth instability
3 = Monetary and financial instability
u = Unemployment rate
w = % growth rate of monetary wages
a = % productivity growth rate
π = Profit rate
v = Income from labour share
I = Investment
X = Balance of trade
Y = National income
E = Aggregate expenditure
D = Public deficit
L = Liquidity
ρ = Exchange rate
r = Interest rate
F = Financial fragility
p = Price inflation

2.1.1 Labour and wage instability

Dynamic instability originating in the labour market mainly brings about four types of disequilibrium: involuntary unemployment, wage inflation, pathological variations in income distribution and labour productivity stagnation (or fall).

The link between functional income distribution and unemployment may be represented through a version of Goodwin's cyclical development model (1967).

Since the formulation of the Phillips curve (1958), the link between wage inflation and unemployment has been one of the most topical issues of the macroeconomic debate. Such debate has pointed out that the link between the two forms of instability is itself unstable and depends on the structural characteristics of both the economy and the economic policy[4].

The variations of functional income distribution are determined by the trend of monetary wages and that of labour productivity, which depends on technological and organisational changes and on industrial relations. Functional income distribution, in its turn, has a crucial influence on the profit rate, which is a key-variable of the economic system, acting both on the accumulation mechanism and on the financial stability of the whole system.

2.1.2 Instability of the accumulation process

Dynamic instability originating in the commodity market is to be found both in the gap between warranted and natural income growth rates (in the sense of Harrod), and in the disequilibrium of the balance of payments. Besides, the State, through public spending and taxation, has a decisive influence on the economic aggregate. This gives the opportunity to regulate the accumulative process more effectively, but may also give rise to distorted forms of intervention. In this respect, the most patent example is given by an ever-increasing public deficit, which brings about a new form of disequilibrium, which may be called "budgetary instability".

---

[4] See Vercelli (1986b).

2.1.3 Monetary and financial instability

Dynamic instability originating in the financial and monetary market takes on the twofold form of monetary instability, which brings about price inflation, and financial instability, which causes liquidity and solvency crises and - ultimately - bankruptcy of one or more financial units.

Being closely related, these two forms of instability are regulated by the same institutions, and especially by the central bank.

The links among liquidity, interest rate and inflation (taking into account the degree of financial fragility of the system) make up the internal circuit which, *ceteris paribus*, originates financial instability.

On the other hand, monetary instability may depend on liquidity increases and/or interest rate reductions. In an open economy, particularly relevant is the difference between the domestic inflation rate and that of the principal foreign competitors. Regulation of the exchange rate by the monetary authorities may have important consequences on monetary stability.

2.1.4 Fundamental interrelations between the main sources of instability

There is a close relationship between the three main sources of instability briefly sketched above. In this framework, the fundamental role is played by profits. High profits, depending mostly - although not exclusively - on industrial relations, favour accumulation and stabilise the economy's financial structure. Thus, investments are encouraged, since profit expectations, as well as opportunities of self-financing, are more favourable. At the same time, more substantial cash flows allow one to control indebtedness, thus ensuring financial stability. Although these are mainly microeconomic mechanisms, the trend of the profit quota on national income, which in the short term essentially depends on industrial relations, is a good index of the average situation the economic agent has to deal with.

Similarly, the interest rate, which is mainly determined by the monetary and financial market, affects both the accumulation process and financial stability. The influences exercised by both the interest rate and the profit rate may find a unified explanation in a generalized theory of portfolio selection (an early example may be found in Keynes, *General Theory*, chapter XVII). In fact, the structure of both real and financial accumulation, as well as the stability of the individual accumulation processes and overall economic stability, are determined through the comparison of profit rates generated by the various (either productive or financial) ways in which capital is employed.

Great relevance should also be given to the links between monetary wages and price inflation, as well as to the interrelations between aggregate spending and unemployment.

There are two policy factors which have considerably affected the Italian economy in recent years:
a) exchange rate regulation (mainly exercised by the monetary authorities) which has a direct influence on the balance of payments;
b) changes in the public debt, which have a decisive influence on the system's financial fragility.

2.2 Structural aspects of instability

The heuristic scheme presented in this paper may be used to analyse the imbalances characterising some industrialised economies and their effects. However, to the purposes of the present paper, the scheme will be used essentially as an introductory approach[5] to the study of the main structural changes which have affected the Italian economy in recent years.

Particular emphasis will be given to the changes of parameters representing the causal interrelations illustrated in the heuristic scheme. In the late 1960s, for example, parameters representing the feedback process between inflation, unemployment and functional income distribution abruptly changed; similarly, in the 1970s the link between aggregate demand and investment (accelerator) was modified.

[5] In order to analyse a structural change, it is first of all necessary to define the characteristics of the structure to be analysed; the heuristic scheme illustrated above serves this purpose.

Structural changes will be considered as endogenous reactions to exogenous stimuli following modifications in the environment in which economic agents operate[6]. Structural reactions will thus depend on a systemic feature of the economy which the system as a whole and its various sectors may possess in greater or lower degree, i.e. structural instability. As a consequence, either physiological or pathological reactions will ensue, which will supply relevant information on the behaviour of economic agents and on the choice of regulatory schemes. Table 1 shows this twofold polarity (flexibility/rigidity and fragility/solidity), with the opposition of the pairs along the diagonal.

For the purposes of the following analysis, particular emphasis will be given to the link among rigidity in the use of productive inputs, technological flexibility and financial fragility, as well as to the link between uncertainty increases and more flexible productive and financial configurations (see Vercelli, 1986).

Table 1: Forms of structural instability and structural stability

	Structural instability	**Structural stability**
Physiological	**Flexibility**	**Solidity**
Pathological	**Fragility**	**Rigidity**

Here is an outline of the scheme proposed in the present paper.

During the second half of the 1960s, the traditional mechanisms of regulation were hindered by an increasing rigidity in the use of the labour-force. This originated a period of economic turmoil characterised by a high degree of uncertainty. Increased uncertainty called for a more flexible technological and organisational paradigm, thus giving rise to a period of deep structural change. This may be considered as a transitional phase, going from the technological and institutional paradigm of the 1950s-1960s towards a new paradigm still to be fully defined.

---

[6] Changes in the environment (such as economic policy rules, degree of uncertainty, political situation, etc.) partially depend on previous modifications of the economic structure, and partially are due to factors which are independent from the economic structure (whose nature may be political, technological, cultural, etc.).

3 Structural changes of the Italian economy

This paper is obviously not intended to give a thorough and exhaustive analysis of the issues being examined, but simply to provide a general outline of the changes which have characterised the Italian economic system from the post-war years to the present day. The present analysis will be articulated according to the main aggregate markets being considered, i. e. the labour, commodity and monetary and financial markets.

3.1 The labour market

The labour market has undergone deep changes. In this respect, the present paper attempts to provide a synthetic analysis of both the occupational structure (examined according to sectors and sex) and unemployment (according to sex and geographical region). Also highlighted is how the variations in the degree of uncertainty of the economic system and of the degree of flexibility of the labour market have influenced both regular and irregular labour demand. Moreover, occupational and wage instability is dealt with in detail, through the study of the links existing between wage inflation, unemployment and income distribution.

3.1.1 Employment and unemployment

The structure of employment according to sectors sizeably changed in the last decades (Graph 1). In this period the employment increased in the tertiary sector, while considerably falling in the primary sector. The employment in the secondary sector grew up to the late seventies, but has gradually shrunk since the early 1980s.

Employment composition according to sex has deeply changed in recent years (Graph 2). In the last two decades, while male employment gradually diminished, female employment progressively grew. However, the gap between the male and female employment rate remains remarkable.

As far as unemployment is concerned, the low unemployment rate of the 1960s was followed by a gradual increase during the 1970s which "explodes" in the 1980s. In recent years the unemployment rate has oscillated between the 10% and the 12% of the labour force (Graph 3).

Graph 1: Employment according to sectors (in thousands of labour units)

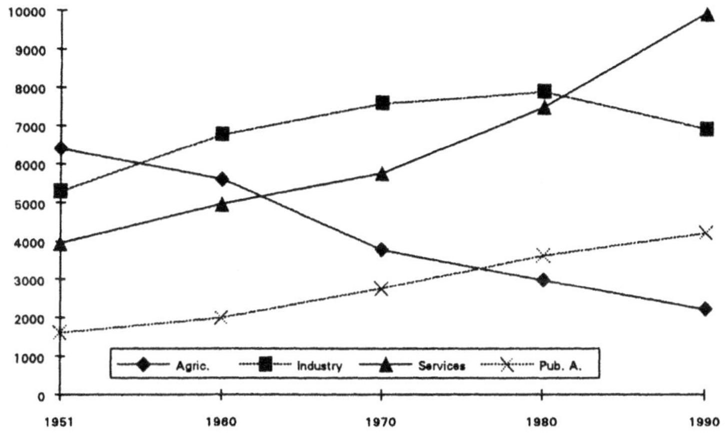

Source: Istat

Graph 2: Employment according to sex (in thousands of units)

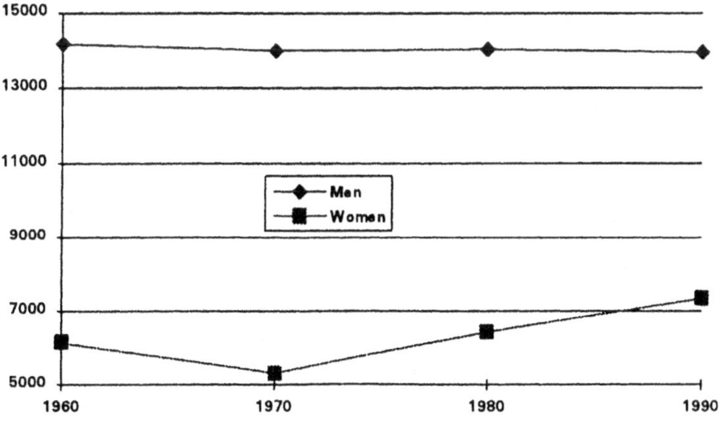

Source: Istat

Graph 3: Unemployment rate (1959 - 1991)

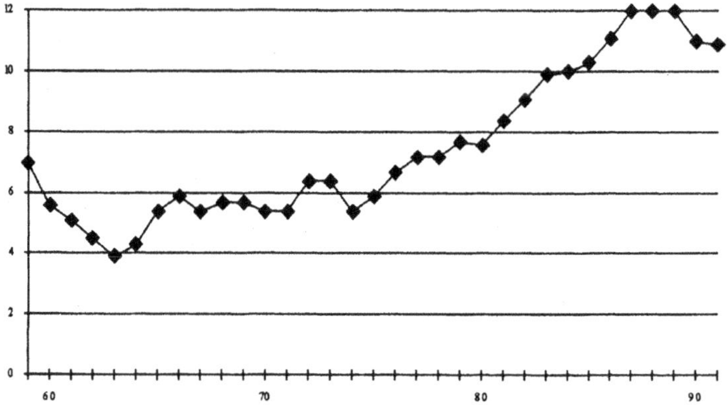

Source: Istat

Graph 4: Unemployment rate according to sex

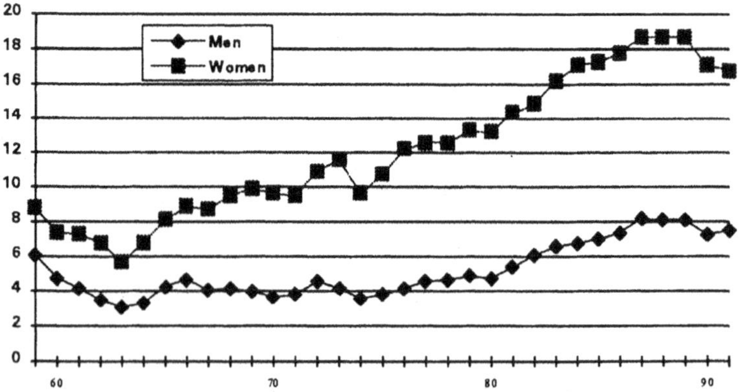

Source: Istat

The unemployment rate has sizeably changed according to sex (Graph 4). In the late 1980s the female unemployment rate reaches the 18%, while the male rate reaches the 8%.

Finally, a well known feature of the Italian labour market is the remarkable gap among the unemployment rates of north, centre and south (Graph 5). This gap worsened during the 1980s. In 1991 the unemployment rate was 5% in the north, 10% in the centre, and 20% in the south and in the islands.

Graph 5: Unemployment rate according to region

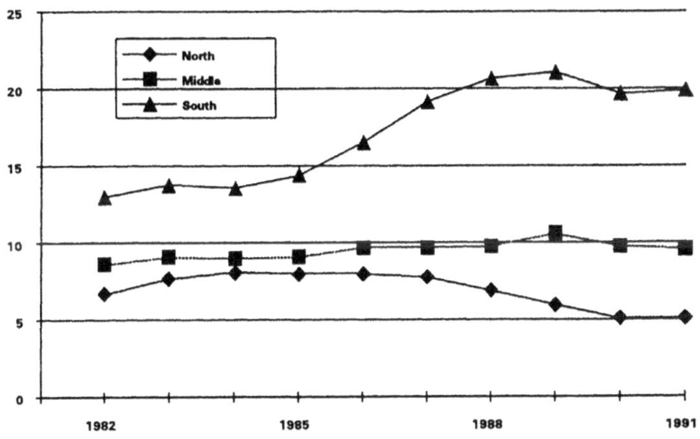

Source: Istat

3.1.2 Uncertainty, flexibility and labour demand

This paragraph provides an interpretation of the development of the quantitative and qualitative structure of employment in Italy in the last few decades[7]. We intend to show how deeply the employment policy of Italian firms was affected by the remarkable changes which influenced both the degree of uncertainty of the economic system and the degree of flexibility of the labour market.

---

[7] See Signorelli (1990, 1992).

a) Uncertainty and regular labour demand

Considerable increases in the degree of uncertainty may be brought about by union struggles, high price variability, political instability, etc. Such increases may have a twofold effect on the entrepreneur's policy: a "risk effect" and a "substitution effect". The former brings about a general reduction of the investment rate, while the latter consists in the (partial) substitution of "more rigid" productive inputs with "more flexible" ones. As a consequence, long-term investments will be cut first, followed by medium-term ones; eventually, if the increase in uncertainty is conspicuous, short-term investments will also be reduced.

The "human capital" may be considered as a medium-term investment, since the time and cost needed to adjust the real "human capital" stock[8] to the desired level are lower if compared to those needed by fixed capital and higher with respect to circulating capital[9].

What the paper intends to highlight is, in conclusion, the probable inverse relation existing between the degree of uncertainty and a desired regular labour demand. The negative effect produced by an increase in uncertainty on the desired regular labour demand increases whenever "human capital" takes on the long-term investment characteristics typical of fixed capital[10].

b) Labour market flexibility and regular labour demand

Labour market flexibility may be of three types: occupational, contractual and wage flexibility.

Occupational flexibility measures the adjustments of the real labour demand to that desired[11]. On the one hand, in the case of maximum occupational flexibility, the entrepreneur will, at any moment, have at his disposal the desired "human capital" stock . Since it is considered in the short run, this stock will hardly be affected by uncertainty variations. On the other hand, in a situation of minimum occupational flexibility, it is

---

[8] The term "human capital" stock indicates both quantitative and qualitative characteristics of regular employment.

[9] W. Y. Oi (1962).

[10] The impossibility (or the remarkable difficulty) in dismissing workers makes the investment in "human capital" irreversible (or long-term), giving it the characteristics of fixed capital.

[11] In both quantitative and qualitative terms.

difficult for the entrepreneur either to hire or fire his workers. Whenever occupational flexibility is low, human capital takes on the characteristics typical of fixed capital, i. e., it becomes a long-term investment. In this context, the desired human capital stock will be considered in the long run, so that the desired labour demand will be considerably affected by the degree of uncertainty.

In short, the theory of long-term positive correlation between the degree of occupational flexibility and a regular labour demand seems to be well-grounded.

The degree of contractual flexibility depends upon the existing institutional arrangements. According to these, the entrepreneur may or may not diversify his labour demand. When there is only one type of contract (for example, full-time and of unlimited duration), the degree of flexibility is minimum. In this case, low contractual flexibility hampers a "diversified" labour demand, such as, for example, demand for part-time or temporary contracts[12]. Hence, a positive relation between this type of flexibility and regular labour demand is also likely to exist.

Non-structural wage flexibility is defined as the degree of correlation between real wage growth and labour productivity growth. Whenever the cost of labour substantially increases while productivity remains practically unaltered, there occurs a functional income redistribution and a consequent loss of profit. The entrepreneur will thus reduce the use of the labour input, by substituting it with others which have become more convenient[13].

Hence, also the degree of wage flexibility probably has a direct relation with regular labour demand.

c) Uncertainty, labour market flexibility and irregular labour demand

Besides reducing the overall labour demand, an increase in the degree of uncertainty induces the entrepreneur to partially substitute "rigid" labour with "flexible" labour. Whenever this flexible labour demand encounters low contractual, occupational or wage flexibility, it generates a (partial) increase in irregular labour demand.

---

[12] At least part of this "diversified" labour demand turns into a demand for irregular labour.

[13] There will probably also be a partial substitution of regular with irregular labour.

Similarly, following a reduction in the degree of flexibility on the labour market, the flexible labour demand which remains unsatisfied will increase. This will produce an increase of the irregular labour demand.

d) The Italian experience

Empirical evidence concerning Italy may provide an illustration of the above causal relations. Indicators referring to union struggles and price variability may be considered (elaboration of data supplied by ISTAT)[14].

The graphs from 6 to 8 show the beaviour of union struggles. All the above indices of the intensity of labour unrest change cyclically according to the concentration of contractual renewals, but their trend clearly increased in the late 1960s and began to decrease only in the late 1970s.

Analogously both the level and variability of prices show a pattern similar to that of labour struggle with a short lag (Graphs 9 -12).

Both these sets of indicators suggest that the degree of uncertainty of the economic system started increasing in the late 1960s, was at its highest in the 1970s and began its gradual downward slope in the early 1980s.

The degree of uncertainty of a given economy is determined by a variety of other factors, such as national and international political instability, imbalances in public finance, disequilibria in the balance of payments, level and variability of both interest and exchange rates, level and variability of GDP growth rate, common and organised crime, etc. For example, the consumption, which during the 1950s-1960s was predominantly addressed towards semi-durable standardised goods, became more diversified during the following two decades. At the same time, the "life spans" of products were considerably reduced. Hence, the system has shifted from a substantially stable demand towards a more variable one, both with regard to quality and quantity.

---

[14] The unbroken lines indicate the annual values, while the dotted lines indicates the triennal moving averages.

Graph 6: Strikes (in units)

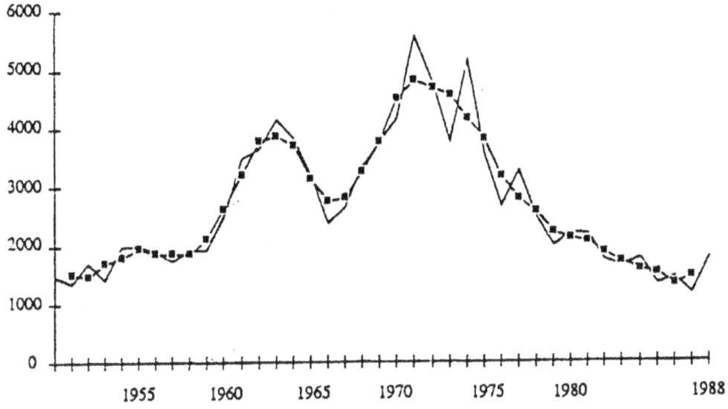

Source: elaboration of data supplied by Istat

Graph 7: Hours lost (in thousands)

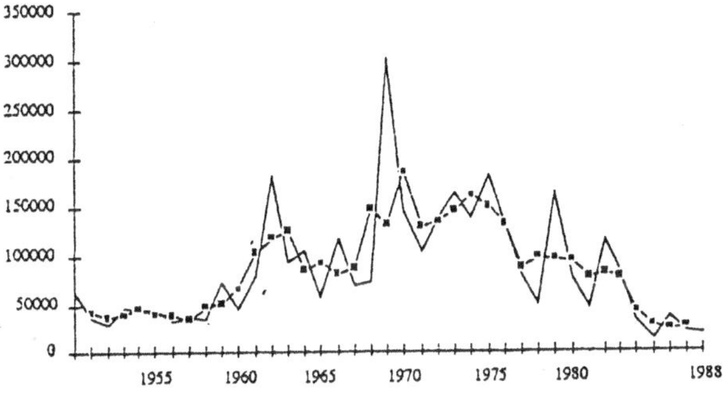

Source: elaboration of data supplied by Istat

Graph 8: Strikes (in thousand of workers involved)

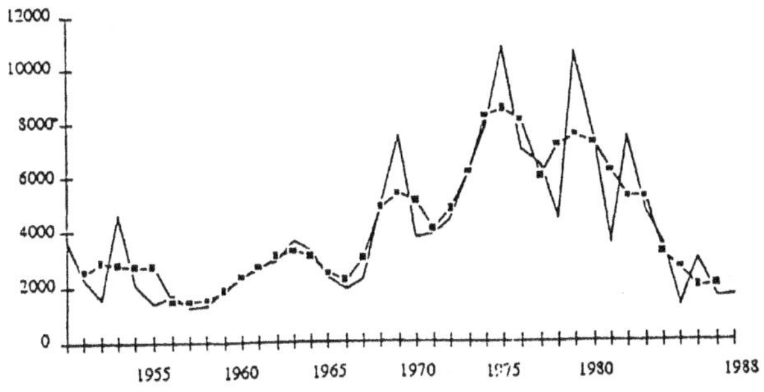

Source: elaboration of data supplied by Istat

Graph 9: Wholesale price index (percentage changes from previous year)

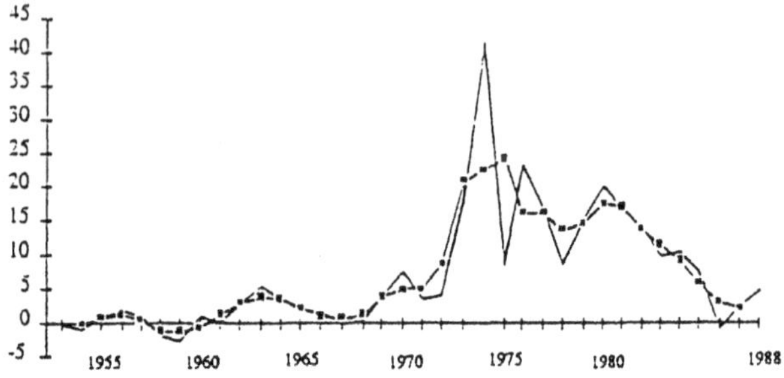

Source: elaboration of data supplied by Istat

Graph 10: Variability of the wholesale price index

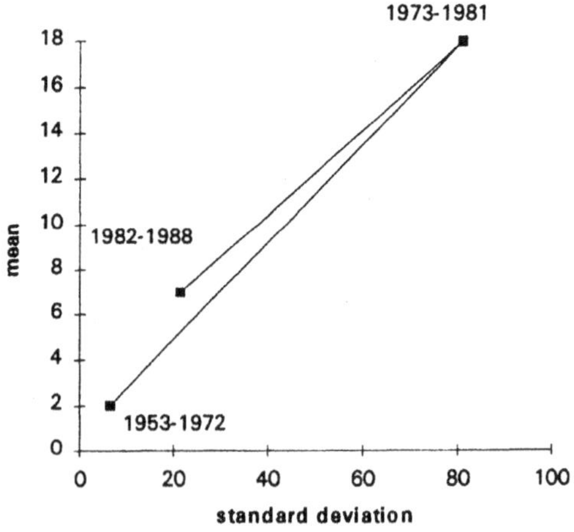

Source: elaboration of data supplied by Istat

Graph 11: Consumer price index (percentage changes from previous year)

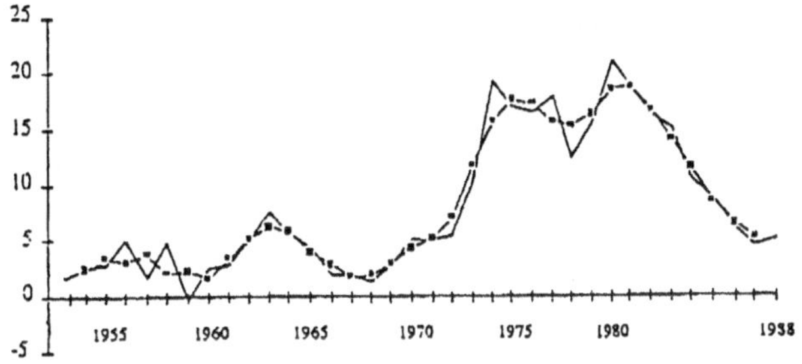

Source: elaboration of data supplied by Istat

Graph 12: Variability of the consumer price index

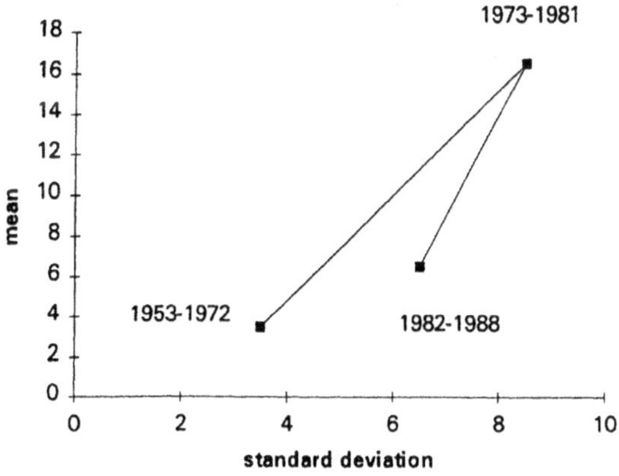

Source: elaboration of data supplied by Istat

As regards the labour market's degree of flexibility, it began to decrease in the late 1960s, and reached a very low level in the 1970s. However, starting from the 1980s, there has been a general increase first in occupational flexibility, followed by similar increases in both wage and contractual flexibility.

In particular, in 1970 a new regulation of industrial relation was introduced under the name of "Worker Statute" (Statuto dei Lavoratori). In practice, the Statute did not allow employers to dismiss their workers, unless for "justified reasons" (giusta causa), and prohibited ad personam hiring. As a consequence, in these years occupational flexibility reached a minimum. Only with the introduction of the "contract of training and work" (Contratto di Formazione e Lavoro[15]) and the promotion of part-time work (Act No. 863/1984) did contractual flexibility begin to rise again. However, the percentage of part-time workers is still very low (about 6% of labour force) as compared to other developed countries.

The 1970s were also characterised by a change in functional income distribution, with a consequent reduction in the profits share. Therefore, non-structural wage flexibility, measured as the difference between the rate of change of labour productivity and the rate of change of real wages, also decreased in this period.

Hence, it can be stated that the 1970s were characterised both by an exceptional degree of economic uncertainty and by a reduced flexibility of the labour market.

Let us now briefly examine the evolution of both regular and irregular labour demand. In the 1960s, as labour supply shrank, the demand for regular labour also decreased. However, in the 1970s labour demand did not keep pace with the increasing labour supply, showing an upward sluggishness which was to become even stronger in the 1980s.

Disaggregation according to sex and geographical region highlights the gap between labour demand and supply, which is particularly evident for women and the South of Italy.

[15] Under the contract of training and work, those under 30 can be engaged for a period of two years at normal salary rates but with very low "social contribution" rates. After the expiry of the two years, the work contract may be confirmed as a normal one or terminated without any particular obligation.

As to irregular employment, the various available estimates show that it was remarkably high during the 1970s, and that its increase slowed down in the 1980s[16].

e) Interpretation of the Italian empirical evidence

The results of the present attempt towards a partial interpretation of the available data are shown in the following paragraph.

A) The 1970s

In the early 1970s, the expectations and management strategies of entrepreneurs were modified as a consequence of the abrupt change which occurred in two major structural parameters of the economy. Labour struggles and price variability contributed to an increase in the degree of uncertainty. This, combined with reduction in the degree of occupational and wage flexibility in the labour market, modified both the qualitative and quantitative characteristics of labour demand.

In particular, due to the reduction in the degree of occupational flexibility, the labour force took on characteristics very similar to those of fixed capital[17].

A reduction in desired regular labour demand did not immediately cause a similar decrease in actual regular labour demand, due to the lower degree of occupational flexibility. In fact, the entrepreneurs drastically decreased the hiring of workers as a response to the constraints to dismiss their workers[18].

Great uncertainty caused an increase in the desired degree of overall flexibility, and also the desired "flexible" labour demand rose. The latter, due to the low flexibility of the labour market[19], was - at least partially - met by irregular labour. Available estimates confirm the growth of irregular labour during the 1970s[20].

---

[16] In the 1980s, especially second jobs and foreign labour increased.

[17] As previously shown, this transformation "increases" negative elasticity with respect to desired labour demand with relation to the degree of uncertainty of the economic system.

[18] In qualitative terms, modifications in regular labour demand (especially due to a lower wage flexibility) brought about negative effects on "marginal" classes of age, which generally have a lower level of labour productivity.

[19] As regards Italy, the low flexibility of the labour market is amplified by the gap between cost of labour and net retribution (the cost of labour is more than double with respect to that of net retribution).

[20] See "Rapporto '89", Ministero del Lavoro, Roma.

In short, the 1970s were characterised by a low desired regular labour demand and by a growing irregular labour demand. These were mainly due to the high degree of uncertainty of the economic system, as well as to a low degree of flexibility of the labour market.

B) The 1980s

In the 1980s the qualitative and quantitative characteristics of labour demand were again modified by a gradual reduction in the uncertainty of the economic system and a new growth of labour market flexibility.

In particular, in the early 1980s a substantial increase in the degree of occupational flexibility brought about a decrease in the actual regular labour demand, which had remained practically "blocked" during the 1970s. At the same time, the degree of wage and contractual flexibility also increased, determining a gradual upward shift of desired regular labour demand. During the 1980s, these transformations slowly led to real employment growth.

On the other hand, irregular employment, although modified in its composition[21], remained at the high level reached in the previous decade.

Hence, in the 1980s higher labour market flexibility reduced the "occupational surplus" accumulated in the 1970s, but did not manage to counteract the upward sluggishness in the demand for regular labour[22].

The Italian economy was affected in various ways by the above-mentioned structural changes. In this analysis, a distinction is to be made between small and large (manufacturing[23]) firms. In the 1970s, large firms were characterised by a more rigid productive and organisational structure, while smaller firms were more flexible in this respect. Moreover, the Workers' Statute of 1970 imposed much stricter obligations on large firms[24] than on smaller ones[25] as regards labour relations.

---

[21] Due to the increase of double and foreign labour.

[22] Obviously, this may also be due to the emersion of irregular labour.

[23] It is held that the considerations here illustrated may refer to the whole economy, with particular emphasis on the industrial sector.

[24] The degree of flexibility (especially occupational flexibility) of the labour market is lower for large firms than for small ones.

[25] In 1990 this difference was reduced through the extension of the Workers' Statute to small firms.

Graph 13: Part- time workers (as percentage of overall employment)

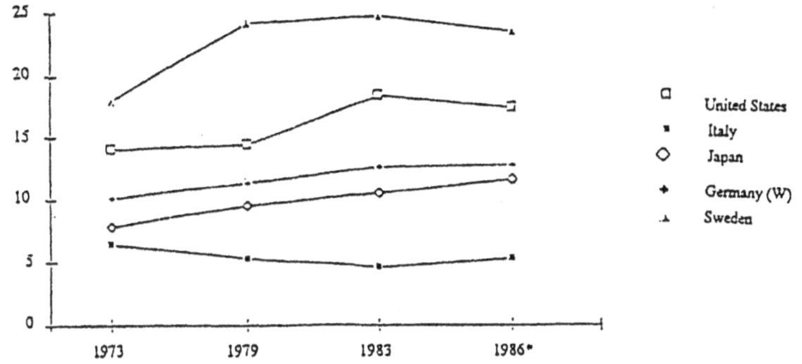

* as regards Italy and Germany

Source: OECD

Graph 14: Non-structural wage flexibility

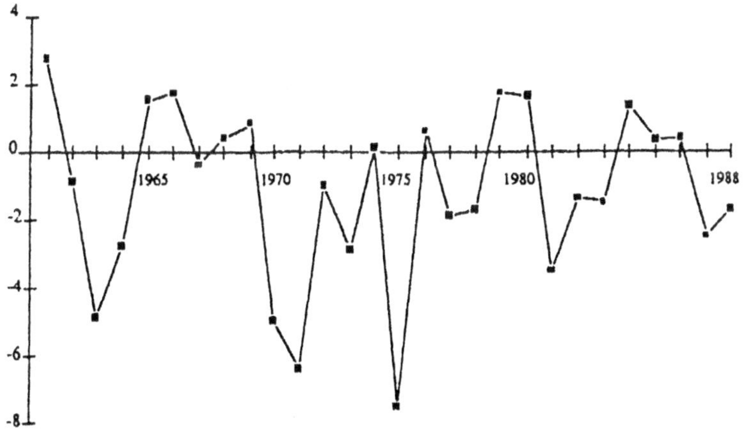

Source: elaboration of data supplied by Istat

Large firms were thus greatly damaged by the increased degree of uncertainty of the economic system and the reduction in labour market flexibility which characterised the 1970s. While, on the one hand, a higher degree of uncertainty led to increases in the desired overall degree of flexibility, on the other hand the reduction of labour market flexibility contributed to lowering the actual overall degree of flexibility.

Hence, the remarkable gap between actual and desired flexibility was one of the main causes of the crisis in large Italian manufacturing firms.

On the other hand, small firms, being more flexible in modifying their own productive and organisational structure, managed to quickly respond to the structural changes occurring in those years. Hence, during the 1970s, large firms accumulated a structural occupational surplus, while in small firms overall employment increased.

Between 1971 and 1981 the number of small and medium-sized firms (with less than 99 workers) went up by 21%, while the number of workers increased by 28.5%. Thus, employment in small- and medium-sized firms increased from 48.5% in 1971 to 55.5% (of total workers) in 1981.

As to large firms, from the early 1980s onwards the gap between desired and actual degree of flexibility gradually shrank[26], due to the lower degree of uncertainty and to the - albeit slow - growth of labour market flexibility. On the other hand, small firms profited far less from their intrinsic flexibility.

3.1.3 Wage inflation, unemployment and income distribution

Up to the late 1960s, the question of functional income distribution was the main cause of both wage and occupational instability. Whenever the issue of contract renewal arose, increased conflict between employers and workers led to phenomena such as strikes and absenteeism, with a consequent increase in wage inflation and in the quota of income destined to labour. These phenomena deserve a more detailed analysis in that they are the first symptoms of the crisis beginning to affect the technological and organisational framework which had led Italy to the "economic miracle" of the 1950s

[26] Therefore, this is true also for the gap between actual and desired labour demand (also with reference to the qualitative characteristics of labour demand: part-time, limited duration, etc.)

and early 1960s. Soaring wages and consequent reductions of profit rates[27] determined a remarkable cyclical increase of unemployment, especially in the years between 1961 and 1969. This was caused by a fall in overall investments, accompanied by an increase in investments aimed at substituting labour with capital. Employment was unfavourably affected by both phenomena, and these negative effects were only mildly mitigated by the cyclical increases in the consumption propensity which were induced by the higher salaries received by employed workers.

On the contrary, a subsequent cyclical reduction of the workers' contractual power boosted profits, accumulation and employment. Goodwin's and Phillips' loops were thus closed, and the ground for their subsequent repetition was laid[28]. This phase was characterised by a "stop and go" economic policy, which played a crucial role in the cycle illustrated above. Such a policy, however, was based on the false assumption that the existing trade-off between inflation and unemployment were stable, so that the economic policy could fully avail itself of the ensuing favourable effects.

In the years between 1969-76 Phillips' loops squeezed to such an extent that they almost disappeared, while the centre of gravity shifted towards higher wage inflation. This was the end of the mechanism which had regulated labour conflicts until then and which was based on both the reactiveness of wage inflation to increases in unemployment and the reactiveness of unemployment to profit variations. In this period, the workers' contractual power was almost totally independent of the labour market's cyclical conditions. Besides, the labour force became a very "rigid" productive input, as a consequence of the important rights ensured to workers by the 1970's Statute. Hence, the cyclical reductions of profits, investments and output did not bring about substantial increases in the unemployment rate. Moreover, since no new regulatory mechanism substituted the old one, the situation became almost uncontrollable. In fact, occupational instability was merely "hidden", rather than under control, while wage instability reached an all-time high.

---

[27] As is well-known, a higher quota of income destined to labour does not necessarily entail a reduction of the quota destined to profits: this happens only *ceteris paribus*. However, in Italy such modifications in income distribution were so quick that this relationship may well be applied, even if only with respect to cyclical short-term fluctuations.

[28] See Vercelli (1986b).

Graph 15: Activity rate (AR) and Employment rate (ER)

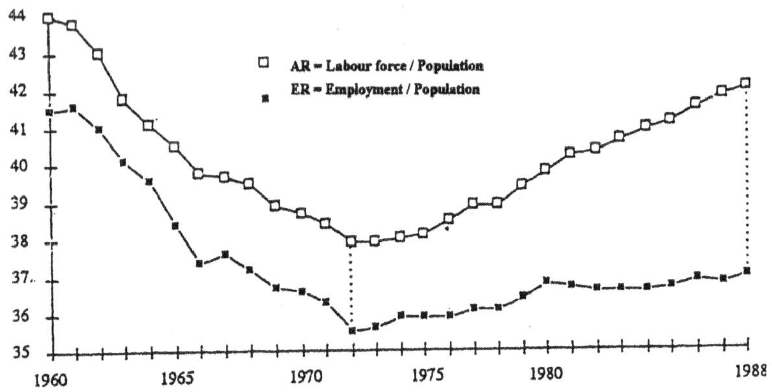

Source: elaboration of data supplied by Istat

Graph 16: Translation motion of Phillips' loops "centre of gravity"

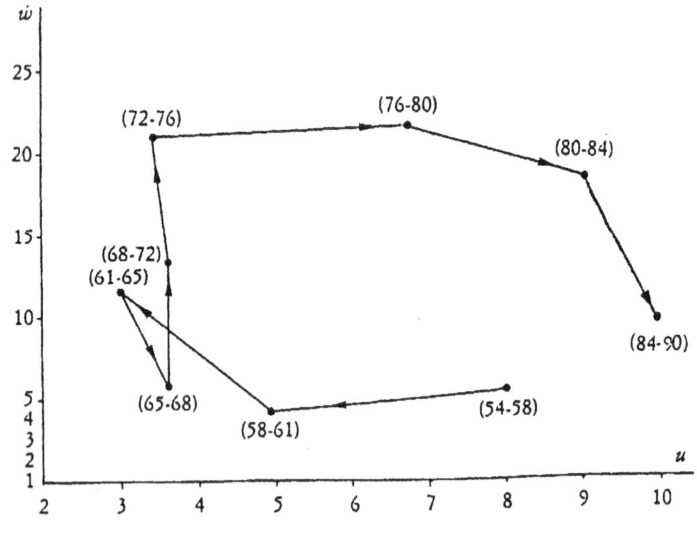

Source: Vercelli (1986b) and elaboration

In order to go deeper in the analysis of labour market structural changes, we may refer to the graph 16, showing the translation motion of Phillips' loops "centre of gravity".

Up until 1961 the translation motion pointed left, thus re-absorbing unemployment without creating wage tensions. Let us examine the shape of the single loops. In the years between 1961 and 1965, full employment brought about a serious increase in inflation, originating the first "explicit" Phillips' loop. The subsequent loop (1965-68) is situated in a position more favourable than the one that could be drawn using data referring to the previous years. This is mainly due to the moderate course taken by trade union policy and by the process of industrial restructuring characterising that period. With the 1968-72 loop, the centre of gravity rapidly shifted upwards. The abrupt increase of inflation brought about by the union struggles of the "hot autumn" (autunno caldo) yields no significant reduction of the unemployment rate. In fact, the consequent loss of profits and international competitiveness limited investments and deterred entrepreneurs from employing new workers. However, unemployment did not rise to the high levels expected, due to the then prevailing optimism over the limited duration of the crisis, and also because of the above-mentioned absence of an efficient regulatory mechanism. Already caught in this predicament, the Italian economy vacillated under the first oil crisis shock. The fourfold increase in crude oil prices caused devastating effects on the productive system: this was due not only to Italy's backwardness compared to many developed countries, nor because of this country's almost total dependence on oil, but mainly because Italian firms were caught in a distributive stalemate position by this unforeseen shock. The unavoidable reduction of actual income following the oil price increase affected wages and profits. This produced an inflationary spiral which gained speed at each phase.In this context, the 1972-76 centre of gravity describes a situation of sky-rocketing inflation accompanied by "hidden" occupational instability. Starting from the mid-1970s, however, a new change of direction took place. The centre of gravity of Phillips' loops shifted towards ever-increasing unemployment rates accompanied by high inflation. Only a decade after, in the mid-1980s, would inflation again be reduced to the levels of the 1960s. As regards the unemployment rate, its slow reduction[29] began only in the late 1980s[30] and was interrupted by the crisis of early 1990s.

---

[29] After reaching levels of over 12%.

[30] In determining the development of the unemployment rate, changes in labour supply are also of primary importance.

3.2 The commodity market

This section focuses on Italy's remarkable economic growth from the post-war years to the present day (with GDP increasing by 500% since 1950 up to 1990, see Graph 17). However the rate of growth progressively decelerated (Graph 18).

A remarkable gap between sectoral employment evolution (as shown in the labour market section) and sectoral production development must also be underlined (see Graph 19). This is mainly due to the different productivity rates of growths in the various sectors (see Graph 20).

While productivity considerably increased in the three private sectors (especially industry), it conversely decreased in the public services sector. The industrial sector reached the productivity levels characterising the sector of marketable services (which showed a moderate productivity growth during the 1980s). On the other hand, the public services sector (whose productivity was the highest until the early 1960s) showed a productivity nearing the - extremely low - levels of the agricultural sector.

At this point, a distinction is to be made between "protected" and "unprotected" sectors. This is mainly based on the different degree of both domestic and international competition which distinguishes the industrial from the tertiary sector (both public and private).

As maintained by recent contributions[31], tertiary backwardness is twofold: on the one hand there is the quantitative and qualitative paucity of the services supplied; on the other, there is a negative contribution to the inflation trend. This situation is mainly due to the "competition deficit" characterising the tertiary sector[32]. An economic policy fostering the creation of higher competition in the public and private tertiary sector is therefore deemed necessary.

---

[31] See F. Barca and I. Visco (1992), "*L'economia italiana nella prospettiva europea: terziario protetto e dinamica dei redditi nominali*", Temi di discussione, Banca d'Italia.

[32] A lower productivity growth, an increase in relative prices and higher profit margins in the tertiary are in part to be explained by the existence of economic and legal barriers (Spaventa, 1973).

Graph 17: GDP expressed by 1985 prices (in billions lire)

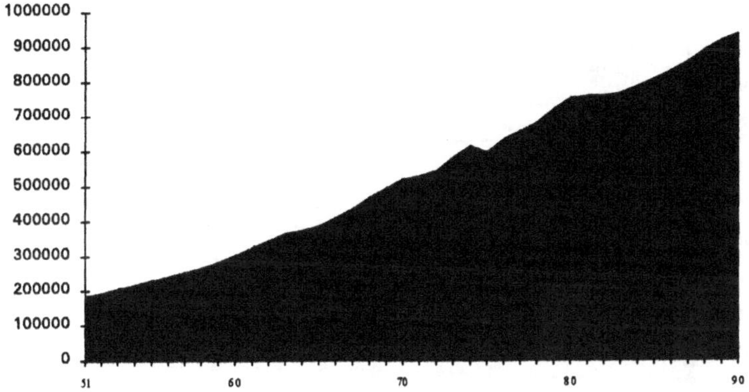

Source: Istat

Graph 18 :GDP % growth rates (divided into time periods)

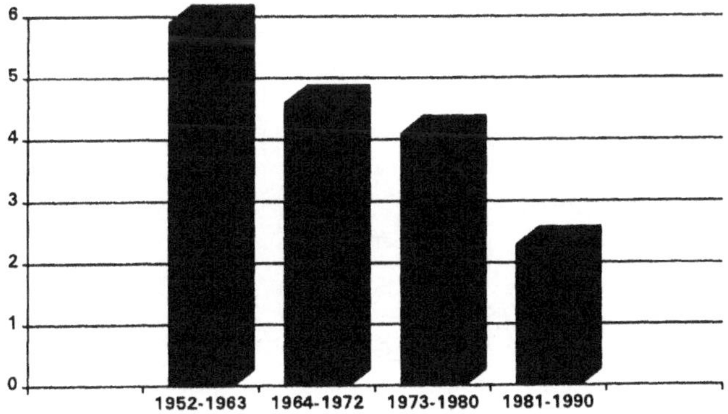

Source: Istat

Graph 19: Value Added according per sectors (in billions of 1985 lire)

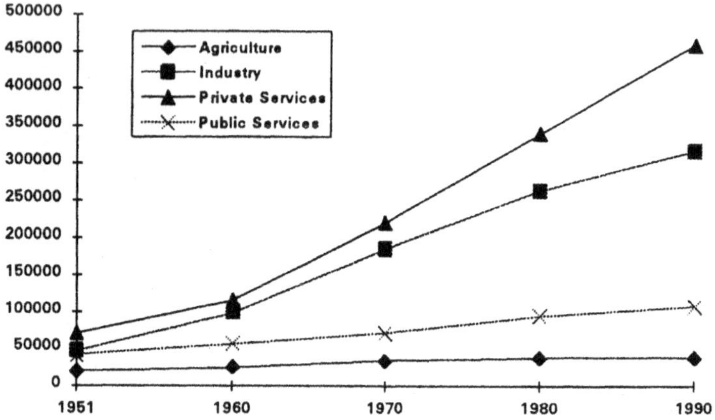

Source: Istat (Toniolo, 1992)

Graph 20: Productivity per sectors (per-capita Value Added in million 1985 lire)

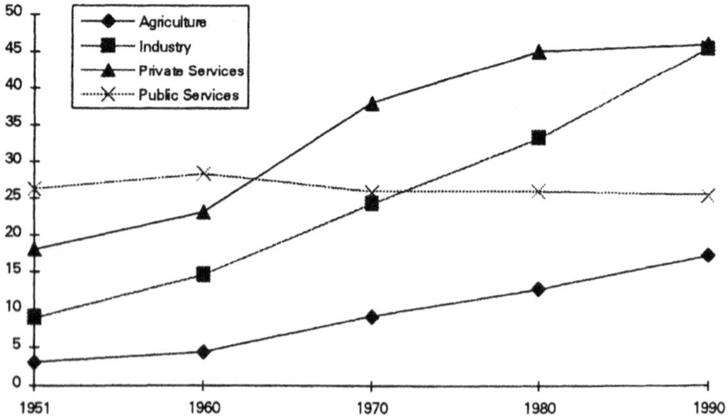

Source: Istat (Toniolo, 1992)

Graph 21: Per-capita GDP according to region (Italy = 100)

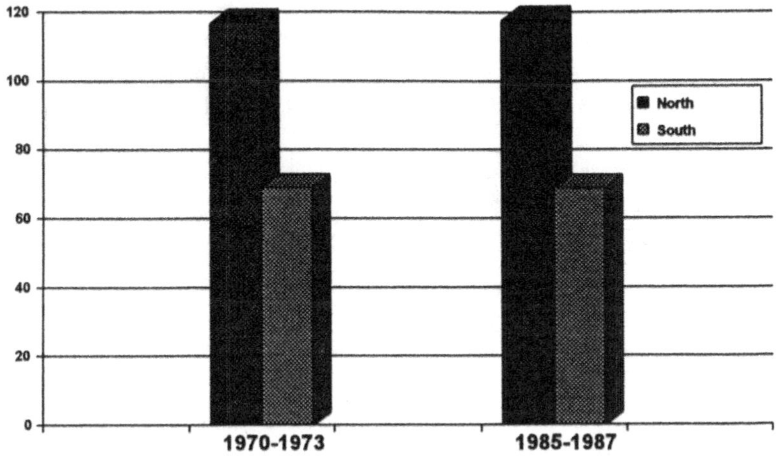

Source: Istat

Graph 22: Per-capita GDP by regions (% annual variations)

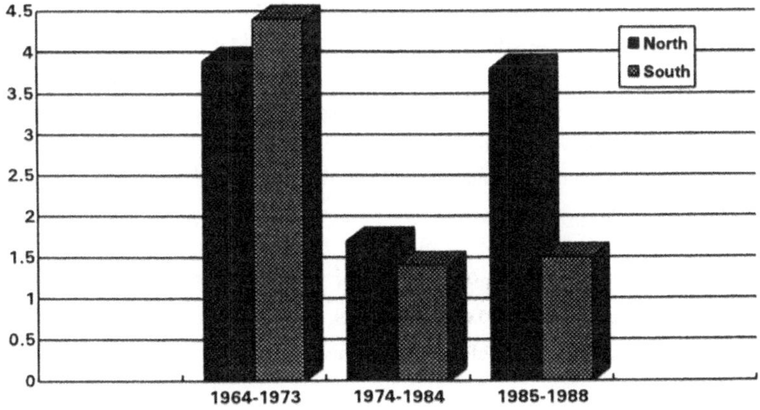

Source: Istat

3.2.1 The "dual" economic growth of Italy

As is well known, the Italian economy is characterised by a sizeable gap between the North and the South. As shown in Graph 21, this gap, in terms of per capita GDP, has remained substantially unaltered in the last two decades.

Per capita GDP variations show that growth was higher in the South of Italy between 1964 and 1973, while in the following years (and especially between 1985 and 1988) the Centre and the North obtained higher growth rates (see Graph 22).

3.2.2 Investment

Although the different theories on growth and development differ under many important aspects, they are unanimous in assigning a strategic role to investment.

Gross fixed investment underwent a remarkable increase in the 1950s and kept high, though oscillating level, in the 1960s. After a marked decline in the 1970s, it stabilized in the 1980s at a lower level (Graph 23).

The evolution of the structure of the investment is revealing. The decline of investment in the last two decades mainly depends on the fall of investment in the building industry and on the gradual reduction of public works expenditure (Graph 24).

As regards Italy, changes in functional income distribution have undoubtedly influenced the qualitative and quantitative trend of investment. The following graph illustrates the evolution of profit margins in industrial transformation over the last forty years (cf. Graph 25).

As shown in the graph, during the 1960s and, above all, the first half of 1970s, the profit margin shrank; this trend was reversed in the 1980s, when the profit margin reached levels higher than those of the 1950s. Only in recent years was there a sudden change of direction.

Graph 23: Gross fixed investment (% of market-price GDP)

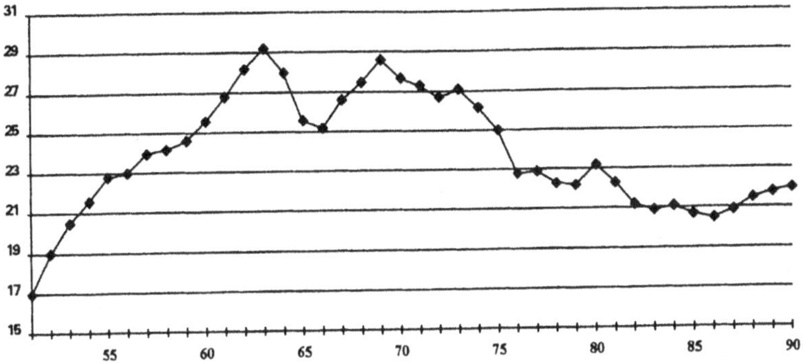

Source: Istat

Graph 24: Gross fixed investment composition (% of market-price GDP)

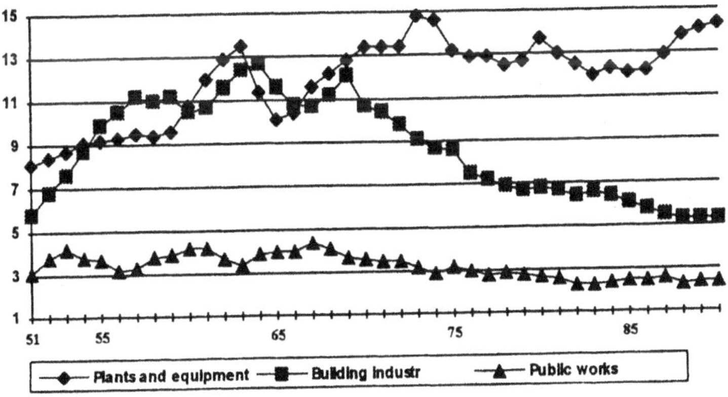

Source: Istat

Graph 25: Profit margins in industrial transformation (as % of Value Added)

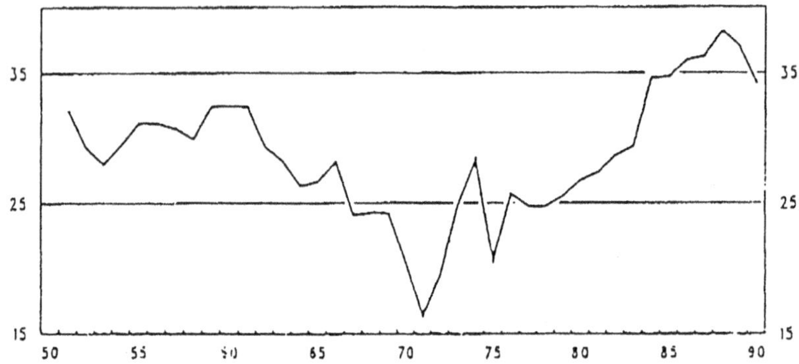

Source: Istat (F. Barca - I. Visco, 1992)

Graph 26: Technological balance of payments (in billions lire)

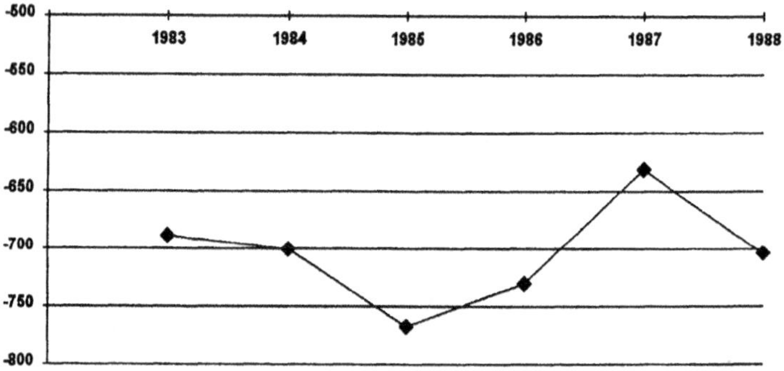

Source: Foreign Exchange Office (UIC)

Capital widening investment, characterising the economy of the 1950s and 1960s, was substituted in the two following decades by capital and labour saving investment. In particular, the 1970s' increase in "structural" uncertainty had a considerably negative influence on long-term investment, whose strategic importance is undeniable. Notwithstanding the difficulty in comparing heterogeneous magnitudes, investment seems yet to be both insufficient in quantity and unsatisfactory in quality. The deepening of the technological gap dividing the Italian economy from that of the major industrialised countries provides further evidence of this thesis.

3.2.3 The foreign trade deficit

The fragility of Italy's accumulation model is highlighted by the analysis of the trade balance evolution. The manufacturing sector faces evident difficulties in counterbalancing the "structural" deficit derived from the agriculture and energy sectors. Italy's specialisation model has been characterised, from the post-war years up to the present day, by a growing contradiction between demand structure, which has become increasingly similar to that of the other industrialised countries, and export structure, which, on the contrary, has proved to be increasingly dissimilar from that of the major industrialised countries[33]. Italy is the only advanced industrialised country which has maintained its specialisation in backward or intermediate industrial technology. The United States and the other main industrial countries, instead, became increasingly specialised in the more advanced sectors. Japan, which in the early 1950s was characterised by lack of specialisation in high-tech sectors as much as Italy was, in the early 1970s had already filled the gap with the United States. Italy's lack of specialisation in high-tech sectors is particularly alarming in the sector of investment goods. This "technological gap" is revealed by the constant deficit of the technological balance of payments (Graph 26).

As shown by the analysis according to geographical areas, Italy's deficit is particularly evident with regard to the USA and, although in lower degree, with the other European countries (Graph 27).

This state of affairs is also partially determined by the scarce human and financial resources allocated to scientific research (cf. Graphs 28 and 29).

---

[33] See Momigliano (1984)

Graph 27: Technological balance of payments according to geografical area (1988 - in billion of lire)

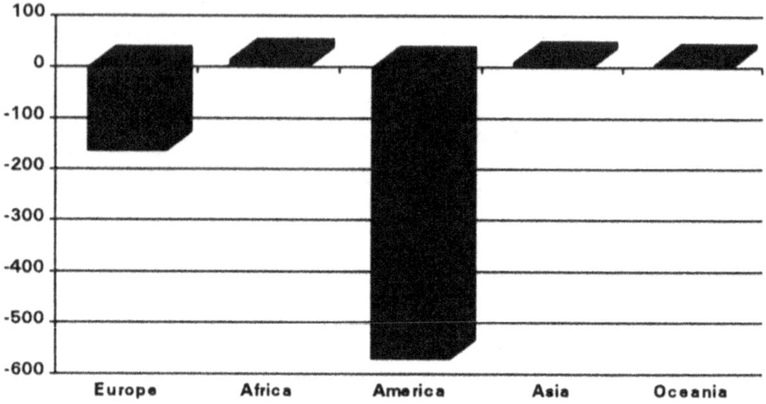

Source: U.I.C.

Graph 28: Staff employed in scientific research (% of active population)

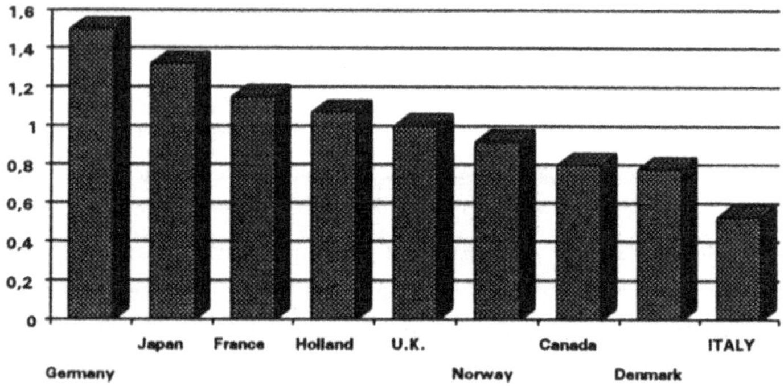

Source: OECD (1987)

Graph 29: Scientific research expenditure (% of GDP)

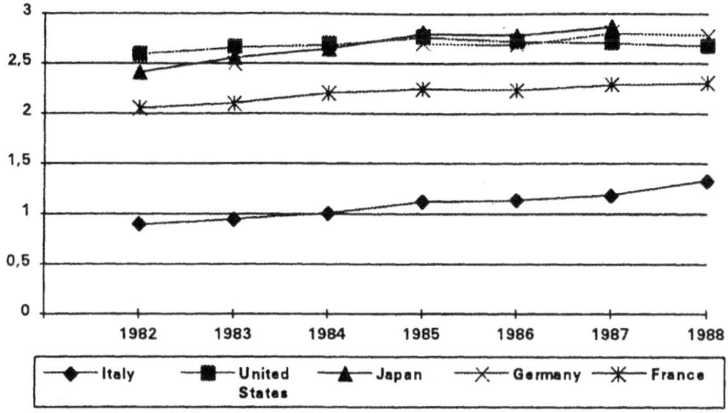

Source: OCDE

Graph 30: Interest rate, official discount rate and inflation

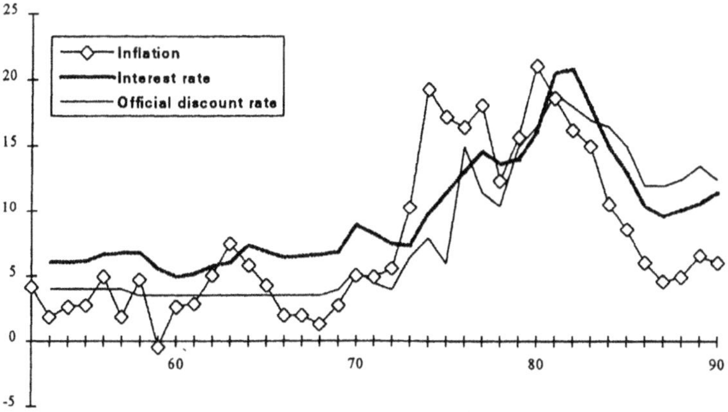

Source: Istat, IFS (Yearbook)

3.2.4 Currency stability

The international monetary system based on the Bretton Woods agreements of 1944 became unstable during the 1960s, and formally came to an end in 1971. Then followed a period of high instability on the currency market, which ended in 1979, when Italy joined The European Monetary System[34]. This, together with the implementation of a "restrictive" monetary policy, led to lower inflation and to a higher foreign exchange stability. Thus, capital movements were liberalised in 1988, and in January 1990 Italy entered the narrow exchange rate band. Subsequently, the Maastricht Treaty (December 1991) paved the way to EMU. However, the monetary turmoil of September 1992 forced the Bank of Italy to an "expensive" defence of the lira (more than 40,000 billion lire in currency reserves "went up in smoke"); failing this, the lira had to be devalued by 7%, and then to leave the EMS. The devaluation and the ensuing free fluctuation of the lira are now leading the economy towards a phase of growing uncertainty. This is especially true considering the circumstances in which these phenomena took place[35].

3.3 The monetary and financial market

In this section the principal structural transformations affecting the Italian monetary and financial market are analysed.

3.3.1 Inflation

In the period examined, monetary instability in Italy never reached the levels of "hyper-inflation". However, wage claims, exploded in 1962-63 and even more in the period which culminated in the "hot autumn" (1968-69). The wage explosion, along with the oil crises (1973-74 and 1979), determined a fifteen-year period characterised by high inflation. A fairly permissive attitude of the Bank of Italy, permitted the 1962-63 monetary expansion and the 1973 decision to let the lira fluctuate, thus favouring the defence

---

[34] The EMS was based on fluctuation bands of various widths and presenting parities which may be re-adjusted following a joint decision of the member countries. From 1979 up to 1992 there have been 12 realignments, the latest of which occurred on 13 September 1992, when the lira was devalued by 7%.

[35] Particular attention should be given to the situation of political instability following the elections of April 1992 and to renewed social conflicting which followed the government's "economic manoeuvre". The latter will also be undoubtedly followed by further measures aimed at a re-equilibration of public finance.

of profit and accumulation at the expense of price stability (see Nardozzi, 1983 and 1985)[36]. However, increasing monetary instability called for an urgent recovery of price control. To this purpose, the Bank of Italy gradually attempted to strengthen its autonomy from the Government, implementing a new policy centered on the development of the monetary market (from 1975 onwards).

As a result of Italy's joining the EMS (1979), the "divorce" of the Bank of Italy from the Treasury (1981) and less conflicting industrial relations, inflation substantially decreased, especially in the first half of the 1980s.

Recently, after the lira had to be devalued by 7% and then quit the EMS, fears of a new increase in inflation have reappeared, but do not yet have materialized in a very depressionary context.

3.3.2 Interest rates

It is well-known that high interest rates slow down the accumulation process, especially with regard to small firms.[37] Graph 30 shows the evolution of the nominal interest rate on long-term State bonds and the official discount rate, compared with the evolution of the inflation rate.

Low nominal rates in the 1950s and 1960s were followed by a steep upward climb in the 1970s, the gradual reduction of the 1980s and the new increase of recent years. As shown in the graph, real interest rates were especially high in the 1980s, and continued to go up in recent years. The "restrictive" monetary policy (revealed, e.g., by the official discount rate trend) has lowered inflation (particularly in the first half of the 1980s) and stabilised the exchange rate (up until mid-1992), but has also brought about negative effects on the accumulation process and on the growth rate of the public debt, since the annual deficit is mainly made up of payable interests.

In the summer of 1992, the - failed - attempt to defend the lira's exchange rate caused an abrupt increase in real interest rates, which only many months after the lira quit the EMS, began to go down.

---

[36]However, it should be noticed that such a policy was hardly avoidable in a period characterised by remarkable imbalances in firms' accounts.

[37] Small firms contractual power cannot be compared to that of larger firms (Barca - Magnani, 1985).

3.3.3 Financial stability

The Italian banking system has been characterised by relative financial stability from the post-war years up to the present day[38]. This is not surprising since the 1936 Banking Law, on which the system was based untill very recently, had as its main aim financial stability, having been enacted after a period of considerable financial turmoil. Financial stability was granted both by a marked distinction between short- and long-term credit and by the oligopolistic form of the market. Oligopolistic control ensured stability even in periods (such as the 1970s) characterised by financial imbalances of both private and public firms, allowing banks to follow a prudent policy, thus avoiding the risks of instability. This result was achieved through an insurance-oriented policy of interest margins. The margins, which were already fairly high (generally more than 3%), went up again from the mid-1970s, in the attempt to control the increasing uncertainty of the system. Moreover, the State protected those firms which were undergoing a critical period, thus curbing the financial crisis from the start. The Bank of Italy followed suit, since "unlike the German banks, it was not inclined to let institution in difficulty go bankrupt" (Nardozzi, 1963). However, it is widely held that this policy, while favouring financial stability, curbed the entrepreneurial capacity of both the productive and financial systems, giving rise to the degeneration of the so-called "aided capitalism". In particular, credit interest rates reached much higher levels than those possible in a more competitive and efficient financial system, with consequent negative effects on productive capital accumulation. In conclusion, it may be said that the Italian financial system has been characterised by "hidden financial instability", bringing about different forms of instability: accumulation slowed down and unemployment rose.

The higher degree of competitiveness gained by the financial market starting from the second half of the 1980s[39], however, entails risks of open financial instability. Increasing bank concentration, which is inevitable in order to gain competitiveness on the international market, should not lead the supervisory authorities to forgetting the beneficial effects of a more decentralised and pluralistic system, both as regards the accumulation of productive capital and the establishment of a pluralistic economy. Defence of a more competitive market, in fact, does entail the safeguarding of such a market through

[38]With some important exceptions, such as the bankruptcies of the *Banca Privata Italiana* in 1974 and the *Banco Ambrosiano* in 1982. However, neither of these episodes caused generalised financial instability.

[39]For example, the prohibition to open new "counters" (sportelli) has now been abolished.

timely regulatory norms of a structural type[40]. Moreover, the strengthening of the monetary authorities and of the co-ordination among the various central banks is even more necessary with the internationalisation of the capital market. In fact, one of the crucial stages of EMU is the creation of a Central European Bank, which is to pursue the goal of price stability.

3.3.4 The public debt

At present, the most serious forms of instability depend on the persisting public deficit and growing State indebtedness. There is now a wide consensus on the necessity of introducing "structural" policy measures aimed at reducing the public debt. However it is still very controversial how the burden entailed in this task is to be divided among the different social groups.

First of all, let us examine the evolution of public debt during the last few decades. State indebtedness started to be particularly serious in the late 1960s. The situation remarkably worsened between 1970 and 1990, when the debt jumped from 35% to 100% of GDP (cf. Graph 31). Between 1960 and 1990 public administration expenditure went up from 30.7% to 52.3% of GDP. Such an increase is mainly due to current spending, in particular social security, interests on public debt and staff salaries (see, e.g., Micossi - Tullio, 1992). The number of employees in the public administration has now reached 18% of the labour force (4,218,000 units), while those who receive a pension are now 19 million over a population of 57 million (there is the possibility of receiving more then one pension).

As to public revenues, they increased substantially only in the last decade, up to almost 43% of GDP in 1990. This increase is mainly a result of direct taxation.

In the comparison with the major EC countries, Italy ranks among the worst, together with Belgium and Ireland, and Italy's Debt/GDP ratio is more than double with respect to France and Germany and threefold with respect to the UK[41].

---

[40] A thoroughly competitive market does not require the central bank to play the role of "playmaker" (which may be advisable in a centralised and hyerarchic credit system), but rather that of "referee", which will make sure that all the players respect the rules (Cassese, 1985).

[41] It must be underlined that one of the present conditions for European monetary union is that the Debt/GDP ratio should not exceed 60% (Italy exceeds 100%) by 1997.

Graph 31: Public debt (% of GDP)

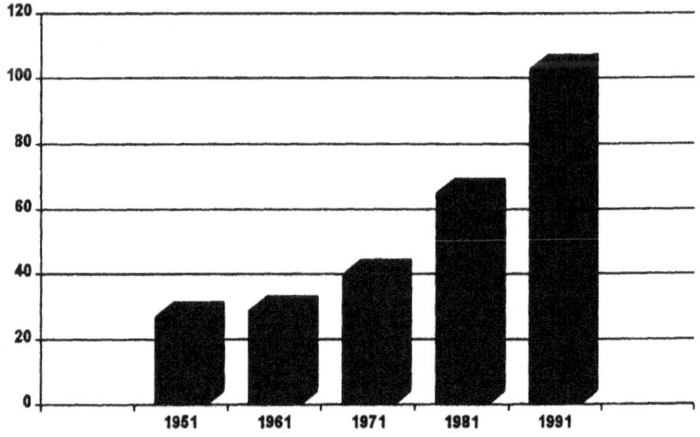

Source: Ministry of Treasury and Bank of Italy

This "structural" imbalance (the growing debt brings about new expenses in order to pay interests; this contributes to increase in the debt, and so on) is becoming one of the most dangerous sources of uncertainty of the Italian economic system, which is likely to have serious effects on the possibility of a balanced and sustainable economic growth.

4 Conclusions

The theoretical nexus between uncertainty and flexibility suggested a few useful insights on the evolution of the Italian economy after the Second World War.

The Italian "economic miracle" (1950s and early 1960s) was characterized by a process of growth led by rapidly expanding big firms and soaring public expenditure. In this period the process of growth was quite stable as unemployment progressively shrank and inflation remained low; even structural change was fairly steady as it consisted mainly in the progressive completion of the productive matrix, and in a progressive concentration of production in big plants run by centralized organisations (both public and private).

Instability and systemic uncertainty began to grow since the wage upsurge of 1963 which triggered the first inflationary episode after reconstruction, and reached very high levels in the period which began with the trade union unrest of 1968-69 (culminating in the "autunno caldo") and extended at least until the adhesion of Italy to EMS (1979). This period was characterized by severe instability in the market for labour (growing unemployment and acute industrial conflict), in the economic aggregates (growing foreign and budgetary instability), and in the monetary and financial relations (high inflation and repressed financial instability). The high degree of instability exhibited by the Italian economy in this period was due in part to international factors (the breakdown of the Bretton Woods system of international payments in 1971, the two oil shocks in 1973 and 1979, the deterioration of cold war), and in part to domestic factors (high tension in industrial relations, introduction of an escalator clause strengthening indexation in 1975, political stalemate). All these factors contributed to induce a high degree of systemic uncertainty which dramatically changed the conditions of economic activity. While big firms, both private and public, found it difficult to adapt to this very uncertain milieu, small firms could exploit a higher degree of flexibility and managed to save the Italian economy by increasing their share of employment, investment and exports.

In the early 1980s the adhesion to EMS was followed by a more restrictive monetary policy, measures of deindexation of wages, and more quite industrial relations. As a consequence inflation began to recede, real interest rates began to rise, and uncertainty progressively fell down. Big firms, which in the meantime had restructured the process of production in a more decentralized and flexible way, succeeded in coming out of the crisis by expanding production, profits, investment and exports, and sometimes also employment. On the contrary, small firms which had lost part of their comparative advantage with the reduction of instability and uncertainty, were particularly hit by the restrictive monetary policy and the ensuing increasing real rates of interests.

In the last two years instability and uncertainty increased again. This is due to international factors (the disequilibria induced by the German reunification, the world depression which hits mainly Europe, the downfall of EMS) and by domestic reasons (a profound political and institutional crisis which interacts perversely with the economic crisis). Also in this occasion, according to the first data, while big firms plunged in a very deep crisis, the small firms were able to exploit their superior flexibility in conditions of high instability and uncertainty. Their resilience was aided by the rapidly falling rates of interests and the devaluation of Italian lira, but big firms seemed to be much slower in taking advantage of the new opportunities.

The high flexibility shown by Italian small firms in an uncertain milieu has stabilized the performance of the Italian economy since the Second World War. This made depressions much less severe than they would have been otherwise, but this also contributed to concealing the increasing weight of some crucial unsolved structural problems. The Italian economy is the only big industrial economy which is still specialized in products having low technological content. The Italian exports are concentrated in sectors characterized by traditional goods, while the Italian economic system is still net importer of high-tech goods. In addition the Italian balance of the technological payments is still characterized by soaring deficits. In the fifties these structural features were shared by Japan that however in the meantime managed to shift to the forefront of high-tech production and to become net exporter of industrial patents. This depends in part on the economic policy pursued in Italy so far, and in part on the peculiar institutional conditions.

The percentage of investment in R&D in national expenditure increased in the 1980s, but it is still much lower than in the other main industrialized countries. In addition, the high degree of economic and political instability, generally higher than in the other main industrialized countries, has discouraged strategic long-term investment which is crucial for developing the high-tech sectors.

Finally, the quality of infrastructures, both material and immaterial, is much lower than that of the main competitors, and this sizeably increases production costs and lowers the quality of products and services. This competitive disadvantage of Italian producers depends in great part on the inefficiency and corruption of the Public Administration. There is a growing consensus on the necessity of its radical reform in order to provide a better environment for productive activity. A rapid success of a radical reform of Public Administration is a crucial condition for the future prospects of the Italian economy.

Graphic appendix of international comparisons

In this appendix we present some international comparisons which may help to understanding better the peculiar feature of the Italian development.

Graph A1: Standardised unemployment rates in the major seven countries (% of total labour force)

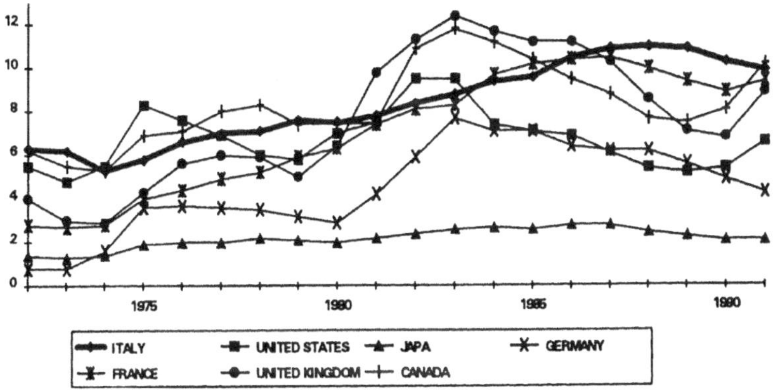

Source: OECD

Graph A2: Growth of real GDP (percentage changes from previous period) (a)

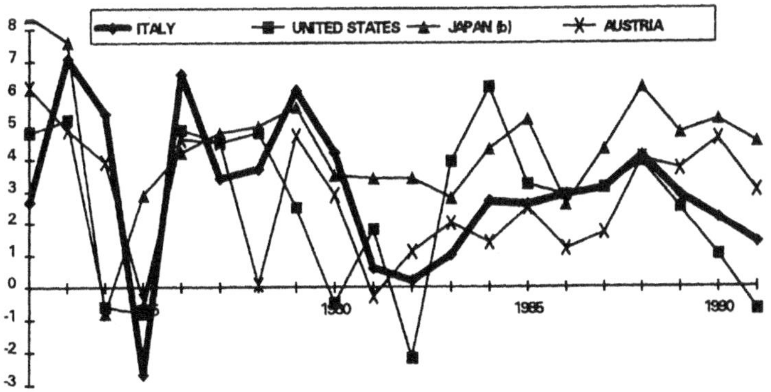

(a) Aggregates were computed on the basis of 1987 GDP weights in 1987 US dollars.
(b) GNP.
Source: OECD

Graph A3: Gross public debt (a) 1993 (percentage of nominal GDP)

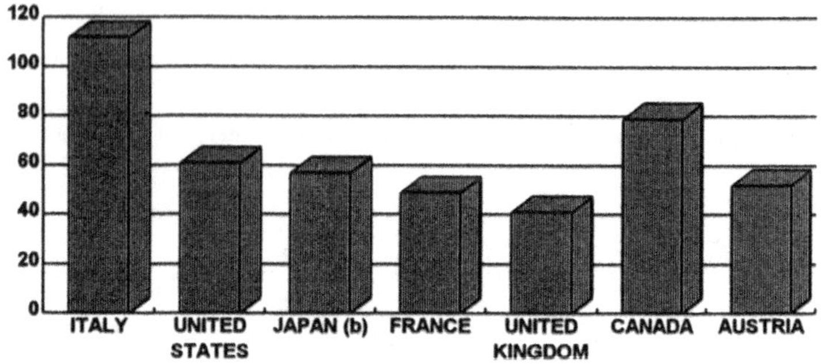

(a) Refers to general government debt.
(b) percentage of nominal GNP
Source: OECD estimates

Graph A4: Central government financial balances (1993) (as a percentage of nominal GDP)

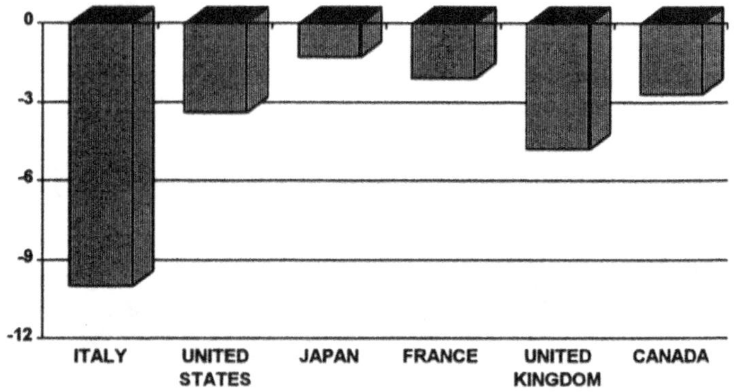

Source: OECD estimates

Graph A5: Productivity in the business sector (1960 - 1973) (percentage changes at annual rate)

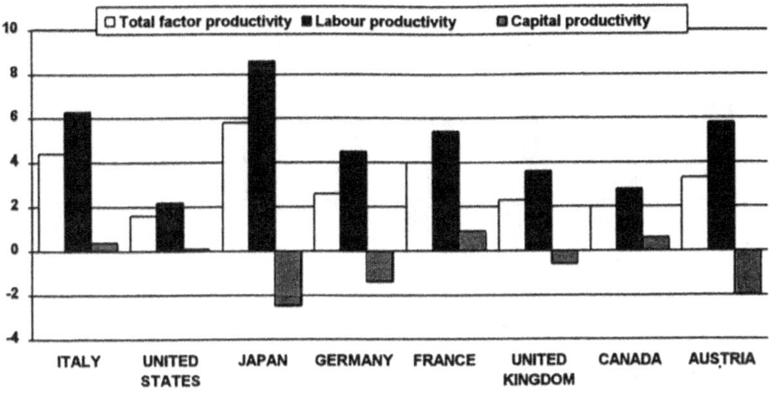

Source: OECD

Graph A6: Productivity in the business sector (1973 - 1979) (percentage changes at annual rate)

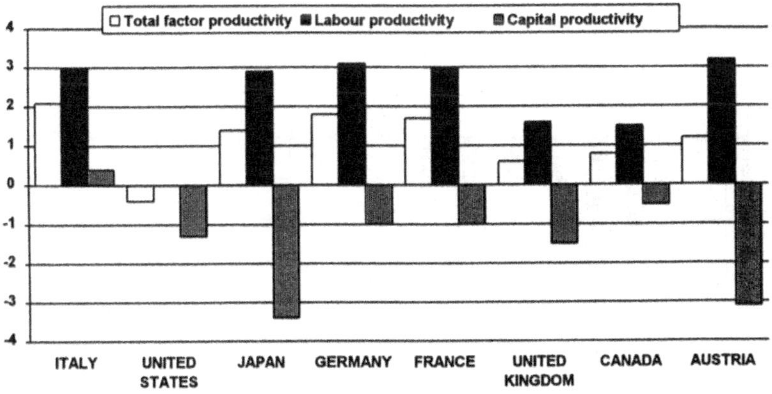

Source:OECD

Graph A7: Productivity in the business sector (1979 - 1990) (percentage changes at annual rate)

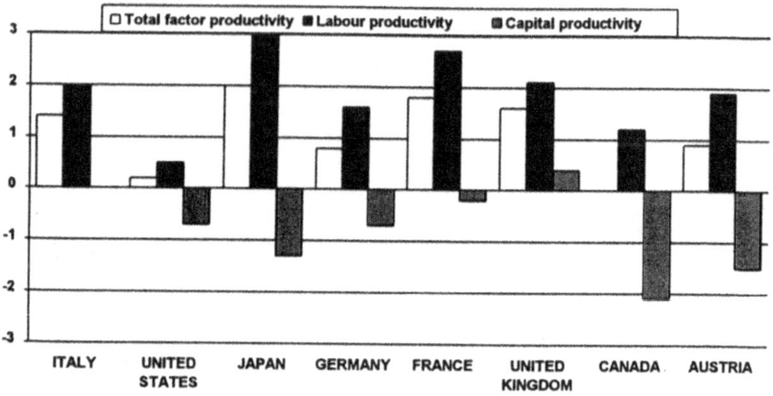

Source: OECD

Graph A8: Current balances (as percentage of GDP)

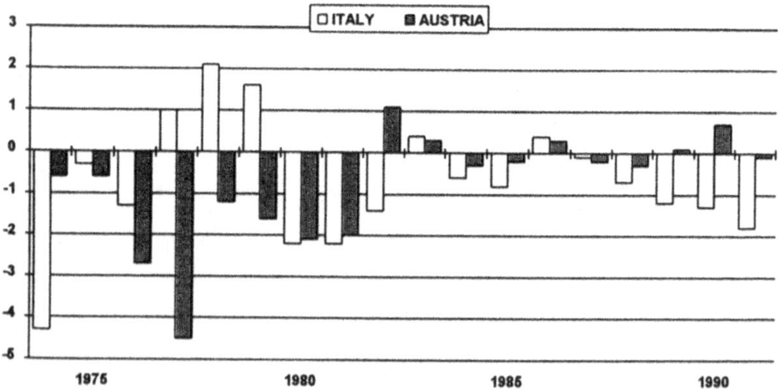

Source: OECD

Graph A9: Private consumption deflators (% changes from previous year)

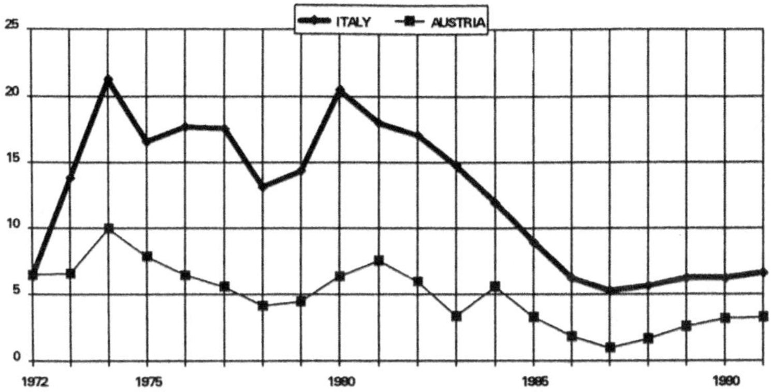

Source: OECD

Graph A10: National saving (as percentage of GDP) 1990

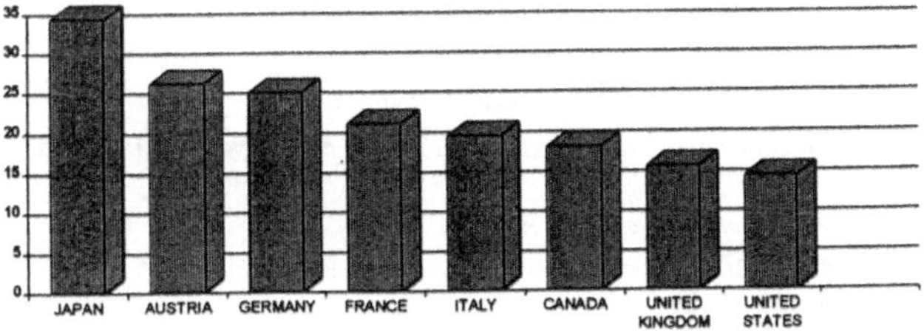

Source: OECD

References

A.I.E.L. (1988): *Flessibilità e mercato del lavoro*, Atti del Convegno AIEL, Arco di Trento.

Alessandrini, L. (1978): *Lavoro irregolare e lavoro nero*, Il Mulino, Bologna.

Aoki, M. (ed.) (1984): *The economic analysis of the Japanese firm*, Amsterdam, North-Holland.

Arcuti, L. (1985): "Intervento", Tavola rotonda su "Le grandi banche e le trasformazioni dei mercati finanziari", *Economia Italiana*, n. 3.

Banca d'Italia, (various issues): *Relazione Annuale*, Roma.

Banca d'Italia, (various issues): *Bollettino economico*, Roma.

Barca, F., Visco, I. (1992): "L'economia italiana nella prospettiva europea: terziario protetto e dinamica dei redditi nominali", *Temi di discussione*, Banca d'Italia.

Barca, F., Caselli, P. (1989): "Competitivita' internazionale e ristrutturazione dell'industria italiana negli anni '80", *Politica Economica.*

Barca, F., Magnani, M. (1989): *L'industria fra capitale e lavoro*, Il Mulino, Bologna.

Bertola, G. (1991): "Labor turnover costs and average lavor demand", *Working Paper Series*, NBER.

Bertola, G. (1991): "Flexibility, investiment, and growth", *Working Paper Series*, NBER.

Bianchi, G., Bruckmann, G., Vasko, T. (1983): *Background material to the conference on "Long waves, depression and innovation: implications for national and regional economic policy"*, Firenze, IRPET.

Bodo, G., Sestito, P. (1991): *Le vie dello sviluppo*, Il Mulino, Bologna.

Bodo, G., Sestito, P. (1991): "Disoccupazione e dualismo territoriale", *Studi e Ricerche*, Il Mulino, Bologna.

Boyer, R., Wolleb, E. (1987): *La flessibilità del lavoro in Europa*, Ediesse.

Bracalente, B., Marbach, G. (1989): *Il part-time nel mercato del lavoro italiano*, F. Angeli.

Bruno, S. (1986): "Incertezza, complessità e crisi dell'economia del controllo", *Economia & Lavoro.*

Camera dei Deputati (1985): *Piano per l'occupazione giovanile*, Ministero del Lavoro, Roma.

Carli, G. (ed.) (1977): *Sviluppo economico e struttura finanziaria in Italia*, Il Mulino, Bologna.

Centro Culturale Congressi (1983): *Il domani della piccola e media impresa*, Saint Vincent.

Centro Studi Confindustria, *Rapporto CSC sull'industria Italiana*, Roma.

Conti, V., Silvani, M. (1984): "Un'interpretazione strutturale del disavanzo dei conti con l'estero", *Economia Italiana*, n. 3.

Dallago, B. (1988): *L'economia irregolare*, F. Angeli.

Dell'Aringa, C. (1986): "Labor market flexibility: the case of Italy", *Discussion Paper C.R.E.L.I.*, n. 1, Università Cattolica di Milano.

Emerson, M. (1988): "Regulation or deregulation of the labor market", *European Economic Review*, n. 32.

Ente per gli studi monetari, bancari e finanziari "Luigi Einaudi" (1986): *Oltre la crisi*, Il Mulino, Bologna.

Ente per gli studi monetari, bancari e finanziari "Luigi Einaudi" (1992): *Il disavanzo pubblico in Italia: natura strutturale e politiche di rientro*, Il Mulino, Bologna.

Giavazzi, F., Spaventa, L. (1988): *Hight public debt: the Italian experience*, Cambridge University Press.

Goodwin, R. (1967): "A growth cycle", in Feistein C. H. (ed.), *Socialism, capitalism and economic growth*, Cambridge University Press, pp. 54-59.

Henry, C. (1974): *Investiment decision under uncentainty: the irreversibility effect.*

ISCO (1984): *Analisi dell'interscambio commerciale con l'estero (1970-82)*, Roma.

ISTAT, (variuos issues): *Supplemento al bollettino - Rilevazione delle forze lavoro*, Roma.

ISTAT, (various issues): *Annuario di statistica italiana*, Roma.

Jones, R. A., Ostroy, J. M. (1984): "Flexibility and uncertainty", *Review of Economic Studies*, pp. 13-32.

Keynes, J. M. (1936): *The general theory of employment, interest and money*, MacMillan, London.

Knight, F.H. (1921): *Risk, uncertainty and profit*, Houghton and Mifflin, Boston.

Krepes, D. N. (1979): "A rapresentation theorem for preference for flexibility", *Econometrica*, n. 47.

Marshak, T., Nelson, R. (1962): "Flexibility, uncertainty and economic theory", *Metroeconomica*, pp. 42-58.

Martini, M. (1978): *La mobilità del lavoro. Un'analisi comparativa*, Milano.

Martini, M. et al. (1987): "L'uomo protagonista dell'economia che cambia", *Synesis*, IV, n.1.

Maruani, M., Reynaud, E., Romani, C. (eds.) (1990): "La flessibilità del lavoro in Italia", *Quaderni di Economia del Lavoro*, n. 41 - 42.

Micossi, S., Tullio, G. (1991): "Fiscal imbalances, economic distorsions and long run performance of the Italian economy", *Quaderni di ricerca*, LUISS, Osservartorio e centro di studi monetari, n. 9.

Micossi, S., Tullio, G. (1992): "Squilibri di bilancio, ddistorsioni economiche e "performance" di lungo periodo dell'economia italiana", *Rivista di Politica Economica*, n. 2.

Mingione, E. (1988) *Underground economy and irregular forms of employment: the case of Italy - Final report*, Commission of European Communities; Program for Research and actions on the development of the labor market, mimeo.

Ministero del Lavoro (1985): *La politica occupazionale per il prossimo decennio. Le analisi*, Brunetta R. (ed.), Roma.

Ministero del Lavoro (1987): *Rapporto '87. Lavoro e politiche dell'occupazione in Italia*, Fondazione G. Brodolini e CER (ed.), Roma.

Ministero del Lavoro (1988): *Rapporto '88. Lavoro e politiche dell'occupazione in Italia*, Fondazione G. Brodolini e CER (ed.), Roma.

Ministero del Lavoro (1989): *Rapporto '89. Lavoro e politiche dell'occupazione in Italia*, Fondazione G. Brodolini e CER (ed.), Roma.

Ministero del Lavoro (1990-91): *Rapporto '90-'91. Lavoro e politiche dell'occupazione in Italia*, Fondazione G. Brodolini e CER (ed.), Roma.

Ministero del Tesoro (1988): *Il debito pubblico in Italia: 1861-1987*, vol. 1, Roma.

Modigliani, F., Padoa Schioppa, F., Rossi, N. (1986): "Aggregate unemployment in Italy: 1960-1983", *Economica*.

Momigliano, F., Siniscalco, D. (1984): "Specializzazione internazionale, tecnologia e caratteristiche dell'offerta", *Moneta e Credito*, n. 146.

Nardozzi, G. (ed.) (1980): *I difficili anni '70*, Etas Libri, Milano.

Nardozzi, G. (1983): *Tre sistemi creditizi*, Il Mulino, Bologna.

Nardozzi, G. (1986): *Autonomia delle banche centrali e rapporti con il governo: il caso italiano*, dattiloscritto.

NOMISMA (1983): *Rapporto sulle tendenze della ristrutturazione industriale in Italia*, Bologna.

OECD (1984): *Perspectives de l'emploi*, Paris.

OECD (1985): *Labor force statistics. 1963-1983*, Paris.

OECD (1986): *Flexibility in the labour market*, Paris.

OECD (1986): *Employment outlook*, Paris.

OECD (1986): "Concealed employment", *Employment outlook*.

OECD (1990): *Perspectives of employment*, Paris.

OECD (1991): *Economic survey of Italy*, Paris.

Oi, W. (1962): "Labour as a quasi-fixed factor", *Journal of Political Economy*.

Onado, M. (1983): "Evoluzione dei criteri di vigilanza nel sistema bancario italiano", *Banca, Impresa Societa'*.

Pierelli, F. (1983): "I mutamenti nella struttura degli scambi mondiali e la "posizione dell'Italia"", *Temi di discussione*, Banca d'Italia.

Piore, M. (1986): "Perspectives of labour market flexibility", *Industrial Relations*, n. 2.

Regini, M. (ed.) (1988): *La sfida della flessibilità*, F. Angeli.

Rey G., M. (1985): *L'influenza del sommerso sulla formazione del prodotto interno lordo*.

Sabel, C. (1985): *A fighting chance: structural change and new labour strategies,* Contributo presentato al convegno su "Stato, politica economica e relazioni industriali in Europa: quale destino?", Facolta' di Economia, Brescia.

Salvati, M. (1988): "Mercati del lavoro e relazioni industriali. Note in margine al dibattito su flessibilità ed occupazione", *Politica Economica*.

Signorelli, M. (1990): "Incertezza, flessibilità e domanda di lavoro. Un tentativo di chiarificazione concettuale", *Economia & Lavoro*, n. 3.

Signorelli, M. (1992): "Incertezza, flessibilità e domanda di lavoro: il caso dell'Italia", *Note Economiche*, n. 1/2.

Spinelli, F., Fratianni, M. (1991): *Storia monetaria d'italia*, Mondadori, Segrate.

Valli, V. (1984): "Flessibilità nell'uso della forza lavoro: la proposta delle fasce d'orario", *Forum Isel*, n. 1.

Vercelli, A. (1977): "The Phillips dilemma: a new suggested approach", *Economic Notes*, VI, n. 1.

Vercelli, A. (1986a): "Stagflation and the recent revival of shumpeterian entrepreneurship", in H. Frisch and B. Gahlen (eds.), *Causes of contemporary stagnation*, Springer-Verlag, Berlin.

Vercelli, A. (1986b): "La "lunga crisi": interpretazioni e prospettive", in *Oltre la crisi*, Ente Einaudi, Il Mulino, Bologna.

Vercelli, A. (1989): "Uncertainty, technological flexibility and long-term fluctuations, in Di Matteo M., Goodwin R. and Vercelli A. (eds.), *Technological and social factors in long-term fluctuation*, Springer, Berlin.

Vercelli, A. (1991): *Methodological foundations of macroeconomics: Keynes and Lucas*, Cambridge University Press.

Vona, S. (1984): "Note per una interpretazione del ruolo del commercio internazionale negli anni della crisi (1973-83)", *Economia Italiana*, n. 3.

European Perspectives for Austria and Italy

Fritz Breuss and Fritz Schebeck
Austrian Institute of Economic Research (WIFO)

1 Introduction

Italy and Austria are facing the intensifying process of European integration in several respects under quite different conditions which do not only depend on the different size of their economies but are also rooted in the political and economic developments in the past. Nevertheless, if Austria will become a member of the European Union (EU) the challenges will gradually converge. Whereas Austria's political system has shown considerable stability, in Italy a process of political change is under way. After the breakdown of Communism in Eastern Europe in 1989 Italy was shaken in its political foundations. The old structures of political parties are in complete reformation with new groupings seeking democratic legitimacy. Hence, Italy's challenge is more of an internal nature, whereas those of Austria is more external.

For both countries the deepening and widening of European integration represents a big challenge. In the years 1993 and 1994 the integration process got a remarkable kick: EC's single market came into operation in January 1, 1993. After a pathbreaking ratification thriller the Maastricht Treaty (treaty of the European Union) became effective in November 1, 1993. The negative vote of the Swiss referendum in December 1992 delayed the begin of the European Economic Area (EEA). In January 1, 1994 the EEA was set into operation between 12 EU members and 5 EFTA countries (with the exception of Liechtenstein and Switzerland). Four EFTA countries (Austria, Finland, Norway and Sweden) started their negotiations for an EU membership in February 1993. Already one year later the talks were successfully finished. Provided that the referenda in those EFTA countries are affirmative, the EU will be enlarged by four EFTA countries on January 1, 1995. After the revolution in Eastern Europe in 1989, EU and EFTA renewed their trade relations with the Visegrad countries (Czech Republic, Poland, Slowakia, Hungary) via asymmetric free trade agreements. The dynamic of the European integration has to be seen also in a world-wide perspective:

The Uruguay Round of the GATT could be finalized in December 1993, the NAFTA between Canada, Mexico and the USA came into operation on January 1, 1994. There seems to be a break-through towards more liberalization of trade on several levels. Although the successes of European and North American integration led to the fear of a dangerous regionalism with potential trade wars, the Uruguay Round is the world-wide umbrella of trade liberalization with new instruments and safeguard rules.

In section 2 the economic position of the two countries, the performance of their economies in the past and the main features of their economic policies are briefly sketched. An assessment of the macroeconomic effects expected to be brought about by the completion of the internal market is presented in section 3. Finally, in a preliminary way, some aspects of the impact of EMU are discussed in section 4.

2 Economic position and performance of the two countries[1]

The Italian economy belongs to the "Great Seven" ("G 7") of the industrialized nations. Having a share of 6% of OECD's GDP Italy ranks fifth among the 24 OECD countries. Austria with a share of 0.9% of OECD's total production – a small industrialized country – occupies rank 14. In 1992, GDP per capita in Austria (18,096 US-$) exceeded those in Italy by 3.5% to 11.2% (depending on the method of calculation); in the same period EC's GDP per capita (16.949 US-$) was surpassed by 6.8% to 13.7%. In relation to EC Italy performed better by about 3% (at current prices and exchange rates/PPP) and 2% (at current prices and exchange rates).

Macroeconomic development

On average, in the last decade (ending with 1993) Italy's real GDP grew nearly as fast as that of Austria (+2¼% per year). While production of services expanded stronger in Italy Austria's industrial production grew annually and averaged by 1½ percentage points faster. Among the components of domestic demand the Italian lead in growth of consumption was more pronounced than that in investment. Contribution of foreign trade (goods and services) to real economic growth was slightly negative in both countries (in Austria closer to zero).

---

[1] This section relies on Breuss (1991, 1992a).

Inflation has developed more favorably in Austria than in Italy. In particular, the impact of the second oilprice shock was significantly stronger in Italy. Afterwards, in both countries inflation could be brought down by disinflationary policies[2]. On average in the last decade the CPI inflation increased by 6½% in Italy and by 3.1% per year in Austria.

Historically, the rate of unemployment has been considerably higher in Italy than in Austria (1992/93 10.5% in Italy, 4% in Austria). During the eighties in both countries labor productivity in the business sector improved by slightly less than 2% per year. Due to a smaller decline in capital productivity in Italy over the last ten years, growth of total factor productivity was stronger in Italy than in Austria (+1% against +¾%).

Economic policy

From a theoretical point of view, Italy as a big country should have a larger scope for autonomous policy than the small open economy of Austria. While Italy's EU membership may impose considerable restrictions on the autonomy of economic policy Austria has – hitherto – not been confronted (at least not formally) with similar restraints as a consequence of being a member of EFTA.

A country's economic policy mirrors also the structure of institutions, the relative power of social groups and the stability of the government. In these respects the political system in Austria is much more stable than in Italy. Since the fifties, Austria has succeeded in resolving social and economic conflicts within the so-called "social partnership" in a cooperative and consensual way, whereas in Italy confrontations between social groups have been harder also resulting frequently in strikes.

Italy has participated in the Exchange Rate Mechanism (ERM) of the European Monetary System (EMS) just from the beginning in 1979, although with wider margins for exchange rate interventions (±6%) until the end of 1989, afterwards normal margins (±2¼% applied also for Italy until the Lira left the ERM in September 1992. Since 1981, by practically fixing the exchange rate of the schilling to the deutschmark Austria has participated passively in the EMS. With this "hard currency option" Austria imports

---

[2] By relaxing the automatic adjustment of wages to prices ("scala mobile") at the beginning of 1983 inflationary pressure in Italy could be reduced additionally.

price stability from its main trading partner Germany, frees a good deal of transactions with foreign countries from exchange rate risks and induces firms operating in the exposed sector of the economy to improve their productivity by restructuring. As a consequence of this hard currency policy Austria's quantity of money is not determined by targets set autonomously; the Austrian National Bank rather accommodates to money demand. Interest rates follow closely the development of the German rates.

For quite a long period the Italian lira was a soft currency experiencing a series of devaluations. Then, since the middle of the eighties up to the big crash in the EMS in September 1992 exchange rate policy has aimed at strengthening the lira. (The arguments for this "relative hard currency policy" are similar to the reasons put forward for Austria's hard currency policy.) Within the EMS there was no realignment between 1985 and 1992. The lira devalued against the ECU by around 1% a year in this period, whereas the schilling revalued by the same amount. With respect to some "fundamentals" the lira was considered an overvalued currency. Thus interest rates are burdened with a risk premium. The interest rate differential to Germany amounts to about 5 percentage points. It has turned out that the monetary targets were too ambitious. Money growth moves at the upper limit of the target zone. After the turbulences in the EMS in September 1992, within two months, the lira lost 12% of its value vis-à-vis the ECU. In the same period the value of the schilling improved by 4%. After the second crisis in the EMS in August 1993 – where the system could only survive by broadening the bands of interventions from ±2¼% to ±15% – the value of the lira improved gradually. In 1993, the adjustment of exchange rates resulted in a considerable improvement of the relative competitive position of Italy by around 15% (measured by the effective exchange rate), whereas Austria lost relative competitiveness by around 3%.

Italian economic policy is heavily burdened by a huge deficit of the general government's budget. It already amounted to 10.9% of GDP in 1990. Since then the medium term strategy for a budget consolidation has proved to be successful. According to OECD estimates, the deficit is declining and will fall below 8% of GDP in 1995. The primary balance (net lending excluding net interest payments) was even positive in 1993 (amounting to 1.5% of GDP). Gross public debt reached a level of 114% of GDP in 1993. In the light of the aim to participate in the project of the Economic and Monetary Union (EMU) of the EU, budget deficits and public debts should – according to the so-called "convergence criteria" – be brought down to 3% and 60% of GDP, respectively.

In 1987 the Austrian government decided to reduce the budget deficit in the medium run. The general government financial balance reached the highest deficit in 1987 (–4.3% of GDP). In the meantime the budget deficit of the general government could be brought down to 2.9% in 1993. Primary balance had a surplus of around 1% of GDP in 1993. Gross public debt amounted to 57% of GDP in 1993. After the big crisis in the nationalized industry, macro economic policy diverted from the so-called "Austro-Keynesianism" and turned towards a more supply-side oriented course (restructuring of the nationalized industry, privatization).

Austria made two steps in reforming its tax system; the first step was set in 1989, the second in 1994. Besides improving purchasing power of consumers and allocative efficiency, one major aim was to relief the tax burden of the entrepreneurs and hence improving Austria's position as an attractive industrial location.

3 Effects of the completion of EC's internal market and of EEA

In a huge effort ("Cecchini Report" (CR); see Emerson et al., 1988) the EC has attempted to quantify the potential economic gains from the completion of the internal market, proposed in the White Paper of 1985. In the CR two approaches were chosen.

The microeconomic (partial-equilibrium) approach aimed at estimating the effects of the completion of the internal market for consumers as well as for producers in several sectors. Relying on special surveys and on consultations of experts effects of the abolition of trade barriers on costs, prices, supply and demand were evaluated. These various assessments of the reductions in costs and prices via lowering non-tariff barriers to trade (NTB), via better exploitation of economies of scale (EOS) and via competition effects were used to quantify the primary effects of completing the internal market.

In addition to the survey approach a series of micro-economic model analyses (partial or general equilibrium models) measured the welfare impact of creating an integrated single market. The basic idea goes back to Smith-Venables (1988) who postulate a specific price segmentation strategy in the pre-single market phase: enterprises set prices like an oligopolist in the sheltered home market and play full competition abroad. After abolishing the border controls and when the regime of common competition law is becoming effective in the single market this price strategy will vanish. As a recent example of such kind of computable general equilibrium (CGE) model studies with imperfect competition one can mention Haaland (1993). The static effects of integration are in the range of less than 1% of GDP, with a higher effect for the EFTA countries if they join the single market.

In the macroeconomic approach the primary effects found by survey studies were taken as inputs for the simulations with macroeconomic models (HERMES model of the EC and INTERLINK model of the OECD; see Catinat et al., 1988). The models were used to simulate the secondary effects (multiplier and accelerator effects, income distribution effects, price competitiveness effects, inflation mechanism, capital accumulation and growth potential) over a time-path of six years. In order to implement the inputs derived from the microeconomic level into the macro models the CR proceeded by identifying four areas of integration:

* elimination of frontier controls
* opening up of public procurement
* liberalization of financial services and capital movements
* "supply effects" (i.e., the strategic reactions of firms confronted with a new economic and financial environment; EOS effects and more competition).

The macroeconomic assessment of the impact of the completion of the internal market on the Austrian economy generally employs the methodology of the CR. The WIFO macroeconomic model was used for the simulations. In contrast to the CR the assumptions and inputs for these simulations could not be derived from specific surveys or studies on the microeconomic or sector level. Such analyses (except for the agricultural sector) had not been available in Austria. Therefore, one had to rely predominantly on the relevant informations delivered by the CR; in some cases they were modified for plausibility reasons in a more or less ad hoc manner.

For Austria, three scenarios were simulated (Breuss-Schebeck, 1991):

1) Outsider position (neither EU nor EEA participation);
2) EU membership;
3) Participating in the EEA

With the creation of the EEA, set into operation on January 1, 1994, scenario 1 has lost its significance, even in the case Austria's EU membership should be denied in a referendum (which actually has not happened). Scenario 1 assumed mainly spillover effects from the internal market via foreign trade; in addition, discriminatory effects of the EU against EFTA countries had to be taken into account to a certain degree. Austria would probably lose its attraction as a location for production if it remained outside the EU.

Simulating scenarios 2 and 3, the four areas mentioned above had to be supplemented by a fifth area: *budgetary effects.* Owing to its stage of development, in the case of EU membership Austria's payments to the EC would exceed that of transfers from Brussels. According to recent estimates net payments would amount to around AS 10 bill. Part of that may be rebated in the phase of adjustment in the agricultural sector in the years 1995 to 1997, so that in the short run the effective net contribution to the EU budget will be lower (about AS 5 bill.). As a consequence of the increased financial needs after Maastricht (Delors II), the EU members may be confronted with higher net contribution in the future. The participation in the EEA will cost Austria no more than AS 1 bill. per year (cohesion fund, contribution to EEA institutions).

As can be seen from Table 1 (second column) most of the effects for Italy are significantly higher than for total EU. In particular, the effect on foreign trade in goods and services will positively contribute to an increase in total production. The reason for these differences are that Italy, due to the existing regional discrepancies, faces considerable catch-up requirements. In addition, elimination of the still prevailing protectionism provides scope for increasing efficiency, and therefore consumer's welfare by a considerable degree.

For Austria, fully participating in the internal market as an EU member would stimulate real GDP growth less than in total EU (+3.6% against +4.5%) and the dampening of inflation would also be weaker than in the EU. The effects on current balance and on financial balance (net lending) of the general government are even opposite in sign. Whereas Austria's current balance and net lending would deteriorate (due to Austria's net payments) the EU could improve these balances, providing scope for expansionary fiscal policy measures, at least theoretically.

Table 1: Macroeconomic effects of European integration (single market and EMU) in the EU, Italy, and Austria (Cumulative effects in year 6 after completion)[1])

	EU	Italy	Austria	
			EU	EEA
	(Percentage deviations from the baseline projection)			
Private consumption	+3.1	+3.8	+3.5	+1.7
Gross fixed investment, real	+5.4	+6.9	+7.4	+5.0
Exports of goods and services, real	+10.5	+12.3	+8.7	+6.1
Imports of goods and services, real	+7.2	+6.6	+9.7	+6.0
Gross domestic product (GDP), real	+4.5[2])	+5.5[2])	+3.6[2])	+2.3[3])
Consumer price index	–6.2	–7.1	–5.2	–3.4
Disposable income of households, real	+2.9	+3.5	+4.1	+2.2
Dependent employment	+1.5	+1.4	+1.7	+1.1
Unemployment rate	–0.7	–0.9	–1.0	–0.6
Current balance (in % of GDP)	+1.0	+1.0	–1.4[4])	+0.3
General government financial balance (net lending in % of GDP)	+2.2	+3.7	–1.0[4])	+0.5

Sources: EU, Italy: Catinat-Donni-Italianer (1988, p. 56, p. 60). Austria: Breuss-Schebeck (1989, 1991). – [1]) To get the average yearly effects, divide the results by 6. – [2]) When EMU is realized, an extra GDP increase by ½ percentage point may result from the reduction in transactions costs. – [3]) May be reduced by ¼ percentage point because of additional discriminatory effects stemming from secondary processing trade. – [4]) Because of less than expected net payments the negative effects on current account and net lending may be lower.

The logic of EFTA countries joining the EEA and the EU can be summarized in the words of Baldwin (1992, p.1)[3]: "The EEA will provide substantial economic benefits for the EFTA countries, with little gain on the political representation side. By contrast, the EU's interest in the EEA is primarily political rather than economic. Full membership will greatly boost EFTA nations' political influence on future EU policy, while the extra economic benefits will be slender. The EU's primary interest in having the rich EFTA countries as members is the extra financial resources that they will provide at a critical time".

In the EEA the "four freedoms" are not completely realized. Since the customs union of the EU does not extent to the EFTA countries border controls are not renounced. Furthermore, the Common Agricultural Policy (CAP) does not apply in the EEA. In general, it has been assumed that by participating in the EEA decreases in costs

3 For a discussion of the possible effects of EC enlargement by countries of EFTA and of Central and Eastern Europe, see CEPR (1992).

and prices will be less pronounced and competitive pressure will be lower than in the case of an EU membership. Therefore, the simulation has produced macroeconomic effects that fall short of the effects received for the case of EU membership. In addition to the costs of border control and those of the system of rules of origin, Austrian firms are discriminated in the EEA compared to EU firms in the case of secondary processing trade with the Visegrad countries. This discrimination results from the fact that the European trade policy has not been harmonized with regard to free trade arrangements of the EU with the Visegrad countries on the one hand and to free trade agreements of EFTA with the same countries on the other hand; a further disadvantage originates from the need of rules of origin in the case of EEA because their is no customs union between EU and EFTA countries. This discrimination only vanishes in the case of full membership in the EU. In the case of the EEA scenario (Table 1) one should therefore take into account this additional discrimination by a reduction of the GDP effect of around ¼ percentage point.

4 EMU – The new challenge

According to the Maastricht Treaty of December 1991 (signed on February 7, 1992) and set into operation on November 1, 1993, the EU is planning to create a European Union. One important element therein is the Economic and Monetary Union (EMU). Whereas the economic union is just the refinement of the "single market" plus more coordination of economic policy (mainly fiscal policy) the monetary union has far-reaching consequences concerning the centralization of exchange rate (single European currency) and monetary policy (European Central Bank – ECB). In the transition period of the second stage (begin on January 1, 1994 with the creation of the European Monetary Institute – EMI)[4] to the third stage of EMU the EU countries are scrutinized whether they fulfill the "convergence criteria" laid down in the Maastricht Treaty. If a substantial part of the UC countries qualifies then the EMU will come into effect on January 1, 1997. If not, the EMU will be created in 1999 at latest, may be only by a block of hard currency countries.

The convergence criteria are primarily oriented to price and monetary stability and to fiscal sustainability (Ovigstad, 1992). The four criteria are:

---

4 The first stage of EMU started on July 1, 1990 with the full liberalization of international capital transactions within the EC.

1) Price inflation of an EC country shall not exceed that of the average of the three best performing Member States by more than 1½ percentage points.

2) No excessive deficits defined as:

- general government deficits shall not exceed 3% of GDP
- general government debt shall not exceed 60% of GDP

3) Normal fluctuation margins (±2¼%) in the ERM and no devaluation during the previous two years

4) Long-term interest rate shall not exceed the average of the best performing countries by more than 2 percentage points.

Ironically, at the beginning of the EU no EU and also no EFTA country could fulfill all the Maastricht criteria. Italy has serious problems with the deficit and debt criteria. In 1993 the deficit was 9.7% of GDP and the debt/GDP ratio was 114%. This implies that Italy would have to be very restrictive in its fiscal policy stance in the next years in order to signal that it is willing to join the EMU.

The EMU aims at creating a single currency in the EU and a ECB which centralizes monetary policy. This implies that the member countries are deprived of exchange rate and monetary policy on the national level. Wage policy and fiscal policy remain as essential instruments to absorb external shocks. Austria has already gathered experience with a two-country monetary union with Germany. The pegging of the Schilling to the DM since 1981 (hard currency option) implies the abandonment of autonomy in monetary policy. During the period of hard currency policy Austria exhibited a surprising convergence with Germany (measured by monetary, price and real variables; see Breuss, 1992b). The EC commission in its study "One market, one money" (EC, 1990, p. 11) mentions the loss of monetary and exchange rate policy as an instrument of economic adjustment at the national level as the main potential cost of EMU. These costs are probably higher in the case of Italy than in Austria, because Austria (hard currency experiment with Germany) has already experience with similar situations. All in all the costs of transition to EMU (in disinflating, reducing budget deficit, loss of autonomy of monetary policy) will be much higher in Italy (EC, 1990, p. 237-238) than in Austria (in case Austria is becoming a member of EU in 1995). The welfare gains from eliminating transaction costs (due to a single currency) will be more or less the same for both countries (EC average is ½% of GDP). Lower interest rates would significantly reduce the debt-service component of the budget deficit in Italy. On the other hand the seigniorage revenue loss will be significant in Italy. According to EU estimates (EC, 1990, p. 122) the gross seigniorage revenues will decline from 1.13% of

GDP at present to 0.51% in EMU. If the productivity of factors of production is improved (as through the single market program) and if the risk-adjusted rate of return is increased (as through EMU), then investment in the EU will be pushed up. There could be a substantial additional growth offered over the long run in the EU as a whole, accumulating to 5% or 10% of GDP (EC, 1990, p. 83). Baldwin (1991) goes even beyond and forecast long run growth effects of EMU in the range of 3% to 45% (average 24%). Similar calculations for Austria result in long run growth effects of 5% to 37% (average 21%; see Breuss, 1992b).

References

Baldwin, R.E. (1992): The Economic Logic of EFTA Countries Joining the EEA and the EC, *EFTA Occasional Paper,* No. 41, Geneva, November

Baldwin, R.E. (1991): "On the Microeconomics of the European Monetary Union", in: *The Economics of EMU. Background Studies for European Economy,* No. 44: "One market, one money", European Economy, Special edition, 1991 (1), 21-35.

Breuss, F. (1991): "Italien und Österreich – Ein Wirtschaftsvergleich", *WIFO-Monatsberichte,* 64 (7).

Breuss, F. (1992a): "Italien und Österreich angesichts der Herausforderung des Binnenmarktes", in: M. Morass, G. Pallaver (Hrsg.), *Österreich-Italien: Was Nachbarn voneinander wissen sollten,* Deuticke-Verlag, Wien, 181-222.

Breuss, F. (1992b): "Was erwartet Österreich in der Wirtschafts- und Währungsunion der EG?", *WIFO-Monatsberichte* 10, 536-548.

Breuss, F., Schebeck, F. (1989): Die Vollendung des EG-Binnenmarktes. Gesamtwirtschaftliche Auswirkungen für Österreich – Makroökonomische Modellsimulationen, *WIFO-Gutachten,* Wien,

Breuss, F., Schebeck, F. (1989): The Completion of EC's Internal Market and its Impact on the Austrian Economy – Macroeconomic Model Simulations, *WIFO Working Papers,* (31).

Breuss, F., Schebeck, F. (1991): "Österreich im EWR. Gesamtwirtschaftliche Auswirkungen", *WIFO-Monatsberichte,* 64 (5).

Catinat, M., Donni, E., Italianer, A. (1988): "The Completion of the Internal Market: Results of Macroeconomic Model Simulations", EC, *Economic Papers,* No. 65, Brussels, September

CEPR (1992): Is Bigger Better? The Economics of EC Enlargement, Monitoring European Integration 3, *A CEPR Annual Report,* London, 30 September 1992.

EC (1990): One market, one money: An evaluation of the potential benefits and costs of forming an economic and monetary union, *European Economy,* No. 44, Brussels, October 1990.

Emerson, M. et al. (1988): The economics of 1992. An assessment of the potential economic effects of completing the internal market of the European Community, *European Economy,* Commission of the European Communities, No. 35, Brussels, March 1988 ("Cecchini Report").

Haaland, J.I. (1993): "Welfare Effects of 1992: A General Equilibrium Assessment for EC and EFTA Countries", *Empirica,* Vol. 20, No. 2, 107-127.

Ovigstad, J.F. (1992): Economic and Monetary Union (EMU): A survey of the EMU and empirical evidence on convergence for the EC and the EFTA countries, *EFTA Occasional Paper,* No. 36, Geneva, March

Smith, A., Venables, A.J. (1988): "Completing the internal market in the European Community. Some Industry Simulations", *European Economic Review,* Vol. 32, No. 7, September, 1501-1525.

II. Structural Dynamics and Industrial Policy

Dynamics of Industrial Sectors and Structural Change in the Austrian and Italian Economies, 1970-1989

Bernhard Böhm[1] and Lionello F. Punzo[2]

[1]University of Technology, Vienna
[2]University of Siena

Introduction

There is a general agreement that changes of major momentum have being taking place in a variety of ways in the last twenty years in all European countries (and elsewhere) and more are anticipated. Such changes involve economic and institutional-political levels, and raise the question as to how to monitor them in the future in order to control processes towards desired policy targets (e.g. cohesion in the European unification is one of the major concerns of EC). To achieve this we need to devise and implement suitable industrial, sectoral and regional policies, and to design institutions as appropriate environments for a complex process of change which is taking place in an increasingly uncertain context.

Often, such discussions are not clear about the meaning of the expression "structural change" they are on. Among other things, this paper discusses the definition implicit in the literature, according to which there exists a functional or causal relationship between structural changes in the Western economies in the two decades of the 70s and 80s, and the exogenous and domestic shocks they had to suffer. Structural changes would be largely the result of adjustment processes exogenously injected, and accomplished via technological change, capital accumulation and innovations, with their institutional and organisational counterparts. (This will be called the "exogenistic view", and it is fair to say that it is the dominant interpretation.)

It is appropriate to treat structural change which is a dynamic phenomenon in the framework of a dynamic theory, and in particular of the theory of system fluctuations. Structural change should be seen as one of the manifestations of severe systemic instability, and to clarify this, we shall explore the disaggregated dynamics of the productive sectors of an economy, while Austria and Italy will supply the empirical applications). We will propose a tentative new approach to analyse sectoral dynamics and to "detect" such instabilities that may lead to phenomena of structural changes, which are treated here as "leaps" in the life of a system discontinuously crossing between two dynamic regimes. Such method is illustrated using the survey-based data from Input-Output National Accounts (for the two countries under consideration). The new method is complementary to the many other established Input-Output methods of sectoral analysis. However, its relationship to the viewpoint (and technical terminology) typical of the modern theory of dynamical systems will appear obvious.

The application to the data for Austria and Italy over the time span 1970-1989 illustrates the type of results that can be obtained with our method. This produces a picture of the transformations of these economies that can be discussed against the existing literature. In particular, the possibility of carrying out international comparisons gives a good perspective to evaluate the dominating "exogenistic view" recalled before. The chapter is organised as follows. We begin by depicting a scenario of stylised facts for the Austrian and Italian economies over the time span of the research. Sect. 2 will put the foregoing analysis in perspective, against the existing (both Italian and Austrian) literature on the 70s and 80s, stressing its structural and disaggregated viewpoint that focuses on technology and innovations. Next, we suggest definitions of structure and of structural change that appear to be better suited to a sectorally disaggregated model of the economy. In the following sections (3 to 5), the approach is compared with more standard methods of Input Output analysis. The analytical framework we propose, comes out as, essentially, an exploratory device to understand (certain features of) the dynamics of capital accumulation and technical change at a sectorally disaggregated level. From Sect. 6 onwards, the pictures of the Austrian and the Italian economies that can be obtained are discussed, in particular in relation to the stylised facts of the relevant literature. Conclusions point out some further extensions.

1 Some stylised facts

Over the time span covered by our research, Italy was sharing in the many difficulties of devising and shaping up the process of European convergence while Austria was formally outside such process, though practically tied up to the German economy by a fixed exchange rate regime very consistently implemented.[1] Its accumulated experience of monetary integration with a "large country" can be very telling on the eve of the European unification, but it is beyond the scope of this article.

---

[1] See Handler (1982) for details.

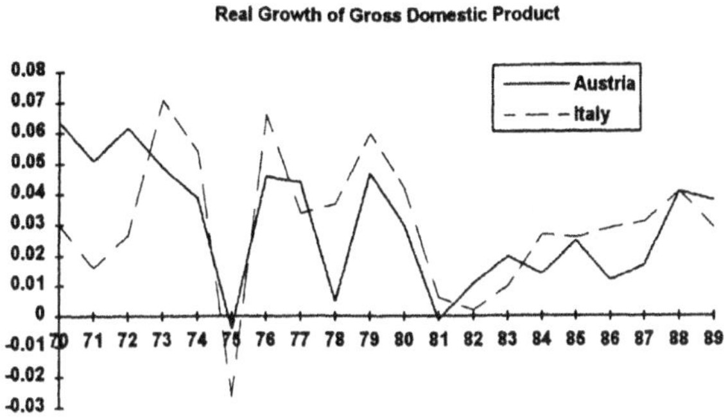

Figure 1: Real GDP growth rates of Italy and Austria

Obviously, the two countries have different economic (as well as both demographic and geographic) "sizes", together with different international positions. Fig.1 shows, however, that they exhibit the same long run pattern of growth of national income. Average growth rates are almost equal . As far as business cycles are concerned, Italy shows stronger fluctuations - troughs are deeper and boom periods stronger than for Austria. These two facts together point out, probably, the role of institutional settings and of the corresponding attitudes to accommodate a variety of shocks by efficient national economic policies. Such macroeconomic differences appear as the classical "tip of the iceberg" where the iceberg is the underlying manifold dynamics of the component sectors.

The Italian economy, on the eve of the 70s, exhibits a rather dramatic landscape. Three stylised facts are generally stressed in the literature[2]:

1. Dualism had lost its traditional geographical dimension (North/Centre versus South) and, rather, was then cutting across regions and industrial sectors simultaneously. The dualistic economic organisation appeared to be have become the very shape taken by the Italian development, rather than a distortion in its historic development. Its frontiers were then more mobile and could move again "on demand".

2. A qualitative change in the performances of sectors usually denominated "traditional" or "technologically backwards" was revealed by a variety of (total and

[2]See e.g. Amendola and Baratta (1978); Cipolletta (1986); Heimler and Milana (1984); Milana (1988); Prosperetti (1988).

partial productivity) indices and a number of other non quantitative observations. This was taken to suggest a re-definition of well established categories of industrial economics and prompt a new consideration of the themes of technology and technological change in relation to the process of capital accumulation.

3. Diversification between geographic regions was often associated with strong sectoral diversification.

On the whole, the setting at the eve of the 1970s suggested the emergence in Italy of the early signs of a crisis in the compact post-war pattern of expansion, with a number of potentially contradicting signs.

An increase in the structural in-homogeneity appears to bee the overall remarkable feature of the mobilised panorama Italy offered at the beginning of the seventies. Moreover, the contour lines of such historic inhomogeneity had been re-designed around the end of the sixties. The same could not be said of the Austrian economy, which on the contrary seemed to enjoy a rather homogeneous and balanced composition, as evidence showed for both the macro and the sectoral levels, giving the impression of "robustness". An unbalanced economic structure, reflected in both regional and industrial imbalances, was generally taken as evidence of fundamental disequilibria, hence of a basically weak Italian economy.

The 1973-4 oil shock violently hit both Austria and Italy and set into motion different forces. The history of the ensuing twenty years has often been depicted as marked by a set of dramatic shocks and a string of induced qualitative changes, in the individual, sectoral and systemic behaviours. Also over this period, Italy exhibits the more dramatic history, which has inspired a large literature and often conflicting interpretations. It is such literature that suggested many themes to our research.

The path of the Italian economy over the two decades is characterised by a shift of weight towards the service industry with a substantial re-sizing of the industrial and construction compartments as measured by employment (their share fell by 36% between 1970 and 1984 alone), value added (-47% in their share over the total of value added in the same period) and fixed investment (-12% for industry alone).[3] This trend was conditioned by the vagaries of the business cycle and of the international conjuncture, given the strong international dependence of the Italian economy. This

---

3 From data in Calcagnini (1986), tab. 1. The author gives a synthetic picture of the structure of the Italian economy at three dates: 1970, 1980 and 1984.

particular portion of the history of the Italian economy has been re-constructed[4] as a sequence of phases: a first period of strong domestic disequilibrium and low profitability (just before 1974); then, a time characterised by attempts to recover profit margins following the competitive devaluation of the lira in 1976-7. The 1980s opened with a phase of industrial restructuring founded upon higher employment flexibility and strong innovation campaigns where investment would have be targeted to the rationalisation of the national production structures. This process of capital deepening rather than widening[5] would have been going on at least until the mid of the decade, enjoying a fair level of productivity and investment demand, while the process of rationalisation by expulsion of labour force from the industrial and construction compartments supported the expansion of the service sector (including government related employment).

The macro economic performance shown by the GDP growth cycle, in fig. 1 above, may explain the remarkable cycle in the interpretations given during those years (and discussed for instance by Cipolletta). However, all throughout that time, there is a general agreement that factors behind the problematic dynamics of the Italian economy are of a structural nature, and that these factors were severely undermining its ability to cope with a troublesome international context. This unanimity of views greatly contrasts with the use of very short term policy measures (e.g. the rate of exchange) as measures of industrial policy. This political and institutional incapacity caused great concerns for a technological increasing lagging behind of the Italian economy in the second half of the seventies, inducing the exploitation of product niches at the margin of the big and booming markets. On the other hand, the literature at the middle of the 1980s unanimously stresses the idea that the widespread reaction to the high environmental uncertainty was a manifold search for more "liquid" or flexible conditions of business operation. Uncertainty discouraged investment decisions and suggested investment plans of lesser sizes and shorter economic lifetime. Productive rationalisation seems to have privileged disembodied technological change or organisational innovations that affect the overall productivity.

The success of this "search for flexibility" characteristic of the beginning of the 80s is apparent from a number of microeconomic indicators, and was overshadowed by the concerns for the long run performance of an economy that was slowing down the process of accumulation of capital stock. Such concern was strongly voiced at the

4 Cipolletta (1986).
5 Calcagnini (1986).

middle of the decade[6].

The well known differences in institutional setting between the two countries was reflected in the orientation and efficiency of the macroeconomic and industrial policies of their governments. During the seventies, Austria actively implemented policies aimed at stabilising employment at a high level. Its approach was based on Keynesian ideas of demand management, coupled with an exchange rate policy which established strong links to Germany, and it is cushioned by the system of social partnership exercising wage and price control.[7] With this policy Austria manoeuvred through the periods of external shocks maintaining moderate growth, moderate inflation and finally also moderate unemployment but accumulating government debts. Eventually, the latter enforced a reconsideration of "Austrokeynesianism" leading to measures for improving government finances, cuts in expenditures and shifts towards indirect taxation. This was practically accomplished at the middle of the 1980s, which is also the midpoint for the set of data available to us and this gives the possibility of following up some of their structural reflections.

From the point of view of the dynamics of the industrial sectors, the Austrian economy exhibits the internationally apparent development of the relative economic weight of the tertiary sector at the cost of the industrial and primary sectors, despite the fact that the share of industry in GDP is larger than on OECD average. It still is a fact that the so called basic sectors and the traditional consumer goods sectors (food, beverages, textiles) are dominating if compared with the international average. On the other hand contributions of sectors with a fast technological development like chemicals and machinery are below the average. However, the rates of growth of R&D intensive branches are above their international averages.[8]

The international competitiveness of all other industrial branches mainly depends on their ability to introduce new basic technology (e.g. microelectronics, biotechnology) with increased interrelations between the activities to the service sector. In this context according to the literature[9], there seems to be no strong supporting evidence that structural change has been less important a phenomenon in the Austrian

---

6 for instance, see Cipolletta (1986), Vercelli and other contributors to the volume Oltre la Crisi (1986))

7 The handbook of Austrian economic policy by Abele et al. (1982) provides an excellent assessment of the potential and actual policy options available during this period. Cf. also the paper by Seidel in the present volume.

8 Cf. the contributions of Aiginger and Schenk in Abele et al. (1982) as well as Seidel (1978).

9 See Beirat (1988)

economy than in other western industrialised countries. Also, no particularly strong evidence of a relatively low flexibility of production in Austria has been provided. However, the proportional use of low qualified workers, of real capital, and predominantly of raw materials is well above the average among the industrialised countries. The presence of a deficit in future-oriented activities may be conjectured: the share of enterprise related services is low; there are still relatively low expenditures and efforts in R&D despite some increases; the impulses of domestic demand for the development of new products and processes are weak.[10] Furthermore, in view of a long tradition in protection, the cost of the sheltered sectors seem to hamper the competitiveness of the exposed branches.

A comparative study of the development of factor productivity in Italy and Austria using the growth accounting technique (Böhm (1989)), tends to support these observations with an aggregative point of view. There is a striking difference in the factor contributions to output growth for the period between 1973 and 1985 in Austria and Italy. In the former country total factor productivity accounts for the entire output growth, negative contributions of labour (dominated by shorter working time) being completely matched by positive ones of capital. For Italy, roughly half of the average growth rate is due to factor input growth with labour dominating and a minor growth contribution of capital.

At the time of writing, the 1989 temporary end in our data set appears to have been the eve of uncontrolled political and economic changes. We should now inquire about the long term tendencies that we are going to observe in our two economies. Over this and related issues the history of past adjustments to shocks may provide the perspective of case studies. This perspective demands us to touch upon a number of questions that would make up for an entire research agenda. Again, the Italian development, the more articulated of the two, will suggest many issues for consideration, only some of which will find a place and a tentative answer in the following pages. It is, however, appropriate to list them here under three general headings.

1. The first questions the place of structural changes as the characteristic dynamic "event" that were observed in the two economies as a result of the joint working of internal and external sources of instability. Structural changes have always been

---

[10] Cf. Schenk (1982)

associated with changing forms and patterns of capital accumulation, with the evolution of the structure of the capital stock and, finally, with the pace of technological advance in the two countries.

2. One, next, asks whether the overall development of such two countries supplies evidence of an increased internal or "structural diversification" which might weaken their capability to cope with shocks and other external and unforeseen sources of disequilibrium.

3. Finally, if we turn to the theory, received growth and development theories consider well behaved patterns of economic development as a unidirectional process of stage climbing from industrial structures characterised by low-tech industries to structures with a high-tech baricenter. The experience of the last twenty years raises serious doubts about this view and calls at least for its qualification.

2 Structural analysis with Input-Output data

The literature, in particular in reference to Italy, stresses the role played in the 70s and 80s, in shaping up a new industrial and economic structure, by technical change and the introduction of both process and product innovations in relation to capital accumulation and the dynamics of employment . Thus, dynamic analysis must be structural analysis, which in turn calls for a description of the economy detailed enough to account for its (sectoral) design and for the functioning of the network of interdependencies. To obtain such description, a vast data bank in sectoral breakdown is available in the national accounts for a large number of countries, Austria and Italy among them.

A discussion of structural change requires, preliminarly, to make clear what is meant by "structure" to be studied. In fact, the notion of structure referred of a social body may lend itself to a whole manifold of distinct definitions, each appropriate to a different level (or rather different layer) of social and/or economic interaction. As a system may have more than one "structure",[11] different notions of structure can coexist if they are used to produce coherent pictures of different interconnected aspects of the same theoretical/empirical "object". And distinct notions of change will be appropriate.

---

[11] For this reason it is becoming a tendency in the literature to accept the notion of the formal identification of a system structure with the structure of its model, or of model in structural form. For this usage typical of the econometrics literature, see Poirier (1991).

In the formalistic identification of structure with model, structural change means change in the set of functions formally describing (or representing) our chosen level of system structure; or, equivalently, as a change of parameter values which go through their bifurcation set. In a specifically dynamic context, we shall treat structural change as a special event of instability, i.e. a discontinuity in the (dis)equilibrium dynamics of the given system. If structural change means a discontinuity in the set of dynamic models of the economy, we must ask ourselves how to "detect it".[12]

Structure, on the other hand, suggests the presence of component parts and of links/constraints induced by functional interdependence with various degrees of hierarchy and levels of strength.[13] We will construct an analytical framework upon the notion adopted in the Input-Output framework, whereby economic structure is a network of stable functional relations in exchange and production between producing sectors and end -users., and thus it is a pattern of qualitative links between those variables which are considered relevant for monitoring the system behaviour.[14] Data in the input-output format have been extensively used for the analysis of structure and structural change.[15] In the conventional interpretation, coefficients derived from their manipulation are treated as production functions; structure and production tend to be identified, and structural change and technical change eventually coincide.

However, caution is required in using Input-Output data for the analysis of the dynamics of technological change and accumulation. The Input-Output model (which is built on such data by using technical coefficients) is not a properly founded production model as it focuses on "exchange" rather than on production, given its conceptual inability to record transactions taking place inside the technological black boxes of the technological transformation processes. (Among other things, capital stocks become "invisibles", because they are sunk deep in those black boxes.)

Thus, we propose to add one more method to the number of methods of structural analysis based on Input-Output tables This "phenomenological" method develops a simple framework for the exploration of diversity in dynamic behaviours, and will be

---

12 see Hackl (1989); Poirier (1991); Rustem and Velupillai (1978).

13 This notion of structure, which does not require an explicit statement of foundations in a choice-theoretic framework, is shared by a number of descriptive models of the general input-output family (at one extreme the Input Output model properly, at the other extreme of aggregation, the elementary Keynesian model of income determination). The definition of structure common to the family is codified by R. Frisch (1933). For a general discussion of these themes, see Goodwin and Punzo (1987).

14 Again refer to Poirier, ibid., for the problems in the econometric approach.

15 Cf. e.g. the studies by Skolka (1977, 1989)

illustrated by the data for Austria and Italy.

Existing Input-Output based methods of structural analysis can be distinguished on the basis of their procedures to identify a core of structural relations. To obtain the latter, one starts with an Input-Output table for a given year, which. can be rearranged as a matrix and decomposed into sub matrices. Aggregating into n produced goods and services, we obtain

$$\begin{bmatrix} Z & Y \\ W & P \end{bmatrix}$$

The (n by n) matrix Z records interindustrial transactions of intermediate goods (which may be split into a matrix of sales or gross output (Q) and a nonnegative matrix (M) of net purchases of intermediate goods sucht that Z = Q - M). On the other hand, matrix Y of size (n by k) , represents the final sector or final demand; the (m by n) matrix W stands for the payments sector, and finally P which will be (m by k) is taken to be a zero matrix for simplicity.[16,17] By performing $Z[q_{jj}]^{-1} = [I - A]$, where $[q_{jj}]^{-1}$ is a diagonal matrix with the reciprocals of the gross output of the j-th good by the j-th industry, we specifically obtain the matrix [I - A] which embodies some of the flow co-ordinates of the production technology in use at the reference date. (We will write A(t) whenever we need to remember that it is a dated matrix.)

Typically, all methods in the Input-Output approach , assume that the production technology reflected in Z, and hence in A, is linear with constant coefficients, i.e. constant returns to scale and a finite number of production processes. Hence, technological properties of the observed economy are entirely described by the net output matrix , or by the input matrix A alone. Matrices Y and W, on the other hand, are given independently of A and exogenously determined. Changes in their entries are considered when we want to obtain comparative statics results. With this conceptual procedure, the "structure of the system" is identified with its technology and with the relative proportions between producing sectors. Thus, in principle, its most relevant structural properties can be revealed directly from observation or via manipulation of

[16] Behind matrices Z, Y, W there are obviously complex statistical procedures to collect and assemble data. Typically, in Input-Output accounting they are collected from survey data and then "simply" aggregated according to the industry principle (see Miller and Blair (1985); Rose and Miernyk (1989)). Alternatively, they can be estimated. As there are some problems at the level of statistical procedures we do not want to go into, we will keep to the former interpretation.

[17] See Miller and Blair, ibid. P is generally a nonnegative matrix. For this derivation also cf. Goodwin and Punzo (1987) pp.176

matrix A. The analysis of structural change, on the other hand, is carried out by comparing the properties of different dated input matrices. Changes in entries will be taken as indication of technological, hence structural change. Although conceptually clear, structural analysis (of a given system over time or of different systems) meets serious difficulties which force the use of indirect methods. They aim at detecting rather than explaining change by studying the functional relationship between matrix Y and A and/or between matrix W and A. With indirect methods we derive indices of structural properties, with a value assigned to each system state, whose time evolution can be followed through time.[18]

It is useful to group them into three distinct classes. In the first two classes are all methods based upon comparing responses of two different matrices A to the same impulse matrices Y and/or W. Working with Y generates indices of the class of output or quantity multipliers, as generalised multisectoral income multipliers. Exercises with W, on the other hand, produce a family of indices supply-based; instead of quantity indices, we obtain value- or price-based indices, for entries in W enter price-cost calculations. Into the third class fall those methods which exploit duality between quantity and value relations holding in equilibrium. (The class is best represented by the indices of labour productivity as used in structural dynamics.)[19]

3 Innovations and capital accumulation

In principle, the Input-Output approach seems to be suitable for an analysis focusing on capital accumulation and technical change. However, in comparisons across time , as opposed to comparison across countries, all existing methods have important limitations., which descend from the fact that changes in the production functions underlying the observed technology cannot be distinguished from changes in the values of a basically stable set of production functions.[20] The description of the system offered by a set of dated input and output coefficient matrices varying overtime, is akin to a set of photographic pictures which cannot capture the intrinsic, dynamic links between system states at distinct dates. Methods suited for international or regional comparisons

---

18 See the notion of descriptive functions (e.g. potential functions) in Luenberger (1979)

19 See Pasinetti (1982). Pasinetti method for the analysis of structural dynamics is contrasted to the synthetic direct method of diagonal coordinates in Punzo (1994).

20 In a similar context, where however structural change is not taken up explicitly, the function is introduced as a potential function. (See Goodwin and Punzo (1987)).

should not be simply applied to comparisons across time of the same economy.

Focusing on the path(s) connecting equilibrium states can unveil some aspects of the process of change. For this purpose we will introduced a notion of structure which is founded on the characteristics of the system disaggregated , in fact sectoral, dynamics. [21] One strategy to "capture" structural change, innovative with respect to the existing approaches, can be to use more than just a single descriptive function. And, to extract information about A, still one possibility is left unexploited, the direct comparison between Y and W . To this purpose, we consider the impulse structures represented by time series of matrices Y and W and we try to identify some of their reciprocal relations, together with properties of their time evolution. Structure will be defined as the description of such dynamic relationships. Our method produces some visually useful descriptive statistics, which can be used as a guidance for more in-depth explorations[22], and for this reason it is "phenomenological" or non-causal, thus in principle compatible with a variety of theoretical models[23].

The time evolution of the "chosen system" , therefore, will be monitored via two bundles of dated matrices that can be paired: e.g. {Y(t), W(t)}, t = 1, 2,..., T, over a fixed time interval.[24] A matrix Y(t) (or W(t)), on the other hand, can be decomposed into a finite set of vectors of economically distinct variables. Thus, Y(t) as the matrix of

---

21 Poirier, ibid, calls for an endogenous theory of structural change.

22 The reason for calling it phenomenological is that only the knowledge of the data matrices Y and W is assumed, but no behavioral functions are discussed, to generate them. The approaches of Input-Output and of Time Series Analysis to structural analysis and structural change are dual to each other and in some ways complementary. In Input-Output we take survey based data which are statistically determined depending upon the statistical procedures dopted. Such procedures are described in many excellent books (cf. e.g. Miller and Blair (1985)), where it is emphasized that they come from census data and in particular from business data. Time series analysis on the contrary starts with the interpretation of time history as realizations from a stochastic process and tries to identify the underlying generating structure. Thus it deals with stochastic variables, rather than aggregate survey variables, and it normally proceeds by decomposing the trend component from the noisy component (the stochastic element that can be introduced into the series as a result of the process being essentially stochastic and/or there being the possibility of measurement errors.) Properties of the trend generating model are identified with structural properties of the generating structure. Thus an estimation problem arises. On the contrary, in the Input-Output approach the notion of the stochastic or deterministic nature of the generating structure does not arise, and it is assumed that the measurement error has been taken care of during the preliminary implementation of the aggregative statistical procedure. Therefore, Input-Output does not take up the estimation problem, and identifies structure with the properties of the structure of the organized data by the Input-Output model.

23 One should compare the foregoing analysis with the new approach to growth proposed by Scott (1989). For a similar approach see also Velupillai, Borpujari and Zambelli (1992), which also offers a critical reveiw of existing alternative approaches to international comparisons.

24 Hereafter, system is taken in the abstract sense, and may be an economy, a region or an industrial secotr in a region or economy, according to the context.

final demand is usually partitioned into a set of column vectors of expenditure by category

$$Y = [\,\mathbf{C\,I\,G\,X}\,]$$

while W for the Payment Sector is further decomposed into

$$W^T = [\,\mathbf{L\,N\,M}\,]^T$$

where all bold symbols stand for vectors, T denotes transpose (which makes row into column vectors), and all vectors in the n by 4 matrix Y and in the 3 by n matrix W are dated, though for simplicity the symbol is dropped.[25]

To analyse the time behaviour of final demand and payment sectors, we may choose some components to monitor. Various options are open and choice must be based upon a preliminary decision about the relative relevance of variables in the context: it must be based upon the problem at hand. Investment, Employment and Value Added (i.e. **VA** = **L** + **N**) are those variables which are more related with the technological information only partly recorded by A . They happen also to be the same macroeconomic and sectoral variables that were chosen as explanatory variables out in the literature about for the two countries but in particular about Italy.

There are, in fact, three basically distinct views on the three-pole relationship between capital accumulation, technological and generally structural change, and productivity behaviour. In so-called neoclassical growth theory, economic performance is evaluated by the method of residuals: net production above factors' contributions is attributed to technological progress. This implies a sharp distinction between movements along a given production function and shifts from one to another as resulting from the exogenous appearance of technological novelties. Production factors are measured in their quantities, and "capital" enters as the stock available at a given date in the system. Without entering into the time old discussion on its measurability, it is important to remark here the static nature of this view. Growth accounting is of this comparative static kind. Via the production function, technological change is connected

---

[25] The scalars 4 and 3 depend entirely upon the chosen degree of aggregation, just like for the number of heterogeneous commodities, the conventional n of much of the literature. The symbols have the usual meaning: **C**onsumption, **I**nvestment, **G**overnment expenditure for goods and services, E**x**ports; dually, **L** and **N** are gross rewards to factor of production (gross as inclusive of taxes), and **M** stands for imports of goods and services. The usual national accounting relationship holds for the row and column double sums: i.e. GNP = L + N = C + I + G + (X - M) , all figures being aggregate values or scalars.

with the capital stock and its time evolution as the result of investment decisions. An alternative view still within the "traditional" approach maintains that investment is the (privileged) vehicle of technological progress. As long as we have a positive growth rate of capital stock, there must be also a positive growth-rate of output. Instead of the capital stock, its growth rate (rate of net investment as a proportion of existing stock) would be monitored. The dynamic nature of this approach relies on the fact that, instead of comparing point values or stock versus flows, to use econometric parlance in a loose fashion, it "regresses" the growth rate of net output g_Y against the growth rate of the capital stock, g_K.

The conception of technical change as a capital embodied phenomenon has many expressions among which we shall single out , for historical reasons, the version based on the so called "technical progress function".[26] With the innovational or neo-Schumpeterian approach, this version shares the rejection of the very notion of a production function. The latter approach, however, also rejects all functional associations between productivity and investment patterns. Any relationship between them is attributed to the fact that a cost pressure induces certain kinds of innovation-driven investments (i.e. those that are aimed at realising a restructuring of the general productive organisation). "Regression" is, therefore, between employment and labour productivity measured by value added (i.e. the difference between cost and sale price).

The production function and the related growth accounting approach rely on the use of a variable (the stock of capital) that Input-Output data does not supply. Figures for stocks must be re-constructed, something that can be done and has been done[27], so that we are not questioning this procedure. If , however, we stick to data made available by Input-Output accounting data, we have to do without that notion, hence without the notion of production functions. This decision , which is consistent with the hypothesis of a limited knowledge of the technology underlying our observations, makes our approach close to those two described above where no stock variables are involved. In the sequel , therefore, we will concentrate on flow variables.

4 The growth and development space

Traditional "flow approaches" (from now, "traditional approaches" for short) focus

---

[26] see Kaldor (1957).

[27] see the data used in Böhm (1989). For Italy see Rosa and Siesto (1989).

upon a single component of the two "non technological" matrices: on vector **I** (which is discussed in relation to matrix Y to which **I** belongs); or on vector **L** (which in turn is related to its matrix W). We will tentatively construct a unifying framework where the two approaches are conceptually "plotted one against the other". According to our hypothesis, important interdependencies between the dynamic behaviours of such variables as **I** and **L** are still to be charted, as it will come out from a multisectoral framework. Much of what we are going to do draws inspiration, at least, from the modern treatment of dynamical systems. Thus, the "state" of a "chosen system " will be identified by the set of values of certain monitoring variables. Comparisons of behaviours of the same system are based upon its history or phase portrait. Comparisons of different systems will be carried on by comparing individual pictures or "photographs" from their respective histories, but also by comparing their whole histories (their phase portraits). All this can be done if, as usual in the mathematical approach, each set of state co-ordinates (the monitoring variables) is labelled with a date t based upon a conventional calendar.

In the specific application illustrated in this chapter, growth rates are chosen as state variables and only two co-ordinates will be used. While reproducing the "simplicity" of dynamical analysis of aggregate macro models, the choice of only two variables allows us to use a unique graphical setting to represent the states of more than one system at each time without cluttering the picture too much.[28] The first co-ordinate (whose values lie on a horizontal, axis) is the rate of growth of value added per capita [29]:

$$g_V \equiv d(VA/E)/dt * E/VA \qquad (1)$$

while the other co-ordinate is supplied by the rate of growth of investment per capita

$$g_i \equiv d(I/E)/dt * E/I \qquad (2)$$

where E stands for the level of employment (in the chosen system at the given date, which is omitted to simplify the notation).

As noted already, the term "system" is generic and its meaning will be different according to the context: eg. it will identify a country like Austria or Italy, or North-

---

[28] A plane is thus the dynamical manifold of a system, i.e. a geometric space where its history is mathematically written.

[29] Notice that "per capita" means "per person employed" (often in the industrial sector associated).

Centre, NC, and MZ, standing for Mezzogiorno, when comparing the two countries. Then, it will indicate administrative or geographical areas, and these systems will be represented by a collection of "producing sectors". But also, quite often, systems will denote individual industrial sectors located in given regions or countries. For each system, we have a growth and development space. Sometimes, the spaces of two or more systems are super-imposed , for contrast and comparison. For a sample picture, the reader may refer to one of the sets of four pictures for Austria or for Italy, at the end of the chapter. Each such set synthesises the history of Austria (of Italy, respectively) in four "photographs"; each of them being a collection of (simultaneous) states of the industrial sectors in the corresponding country. (In a picture taken at time t, the dynamic state of the j-th sector/system is described by its values for $g_v(t)$ and $g_i(t)$).

The seemingly unconventional use of such two variables requires some important modifications of the theoretical arguments recalled in the previous section. With the Input-Output accounting data, the process of capital accumulation can only be monitored through time series of gross Investment, hence it is indirect. Without direct figures for the capital stock or for net investment, the rate of capital accumulation : (dK/dt)/K, (which appears e.g. in the Kaldorian technical progress function) cannot be defined, at least empirically at a sectorally disaggregated level. However, gross rather than net investment figures are relevant as indicators of the pace at which new techniques are being introduced.[30] Thus, capital accumulation is monitored via the rate of growth of investment. Under the usual assumptions, the latter is a proxy for the rate of acceleration in the process of capital accumulation.[31] Investment (hence, its growth rate) is taken in intensive form as investment per capita to "neutralise" the effects on the process of capital accumulation related to employment's own dynamics.

Sectoral value added figures seem, on the other hand, to provide a better index of productivity in a context of technical change and innovation, than productivity as measured by gross output. It is employed in the technical progress function approach ; it is used also in the theory based upon the notion of innovations and innovative behaviours, and therefore it seems to be a common ground for a comparison of them. Theories based on production functions would rely on gross output productivity measures. Also for productivity we prefer to work in intensive form, with productivity

---

[30] This casts serious doubts on the empirical relevance of approaches requiring net investment data. The problem is particularly evident when working with the level of disaggregation chosen in this paper, it may prove less serious at the macroeconomic aggregative level for which the function was conceived. Theoretical appeal and elegance seem to conflict the practical problems of applying such concepts.

[31] Note that instead of the rate of growth of capital stock, we use its acceleration over its velocity.

per capita.[32]

With each of the two co-ordinates (1) and (2) , one can associate a distinct real line which provides one axis in a plane, when we will put them together. Taken alone, each such line records synthetically dynamic behaviour in two dimensions. So, for instance, in any of the tables of say the Austrian economy between 1970 and 1989, we may isolate for instance the vertical axis recording the rate of growth of gross investment per capita in 10 Austrian industrial sectors. The history of the investment behaviour in a chosen sector is obtained by putting together four points each belonging to a different table. (Hence, the data for the j-th sector are derived from its phase portrait (cf. Figures 7ff.).

The value of the rate of growth of gross per-capita investment is a real number, or a point on the vertical axis, labelled with the conventional sector number and its date. Thus, for a generic sector, it may be written

$$g_i \equiv (di/dt)/i = \alpha \qquad (3)$$

(with $i \equiv I/E$, and dropping the j-th suffix as there is no ambiguity).

For given value $\bar{\alpha}$, (3) can also obviously be re-written

$$di/dt = \bar{\alpha}\, i \qquad (4)$$

which is a first order linear differential equation in the variable $i = i(t)$, with a solution

$$i(t) = i_0 \exp(\bar{\alpha} t) \qquad (5)$$

(where i_0 is some initial value of gross investment per capita.)

On the other hand, the time behaviour of per capita investment, recorded by the set of values of i(t) , is itself the result of putting together the time series of investment with the time series of employment. Hence, the rate of change of i in (4) reflects the dynamic behaviours of both investment and employment on a sectoral basis.

32 About the employment level: In a different study one should discuss employment dynamics, rather that capital accumulation, explicitly. Our decision for the variables in intensive form makes such dynamics only "implicit", while surely in the time span of our interest it has been important.

The origin of the g_i-axis describes a dynamic behaviour analogous to steady state because, with gi = 0, the initial investment/employment ratio would remain unchanged through time at its initial value. This property is associated with Harrodian (aggregate) dynamics, where there is neither technological change nor capital/labour substitution and the expansion path is one of balanced growth with a fixed technique. Harrod's own steady state path is one in the set of paths with constant I/E ratios: it is the one where the pace of capital accumulation is homogeneous throughout the sectors (a balanced growth path where the ratio i is equal in all sectors), or they over time average out around a constant aggregate value of i . Thus, we shall call the origin of the g_i - axis the "Harrodian set" spanned by sectoral paths parameterized by their initial values i_0. A quick glance at the tables in this chapter shows that this and similar other states as dynamic behaviours are defined for theoretical convenience rather than their own empirical relevance.[33]

A non zero value on the g_i -axis indicates a positive or negative rate of growth of I/E. In contrast with the balanced growth behaviour, the level of per capita investment would then be changing over time at a steady rate (as dynamic equation (4) is linear). For any value of g_i, we would have a process of continuous change in investment intensity at a constant rate, as indicated by the solution (5). The corresponding path would be explosive or implosive according to $\alpha > 0$ or $\alpha < 0$, and it would "fly away" from any balanced growth path, once started. The "distance" between the current value of i(t) and the corresponding value on a balanced growth path would increase exponentially as time goes by.[34] Thus, all points on the g_i -axis except the origin represent paths deviating from balanced growth. Above the origin, gross investment per man increases steadily: thus, as $I \equiv dK/dt + A$, if A is a constant fraction of existing capital stock, per-man-capital would be increasing steadily at an ever faster pace. The opposite dynamical situation is associated with points below zero.

---

33 Note that (4) is defined only for $i > 0$, as I stands for gross investment. Thus, a given value of i is mapped into the origin of the g_i-axis only if $di/dt = 0$, and i remains constant. Now, if i is taken to be a proxy for the rate of net accumulation, i.e. if we take $i \cong dk/dt$, for $k \equiv K/E$, a given value of i is mapped into $di/dt = 0$, only if the system is on a balanced growth path. Thus $g_i = 0$ for all initial values $i_0 > 0$ of Harrodian-like balanced growth paths. In a general multisectoral framework dK/dt may be zero and $I < A$ (A for replacement). In these cases we would still have balanced paths, characterized however by contraction rather than growth. (In a multisectoral context, like ours, the possibility of a sector of following a contraction path, should not be ruled out, as it is empirically relevant.) This provides theoretical support to the use of gross investment for dynamic analysis. For practical difficulty one should give some value to A and derive from it the net investment behavior.

34 This is again reminiscent of another property of Harrodian dynamics, knife-edge instability. See below.

Equation (4) and its graph (or state space, in a moment), taken by themselves, represent a state with constant output level, and thus with no productivity changes. This use, is obviously closest to the production function approach, where a variable value of di/dt would be plotted against the constant values dq/dt = 0 or dy/dt = 0, indicating constant productivity measured by gross output $q \equiv Q/E$ or by net output per man, respectively. To describe "dynamics" requires only the g_i - axis. Taken alone, then, this is the axis of dynamic capital/labour substitution for the production of a constant rate of output per man.[35]

If , instead, we plot g_i against the axis of the productivity growth and allow the latter to take up values different from zero, the g_i -axis becomes the axis of technical progress functions in a dynamic version. Any of such functions in fact are allowed to shift overtime, and each point on the axis stands to indicate a process of shift from one function to another.

A connection can be established in the following way. In the theory of embodied technological progress, increases of (labour) productivity ensue from transfers of exogenous technological advances into the economy. The rate of technological progress is therefore functionally dependent on the pace of capital accumulation. In terms of our construction we need a function from the vertical axis and the rate of change (and of growth) of the values of our productivity-per-man index function. Taking I as a proxy for net investment, I/E is positive if the rate of capital accumulation is positive. On the other hand, when the latter is positive, we have a positive rate of change of productivity. We would accordingly expect a positive (i.e. non-zero coefficient, in linear form) correlation between increasing investment intensity and productivity increase: any value on the vertical axis associated with a positive value of the productivity index, would then represent a movement along a given technical progress function. Any point on the g_i - axis which is associated with a positive value of an index of productivity growth describes properties related to the slope of the sectoral technical progress function, available at that date.

In the same fashion as we did with g_i , the horizontal axis of values $\{ dv/dt * v^{-1} \}$ can be conceived as having being constructed from a one-parameter family of linear first order differential equations

35 Note that in the present framework this is a process rather than a once-for-all adjustment, therefore, to be monitored by its pace.

$$dv/dt = \bar{\beta}\ v \qquad (6)$$

where v = VA/E (VA for value added) and is some given scalar value. (Again a look at the end of the chapter would be helpful to remind oneself that both v and dv/dt in (6) carry the label of a sector or a region, and a date.)

Solutions are of the familiar form: $v = v_0 \exp(\beta t)$, where economically meaningful cases require $v_0 > 0$. Just like before, each point lying on the g_V - axis is itself a path, monitored by the time (constant, explosive or implosive) behaviour of the v variable alone. All paths with a given and time constant value for per capita value added would be to go with a value $\beta = 0$. All such paths correspond to the case of no productivity change; if moreover, they are associated with values on the vertical axis, we would obtain the equivalent of movements along a given production function.[36] Otherwise, productivity per man would be changing over time at a given steady rate, β itself, (whatever that value happen to be sector wise at the given date). Then, these paths may result from technical change of some sort: technical progress, as is usually called in the literature, if $\beta > 0$, technical regress, one should say, when $\beta < 0$. Again, a glance at the diagrams shows that the latter is more frequent than is normally thought in the literature.

The literature suggests to associate the g_V -line with innovative behaviours. At each point to the right of the origin, the state of the system is really a process of productivity growth as unit costs are being continuously reduced (given sale prices) through process innovation; and/or, at possibly constant unit costs, (relative) sale prices keep increasing as a result of product innovation. There is no clear cut, or unique expected causal relation between innovations and investment behaviour. The now extensive literature would monitor changes in value added to follow the dynamics of innovations.

The difference between the two approaches we are discussing, can be reduced to a matter of different intensity assigned to the relationship between v and i. The innovational viewpoint would expect to find a weak or even nil correlation factor between the dynamic behaviours of the two variables. The approach stressing the existence of a clear-cut causation between pace of capital accumulation and productivity change expects strong functional relations between them. Both approaches

---

[36] In fact, $I/E = dK/K * K/E$

seem to "miss something" and produce partial accounts of factual histories. Our figures for Austria and Italy supply strong support for this conclusion.

5 Histories of countries and of sectors

The theories reviewed in Sect. 4 above single out, each, only one of the two axes introduced in the previous section, and it is for this reason that they can give a partial account of actual development of the two economies, Austria and Italy. Our innovation is that, in interpreting this development, we monitor both the dynamics of investment and that of value added per capita.(hence, the dynamics of employment, implicitly). Accordingly, the two axes are put together in our graphs, as co-ordinate axes of a "growth and development plane.

The information on the system states that is recorded in this framework, is of structural nature for the time behaviours of the rates of growth signals the its responsiveness to solicitations and its "natural attitude" towards undertaking changes Now, a glance at the graphs shows important differences of dynamic behaviours between the two countries and over the two decades, 1970-1989. They are, moreover, coupled in a complicated and variable fashion.

Let us begin with Austria (tables 2 - 5). Each table contains a number of dots, one for each sector (or industry, as defined in the input output format). If we follow one sector in its behaviour across the four tables, say sector # 37, and report its co-ordinates on a single diagram, we obtain the history of the sector monitored via the chosen co-ordinates. One should remember that a state is itself a zoomed-in path with two rates of growth in the two co-ordinate directions. A change of state is a movement across paths (via a discontinuous "jump"). In principle, each state as a path is a candidate for being an equilibrium path, i.e. a state which may "continue in real time". In other words, a "path across states" is our equivalent for a "traverse".[37]

---

[37] As it should be if one follows Hicksian terminology. Hicks (1973) is the classical reference. In fact, the notion of a traverse does not imply stability towards a new equilibrium, with its related supporting new structure, and descriptive model; it only requires the milder notion of a gravitation process, which itself can be interrupted by "new emerging states" that become system feasible. Thus, traverses changing directions (as made up of more elementary traverse) are not to be excluded. Our data, however, seem to underline that this has been the dominant phenomenon between the seventies and eighties. This fact demands an empirical explanation. At this point it should be obvious that a number of typical notions of economic dynamics have their analog (sometimes, their equivalent) in our framework. We shall suggest appropriate translations.

The existence of a traverse can be visually reconstructed by following the same (labelled) dot over its history, from table to table. Thus, one can see that, between 1970 and 1989, there is no dot, or no sector (either in the Austrian or in the Italian economy, see tables 6 - 9) which did not cross from path to path. Traverse behaviour is the generic behaviour in both countries. Actual histories appear as made up of a set of traverse paths for each system, or traverses made up of a set of simpler ones, over a shorter time span. This is important in a dynamic context: traverse behaviour exhibits system instability with respect to given path; repeated traverses show that such instability is with respect to any specific (virtual) path. Instability is a qualitative property.

Representing paths as states allows us to represent dynamic behaviour immediately as disequilibrium behaviour. Structural change must then appear as some form of extreme disequilibrium founded on that qualitative instability noted above. In the diagrams, a marked tendency to "change dynamic direction" along transitions paths from period to period seems to be characteristic of all "systems", regions or industrial sectors. This can be as wild a phenomenon as with the metal producing sector # 13 in Austria or the Italian construction sector # 53. It demonstrates the greater instability of the Italian economy compared to the Austrian during the 1970s and 1980s: structural instability emerges as sequence of changes in development models. Obviously, such instability may simply reflect data distortion (i.e. of the high investment instability which our smoothing technique did not manage to reduce). Or rather, as we are inclined to believe, it is indirect evidence of a drive towards an increased flexibility as a response to increased economic environmental uncertainty, that the literature attributes to sectoral behaviours, in particular of the Italian economy. This demonstrates the generality of an extreme uneasiness and mobility in the economic situation over those two decades. One of the stylised facts that belong to the established literature is captured by our framework, and might account for the general dispersion of the sectoral behaviours in the Italian economy, for instance. A comparison from this viewpoint of the two economies shows that this phenomenon has been less important in Austria.[38] Moreover, at least for the time interval 1970-89, the notion of virtual paths, i.e. equilibrium behaviours over a short period, seems to have little empirical relevance, for practically no observed dynamics conforms to it.

These few remarks show that a re-consideration of the traditional categories of

[38] For instance, see Vercelli (1986). At any rate, high investment volatility when environmental uncertainty is high, is itself a signal of an active search for liquid (more flexible) positions.

growth theory and technical change is in order. In the language of the mathematical theory, with each initial state of a (traverse) path we can associate the incremental value of the two state variables, i.e. (the values of) time derivatives for both g_V and g_I . The observation that traverse behaviour is in a sense typical in the country histories under investigation, confirms the original intuition behind our framework: the growth and development plane, filled with states labelled by the pairs of values (g_V, g_I), may be treated as a phase-space.

Cross checking of the phase portraits of a sample of sectors in the two countries demonstrates that differentiation and dynamic inhomogeneity are the peculiar features that produce the different performances. We shall have to look into it later.

Finally, we have to account also for relevant differences in country behaviours, or "country traverses" which are the closest notion to structural changes. Here we should exploit at its best what pretends to be the novel feature of the present framework. The state of each country requires 10 dots (for the 10 common industrial sectors) at each date, and one pair of co-ordinates for each dot. Therefore, the history or phase portrait for Italy or for Austria is obtained by super-imposing four tables each recording a distinct behaviour resulting from all sectoral behaviours.

Again, comparing the two sets of tables for the two countries the reader can begin to "feel" how different has been each country's own response to the same set of shocks of the 70s and 80s. Vivid confirmation of how essential is sectoral differentiation is provided by the clear visual fact that the "maze of dots/sectors" in neither country flows together: their relative distances change overtime.

6 A taxonomy of regimes

A sector with all of its states along the g_V -axis would have a history of innovation processes only, where new production functions not existing before appear.[39] Likewise, a system whose preferred direction was along (or sufficiently close to) the g_I -axis would behave "traditionally", i.e. would move along a given production function or shift between known production functions (with basically no dynamic productivity changes). Very few sectors in either country exhibit such unilateral behaviour; those which do (e.g. Austria # 35 or # 38 in the fourth period, 1984-89), would exhibit it only

[39] Nelson and Winter (1977).

for a very limited amount of time, the most remarkable exception being Italy # 42. While states in the north-east quadrant seem to conform to the predictions of either one of the two traditional theories reviewed above, there is a large number of states which lies in "theory-forgotten" regions. Thus, we must make use of the whole growth and development plane and not just two of its quadrants.

This is however, what we should expect, in a sense. Mathematics says that it is "hard" to find a dynamical system sticking close to anyone axis in the plane for a relevant time span, or resting on a point equilibrium. In general, actual dynamics is a varying mixture of movements along both axes, with time-varying weights of the two co-ordinates. "Equilibria" as steady paths are likewise rarely observed. The construction incorporates these generic properties, and one can just look at the history of either Austria or Italy (or the history of any sector) to find this out.[40]

Some mathematical cases empirically rare can be used to give some structure to the plane of paths (g_V, g_i). The origin in the plane is the unique state which, if ever occupied and never disturbed, would not change in any direction for endogenous causes. It is an equilibrium or a time constant state: its characteristics relevant here is that both rates of growth are equal to zero. In traditional growth theory steady state represents behaviour characterised by the absence of innovations and of changes in the pace of capital accumulation. In the state space of our systems, growth rates are unrelated to each other at least in principle . It seems natural to generalise the notion of steady state dynamics to comprehend all states lining along the 45-degree line through the first and third quadrants. (There the two rates are equal to each other. The fact that they go through the origin guarantees that steady states as traditionally thought belong to the set, which can therefore claim to be a generalisation.) Steady state is any path whereby innovative and traditional behaviours in a sense "compensate" each other.

Some "order" or classification must be introduced into the (g_V, g_i)-plane which in fact summarises diverse dynamical behaviours. By classifying sets of paths into "regimes", one may hope to distinguish qualitatively different kinds of dynamic

---

[40] Note that, while a "traditional" steady state is an equilibrium, this is no longer necessarily true in the present framework: the two notions being logically distinct if we define, as appropriate, equilibria over a time span [t, t+z] as those states (paths) such that : i(t, t+z) - v(t, t+z) = constant, where the average rates of growth i(.,.) for investment per capita in period t and t+z , and z is a nonzero integer. On the other hand, our steady states have the property that certain system proportions (between traditional and innovational patterns) at a given date do not change overtime. One such steady state can be an equilibrium only if it lasts for some time z > 0 .

behaviour. Classifications are always, to a certain extent, arbitrary: ours intends to be an instrument to discriminate between different types of traverse behaviours and, hopefully, it will produce a notion of structural change adequate in the context of sectoral dynamics. The classification scheme that seems to fit these twofold purpose makes use of the theoretically-interpreted histories of the seventies and eighties: it will have to allow for the technical progress function and the innovation models as special cases.

At this point, the space of growth and development can be partitioned via a taxonomy of behaviours. Without counting the rare states (that is: the origin, the distinct axes and the 45-degree line), there are four quadrants which can be coupled in pairs. The first and the third quadrants, A, A', are characterised by the fact that the signs of two growth variables are the same; for quadrants B and B' a positive value of either one is matched with a negative value of the other. Otherwise, A' and B' are the polar regions of A and B , respectively.[41]

Using a classical Schumpeterian distinction, the pair (A, A') collects the set of paths of "growth" and of its opposite, "contraction", as they are understood in traditional theory of growth. Its complement would then be the set of states (in B or B'), where we collect all paths of "development" (and of its opposite, for which we have no better name). Intuitively speaking, the qualitative difference between these two pairs of regions of dynamic behaviours can be expressed in this way: development paths are normally (see e.g. the diagrams below) associated with systems which are in search of a stable internal structure and dynamic behaviour. Restructuring is the structural synonym for this kind of Schumpeterian dynamics of changing proportions. As a consequence no system (e.g. an economy, a sector) can stay "forever" in the "development" region. Received theoretical wisdom asserts that it can "grow" or "contract" for a long time span. Unfortunately, traditional analyses of the inter-play between technological transformations and the related structural changes, and the like, used just this as an excuse to confine to states in (A, A'). Thus, they also claimed for themselves the status of long run theories.

A "regime" is a class of dynamic behaviours which are sufficiently similar from a qualitative point of view, that they can be considered variants of the same basic model. In a slightly more formal fashion, one can say that dynamic behaviours in the same

41 Geometrically, the origin does not belong properly to either pairs. If interpreted as we suggest, as a zoomed-in Harrodian set, it falls into (A, A').

regime would be represented by mathematical models that belong to the same parameterized family. One can be more sophisticated but we do introduce the distinction at this stage by taking advantage of the definition of the steady state set. Earlier, a steady state was introduced as a kind of generalised Harrodian path. Being confined to a one dimensional manifold in the plane (a line), steady state behaviour can only be considered for reference and has a purely theoretical interest. In practical terms, a system can be sufficiently close to it for some time: it is natural to consider the steady state behaviour as a corridor or a band around it that is not practically distinguishable from its mid path.

Dynamics in the Steady State Corridor is one of either growth or of contraction, as the literature requires. Inside the corridor the two tendencies towards traditional and innovative behaviours compensate each other at least approximately. Sectors and/or economies with a long permanence in the corridor, are reasonably called mature. Dynamics of empirically relevant systems should not be expected to exhibit peculiar behaviours. In the light of this structural stability criterion behaving like a mature system is expected to be a transient phenomenon. Again, mathematical intuition finds sufficient support in our diagrams: many a sector in both countries have episodes of steady state dynamics, but it is hard to extrapolate from this any long run, stable tendencies. This might be the effect of the general environmental instability of the seventies and eighties. It can also be conjectured that this is a characteristics of sectoral, as opposed to aggregative, dynamics .

Six regimes can then be clearly distinguished while the Steady State Corridor and the innovation and the technical progress axes belong to a bifurcation set. The ordering of the regimes begins with the Innovational regime numbered in Roman I , and continues clockwise. (For this refer to Figure 2). With each regime is associated a distinct canonical model . Regimes I and IV (Regimes VI and III) are the mirror image of each other.

Growth theory (and all other theories based on the notion of embodied technical progress channelled by capital accumulation), "predict" dynamical states belonging to regime VI (and may consider its theoretically possible polar, III). Theories where technical progress is the result of innovational activities focus on Regime I (and, symmetrically, regime IV). Typically, either the two overlook or disregard states belonging to regimes II and V: the latter are what we have called the theory-forgotten regimes. They find a location in the above theories only as rare perverse cases, to be handled with ad hoc explanations and case studies. In our approach they are the key to understand the manifestations of system structural instabilities.

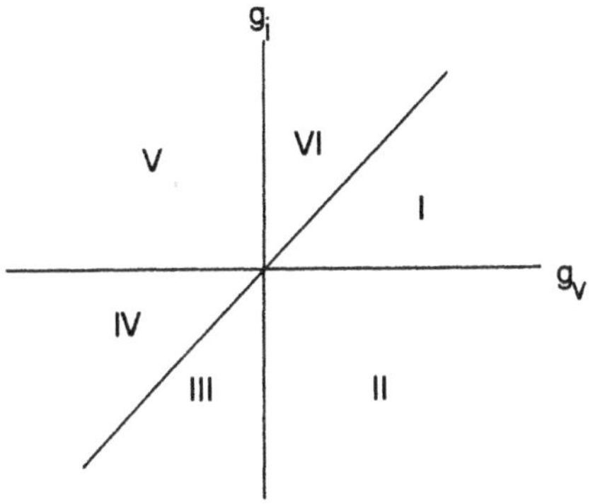

Figure 2: Regimes in the space of growth and development

There is no division of labour between the two approaches, which might guarantee their compatibility. For instance, the former classifies industries as traditional or modern as their paths belong to I or VI; for the latter, it is exactly the other way around: modern, innovative sectors are those that belong to regime I ; traditional ones to the regime VI . This is because the former only focus on capital accumulation, the latter only on value productivity. The generalised instability already remarked, whereby systems are "always" on some traverse bringing them tendentially to cross from regime to regime, points out that classification must depend of qualitative dynamical properties and must allow for their evolution. Their basic difference can be expressed in terms of the signs and the value of the angular coefficient, say a, of the hypothetical line $g_i = a\ g_v$ relating the two growth rates. Traditional capital embodied and technical progress theory predicts a high positive coefficient between accumulation and productivity growth: regime VI is typical in representing this situation. On the contrary, innovation-based theories argue for a low value of the same coefficient and expect typical behaviours in regime I. Thus regimes I and VI are the typical representatives of the two theories if we think of them as alternatives to each other.

For the two "traditional theories" that we have identified, in regimes II and V , growth rate variables have both the "wrong signs". In the former, a pace of productivity increase (at various speeds) is matched by processes of reduction of capital stock per man employed, which can itself be the result of slower accumulation or of a higher rate of employment growth, or of both. This could be interpreted as capital/labour substitution (according to classical growth theory canons) were it not going together with productivity increases as measured by the growth rate of value added. We have, here, something in the nature of a process of "business restructuring" going together with overall productivity expansion. Perhaps, one could characterise these paths as processes of "capital expulsion". Regime V is basically the mirror image of II. Both classes of behaviours, in reality, will reflect diverse micro-behaviours, and the actual forms of realisation of either regime can vary substantially from sector to sector, from country to country, etc. This gives scope for ad hoc case studies. It makes sense, then, to call them altogether as two "black holes": where more in-depth analysis is needed before proceeding to any other generalisation. Allowing for diversity can become a constituent part of the interpretation: A glance at the histories of our two countries provides good reason for spending some time trying to understand them rather than treating them as perverse cases.

These behaviours appear to be empirically relevant. Therefore, here, structural change is a change of dynamical model. It requires a regime switch: geometrically, it is a discontinuous traverse or a "jump" from one to another of the six canonical regions, hence, crossing the bifurcation set. Vice versa, a development pattern is a set of states which may or may not be described by the same model. It is a more general notion and represents the structural translation of the notion of a business cycle.

7 Austria and Italy, 1970-1989

The framework outlined in the previous section is an exploratory device, for it can only "chart out" the observed variety of dynamic behaviours, suggest some plausible interpretations, but in particular indicate where these are missing. Although with each regime we are associating a distinct canonical model, we are not explicit about its mathematical formulation and we are going to suggest only some generic or typical characteristics. Modeling traverses as dynamics linking paths that belong to different regimes would be most interesting, but. this is postponed for another occasion.

Figures 3a to 3d and figures 4a to 4d depict the parallel histories of Austria and Italy as monitored by the movements of clusters of points/paths over time. Each path is associated with an industrial sector, over the time interval 1970 to 1989 which has been sub-divided into four sub-periods for statistical convenience. (The other tables, instead, suggest elements for the comparison of histories of individual sectors across the two countries and their traditional regional divisions. They will be commented in the next section.) The selection of periods was based on the overall economic development of Austria and Italy as measured by the growth rate of real GDP (cf. Figure 1 above). Starting from 1970 the first sub period has been chosen to extend until 1974, the first year to experience the increase in oil prices and a problematic year for economic policy in view of the impending inflation which materialised in the second sub-period 1974 to 1980. Including the crisis year of 1975 and the experience with different types of political management of the national economies this period is characterised by heterogeneous growth as visualised in the GDP growth rates. 1980 to 1984 marks a recession period which world-wide ended in 1984 where only special (tax) policy effects prevented Austria from joining the upward trend in growth. The final period considered is from 1984 onwards until the last period where data were available (1989). This period can be regarded as a time of recovery. The basic set of data for Austria and Italy is somewhat heterogeneous. The reason for this lies partly in changes of the statistical framework used by the national statistical offices and partly in differences of classification across countries. The appendix will state all necessary details on data which are relevant for the interpretation of the results.

A number of considerations suggested to lump together the nineteen years into sub-periods corresponding to the phases of the various business cycles and the timing of the exogenous shocks. Then, average growth rates of investment intensity and of labour productivity are computed for each of the four sub-periods, as simple averages of the annual growth rates. The statistical procedure is very crude and can only be justified as a first attempt at handling such data; it can surely be improved on a second attempt. The reason is obviously one of smoothing the investment time series, specially needed in comparing that time series with the normally smoother time series of productivity. However, smoothing should not be excessive in the present context for investment volatility is itself a signal of business reactivity to changes in economic environment.

Not all the issues which have been raised in previous discussions in relation to the recent dynamics in the two countries, can be addressed in the framework above. The most important of those which escape, refers to the existence and the extent of processes of de-industrialization: not much can be added to the casual remarks that are recorded in Sect. 2 above, as the data available refer only to the manufacturing compartments.[42] Two general issues, however, can be briefly discussed now.

---

[42] See Momigliano and Siniscalco (1982) for an interesting discussion of the issue in the framework of

Immediately after, we will focus on the comparison of the histories of the two countries.

The first of these issues concerns the relevance of "flexibility" considerations that would have determined or at least conditioned business and in particular investment decisions that had to be taken in an increased environmental uncertainty (see the section 2 on stylised facts). In our framework, they would give rise to behaviours in regime II where capital is being expelled and its link to productivity dynamics is "perverse". We have pointed out that such regime proves to be very important from an empirical viewpoint: a quick look at the tables for both countries does show that many sectors followed paths in regime II , and lingered on in them for a non negligible length of time. Moreover, in both countries this behaviour was prevalent in the first half of the eighties when industrial re-structuring began in earnest and went on fast. One has the impression that, on the whole, flexibility has been a property relatively more important in the Italian rather than in the Austrian history. This perhaps might explain why this theme appears as a leit-motif in the mid-1980s literature on the Italian development.[43] We will come back to this issue later.

The next question concerns the existence of recognisable technological trajectories.[44] This is a difficult item to discuss: although the notion of a trajectory sounds dynamic, we have no way to fit it into our framework. The existence of a trajectory should emerge as a consistent behaviour of the cluster of points indicating the various sectors of a given country: i.e. it would manifest itself as form of homogeneity of dynamic behaviours among the sectors in a given country, all of them sharing the same canonical model. Again, our tables do not support such idea. It is, rather, dis-homogeneity (to various and time-varying degrees) that appears to be the most relevant and interesting feature of sectoral dynamics. If a "typical dynamic model" has to be defined, as implicit in the notion of a predominant trajectory, it would be an artificially constructed, weighted average of various regimes. In a sense, we simply fail to see the practical interest in that conceptual construction for it is in sharp contrast with the philosophy behind classifying variety of regimes. Moreover, a comparison of the forms of in-homogeneity across the two countries is our evidence to support an important

vertically integrated sectors; see also Calcagnini (1986), ibid.

43 Barca and Magnani (1985) must be credited for pointing out the emergence of new characteristics in business investment behaviors. For flexibility, see again Cipolletta and Vercelli, both already often cited.

44 see Dosi (1988), and the bibliography cited there.

idea: that reactions to the same changes in economic environment were quite different. The notion of a unique technological trajectory (and related notions, of paradigm, etc.) do not seem very useful in a sectoral dynamic context. We will argue that they suffer from the macroeconomic distortion typical of many versions of the long run approach.

The existence of a long run cycle is a visual distortion due to the still too aggregated description of the system that we are using. Technological trajectories are to the theory of innovation what trends are in the linear theory of business oscillations: they pre-assume long run tendencies, which would not depend on the actual paths followed by the economy. As we know by now, a set of co-ordinated tables makes up the equivalent of the state space for the corresponding country, which is represented by 10 pairs of co-ordinates (i.e. one for each sector). Unfortunately, we could not have the same data for all sectors, so that the pictures only represent the industrial sectors. Following a cluster of points across time, we have the impression that in both countries an important growth cycle was the essential characteristics of the two decades. In fact, one way to support the existence of a technological trajectory relies on the optical illusion connected with such cycle. In both countries, the cluster of sectoral behaviours seems to come back full circle at the end of the eighties to where it was at the beginning of the seventies. This, however, hides the important fact that the two economies emerge after almost twenty years profoundly changed from a structural point of view. This, only the analysis of the intervening history can tell us.

It is startling how the histories of the two countries are different from one another. It is this feature that we need to understand. In the first two sub-periods, Austria shows a relatively stable clustering around the steady state corridor. (Exceptions are Energy Production (# 4), Basic Metals (# 37) and possibly Mining (# 2).) In the beginning eighties, most sectors have reduced the rate of growth of investment as measured per man employed, still maintaining some, though small, productivity increases. (The exception here is the Paper industry (# 34) with anti cyclical investment deepening at the highest average productivity growth.) Mid-eighties sees Austria's major industrial sectors engaged in a revived investment activity, while its "traditional sectors" of Food production and Construction stick to a steady state expansion: this is expected on the basis of our interpretation of dynamics of mature sectors. After the overall investment slump during the recession years in the early eighties and the rise of unemployment soon after, going hand in hand with attempts to re-structure the nationalised industries, Austria has entered a phase of fast investment growth with an emphasis on rationalisation. Thus, over the whole period Austria has on average moved full circle from a more steady-state-like movement through a phase of mild restructuring back to a rather traditional regime of increased dependency on capital accumulation. In fact, at the end of the eighties, the result of the impetus in investment does not yet exhibit positive results in terms of dynamic productivity gains.

Rates of productivity did not change sensibly over the almost twenty years of our period of observation so that the overall picture of development patterns is dominated by movements along the investment growth/production function axis: this brings us to conclude that the relative weight of innovative activities has been on the whole moderate. As pointed out in Sect.2, the search for flexibility does not seem to have been preponderant in determining reactions to inflation in the seventies or to the slump of the beginning eighties. These responses resulted basically in changes in the pace of accumulation, hence in acceleration and decelerations of the investment dynamics. Among the "traditional branches", we find also a prevailing of paths in the neighbourhood of the steady state corridor. With only the textiles industry showing major variations in its investment rates (in the first and last sub-period), it can be seen that character and attitudes in those branches have hardly changed.

Phasing in the cycle is fundamentally different in Italy and Austria, something which emerges looking at the sectoral scenarios behind the macroeconomic similarity of a common, low average growth rate of GDP. In contrast to the quiet industrial atmosphere of the same years in Austria, the Italian economy presents itself on balance in the seventies as an economy going through a process of accelerated and wide spread innovation where productivity gains are speedily harvested. The picture of its sectors basically all in regime I, with moreover high values of sectoral g_V's , dramatically contrast with Austria's balanced distribution close to the Harrodian set and around the steady state line, both slow accumulation and slow productivity increases.

Italy has problem sectors like Basic Metals (# 13) and Energy Production (# 06); on the other hand, its traditional exporting sectors (Food, Textiles) are among those realising the greatest productivity gains compared with the low cost incurred in terms of investment: basically these sectors are continuing on the surprising performance of the end of the sixties. This confirms the scenario described at the opening of the seventies (see Sect. 2) and demonstrates how the classification of industrial activities on the bias of technological presumptions, contrasts with the mobility of the borders between sectors.[45]

Thus, the Italian economy was hit by externally originated shocks at the "wrong moment": this shows up in the generalised fall in the productivity index in the second period. The reaction of the Austrian economy is comparatively sluggish, or non-existent; however, while Italy preserved a certain overall homogeneity (but here one should better consider the internal regional division of the country), the first Austrian reactions were rather disorderly. Only at this point was the distance between the two countries' dynamics reduced, rather suddenly. Restructuring on a grand scale was undertaken in both countries in the early eighties. However, while there seems to be a continuity in this direction of the Italian economy, the same cannot be said of the Austrian and its change of regime is rather more dramatic. On the whole, the early eighties in Italy are dominated by a regime of restructuring with higher productivity growth than Austria on average. The role played in shaping this overall process by the events in the mechanical and the chemical industries cannot be over-emphasised. This was followed by expansion along the steady state with some sectors involved in accelerated capital deepening (this confirms the literature). Eventually, the sectoral cluster seems to spread evenly across the two regimes in the first quadrant. Thus, on the whole, the phase portrait for Italy seems to confirm with the picture of a dynamics driven by flexibility targets and constraints, with low values of the rate of growth of investment coupled with rapid productivity growth (relative to employment growth). This "model of development" seems to have been abandoned in the second part of the eighties. We are not in a position to say anything more precise, now.

As expected, Austria emerges as the more effectively "protected" of the two economies, especially during the seventies. The Austro-Keynesian policy approach managed to stabilise the productive and general economic structure by substituting for deficiencies of private demand particularly in a period when larger changes of the structure were called for (e.g. in the post oil-crisis years). The crisis in this policy began in the eighties when budget limitations became stringent and restructuring could not be postponed any further: shocks were essentially domestic. This gave rise to massive lay-offs in the state owned industries too and brought about issues of privatisation which are playing a major role today. On the whole it seems that short term policies have inhibited structural changes required to adjust to exogenous shocks.

---

45 Cf. Prosperetti (1987) and Milana (1988)

At the end of the 80s, Italy seems to have eventually the better balanced structure as a result of its inability to protect the economy against such shocks. The histories of the two countries are histories of repeatedly emerging structural instabilities, with sudden re-directions in dynamic behaviours and with a greater instability for Italy, largely explained by political inefficiency. Ironically, in a sense this left that economy to rely on itself, and get organised, while efficient government intervention in Austria delayed much needed structural adjustment. The consequences for the developments of the two economies in a larger Europe seems to be obvious but will not be elaborated further.

We need to have a look at the distinct developments of the North and the South of Italy. The Italian structure diversified dramatically while going through a long period of shock adjustments. The behaviour of the North/Centre in many ways mirrors that of Italy as a whole. This is a consequence of the large share of the North/Centre in the industrial sectors. The South maintains a scattered structure over all sub-periods of our analysis. The distance in development between the North and the South has increased because the North has shown a stronger innovative and adjustment capacity compared to the South. This will become clearer looking at individual sectors more closely.

In the seventies the Mezzogiorno shares with Austria a somewhat ossified industrial structure. However, while changes did eventually take place in Austria in the eighties, the same cannot be said of the Italian South. Comparing overall performance, one perceives that the real problem with the region is the great unbalancedness in the dynamic structure of the regional economy, with sectors following totally diverse and heterogeneous paths. The maze of macroeconomic and structural policies implemented in the area, unfortunately, never have been aimed at increasing regional homogeneity, notwithstanding various battle cries to the contrary. If they were attempted, they did not succeed. Uneven development within the South rather than between the South and the North, or the promotion of cohesion within the regional and economic structure, seems to be the relevant policy target.

Although in many ways partial, the previous observations agree in indicating the delicacy of the structural situation on the eve of the European market unification and of the adhesion of Austria to it. The unexpected events at the end of the eighties have only increased the already great uncertainty.

8 Sectoral histories

Re-considering the prevailing interpretations of the 70s and 80s, it is true that the Italian economy was going through a delicate phase at the beginning of the decades; it is not true that it was faring terribly bad, with basic disguised and open disequilibria (except for the historic problem of Mezzogiorno). Comparison to Austria suggests a more dynamic and innovative attitude, and indicates that the tendencies in industrial re-structuring that appeared at the end of the sixties, had not yet lost their impetus. This continues during the second half of the seventies, showing a dynamism constructed on the so called traditional sectors (perhaps under the umbrella of the devalued currency), that has again no match on the other side of the Alps. Instead of deep-freezing in a technological-retarded path the structure was able to go through the difficult period of the early eighties by dramatically re-considering investment strategies and employment relations: this strategy of flexibility did not hamper the solidity of the Italian structure (as was feared by many at the mid of the eighties). On the contrary, the industrial structure was apparently prepared for the period of fast international expansion which was to follow, perhaps a result of capital deepening, as stressed by some, and/or of the re-location of labour force from the industrial sectors to the service sector. This would be demonstrated by its fairly balanced distribution along the steady state corridor. The sectorial clustering of the Austrian economy all along the vertical axis in the VI regime seems to show that the latter was still in the middle of a process of technological investment-driven process of transformation. On the whole it seems that capital accumulation is less suitable as indicator of economic performance in Italy than in Austria. Some sectoral cases will show this.

In fact, a quick look at the history from the sectoral viewpoint, rather than that of the country, reveals that a pattern of growth cycle goes together with some form of "repeated structural change". This follows from the choice of the sub-periods which yields insights into country- and sector- specific cyclical properties. It would be desirable to have a model for the properties of these oscillations. The fact that the time sequence of such changes does not follow an established pattern shows that a more refined framework is needed to describe them. Moreover, it shows that the appropriate level to formalise the notion of structural change is the economy itself rather than a sector. This is one of the themes for future research.

A model case in this international comparison is offered by the Textiles industry (# 42), which is usually regarded as a traditional and mature industrial sector on the basis of some technological characteristics and the presumed impossibility of important innovations. The history of that sector is quite different in the two countries. In Austria we notice an up and down movement along the investment growth axis with slightly smaller productivity growth rates during the seventies and beginning eighties, whereas the Italian experience is dominated by a strong move towards innovation, especially after the mid-seventies. It is just in the first sub-period that we find relatively high investment rates paired with higher productivity growth, a development which prevails in Austria only in the late eighties. Since the mid-seventies both the North and the South have moved into a re-structuring phase, dominated by productivity growth changes rather than by investment dynamics. Although the deviations from the steady states corridor, especially for the North, are not large - as expected for a traditional sector, we must notice that innovative elements have been at work in Italy for more that one decade. This industry case has attracted a great deal of attention in the past. Its development was a matter of concern in the country for the long run tendencies that seemed to signal: a dangerous tendency for Italy as a whole to leave the race with all other advanced countries for high-tech, and to join the legions of upcoming LDCs.

The textile industry is one of the industrial instances showing that development patterns are related to location and environment. Although not reported here, regional comparison at the end of the seventies and early eighties indicate that, even within Italy, patterns of development of the same sector could be quite different, sometimes in locations a few miles from each other. In particular, this is true of "mature sectors" which seemed to have provided the innovational laboratory of those years. Perhaps, their long run contribution to high-tech development will eventually not be great, but they do contribute models of survival in increasingly competitive markets and tough business conditions.

In terms of their contributions to total value added in real terms, there is a rough similarity between the sectors in the two countries. The dominating contribution among the industrial sectors comes from Metal Production and Machinery followed by Chemical Products and Food, Beverages and Tobacco. Construction sector and Energy Production come next. We shall begin however again with some exemplary cases.

In Metal and Machinery Production (# 24), Italy and essentially its North/Center regions have been in an expansionary restructuring phase in the 70's and moved finally to a steady state growth after a phase of fairly slow capital accumulation. In contrast, Austria remains in a rather traditional development close to the steady state corridor in the first two sub-periods and moves into a restructuring phase only at the beginning eighties. The mid-eighties are characterised by a dramatic increase in the investment/capita growth rate with a practically unchanged growth rate for productivity. Thus, increases in the investment intensity in this sector which incorporates also means of transport tend to imply purchases of new technology especially for the increasingly important branch of suppliers to the automobile industry. A look at Sector # 28 (Motor vehicles) of the Italian economy, which is available in a separate evaluation, indicates that this happened in Italy too during that very period. So, considering the commodity composition, the pattern of development in both countries seems to be fairly similar but it shows a different degree of variability. Both find themselves near the steady state in the beginning and in a process of an increased deepening of investment towards the end of our period of investigation. Both underwent temporary restructuring with maintained productivity growth therefore supporting the hypothesis of being among the innovative branches. They tend to the role of mature sectors.

Striking differences between the South and the North/Center of Italy can be confirmed. The Mezzogiorno for the first three sub-periods remains in a situation of decreasing investment rates but with maintained productivity growth in terms of value added per employed, while the North/Centre - with one exceptional period remains in an expansionary restructuring movement. In the production of vehicles the South even shows a phase during the second half of the eighties of deepening investment with decreasing productivity - certainly a critical one. The North/Centre on the other hand mirrors the above mentioned development of total Italy providing the larger share in the regional distribution of Italy in this sector.

Sector # 17 of Chemical and Pharmaceutical industries is generally dominated by large and extreme movements. Particularly the South of Italy shows extreme shifts between "regimes". Moderately increasing investment and relatively large productivity rates in the beginning of the seventies are followed by a strong fall in the investment intensity with hardly much consequences for productivity growth. In the early eighties the investment intensity remains almost unchanged at a productivity growth of some 20 percent which later falls to below 5 percent at a 10-percent increase in real investment. The development in the North and Centre is somewhat steadier: increases in productivity growth during the seventies at slightly falling investment rates. The eighties show decelerating productivity growth with accelerating capital deepening. The development of total Italy follows the North/Centre except for sub-period two where the large negative growth rate of investment of the South exerts its influence.

The great volatility in the pace of per-capita investment which characterises also the development of the Austrian Chemical industries, may be empirical evidence of a re-definition of the role and strategy of the sector at the international level during the years of our research. Rates of productivity growth remain moderate and quite similar throughout. Average investment growth during the last sub-period almost stagnated, although annual investment rates fluctuated widely. Strengthened environmental consciousness motivated some innovative efforts paired with occasional investment in an industry which for most of the past must be considered as a centre of innovative activity. The Austrian evidence at greatly reduced productivity rates mirrors the Italian development with an approximate time-lag of one subperiod.

Food, Beverages, and Tobacco industries (# 36) are normally classified as traditional. The diagrams for both countries, however, suggest again an unexpected mobility. Except for the South of Italy, movements tend to be in the neighbourhood of the steady-state corridor. All regions undergo a short phase of mild restructuring after the oil shock. The South, however, presents itself as moving between processes of strongly increasing and decreasing (or stagnant) investment rates. Changes is productivity growth are generally more pronounced in Italy than in Austria.

The development pattern of Construction (# 53) follows a relatively clear line which could be regarded as approximating an almost linear technical progress function. The movements along it over the business cycle affects all countries alike. All have undergone some restructuring in the early eighties and have moved back into the neighbourhood of a steady state later.

The Energy Production sector (which in Austria also includes water supply) may typically be characterised by the fact that large investment projects with long duration are the rule rather than the exception. From this point of view it should not be surprising to encounter phases of high investment growth coupled with decreasing output or productivity. A view of the graph yields a bewildering variety of process states. A common feature may be found in sub-period three (the beginning eighties) where decreasing productivity rates are indeed linked with positive investment growth rates, though not very high ones. For Italy this situation had already occurred in the late seventies but to a different extent in the North/Centre (with large investment rates) and the South (with large negative ones). Just the opposite situation existed in the beginning seventies. In Austria a rather critical phase of energy policy has been entered in the beginning eighties (with a rejection of the atomic power plant and a hydropower plant on the Danube) but Energy Production has later on, just like Italy, moved towards the steady state corridor.

For completeness, we shall quickly review the remaining industrial sectors which account for smaller shares in the composition of output. The Textiles Industry was discussed above. Paper, Printing and Publishing (# 47) underwent a critical phase with the introduction of electronic publishing on the one hand and the increasing consciousness about environmental issues on the other. The graphs represent typical movements for each country considering the relative share of the components of this sector. In Austria paper production is dominant, followed by printing. The exceptional investment rates in the beginning eighties may be explained by the efforts to install pollution reducing equipment, all other periods show a steady state development. Italy remains near the steady state path until the mid eighties were - after some restructuring in the South - investment rates picked up possibly reflecting increased computerisation. For Sector (# 50) of Wood, Rubber and Other Products, one observes heterogeneity across countries including both Italian parts. The Italian South largely maintains its productivity growth. Restructuring in the seventies brought about some drive towards increased investment. The North - dominating the result for total Italy - started from a path in regime I and settled in regime VI after some restructuring during the early eighties. Austrian data relate only to wood processing and indicate some attempts at innovation especially during the eighties. The two sectors of Basic Minerals and Metals (# 13, # 15) present a similar picture for Austria - investment cycles at slowly decreasing productivity growth rates. Innovative phases in these state dominated sectors are therefore called for, in particular after the reduction of controlling influences by the government. Italian sector # 15 exhibits movements along the steady state corridor which deviate a bit in the early eighties. The paths followed by the southern regions of Italy, however, indicate some degree of innovative activity. Sector # 13 , on the contrary, presents movements from highly capital intensive - low productivity - growth regime, V, in the beginning seventies towards a decade of restructuring ending with high investment growth in the North/Centre. This sector is again a good example for a forceful dynamic motion out of problematic regimes into phases of maintained productivity growth rates with or without investment deepening.

9 Some tentative conclusions

In this chapter, sectoral dynamics has been cast into a uniform, though highly simplified, framework, that accounts in principle for both disequilibrium adjustments and regime switches. The Austrian and the Italian economies are described by ten dynamic indices, each of them with two values or dynamic co-ordinates in a growth and development plane. They are represented as two multidimensional oscillators, each requiring 20 state co-ordinates. Fluctuations dominate their dynamic behaviours.

The dynamics that can be captured and partly described in this way, offers interesting suggestions for the evaluation of the performances over time of the two countries and for their comparison. In the light of sectoral dynamics, structural change is a discontinuous step in the predominantly oscillatory phase portraits of both countries. It has taken place either in the second 1974-80 period (for Italy) or in the third , 1980-84. The time period 1984-89 therefore could be the beginning of a new cycle in the histories of the two countries. However, the individual pictures taken from the two country histories exhibit remarkable differences and offer interesting hints for the interpretation of the evolution in the intervening time period.

This paper reports tentative results along a new line of research. Further steps may now be made, beginning with the refinement of a number of analytical details, in particular the statistical methods which are rather crude. As for the empirical part of the study, the histories of individual areas and administrative regions and into key sectors, as well as the detailed analysis of regional developments can be a promising line for future research. Finally, a major limitation to be removed refers to the absence of all analysis of the functional connections, or dynamical coupling, between the two countries and with other countries and economic areas. For the moment, interdependence is only implicitly present in the framework above.

From the theoretical viewpoint, this representation of an economy borrows from the theory of dynamical systems. Each sector is in fact an oscillator and the picture for the whole country is obtained by putting together the behaviours of all 10 oscillators (industrial sectors, properly) for which we had data. As such oscillating sectors are coupled with each other in a variety of ways, the next step is to explicitly model this relationship. A dynamic model of producing sectors could be used for a variety of parameter sensitivity analysis and for theoretical simulations.

Bibliography

Abele H., E. Nowotny, St. Schleicher, G. Winckler (eds.) (1982): Handbuch der österreichischen Wirtschaftspolitik, Wien, Manz

Aiginger K. (1982): "Industrie", in Abele et al. (eds.)

Amendola, M., P. Baratta (1978): *Investimenti Industriali e Sviluppo Dualistico*, Milano, Svimez, Ass. per lo Sviluppo dell'Industria nel Mezzogiorno

Amendola, M., J.L.Gaffard (1988): *The Innovative Choice*, Oxford, Blackwell

Barca, F., M. Magnani (1985): "Nuove Forme dell'Accumulazione nell'Industria Italiana, Banca d'Italia, Temi e Discussioni

Bayer K. (1978): "Charakteristika der österreichischen Industriestruktur - Ein Vergleich mit der BRD", in Monatsberichte des Österreichischen Instituts für Wirtschaftsforschung 51(8)

Böhm, B., "The Development of Factor Productivity: Some new results on Austria and Italy", Research Report N.94, Inst. of Econometrics, TU-Vienna, Oct. 1989

Böhm, B., L.F. Punzo (1992): "Detecting Structural Change: A Scheme for the Comparison of Austria and Italy in the Seventies and Eighties", in Clauser, O.; P. Kalmbach; G. Pegoretti; L. Segnana (eds.),: *Technological Innovation, Competitiveness, and Economic Growth*, Berlin, Duncker & Humblot

Calcagnini, G. (1986): "I Principali Parametri dell'Industria Italiana", in *Struttura Industriale e Politiche Macroeconomiche in Italia,* I. Cipolletta (ed.),Bologna., Il Mulino

Carter, A. (1970): *Structural Change in the American Economy*, Cambridge, MA, Harverd University Press

Cipolletta, I. (1986): "Le Politiche Congiunturali e la Ristrutturazione Produttiva", in Cipolletta I. (ed.): *Struttura Industriale e Politiche Macroeconomiche in Italia*, Bologna, Il Mulino.

Dosi, G. (1988): "Sources, Procedures, and Microeconomics Effects of Innovation", in *Journal of Economic Literature*, vol.XXVI, September

Frisch, R. (1933): "Propagation Problems and Impulse Problems in Dynamic Economics", in *Essays in Honour of Gustav Cassel*, London, George Allen & Unwin

Goodwin, R.M., L.F.Punzo (1989): *The Dynamics of a Capitalist Economy. A Multi-Sectoral Approach*, Cambridge, Polity Press; and Boulder, Westview Press

Hackl. P. (1989): *Statistical Analysis and Forecasting of Economic Structural Change*, Berlin, Springer-Verlag (IIASA)

Handler H. (1982): "Die österreichische Hartwährungspolitik", in Abele et al. (eds.)

Hicks, J. (1973): *Capital and Time*, Oxford, Oxoford University Press

Heimler, A., C. Milana (1984): *Prezzi Relativi, Ristrutturazione e Produttività. Le Trasformazioni dell'Industria Italiana*, Bologna, Il Mulino

Heimler, A. (1988): "Crescita produttiva e processi di ristrutturazione", in. Milana C. (ed.)

Kaldor, N. (1957): "A Model of Economic growth", in *Economic Journal.*

Luenberger, D. (1979): *Introduction to the Theory of Dynamical System*, New York, John Wiley & Sons

Milana, C. (ed.), (1988): *Ristrutturazione e Produttività nei Paesi Industriali*, Bologna, Il Mulino

Miller, R.E., P.D. Blair (1985): *Input-Output Analysis. Foundations and Extensions*, New Jersey, Englewood-Cliff, Prentice-Hall

Momigliano, F., R. Siniscalco (1982): "Nota in tema di terziarizzazione e deindustrializzazione", in *Moneta e Credito*, N.138

Nelson, R.R., S.G. Winter (1977): "In Search of Useful Theory of Innovation", in *Research Policy*, vol.6, pp.36-76

Nelson, R.R., S.G. Winter (1982): *An Evolutionary Theory of Economic Change*, Cambridge, Mass.

Poirier, D.J. (1976) : *The Econometrics of Structural Change*, Amsterdam, North-Holland

Poirier, D.J. (1991): "The Econometrics of Strucutral Change: a Retrospective View", in *Structural Change and Economic Dynamics*, vol.2

Prosperetti, L. (ed.), (1989): *Struttura Produttiva e Relazioni Industriali*, Quaderni di industria e sindacato, 21, Roma CEDIS editrice

Punzo, L.F. (1985): "Issues in Multisectorial Modeling ", (Lecture Notes), Institutsarbeit Nr.224, Wien, Institut für Höhere Studien

Punzo, L.F. (1994): "Economic Dynamics and Structural Change in Different Coordinate Systems", (forthcoming)

Rosa, G., V. Siesto (1989): *Capitale Fisso e Industriale. Stime settoriali e verifiche dirette*, Quaderni dell'Industria, Bologna, Il Mulino.

Rose, A., Miernyk, W. (1989) : "Input-Output Analysis: the First Fifty Years" in *Economic Systems Research*, Vol.1

Rustem, B., Velupillai, K. (1978): "On Detecting Time Varying Structures", LSE Econometrics Programme, Discussion Paper N.A19

Schenk W. (1982): Technologie-Politik, in Abele et al. (eds.)

Scott, M.F. (1989): *A New View of Economic Growth*, Oxford, Clarendon Press

Seidel H. (1978): *Struktur und Entwicklung der österreichischen Industrie*, Schriftenreihe der Bundeskammer, Wien, No.32

Skolka, J. (1977): "Input-Output Structural Decomposition Analysis for Austria", in *Journal of Policy Modelling,*

Skolka, J. (1989): "Input-Output Anatomy of Import Elasticities", in *Empirical Economics*, vol.2.

Velupillai, K., J. G. Borpujari; S. Zambelli (1993): "The Economics of Kravis-Heston-Summers. Purchasing Power Parities (PPPs) and Production-Based Indices for the International Comparison Programme (ICP)" UCLA, Center for Computable Economics Discussion Paper, March.

Vercelli, A. (1986): La 'Lunga Crisi': Interpretazioni e Prospettive", in Ente Einaudi, *Oltre la Crisi*, Bologna, Il Mulino

Appendix

1. The data

Since there have been changes in the compilation of data we have been forced to work with two different sets for Italy of which the first covers observations from 1970 to 1980 and the second the years from 1980 to 1989. While data on investment and value added were provided already in real terms for the latter period, we had to use national deflators for the former one. This fact will hardly bias the data used in this study as we are concentrating only on two large regions of Italy (the North/Centre and the South) besides Italy as a total. The deflation may however distort somehow data relevant for a more disaggregated analysis pursued elsewhere.

Italian data for the period 1970 to 1980 are taken from the ISTAT publications "Annuario di contabilita Nazionale" Tomo 2, tav. 1.7 and following ones, for investment, value added and employment data. Figures in constant prices were calculated using deflators for the total economy based 1980 = 100. For the period 1980 to 1989 all data are obtained from the ISTAT data bank, investment and value added already at constant prices of 1980.

The deflators for the sectors of the North/Centre and South of Italy (1970-1980) have been estimated on the basis of implicit sectoral price deflators from the UN National Accounts for Italy.

Data for Austria are from the National Accounts Statistics "Oesterreichs Volkseinkommen 1991, Tables 6, 6a, 8, and 25" and earlier volumes. Sectoral investment deflators were constructed from deflators according to the type of capital good. As investment data for the service sectors as well as agriculture were not readily accessible the data set covers only the manufacturing sector, energy production and construction.

For Austria no regional subaggregates were available. The sectoral breakdown (as shown below) does not conform to the Italian one in general. Furthermore, as there are no reliable figures for the investment of service sectors the comparison between the two countries have to be restricted to the ten manufacturing sectors only. Major differences between the classification of sectors concern the following ones:

• Production of machinery and metal products also include vehicles which are covered in Italian sector 28 separately.

• Mining is included among the relevant industrial sectors in Italy. It is a separate sector in Austria. This seems to be relevant in the assessment of sector 15 (IT) and 36 (A).

• Sector 50 of Italy contains wood processing (to a minor extent) together with rubber and other products whereas the corresponding Austrian sector (33) only contains wood processing.

• The relative share of certain products could be substantially different in both countries reflecting different endowment with resources as well as differences in tastes. This fact suggests a cautious interpretation of the empirical evidence.

2. The sectoral classification

Table 1: Classification of the relevant sectors of the Austrian economy (national income accounts)

2	mining	Bergbau
3	total manufacturing	Sachgüterproduktion
31	food, beverages, tobacco	Erzeugung von Nahrungsmitteln u. Getränken, Tabakverarbeitung
32	textiles and leather	Erzeugung und Verarbeitung von Textilien und Leder
33	wood processing	Be- und Verarbeitung von Holz
34	paper, printing, publishing	Papierindustrie, Druckerei, Verlagswesen
35	chemical industries	Chemische Industrie
36	production of stone- and glassware	Erzeugung von Stein- und Glaswaren
38	metal processing	Metallverarbeitung
4	energy and water supply	Energie- und Wasserversorgung
41	electricity, gas and heat supply	Elektrizitäts-, Gas- und Wärmeversorgung
42	water supply	Wasserversorgung
5	construction	Bauwesen

Table2: Classification of the relevant sectors of the Italian Economy

06	energy supply	Prodotti energetici
13	basic metal industries	Min. e meta. ferrosi e non ferr.
15	non-metal. mineral products	Min. e prod. non metallif.
17	chemicals and pharma.	Prodotti chimici e farmac.
24	metal products and machines	Prod.in metallo e Macchine
28	vehicles	Mezzi di trasporto
36	food, bever.,tobacco prod.	Prod. alim.,bev.,tabacco
42	textiles,leather,furs,shoes	Tessili,cuoio,pelli,calz.
47	paper, printing, publishing	Carta,cartotec.,editoria
50	wood, rubber, and other industrial products	Legno, Gomma ed altri prod.indust.
53	construction	Costruzioni

The Italian sector numbers are used in all graphs which contain both countries. For comparison purposes we list the sector numbers which may be considered to be roughly equivalent:

Austria	Italy
31	36
32	42
33	50
34	47
35	17
36	15
37	13
38	24
4	06
5	53

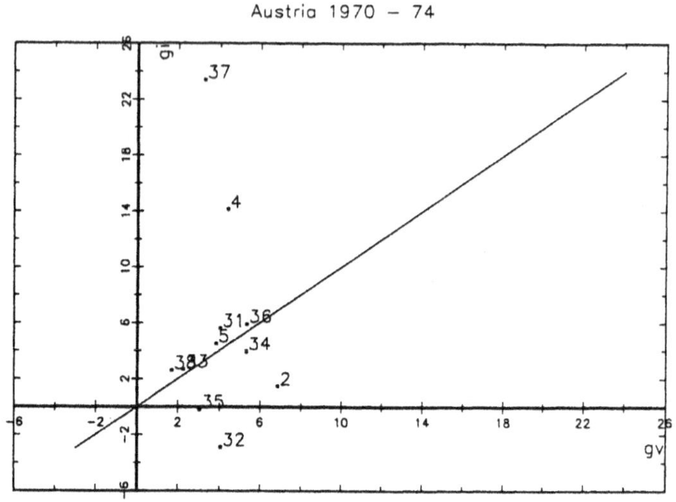

Figure 3a

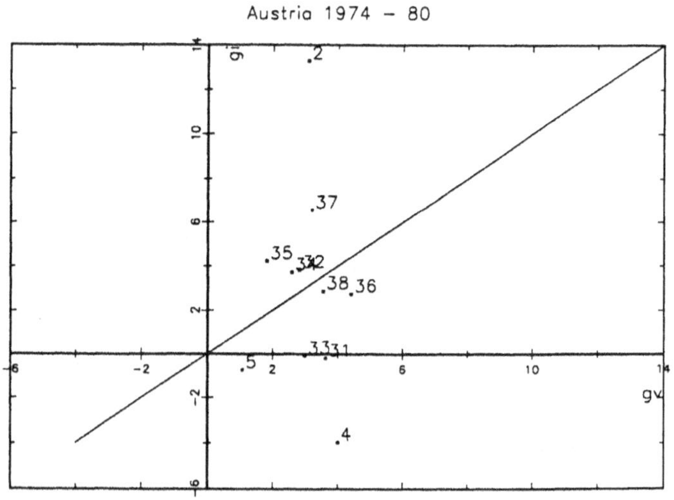

Figure 3b

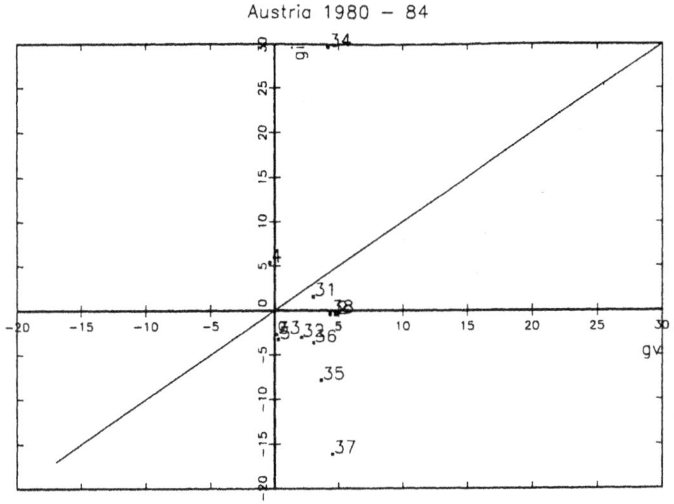

Figure 3c

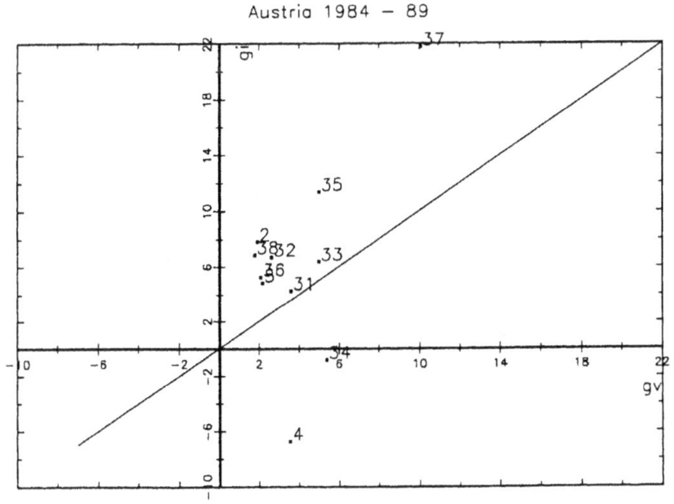

Figure 3d

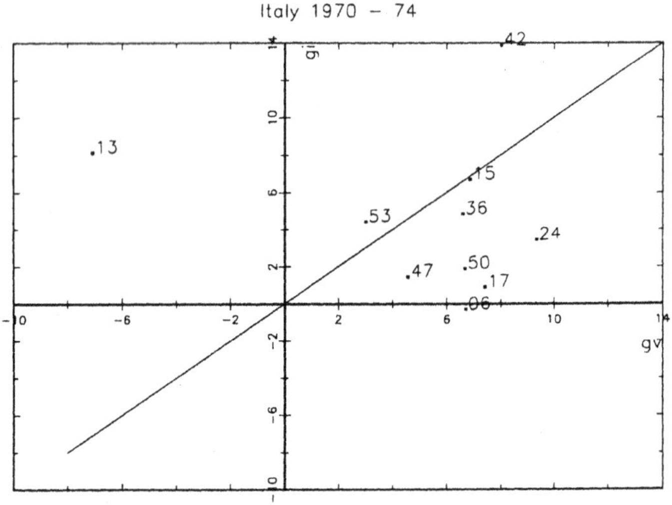

Figure 4a

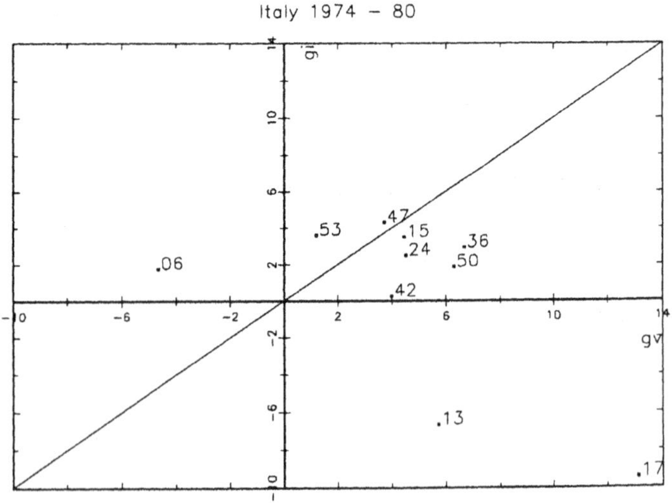

Figure 4b

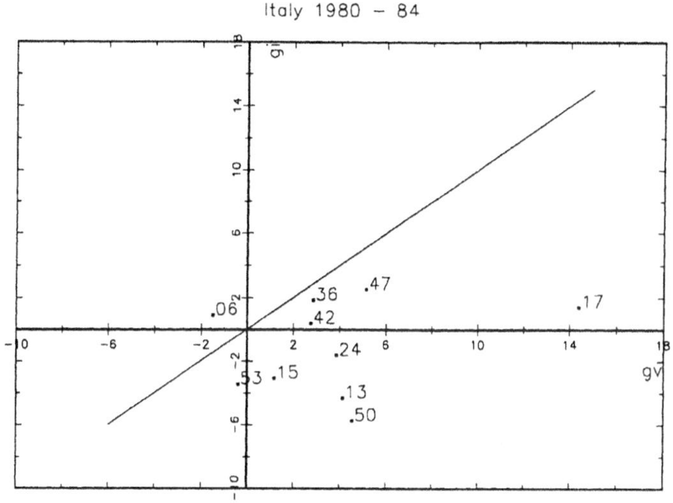

Figure 4c

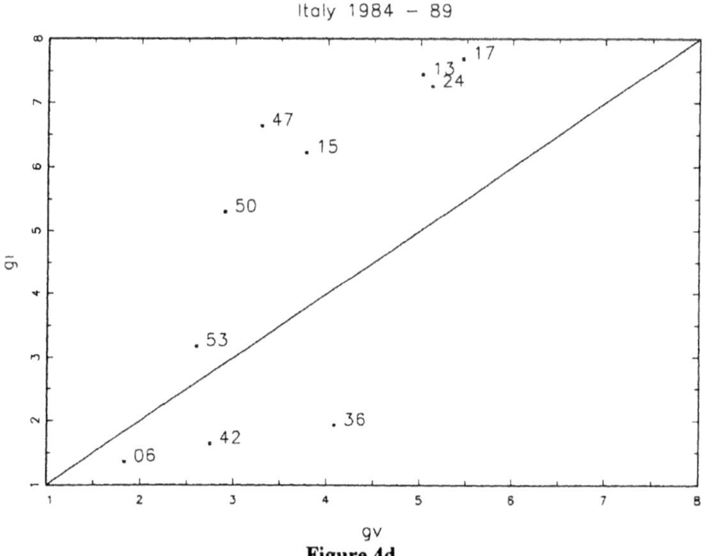

Figure 4d

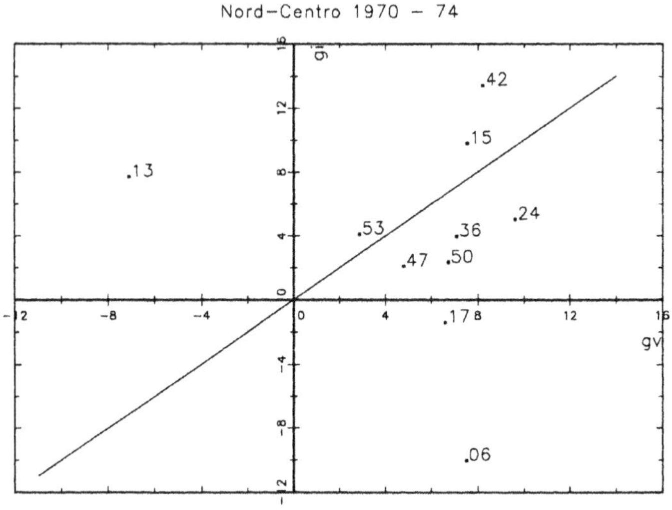

Figure 5a

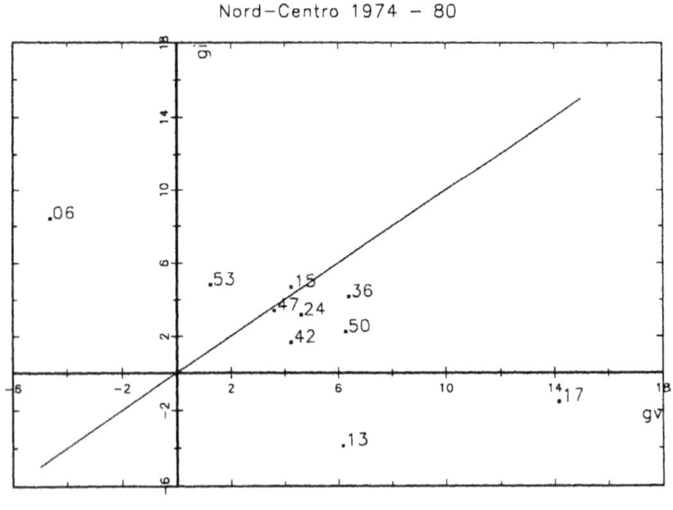

Figure 5b

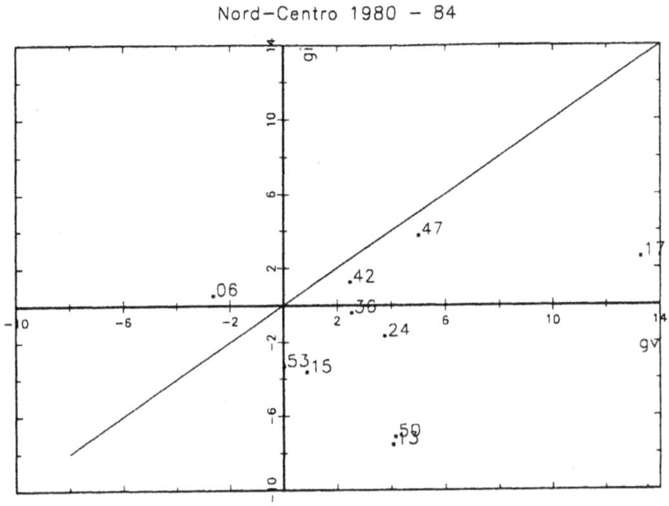

Figure 5c

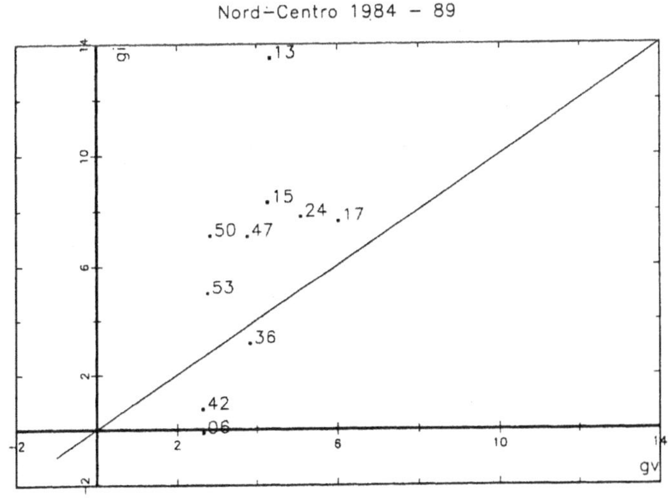

Figure 5d

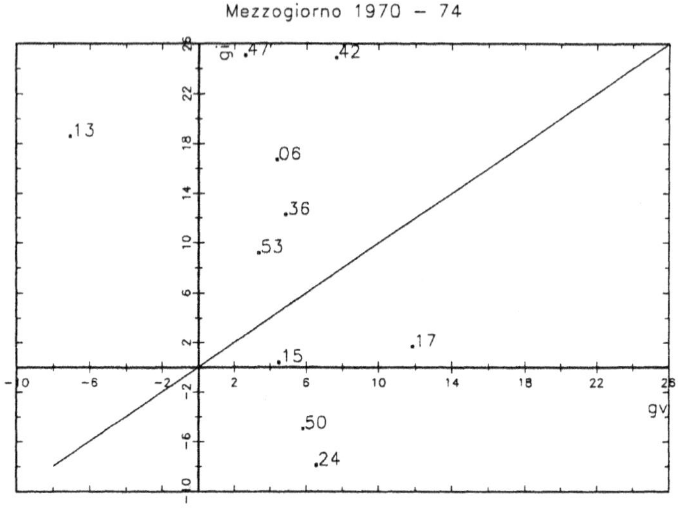

Figure 6a

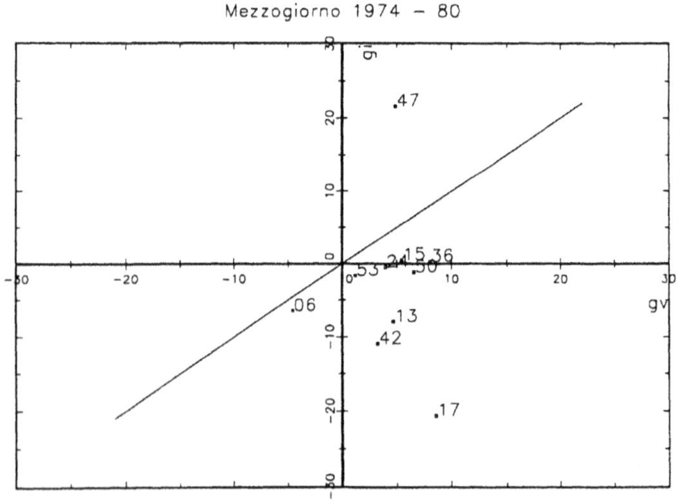

Figure 6b

Mezzogiorno 1980 – 84

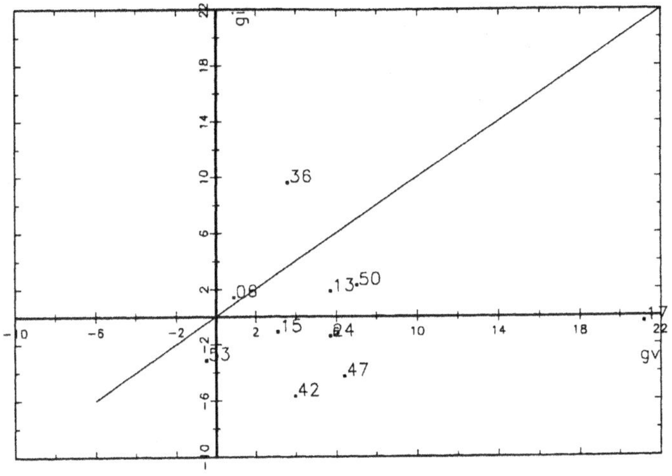

Figure 6c

Mezzogiorno 1984 – 89

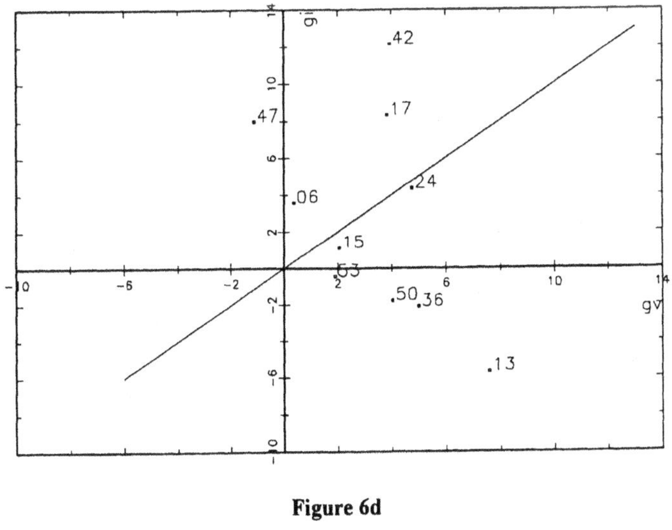

Figure 6d

The following figures exhibit the development in specific industrial sectors. We employ the following notation: A-j, IT-j, NC-j, MZ-j, relating to Austria, Italy, North/Centre of Italy, and South of Italy. The index j refers to the subperiod, j = 1, 2, 3, 4, where subperiod 1 extends from 1970 to 1974, subperiod 2 from 1974 to 1980, subperiod 3 from 1980 to 1984, and subperiod 4 from 1984 until 1989.

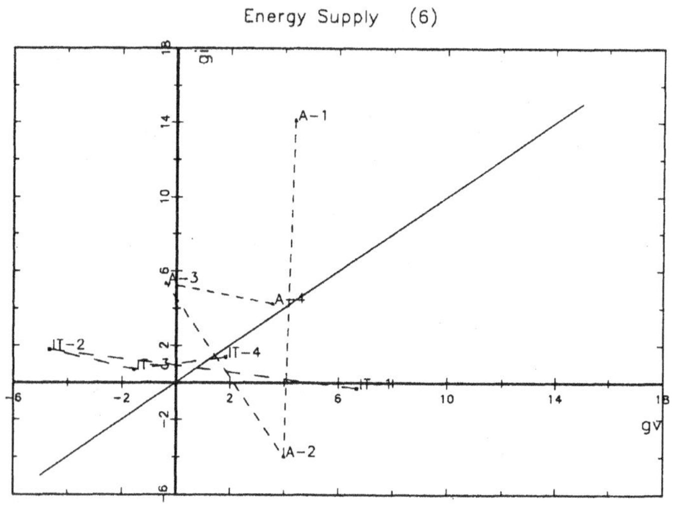

Figure 7a: Austria (A) - Italy (IT)

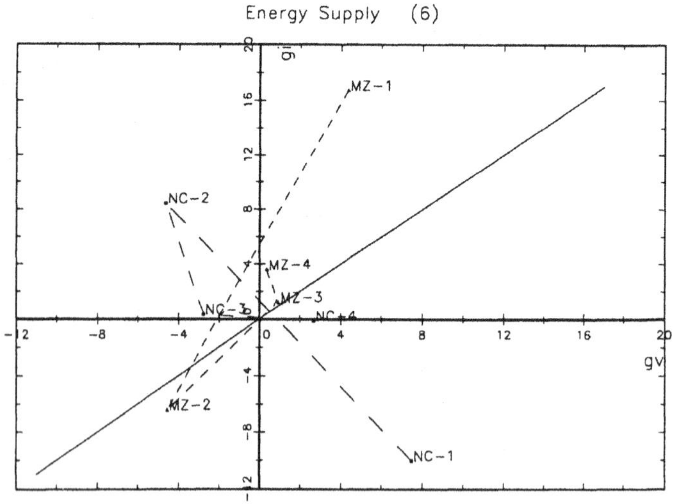

Figure 7b: North-Centre Italy (NC) - South Italy (MZ)

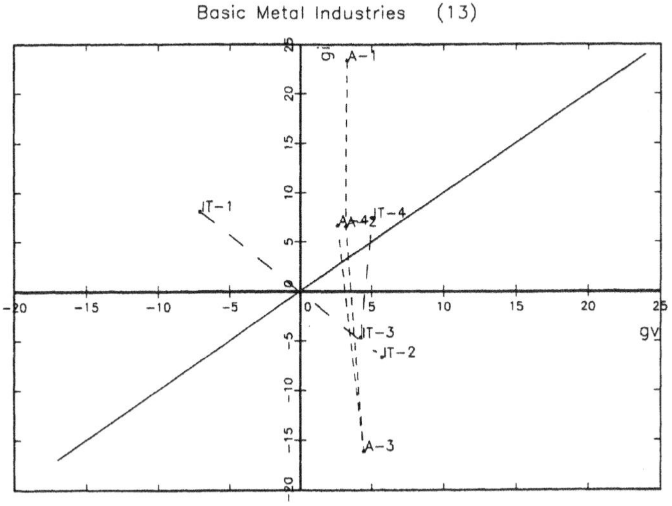

Figure 8a: Austria (A) - Italy (IT)

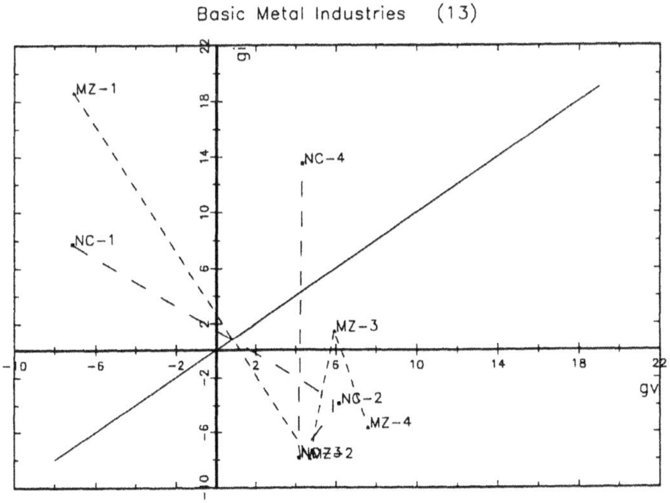

Figure 8b: North-Centre Italy (NC) - South Italy (MZ)

Non-metal Mineral Products (15)

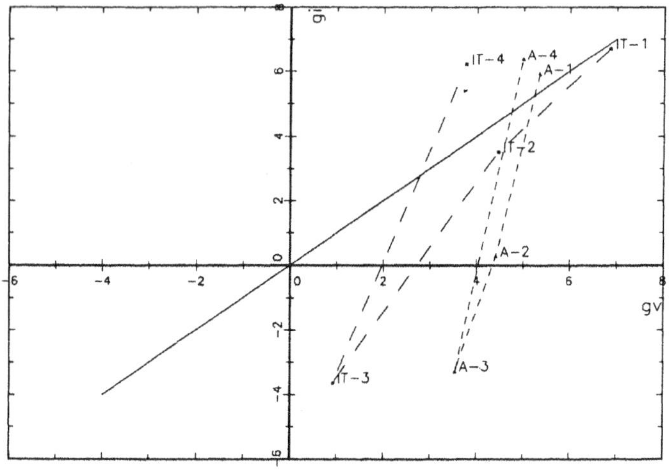

Figure 9a: Austria (A) - Italy (IT)

Non-metal Mineral Products (15)

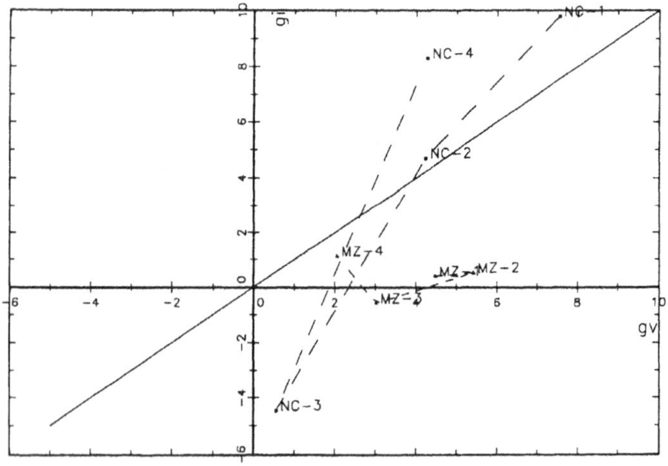

Figure 9b: North-Centre Italy (NC) - South Italy (MZ)

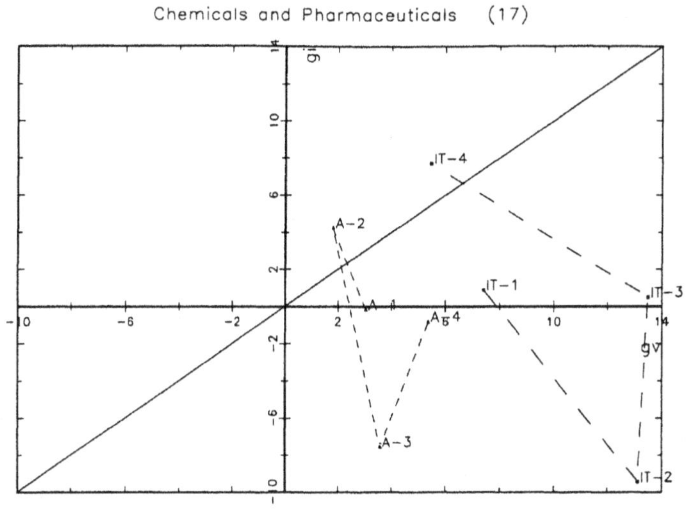

Figure 10a: Austria (A) - Italy (IT)

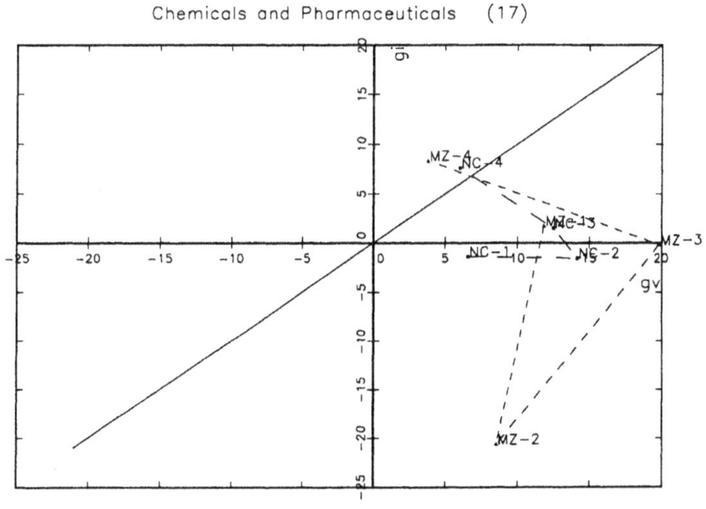

Figure 10b: North-Centre Italy (NC) - South Italy (MZ)

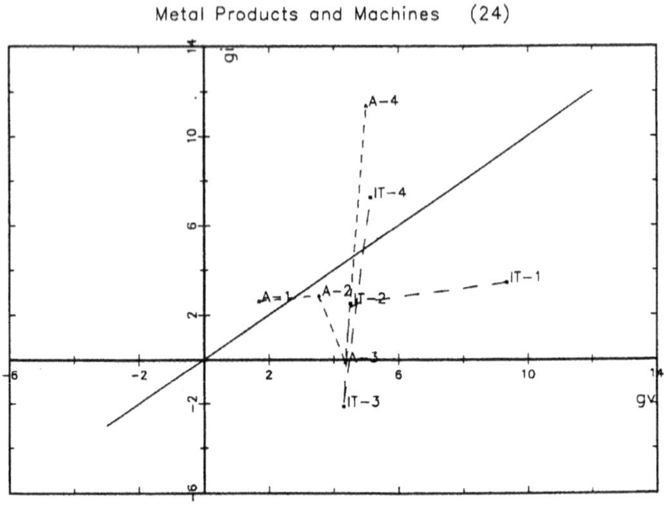

Figure 11a: Austria (A) - Italy (IT)

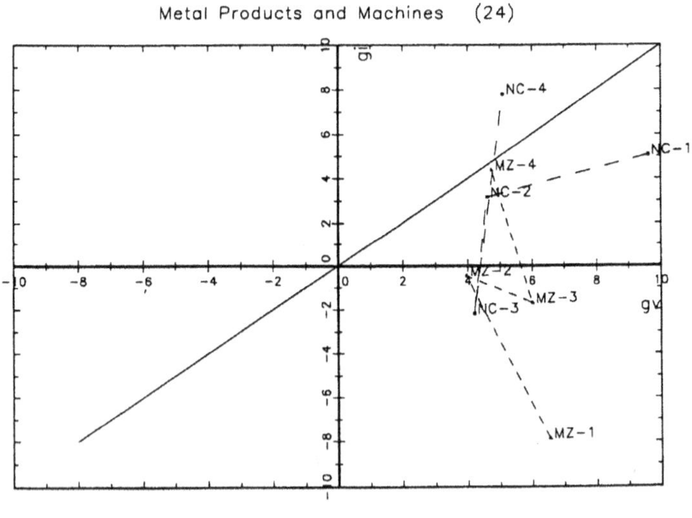

Figure 11b: North-Centre Italy (NC) - South Italy (MZ)

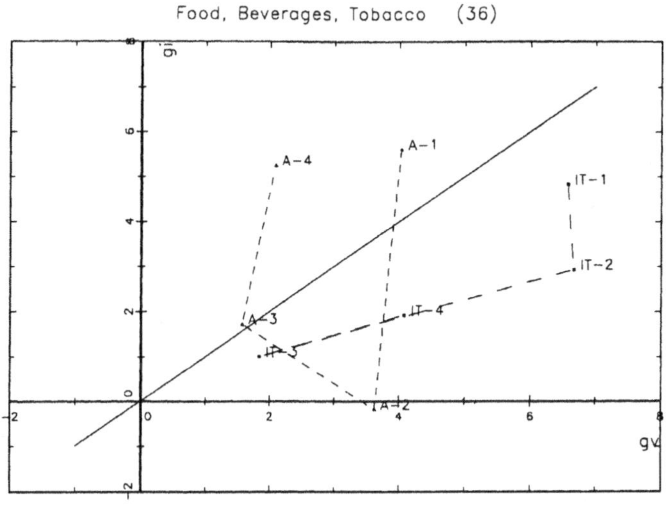

Figure 12a: Austria (A) - Italy (IT)

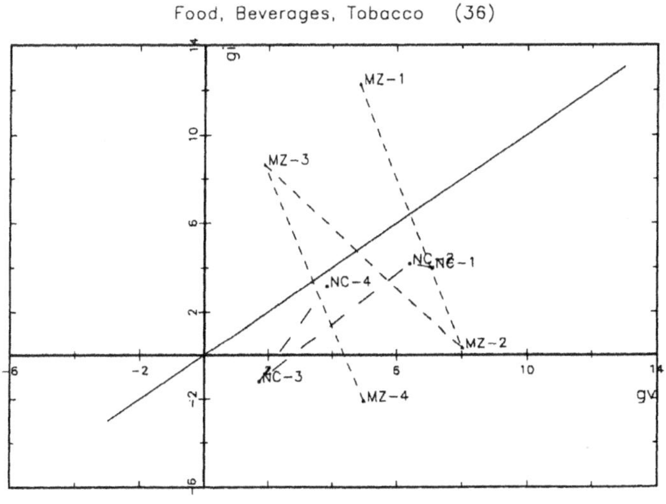

Figure 12b: North-Centre Italy (NC) - South Italy (MZ)

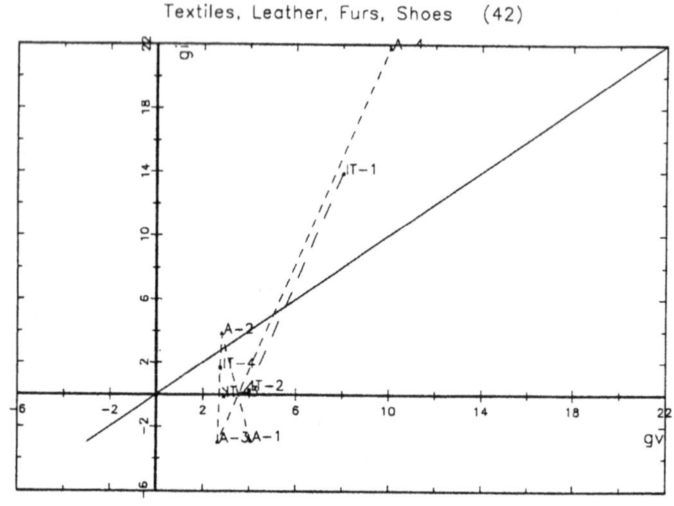

Figure 13a: Austria (A) - Italy (IT)

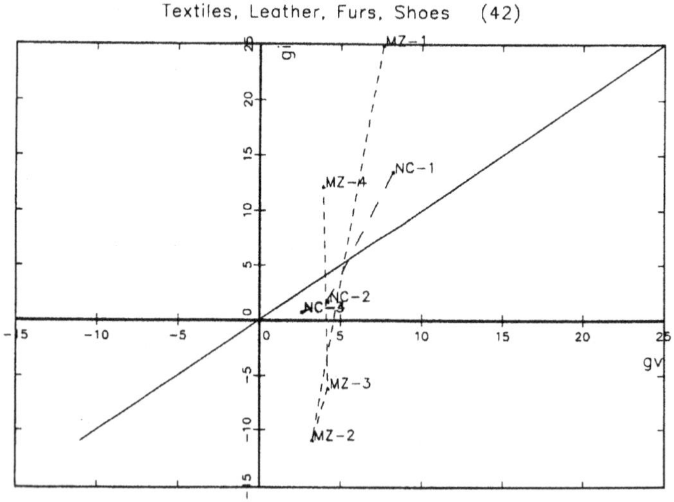

Figure 13b: North-Centre Italy (NC) - South Italy (MZ)

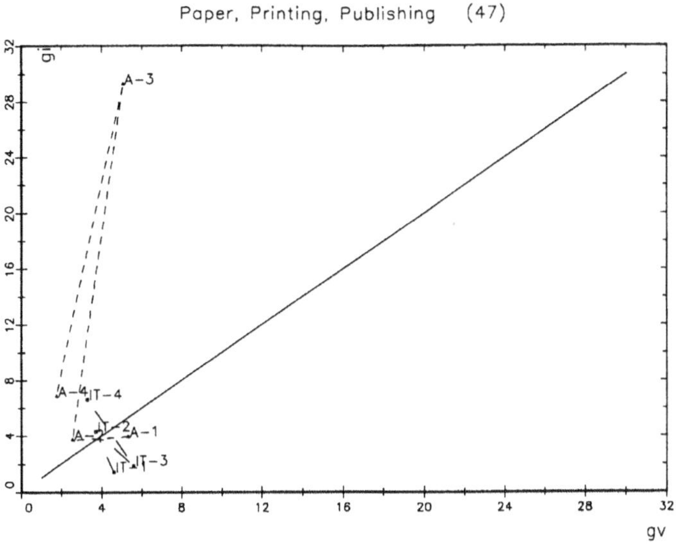

Figure 14a: Austria (A) - Italy (IT)

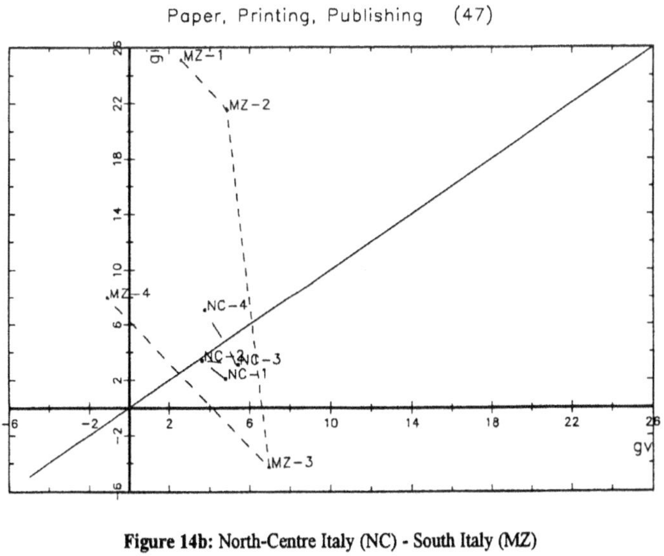

Figure 14b: North-Centre Italy (NC) - South Italy (MZ)

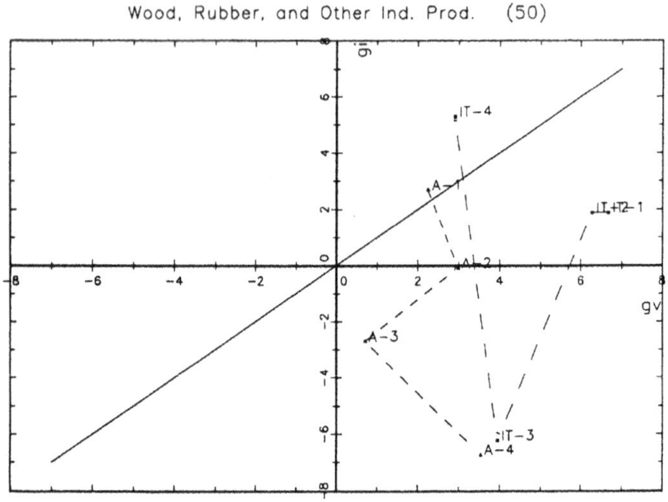

Figure 15a: Austria (A) - Italy (IT)

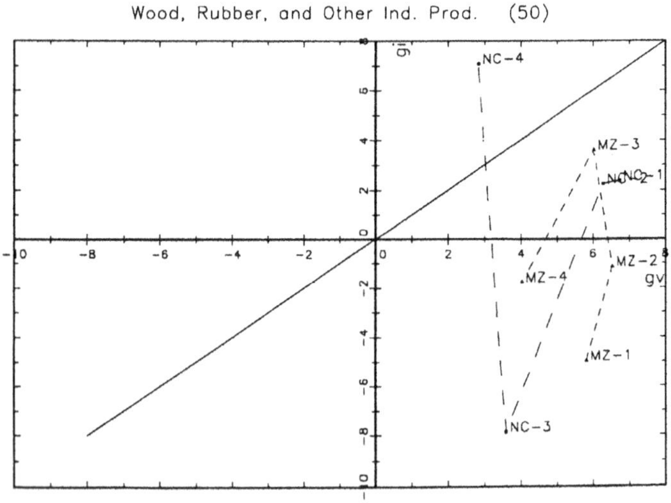

Figure 15b: North-Centre Italy (NC) - South Italy (MZ)

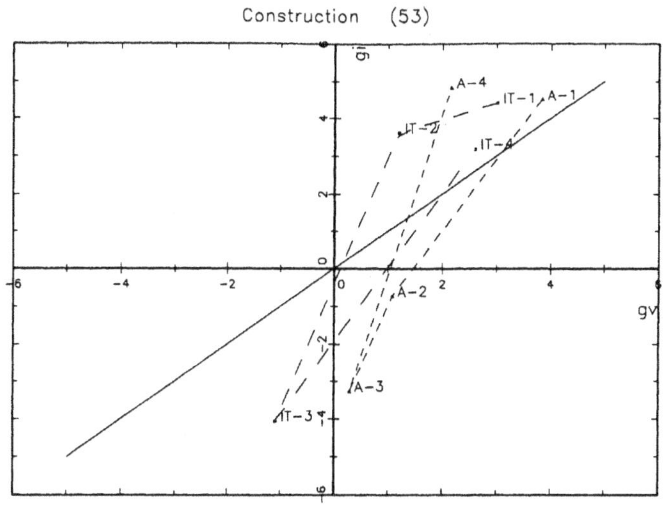

Figure 16a: Austria (A) - Italy (IT)

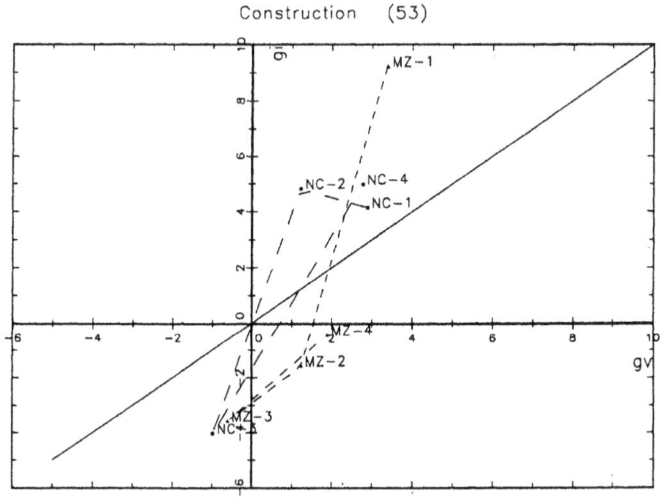

Figure 16b: North-Centre Italy (NC) - South Italy (MZ)

Technological Position and Industrial Structure of Austria

Hannes Leo

Austrian Institute of Economic Research

1 Introduction

The opening up of the East bloc countries changed the political location of Austria substantially: before 1989, Austria was - as a neutral country - directly in between two major blocs. Nowadays Austrian is right in the centre of a region called Central Europe. As old relationship are renewed and new co-operation are ventured, the impact of this process can already be identified. Overall Austrian exports to the surrounding former East bloc countries have been augmented substantially. At the same time numerous joint-ventures (Stankovsky, 1993) have been established taking advantage of the huge local demand and the favourable labour costs (not exceeding 1/10 of the Austrian labour costs). However these cost advantages of the producers in the former East bloc countries also make them serious competitors for Austrian firms on Austrian and international markets in more labour intensive, low technology industries (textiles, steel, cement).

Simultaneously Austria applied for EC membership. In preparation of this step, the already strong relations with Western European countries have been further strengthened. A look at the trade flows demonstrates that Austria is already strongly interwoven with the European Community, the latter being Austria's most important export region as well as the origin of most of its import. Although full integration will result in a positive balance for Austria (Breuss and Schebeck, 1989, and in this volume) it will also lead to a restructuring of the high end of Austrian industry and of the still sheltered sectors of Austrian economy.

These developments and the ever increasing competition within Triad countries has led to an intensified discussion of both the industry structure (speed of structural change) and the technological position of Austria. Although the discussion focuses mainly on short-term issues (related to increasing competition from producers with marked cost advantages), medium and long-term issues are gaining in importance. EC integration, GATT-membership, etc. already indicate that the opportunities for policy actions favouring national industry are rather limited and have the chance of being sanctioned. Therefore the centre of activity in industrial policy already has and will have to continue to shift even further towards "allowed" medium-term policy strategies in the fields of technology, environment and regional development. The policies will be centred towards changing industrial structure and technological position in a medium term period.

The following paper tries to describe the industrial structure, structural change and the performance of Austrian industry. Furthermore the technological position is described and analysed in detail. Both strands lead to concluding remarks on future challenges and necessities for Austrian industry.

2 Structure and structural change of the secondary sector

2.1 Industry structure

Austria has one of the largest secondary sectors[1] among OECD countries (surpassed only by Japan and Germany). In 1989 36,7 % of total value added (at 1985 prices) were created in the secondary sector which employed 37,0 % of total labour force (OECD 1993). Nevertheless the share of the secondary sector decreased considerably in the last decades: in 1960 it accounted for 47 % of total value added and of 40,3 % of civilian employment. However, this reduction of the secondary sector was - due to a good industry performance in the past 20 years - smaller than in most other OECD countries. Compared with western European countries the growth of Austrian industrial production has been continuously higher throughout the seventies and the eighties. It was not until 1986 that Austria was outperformed by these countries. The period afterwards was marked again by high industrial growth in Austria with a peak in 1990 (+7,4%).

The overall structure of Austrian industry is still burdened by an above average share of the basic goods sector. Due to the great importance of the steel and pulp and paper industries this sector accounts for 15,3 % of industrial value added. 11,3% of value added are produced by the chemical sector, 12.3% by building supplies, 22,5% by traditional consumer goods and 34,0% by engineering goods. In EC countries, the basic

---

[1] The secondary sectors encompasses manufacturing, electricity, gas and water, and construction

goods sector (10,6%) and the building supplies sector (8,4%) are well below the Austrian level, whereas chemicals (16.3%) are more important among EC countries. The traditional consumer goods sector and the engineering sector are equally important among EC countries and Austria.

2.2 Structural change

The positive growth performance of industry in the past decades is to some extent due to structural change from basic goods to engineering goods: the net production value of the basic goods sectors amounted 65,1 % of net production value of the engineering goods sector in 1960 and was reduced since then to 46,2 % in 1989. The new activities coming out of this incremental rather than radical change could mostly be described as "medium tech" activities leaving still a gap in high-tech, science based industries.

In Austria small and medium sized enterprises performed much better than large enterprises. In 1976 the 12 largest enterprises accounted for 14,3% of total employment in industry. This number fell to 13,9% in 1983 and to 7,9% in 1988. But what is large in Austria is not necessarily large internationally: the average number of employees of the 10 largest enterprises in Austria is 12.000 and therefore considerably under the Swiss average of 60.000 - not to mention the United States, where the an average employment among the 10 largest enterprises is 311.000 (Aiginger, 1992).

On the industry level, structural change for the period 1980 - 1991 has translated into the expansion of the electronics industry, transport equipment industry, glass industry, pulp and paper industry, and metal products accompanied by a reduction leather and leather products, mining, basic metals and textiles (see table 1). The growth of the transport equipment industry was fuelled to some extent by foreign investments (i.e. General Motors producing engines and gear boxes and BMW establishing an engine production line and a R&D lab for diesel engines to mention the most important) and the enforcement of an indigenous car component supply industry working in close co-operation with European car producers, located mainly in Germany. Pulp and paper, on the other hand made large investments into pollution control and production equipment throughout the eighties. This investment cycle was partly triggered by enforced environment regulation alongside with public support schemes for environmental protection investments and led not only to better environment conservation but also to an improved competitiveness of the industry. Altogether the pulp and paper industry has increased its production capacity by more then 80% since

1980[2]. The electronic industry - the third major industry with a huge expansion - expanded at a fast pace due to the rapid diffusion of electronic equipment in all parts of the economy and of daily life.

Table 1: Austrian industry production index*) between 1980 - 1991 (1980 = 100)

Electrical machinery	200.7
Transport equipment	186.6
Glass	176.7
Pulp and paper	171.8
Paper products	171.5
Metal products	155.7
Wood products	149.7
Food and beverages	138.5
Chemicals	141.3
Castings	141.2
Machines	134.6
Non ferrous metals	127.8
Textiles	111.2
Iron and steel	98.7
Leather	91.4
Oil	87.7
Mining and quarrying	84.2
Clothes	82.5
Clothes	83.3
Leather products	68.1
TOTAL INDUSTRY	136.7

Source: ÖSTAT. *) Reflects the volume of industrial production in physical units (weighted by share in value added).

2 The increased capacity is one of the reason why Austrian pulp and paper industry has been severely hit by the present recession and the devaluations of major competitors (Finland, Sweden) and customers currencies (Italy).

2.3 Productivity growth

The growth of industrial production was supported by an above average productivity growth during the post war period. Because of Austria's underdeveloped state at the end of the second world war, the rapid increases in productivity therefore can be seen as a catching up process fuelled by high investments into capital goods (Hahn 1991, Aiginger 1987). The average annual growth of productivity per labour hour of 5,5% in the seventies and of 4,8% in the eighties was considerably higher than in Germany and was surpassed by only few countries (Bayer 1983, Guger 1991). Manufacturing industries in particular reduced the productivity gap with other advanced industrial countries within the last two decades. For example, in 1991 Austrian industry almost reached the German labour productivity level. This is noteworthy as, at the beginning of the seventies, there was a 30 % productivity gap. Yet one must mention that capital productivity - although the gap has been narrowed in recent years too - is still significantly lower than in Germany (Aiginger, 1992).

At the industry level pulp and paper, transport equipment, metal products, castings and electrical machinery showed the highest productivity gains during the eighties (see chart 1). The same industries also reveal the highest increases in output in that period (R^2 = 0,54). This relationship was first explained by Verdoorn (Verdoorn's law) who deduced a constant elasticity of labor productivity with respect to output in an expanding industry. This relationship is due to economies of scale, technological progress and learning by doing and is particularly associated with secondary activities (manufacturing, public utilities, construction, (see Mitter, Skolka 1984)).

2.4 Export performance

The free trade agreement with the EC at the beginning of the seventies led to a significant internationalisation of Austrian industry: presently 54,4% of the industrial goods produced in Austria are exported (1970: 33,3%); 59,8% of the industrial goods used are imported (1970: 39%). Chart 2 shows the export ratio and the trade balance (as a percentage of production volume) on an industry level. Austria is a net exporter of leather and leather products, pulp and paper, steel, glass, castings, paper products and machines. The main trading partners (either import or export) are located in western Europe (amongst whom Germany plays a dominant role accounting for 40% of exports and 43% of imports in 1992). The share of foreign trade with overseas countries is - in contrast with European countries - low and shrinking.

The trade balance of Austria is chronically in the red (1991: 113 billion AS). Furthermore the unit values (price per kilogram) of Austrian imports (45,6 AS per kilogram) are continuously higher than the unit value of Austrian exports (32,7 AS per kilogram). According to Aiginger (1992), this situation is due to Austrian deficits in the fields of industrial design, know-how, organisation and industry related services which enable firms to charge higher prices on the international market.

Chart 1:

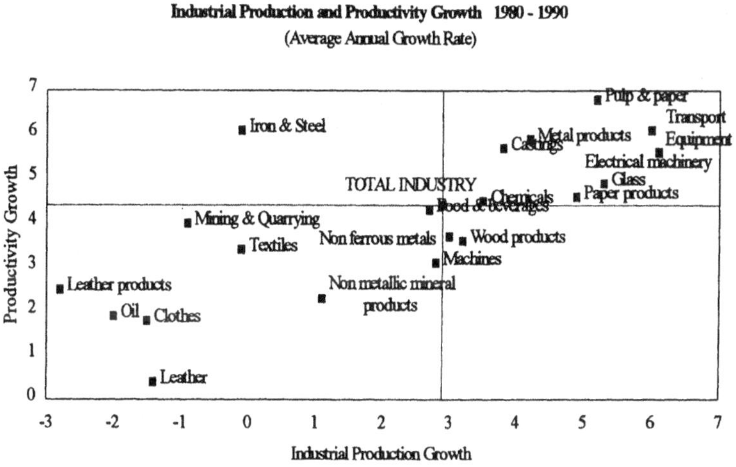

The stock of foreign direct investment of Austrian industry amounted to 4,1% of GNP and is currently well below the 10% level which is the average among advanced industrial countries. The fact that the stock of foreign direct investment of Austrian industry (ADI) was only 1,4% of GNP in 1985 illustrates the rapid catching up process in this field. Consequently the Austrian balance of ADI/IDI was in the black for the first time in 1990 and still is (1990: 11 billion AS, 1991: 12 Billion AS surplus).

Chart 2:

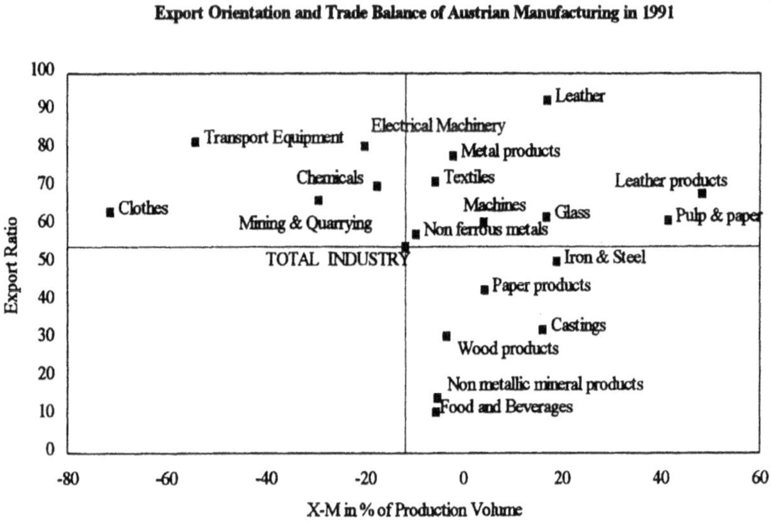

3 Technological position

3.1 R&D expenditure

Research and development expenditures measure the input of firms and government for the "production" of new knowledge, which eventually materialises in new products, processes and services. Although the explanatory power of R&D expenditures is doubted by some analysts, it is still the most important indicator for the technological position of a country. This is due not only to common data gathering practices (which were laid down by the OECD in the Frascati Manual) but can also be attributed to the obvious interrelation between R&D activities and technological progressiveness of a country[3].

[3]The basic critique centers on the high level of aggregation of R&D data. When interpreting R&D figures one has to consider the following limitation to the data:

- o The comparison of R&D spending on a national level is distorted, by the military R&D expenditures and spending on space programmes included in these figures.

Austria's expenditure on research and development in 1992 reached 1,52 % of GDP. This level is clearly below that of OECD as a whole (1985: 2,3%) and of the EC (1990: 2,0%). A comparison with Switzerland (2,9 %), the Netherlands (2,3%), and Finland (1,9%) also shows that Austria is lagging behind..

Table 2: Gross Domestic Expenditure on R&D (GERD) as a percentage of Gross Domestic Product

	1975	1981	1985	1987	1988	1989	1990
United States	2,3	2,5	2,9	2,9	2,8	2,8	2,8
Japan	2,0	2,3	2,8	2,9	2,9	3,0	3,1
Germany	2,2	2,4	2,7	2,9	2,8	2,9	2,8
France	1,8	2,0	2,3	2,3	2,3	2,3	2,4
Italy	0,8	0,9	1,1	1,2	1,2	1,3	1,3
Netherlands	2,0	1,9	2,1	2,3	2,3	2,2	2,1
Belgium	1,3	·	1,6	1,6	1,6	1,7	1,7
Sweden	1,7	2,3	2,9	3,0	·	2,8	·
Switzerland	2,4	2,3	·	2,9*)	·	2,9	·
Denmark	1,0	1,1	1,3	1,4	1,5	1,5	·
Norway	1,3	1,3	1,6	1,8	·	1,9	·
Finland	0,9	1,2	1,6	1,7	1,8	1,8	1,9
Austria	0,9	1,2	1,3	1,3	1,4	1,4	1,4
OECD total	1,9	2,0	2,3	·	·	·	·
EG total	1,6	1,7	1,9	2,0	2,0	2,0	2,0

Source: OECD, STI. *)1986.

o R&D expenditures measure the input for research and development and comprise about 30 to 40% of the total expenditure for the development of a product (Volk 1988). Not included are expenses on engineering, design, market introduction etc.

o R&D spending in small countries is heavily influenced by the presence of multinational enterprises. It should be noted, however, that a major part of the high expenditures in Switzerland and in the Netherlands is accounted for by high-tech companies operating internationally. In the Netherlands, for example, the five largest multinational companies account for 70 % of the business sector's R&D expenditure.

Despite these critical remarks most researchers - including myself - assume that the level, structure and change of R&D expenditures are valid indicators for cross country comparisons which allow a rough estimation of the technological position of a country.

The gap between OECD or EC levels is due to the large share of the basic goods sectors (with a small outlay for R&D), the small expenditure on military[4] and space projects and the non-existence of large multinational enterprises. In the Austrian context "large" industrial producers are 1) Austria's nationalised industry - historically strong in basic industries; 2) subsidiaries of multinational enterprises, where - despite a tendency towards the increasing internationalisation of R&D activities within MNE - R&D remains concentrated at corporate headquarters (Dunning (1990); and 3) the remaining "large" industrial producers are often to be found in less R&D intensive consumer goods or basic industries (e.g. pulp and paper, for an investigation into the size/innovativeness relationship see Hutschenreiter, Leo (1992)).

The restructuring of nationalised industry in the eighties was seen by some analysts as an opportunity to build up large, internationally competitive and technologically advanced enterprises which in turn could also stimulate the technological progress of wider segments of Austrian industry. Presently nationalised industry contributes 18.6% of private R&D expenditure with a rather modest R&D ratio (R&D in per cent of sales) of 1,9% (as opposed to 3% for total industry). In the meantime, restructuring difficulties has led to a modification of the strategic concept of nationalised industry: instead of growing into high-tech areas a concentration on the basic good sector activities is occurring. Although this tendency will be coupled with the technological upgrading in these areas, in the future only a weak impetus on the overall technological position and progress of Austria can be expected to come from nationalised industries.

3.2 Patent statistics

Overall R&D statistics suggest that Austria resembles a medium-tech country. An analysis of the US patent statistics (see table 3) supports this view[5]: in the United States,

[4] Compared with other countries (e.g. USA, France, UK) Austria participates in research-intensive defense and space projects only to a very limited extent . While this leads to a lower research ratio, it has hardly any effects on the economy's performance (Leo, 1991, Tichy, 1992).

[5] There are two reason for using US patent statistics for an international comparison of the technological performance of a country:

1. If one takes patent grants in the home countries one has to cope with the problem that the propabiltiy that a patent is granted varies. For example, in France 90%; in Great Britain 80%; and in Germany 35% of patent applications will receive a patent (Griliches 1990, S. 1663). It therefore is not advisable to compare patent grants in Germany with patent grants in France. Furthermore it can be assumed that the large market in the US will induce firms to apply for a US patent if they do have an economically

most patents granted during the period between 1963 and 1989 were obtained by American companies, while some 35 % of the patents were of foreign origin. In the international ranking list, Austria places 11th, behind Sweden, Italy and the Netherlands, but ahead of Belgium, the USSR and Australia.

Table 3: Patent activity by date of patent grant in the USA (1/1963 - 12/1989)

	1963-1975	%	1963-1989	%	Average annual growth 1975-1989
TOTAL	854537	100,00	1812419	100,00	5,52
US ORIGIN	629930	73,72	1180012	65,11	4,59
FOREIGN ORIGIN	224607	26,28	632407	34,89	7,67
JAPAN	36936	4,32	184075	10,16	12,16
WEST GERMANY	57124	6,68	145127	8,01	6,89
UNITED KINGDOM	35893	4,20	70727	3,90	4,96
FRANCE	22683	2,65	54635	3,01	6,48
SWITZERLAND	13911	1,63	31340	1,73	5,97
CANADA	13484	1,58	31073	1,71	6,14
SWEDEN	8495	0,99	19646	1,08	6,17
ITALY	7424	0,87	19570	1,08	7,17
NETHERLANDS	7158	0,84	17324	0,96	6,52
AUSTRIA	2494	0,29	6577	0,36	7,17
BELGIUM	2908	0,34	6554	0,36	5,98
U.S.S.R.	2701	0,32	6404	0,35	6,36
AUSTRALIA	1999	0,23	6391	0,35	8,66
DENMARK	1624	0,19	3858	0,21	6,38
FINLAND	652	0,08	2884	0,16	11,21
ISRAEL	699	0,08	2876	0,16	10,63
CHINA (TAIWAN)	24	0,00	2336	0,13	38,68
NORWAY	865	0,10	2185	0,12	6,84

Source: U.S.Patent and Trademark Office.

Since 1975, total patent grants have increased by an average of just over 5,5 % per cent per year. Given the discussions about the technological "decline" in the United States, the lower growth rate of patents granted to American companies is not surprising. While patents of US origin grew by an average of 4,6%, patents of non-US

important invention. Using US patent statistics therefore assures that all firms have the same conditions to receive a patent and that the most important innovations will be patented in the US (Schiffel/Kitti 1978).

2. Pavitt (1980) showed that "each country has the same propensity to patent in the USA in relation to the size of its innovative activities" thus making such data a useful technology indicator for cross-country comparisons.

origin increased by 7.7%. Japan recorded a particularly dynamic development (+12,2%). Large increases were also achieved by Taiwan (+38,7%), Finland (+11,2%) and Israel (+10,6%). Austria holds 0,36% of all patents in the United States and saw above-average growth of 7,2% in the number of patents granted during the period from 1975 to 1989.

Both - R&D and patent statistics - indicate that the technological gap between Austria and the most advanced countries is narrowing although at a modest speed. This catching up proceeded with varying intensity: after the second world war technological progress was mostly imported through investment goods. The unrestricted availability of technologies developed abroad led to huge productivity improvements in Austria[6] but also created the opinion among managers that in-house R&D was unnecessary due to the easy access to foreign technology.

A change of mind did not occur until the end of the sixties. In the seventies Austria launched a major initiative to catch up with other countries. The growth rates of R&D expenditures in that period were above OECD average, though starting from a low level. At the beginning of the 1980s, this trend came to a standstill. While the development in other countries was gaining momentum, growth rates in Austria were relatively modest. The reason for the sluggish development in Austria was the restraint exercised by companies in the field of their investment in R&D. Nevertheless, growth was achieved, with most the increase resulting from additional government expenditure. At the end of the 1980s, however, the growth pattern changed again: the main contribution to the higher R&D ratio came from the corporate sector, which substantially increased its R&D expenditure.

A recently conducted innovation survey in Austria (Leo - Palme - Volk, 1992) shows fundamental changes in the attitude of firms toward innovation: not only have R&D expenditures increased considerably but firms also have shifted the objectives of the innovation process from process optimisation towards product innovation. This development should reduce the dependence of Austrian industry on technologies developed abroad and increase the room to manoeuvre under fiercer international competition.

---

[6]Steindl (1977) showed that the productivity growth induced by imported capital goods was in Austria twice as high as in the countries of origin - mainly the USA.

4 Conclusion and policy recommendations

Industrial structure and the technological position of Austria have improved in recent years. The changes in both fields were incremental rather than radical. Industrial structure improved in the sense that the importance of the basic goods sector has been continuously reduced and medium and high-tech activities enforced. Simultaneously, the technological position measured in R&D expenditures and patent grants has also improved. Nevertheless the upgrading of the Austrian structures will have to proceed at a faster pace in order to be able to react to new competition from the former East bloc countries as well as to respond to the challenge of the EC integration. Under the present environment the only feasible goal for economic policy is to reinforce convergence on the most advanced countries.

But knowing ones goal and implementing it through economic policy are two different things. For policy action under a rather corporatist framework such as in Austria you have to have a broad consensus regarding the present situation and you need efficient institutions for implementing your policy. Although this sounds quite simple it is not: Presently the relevant institutions keep a low profile on their "visions" of the Austrian economy and therefore no discussion takes place on economic strategies. Furthermore, not taking in account other policy fields, four ministries claim to be responsible for industrial policy. Not surprisingly you find a lack of co-ordination and areas of overlap, etc.. A clear-cut plan designating responsibility for industrial policy and broad discussions of the economic situation are much in need.

Apart form an adequate institutional setting industrial policy has to offer stable conditions for the upgrading of existing structures. Structural change should be seen as a kind of "natural process" which should be eased but not controlled by industrial policy. When improving the working condition for industry, one should more or less try to aid the expanding segments and cushion the decline in the sectors of your economy which can not be upgraded. For that kind of "evolutionary" policy approach (i.e. supporting the adaptation to a new environment and not simply achieving goals set under a mission oriented policy paradigm), you need to influence quite well-known subsystems of your economy, e.g. improving the school system, reducing bureaucracy in public sector, conserving social peace, environment protection and so on.

With this "evolutionary" strategy, the structure of industry does not change dramatically although the significance of medium and high-tech productions should increase. For activities in new fields (e.g. "emerging" technologies) quite different strategies are necessary. A small country like Austria has to limit its fields of activities and therefore to make choices among possible alternatives. The exploitation of "emerging" technologies can be done by investing first into scientific infrastructure and then trying to foster spin-off enterprises, rapid technology transfer, etc. It should be mentioned that this approach is rather risky as the selection of fields of activities must be made at a time when neither the technological nor the economic potential on an emerging field is fully known. Furthermore the management of such ventures is not yet well understood.

Under the present situation the impression prevails that the enterprises in Austria were and are prepared to adapt to and exploit the new possibilities brought about by the changes in the environment. Unfortunately the sluggishness of the institutional setting in many ways hinders rather than enforces structural change.

Bibliography

Aiginger, K. (1992): (Koordination), *Industriepolitik 2000*, vorläufige Fassung, Wien

Basberg, B. J. (1987): "Patents and the measurement of technological change: A survey of the literature", in Freeman (1987)

Bayer, K. (1983): "Produktivitätswachstum österreichischer Inudstriebranchen im internationalen Vergleich", *WIFO Monatsberichte* 10

Breuss, F., Schebeck, F. (1989): Die Vollendung des EG-Binnenmarktes. Gesamtwirtschaftliche Auswirkungen auf Österreich, Makroökonomische Modellsimulationen, *WIFO-Gutachten*, Wien

Dunning, J. H. (1990): "Multinational Enterprises and the Globalisation of Innovatory Capacity", Discussion Paper in International Investment and Business Studies, No. 143, University of Reading, Department of Economics

Freeman, C., (1987): *Output Measurement in Science and Technology*, Elsevier Science Publishers, North Holland, Amsterdam

Griliches, Z. (1990): "Patent Statistics as Economic Indicators: A Survey", *Journal of Economic Literature*, Vol. XXVIII

Guger, A. (1992): "Ein absoluter Produktivitätsvergleich Österreich - BRD", in Aiginger (1992)

Guger, A. (1991): "Lohnstückkostenposition der Industrie 1990 verschlechtert", *WIFO-Monatsberichte*, 64(7)

Hahn, F. (1991): Kapitalproduktivität in der österreichischen Industrie 1970 bis 1989, *WIFO-Monatsberichte* 64(7)

Hutschenreiter, G., Leo, H. (1992): "Empirical Evidence on Schumpeterian Hypothesis in Austria", Paper presented at the Industrial Organisation Conference, Vienna

Mitter, P., Skolka, J. (1984): "Labour Productivity in Austria between 1964 and 1980", *empirical economics*, Vol. 9

Leo, H.(1991): , Die österreichische Weltraumindustrie, Ausmaß und Perspektiven, *WIFO-Gutachten*, Wien

Leo, H., Palme, G., Volk, E. (1992): *Die Innovationstätigkeit der österreichischen Industrie, Technologie- und Innovationstest 1990*, Wien

OECD (1992): "Science and Technology Policy, Review and Outlook 1991", Paris

OECD (1993): "National Accounts", Vol. 2, Paris

Pavitt, K. (1980): *Technical Innovation and British Economic Performance*, London

Schiffel, D., Kitti, C. (1978): "Rates of Invention, International Patent Comparisons", *Research Policy*, Vol.7, Number 4

Stankovsky, J. (1993): "Marktstellung in Ost-Mitteleuropa bedroht", *WIFO-Monatsberichte* 6

Steindl, J. (1977): "Import and Production of Know-How in a Small Country: The Case of Austria", in Saunders, C. T. (ed.), *Industrial Policies and Technology Transfer between East and West*, Springer Verlag, Wien, New York

Tichy, G. (1992): "Forschungs-, Technologie- und Industriepolitik", *Arbeit und Gesellschaft*, Wien

Volk, E. (1988): Die Innovationstätigkeit der österreichischen Industrie, Technologie und Innovationstest 1985, *WIFO-Gutachten*

Endogeneous Technical Progress in a Macroeconomic Model. A Comparison between Italy and Austria

Gerhard Hanappi
University of Technology of Vienna

1 Introduction

The objective of this paper is to discuss the effects of an innovation promotion program in two European countries, Italy and Austria. To do so, a highly aggregated macro-economic model is used, which has been successfully applied for similar policy questions in the FRG (see Frühstück, Hanappi, Wagner (1990)). The model will be introduced briefly in chapter 1. Some analytical features of this formulation will also be mentioned. Chapter 2 reports the results of the estimations of the behaviourial functions for the Italian and the Austrian economy. Some preliminary conclusions from the comparison of important parameters are drawn. In the following chapter 3 a simulation experiment is carried out: If government increases its expenditure on the advance of technical knowledge, then deviations of major economic variables from their trajectories in a reference scenario are computed. Again, results are interpreted and the case of Italy is compared to Austria. In the final chapter the validity of the findings is discussed and some possible extensions are mentioned.

2 A macroeconomic model with endogenous technical change

The model used to explain endogenous technical change in an economy is given in table 1. The key idea is to treat technical knowledge of an economy as a stock variable (KRD), which enters the aggregate production function [1] analogous to the capital stock. Since the inverted production function is used as labour demand function [1.1], a higher level of technical knowledge implies lower labour demand.

Technical knowledge is increased by a specific investment (IRD). Investment function [4] explains investment in R&D with the same arguments as function [3] does for regular investment: In both cases on the one hand expected growth, the accelerator, and on the other hand relative factor prices, interest rate versus wage rate, induce investment. Notice that the first argument, the accelerator, can be interpreted as an indicator of the expected profit rate, if the latter depends on the ratio of capacity utilization to output. The difference between the two investment functions stems from the assumption, that R&D investment is less volatile compared to regular investment. Research and development, once induced, is a long-term project. Equation [4] takes care of this assumption by the use of lagged terms.

Other equations of the model are fairly conventional. Consumption function and equilibrium condition in the goods market need no explanation. Government expenditure plus net exports is captured in variable G, which follows output according to the simple relationship [5]. Capital stock and technical knowledge decrease with their depreciation rates and increase with investment (equations [6] and [7]). As is standard in Keynesian macro-models, the labour market can be in disequilibrium if the exogenously growing labour supply exceeds labour demand (equations [8] and [1.1]).

Nevertheless there are forces to drive the labour market at least partially back to equilibrium. In the wage-price-system the wage equation [10] contains a feedback from labour market disequilibrium to the wage setting process. With higher unemployment wages will be lower and, as a consequence, relative factor prices change and encourage firms to substitute labour for capital, employment increases. Prices increase either due to imported inflation or due to a mark-up over wage increases (equation [9]). Since there is more or less central wage-setting in most industrialized countries mark-up behaviour seems to be applicable for wages too.

In both equations [9] and [10] the influence of changing labour productivity is brought into the picture explicitely. The suggestion is, that part of technical progress has to be distributed to wages ($a_{10,3}$ in equation [10] should be positive), while on the other hand increasing competition in times of fast increasing technology should dampen inflation ($a_{9,3}$ in equation [9] should be negative).

As the analytical treatment of this model in [Frühstück, Hanappi, Wagner (1990) pp.64-78] shows, the stability of the model can only be determined if specific parameter values are assumed. Keeping in mind, that parameter values express economic behaviour, this implies, that for slowly changing parameter values the model might change from a stable region to an unstable one, and vice versa. For a mid-term simulation approach however, questions of stability seemed to be of less importance.

Table 1: MODEL EQUATIONS

Goods market

Equilibrium condition:

[0] $Y_t = C_t + IR_t + IRD_t + G_t$

Behavioural equations and technical relations:

[1] $\ln Y_t = a_{1,1} \ln (cu_t K_t) + a_{1,2} \ln KRD_t + a_{1,3} \ln L_t$ (used only as in [1.1])

[2] $\ln C_t = a_{2,1} + a_{2,2} \ln Y_t$

[3] $\ln IR_t = a_{3,1} + a_{3,2} (\ln Y_t - \ln Y_{t-1}) + a_{3,3} (\ln r_{t-1} - \ln w_{t-1})$

[4] $\ln IRD_t = a_{4,1} + a_{4,2} (\ln Y_t - \ln Y_{t-1}) + a_{4,3} (\ln r_{t-1} - \ln w_{t-1}) +$
$+ a_{4,4} (a_{4,2} (\ln Y_{t-1} - \ln Y_{t-2}) + a_{4,3} (\ln r_{t-2} - \ln w_{t-2}))$

[5] $\ln G_t = a_{5,1} + a_{5,2} \ln Y_{t-1}$

Definitions:

[6] $K_t = K_{t-1} + IR_t - a_{6,1} K_{t-1}$

[7] $KRD_t = KRD_{t-1} + IRD_t - a_{7,1} KRD_{t-1}$

Labour market

Disequilibrium

[8] $U_t = L^S_t - L^D_t$

Behavioural equations and technical relations:

[1.1] $\ln L^D_t = (\ln Y_t - a_{1,1} \ln (cu_t K_t) - a_{1,2} \ln KRD_t) / a_{1,3}$

Wages and prices

Behavioural equations

[9] $\ln P_t = \ln P_{t-1} + a_{9,1} \ln P^M_t + a_{9,2} (\ln w_t - \ln w_{t-1}) + a_{9,3} ((\ln Y_{t-1} - \ln L_{t-1}) - (\ln Y_{t-2} - \ln L_{t-2}))$

[10] $\ln w_t = \ln w_{t-1} + a_{10,1} (\ln L_t - \ln L^S_t) + a_{10,2} (\ln P_{t-1} - \ln P_{t-2}) +$
$+ a_{10,3} ((\ln Y_{t-1} - \ln L_{t-1}) - (\ln Y_{t-2} - \ln L_{t-2}))$

List of variables:

Endogenous:

C .... private consumption
G .... government expenditure plus net exports
IR .... investment (regular)
IRD .... investment in research and development
K .... capital stock
KRD .... capital stock in R&D (technical knowledge)
L .... employment
P .... GDP deflator
U .... unemployed persons
w .... wage rate
Y .... national income

Exogenous:

cu .... capacity utilization
L^S .... labour supply
p^M .... import price index
r .... interest rate

3 Simulation models

Estimating the behaviourial functions of the model for Italy and for Austria did not lead to great surprises. Basically economic intuition proved to be justified. Table 2 gives the results for Italy, table 3 for Austria[1].

For the estimation of the production function, the parameter restriction that $a_{1,1}$ plus $a_{1,3}$ equals one has been assumed. That is, increasing returns appear only via growth in technical knowledge[2].

The estimation of [4] is based on the restriction that $a_{4,4}$ equals one. This assumption can be justified by the argument that firms take a long term view on investment in R&D; they attach the same weight to recent experiences as they do to current ones[3].

An interesting result is the negative influence of lagged output growth on investment in R&D. A Schumpeterian interpretation would state, that firms start innovation during the recession. As equation [3] shows regular investment behaves pro-cyclical.

Suggestions about signs of the wage-price-systems' coefficients proved to be correct.

The case of Austria nevertheless lead to difficulties, which caused a slight change in the model structure. Labour demand could not be estimated as inverted Cobb-Douglas production function. To arrive at reasonable results a constant capital-output-ratio had to be estimated (equation [1]). This is the reason why instead of the two independent variables K and Y only one variable, namely Y^*, enters the labour demand function [1.1].

---

1 Since the emphasis of this paper is not on the econometric estimation of the model, all measures of significance of the single equation OLS estimations are omitted. In general parameters are significant at a 95% level. As data source OECD series were used, Austrian capital stock data was taken from the WIFO database, the Italian capital stock was derived from the estimations of Maddison [Maddison A. (1986)].

2 For recent industry specific estimate of a similar function for the FRG see [Blazejczak, Erber, Horn (1988)].

3 On long term orientation of R&D investment see [G.Dosi (1988)].

In equation [5] the introduction of a time trend improved the estimation tremendously, suggesting that the growth of this variable in Austria depends less on output growth.

Comparing some key parameters gives the following picture. As the output elasticity shows, the Italian stock of technical knowledge contributes more to output than the Austrian does. The fact, that substitution between capital and labour is much more rigid in Austria might have contributed to this.

On the other hand investment behaviour, in particular the accelerator mechanism, seems to react much more sensitive in Austria than in Italy. For relative factor prices the long prevailing stability of distribution between labour and capital could have lead to higher sensitivity.

Equation [9] shows that Austria could be hit by international inflation slightly stronger than Italy. Austrian firms meet less favourable circumstances than Italian firms do to compensate wage increases by price increases. On the other hand Austrian entrepreneurs are better off in preventing increasing competition from driving down their prices.

Austrian labour unions react with their wage setting process more sensitive to labour market disequilibria than Italian unions do. Austrian workers seem to receive their wage increases rather in relation to increased productivity, whereas Italian workers seem to get higher wages as compensation for inflation.

Evidently suggestions like these are only as good as a highly aggregated model can picture a complex economy. Nevertheless most of them sound quite plausible.

Table 2: ITALY

Goods market

Estimated equations:

$$[1]\ \ln Y_t = 0.163 \ln (cu_t K_t) + 0.272 \ln KRD_t + 0.873 \ln L_t$$

$$[2]\ \ln C_t = -2.257 + 1.131 \ln Y_t$$

$$[3]\ \ln IR_t = 11.862 + 0.515 (\ln Y_t - \ln Y_{t-1}) - 0.103 (\ln r_{t-1} - \ln w_{t-1})$$

$$[4]\ \ln IRD_t = 8.331 - 0.223 (\ln Y_t - \ln Y_{t-1}) - 0.226 (\ln r_{t-1} - \ln w_{t-1}) - \\ - 1 \cdot (0.223 (\ln Y_{t-1} - \ln Y_{t-2}) + 0.226 (\ln r_{t-2} - \ln w_{t-2}))$$

$$[5]\ \ln G_t = -4.9072 + 1.23 \ln Y_{t-1}$$

Assumed:

[4] $a_{4,4} = 1$

[6] $a_{6,1} = 0.025$

[7] $a_{7,1} = 0.025$

Labor market

Assumed:

Nominal wages are downward rigid.

Wages and prices

Estimated equations

$$[9]\ \ln P_t = \ln P_{t-1} + 0.0129 \ln P^M{}_t + 0.9116 (\ln w_t - \ln w_{t-1}) - 0.288 ((\ln Y_{t-1} - \ln L_{t-1}) - \\ - (\ln Y_{t-2} - \ln L_{t-2}))$$

$$[10]\ \ln w_t = \ln w_{t-1} + 0.2829(\ln L_t - \ln L^S{}_t) + 1.15(\ln P_{t-1} - \ln P_{t-2}) + \\ + 1.362 ((\ln Y_{t-1} - \ln L_{t-1}) - (\ln Y_{t-2} - \ln L_{t-2}))$$

Table 3: AUSTRIA

Goods market

Estimated equations:

[1] $\ln Y^*_t = 0.2184 \ln K_t$

[1.1] $\ln L_t = \ln Y^*_t + 14.77 - 1.37 \ln KRD_t$

[2] $\ln C_t = -0.656 + 1.0057 \ln Y_t$

[3] $\ln IR_t = 9.889 + 0.741 (\ln Y_t - \ln Y_{t-1}) - 0.301 (\ln r_{t-1} - \ln w_{t-1})$

[4] $\ln IRD_t = 2.726 - 2.304 (\ln Y_t - \ln Y_{t-1}) - 0.564 (\ln r_{t-1} - \ln w_{t-1}) -$
$- 1 \cdot (2.304 (\ln Y_{t-1} - \ln Y_{t-2}) + 0.564 (\ln r_{t-2} - \ln w_{t-2}))$

[5] $\ln G_t = 9.68 + 0.13 \ln Y_{t-1} + 0.033 \cdot t$

Assumed:

[4] $a_{4,4} = 1$

[6] $a_{6,1} = 0.025$

[7] $a_{7,1} = 0.05$

Labour market

Assumed:

Nominal wages are downward rigid.

Wages and prices

Estimated equations

[9] $\ln P_t = \ln P_{t-1} + 0.02736 \ln P^M_t + 0.6634 (\ln w_t - \ln w_{t-1}) - 0.019 ((\ln Y_{t-1} - \ln L_{t-1}) -$
$- (\ln Y_{t-2} - \ln L_{t-2}))$

[10] $\ln w_t = \ln w_{t-1} + 0.311(\ln L_t - \ln L^S_t) + 0.79(\ln P_{t-1} - \ln P_{t-2}) +$
$+ 1.197 ((\ln Y_{t-1} - \ln L_{t-1}) - (\ln Y_{t-2} - \ln L_{t-2}))$

4 A simulation experiment

Forecasting the two economies for five years by the use of the two simulation models gives an idea of the highly interdependent structure of these models. In this chapter only one policy experiment is carried out, and the results of this experiment in both countries is compared.

Assume that instead of following equation [5], government suddenly adopts an innovation promotion program. More precisely, one percent of GDP are taken away from government expenditure, lowering variable G, and are added to investment in R&D, increasing variable IRD. Moreover this policy shock is permanent, that is, it appears in each year.

Table 4 compares the deviation of the performance of the two economies if they are hit by such a policy shock. Figures given are the differences of the growth rates of the respective variables, measured in percentage points. In other words the growth rate of a certain variable in the reference run (without policy shock) is subtracted from the growth rate of this variable in the policy run.

Table 4: Results of the simulation experiment

Year	1989	1990	1991	1992	1993
ITALY:					
GDP	0	-0,02	0,02	-0,02	-0,01
Unemployment Rate	1,55	1,55	3,2	3,19	3,4
Prices	-0,46	-0,24	-1,18	-0,48	0,02
Wages	-0,52	1,07	-1,32	0	-1,65
AUSTRIA:					
GDP	-0,58	0,53	-0,71	0,6	-0,55
Unemployment Rate	0	2,3	2,18	4,45	4,18
Prices	0	-0,99	1,37	-0,92	-0,05
Wages	0	-1,53	2,14	-1,4	0

As this table shows, the Italian economy is hit by such a policy shock much less severe than the Austrian. Growth of GDP remains almost unaffected, while Austrian growth rates start to oscillate. This might have been caused by the long stable development of Austria, which somehow taught Austrian agents to react stronger on slight changes.

In both cases employment suffers from labour saving innovation in a very significant way. While Italian consumers will benefit from lower prices, Austrians in generally will not. In both countries wage growth will become unstable, higher unemployment surely will drive down wages in the long run.

5 Conclusion

As this paper shows, even small and highly aggregated macroeconomic models can reproduce plausible features of inter-country comparisons. Extensions of this type of models, incorporating international trade, money markets and exchange rate dynamics have been tested for the FRG [Hanappi, Wagner (1990)] and for Austria [Hanappi (1990)]. A model with a more elaborated public sector is in preparation.

Comparing Italy and Austria shows certain advantages of Italy as far as its capacity to translate higher productivity into lower prices is concerned. On the other hand Austrian workers seem to be in a better position if technological unemployment starts to increase. For both countries the disadvantages of a forced technology policy, which is not encompassed by a complementary employment program, probably outweighs its benefits[4].

References

Blazejczak J., Erber G., Horn G.A. (1988): "Sectoral and Macroeconomic Impacts of Research and Development on Employment." In: *International Conference on New Technology: Its Impact on Labour Markets and the Employment System*. 5th-7th December 1988, Berlin. 83-102.

Coe D.T., Helpman E. (1993): "International R&D Spillovers", *IMF Working Paper* 93/84.

Dosi G. (1988): "Sources, Procedures, and Microeconomic Effects of Innovation." In: *The Journal of Economic Literature* XXVI(1988), 1120-1171.

Hanappi G. (1990): "Zinssätze und Kapitalverkehr im internationalen Zusammenhang.", *Schriftenreihe Volkswirtschaft der österreichischen Postsparkasse*.

Hanappi G., Wagner M. (1990): "The Nexus between Innovation and Growth in the Federal Republic of Germany", in E.Matzner/M.Wagner (Hrsg.), 1990, *The Employment Impact of New Technology. The Case of West Germany.*, Avebury, Aldershot, Brookfield, USA.

Frühstück W., Hanappi G., Wagner M. (1990): *Tandem. Innovationsaktivitäten im wirtschaftlichen Funktionsgefüge der Bundesrepublik Deutschland.*, Berlin: De Gruyter.

Maddison A. (1986): *The Phases of Capitalist Development*, Prentice Hall.

[4] An interesting question not touched in this paper is how domestic R&D efforts affect the economic performance of important trade partners (compare for example [Coe D.T., Helpman E. (1993)].

III. A Perspective on Monetary Policy and the Balance of Payments

On the European System of Central Banks: A Note

Marcello de Cecco
University of Rome "La Sapienza"

1. As we got close to the Maastricht Conference, a scramble to work out an agreement to start the second phase of European Monetary Unification was taking place. In addition to the Maastricht meeting, the publication, at the beginning of 1991, of a tentative outline for a European System of Central Banks has given free rein to academic reflections on the most important features to be conferred to the ESCB, which it is asssumed will be the core around which the European Political Union will be aggregated.

The Apeldoorn meeting, however, showed with utmost clarity how little was the area of agreement of the EC partners on the issues concerning the content of the future European Monetary Union, as suggested by the Delors Report. A compromise seems to be emerging on the proposed European Monetary Institute, which should precede the ESCB. This looks like one of those extremely long lived temporary solutions Europeans are so good at devising.

Undoubtedly, the succession of phases suggested by the Delors Report had the benefit of scant historical experience. In real life political sovereignty seems to have preceded monetary sovereignity in the vast majority of cases. The phases suggested by Delors, however, could be seen as a progressive erosion of national sovereignty and in this light it is possible to see that easy things are done before the difficult ones. In this list, political union can be seen as the last step on the long road covered by the European Community since 1958, and the fact that the monetary union is the one step before the last makes it like a stepping stone which makes it easier to reach a higher ground.

Perhaps because it has been suggested that monetary union precede political union may be the reason why discussions about the the ESCB have shown the nature of a traditional dispute on the monetary standard. In the past century ,as well as in previous ones, national and international disputes about the choice of the monetary standard were numerous and fascinating. The nature of internationally traded commodities of the standards in question made international discussions on the standard easier.

The transition to monetary systems based on paper and therefore of a completeley fiduciary nature has made the discussion on the monetary standard difficult. This applies to the European monetary standard. The current debate therefore becomes more and more similar, also for reasons of historical analogy, to the dispute on monetary standards which involved theoretical and practical economists after the first world war. The problem was then that of stabilising most of the European national monetary systems, after the deep disturbances they had suffered because of the war, and of war finance.

A return to the Gold Standard seemed then a universalistic and free-trade choice, which cristallised around it all those who identified the pre-war era with monetary stability and the latter with the gold standard. Gold monometallism, however, was advocated by some as a solution open only to the economically stronger nations. Those should have created a trade and capital circuit totally free from any control, and around that core a periphery would come about, formed by countries in worse financial conditions, which would prefer to adopt floating exchange rates.

It is easy to understand that the debate was about which countries could and should adopt which price indexes. The paladins of a swift and generalised return to the gold standard believed that all could index their currencies to the price of gold. Those on the contrary who believed that some countries, even the majority of countries, were not in a position to go back to gold immediately, advocated the two speed center-periphery solution, which suggested that peripheral countries adopt a freely floating exchange rate, tied, as it were, to the domestic price level. Monetary policy would then be free from all ties to gold, and could be targeted to the stability of domestic prices, since the choice of a gold peg would probably mean rapid and deep deflation. A floating rate would also tie monetary policy to political decisions on production and distribution taken domestically in as complete as possible isolation from international conditions.

In the current discussion on the second phase of the European monetary unification process, the subject is of course no more, as in the aftermath of world war I, what commodities or baskets of commodities to choose as monetary standard. It has become instead the feasibility of a complete join-up of very different domestic price systems. The debate is thus on what will be the likely results of such a drastic operation.

If exchange rates are fixed the various European moneys must be all subjected to the same rules of issue, since complete intercirculation will otherwise see Gresham's Law at work. It was so in the case of the Latin Monetary Union, which allowed intercirculation of subsidiary coins within certain limits, and also allowed individual countries to produce such coins at different rates, and said nothing about public deficits rules, or about suspension of convertibility. Fixed rates would of course not last if rules of issue differed, but before the intercirculation rules were repealed, Gresham's Law would work and bad currencies would replace good ones. For at least a considerable while, citizens of unruly countries would enjoy the right to preempt the national product of well run countries. Historical experience has shown with great regularity the disappearance of good coins and their gradual repalcement by bad coins, at the domestic as well as at the international level. Good coins were used to save, bad coins were used to spend.

In paper standard systems, before the arrival of a single currency, the fiscal deficit of the more spendthrift countries determines the monetary policy of the whole currency area, and thus the level of effective demand and the conditions of production and distribution. It is true that in such a case, fixed exchange rates would not last very long, but in the meanwhile the spendthrift countries would be able, by paying high interest rates on their debt, to keep the game going for a considerable time, before their creditworthiness became so compromised that lenders would refrain from lending to them and even scramble out of currencies of the high interest countries. Fixed exchange rates without a common set of economic policy rules would thus probably see first a build up of international debt and then the dramatic collapse of the system.

It is exactly this fear which motivates the actions of the German economic authorities and their stand on the subject of the further phases of European Monetary Unification. They see the immediate adoption of a fixed exchange area as large as the present EC as totally unrealistic and fraught with the considerable danger that the German economy will be subjected to a level of effective demand incompatible with the preservation of price and credit stability, exactly because spendthrift countries will be able to raise interest rates to the level required to maintain fixed exchange rates through capital imports. The unraveling of this process they believe will be dramatic and inevitable, bringing in its train financial instability and excessive deflation, as lenders realise that exchange rates cannot remain fixed as countries cannot carry on borrowing without impairing their creditworthiness. German authorities are convinced that a prematurely established and too generalised fixed exchange rates system among

European countries will inevitably sow the seeds of its own dramatic destruction. They believe this scenario will not come about only if a dual system is established, which will allow fixed rates only among politically and economically homogeneous countries, while politically and economically heterogeneous countries will be on floating rates.

This debate is very similar to the one held at the end of the second world war, when J. H. Williams launched the idea of the key-currencies. It is also similar to the debate that took place at the end of the first world war. Then like now many European countries were struggling with large public debts and excessive currency creation stemming from unbalanced state budgets. Then like now the self appointed defenders of private savers had to struggle against the proclivity of parliaments to vote expenses without securing adequate revenues by politically unpopular tax increases. Then like now a way out seemed to have been found in the creation of a European system of central banks, which would be by statute totally independent from political influence and dedicated to the single minded pursuit of price stability and the preservation of the gold standard.

As is well known, this interwar progenitor of the European System of Central Banks was the creature of Montagu Norman, Governor of the Bank of England. He wrote down in 1920 the Ten Commandments of central bank independence and saw to it that only countries whose political authorities swore their allegiance to the Tables of the Law received the large loans necessary to buttress their stabilisation policies. He also made sure that the successor states to the defeated central European empires established new central banks whose statutes contained his Ten Commandments in form and substance.

Norman's grand stabilisation plan came unstuck when his basic premise failed to realise itself. This was that U.S. prices would grow more than British prices, thus allowing Britain and the rest of Europe to stabilise at a decent level of effective demand and at balanced current accounts. But U.S. prices refused to oblige, and U.S. competitiveness remained too great for European economies to bear, and especially for the Pound Sterling to go back to the pre-war parity without sacrificing full employment in Britain and elsewhere.

As European countries faced the post-stabilisation threat of mass unemployment and financial crisis, the Ten Commandments of central bank independence came crushing down. But not before they had engendered financial crisis everywhere, as one of them was the prohibition to use open market operations. This had been put there in order to prevent central banks from financing deficit spending governments, but it prevented them from giving help to financial markets when banking crises exploded and spread to the whole of Europe.

Montagu Norman had tried to make sure that his Ten Commandments were adopted by as many central banks as possible to guarantee that they would be respected especially by his own British political authorities. This urge seems to be very intensely felt even today, by the central banks of countries like Germany, Britain and the Netherlands, which expect a worsening public finance situation at home, and want to erect a barrier against it by establishing central banks absolute dedication to price stability as a rule of international good conduct.

By preaching a dual system of exchange rates in Europe, moreover, they make sure that such a code of international good conduct be adopted only by the countries most likely to be able to stick to it in the long run. A dual system allows core countries to maintain price staibility and the periphery to ensure full employment for the whole system by fiscal deficits which will generate trade imbalances and devaluations, whose evil effects will however only be felt in the peripheral countries. This state of affairs would reproduce much more closely the international economic system as it existed before 1914. It was the bimetallic and silver part of the system which generated a level of effective demand sufficient to ensure full employment everywhere and relative price stability in the gold part of the system.

The recent re-unification of Germany has made things relatively more difficult to manage for German authorities. The Delors report is a pre-unification document, which is predicated upon the permanence of a German vocation to price stability coupled with a French and Italian vocation to full employment and deficit spending. In the ideal Europe of Delors, France and Italy generated demand, and Germany generated stability, a virtuous mix which allowed monetary unification to proceed. But German unification has now given Germany an endogenous source of effective demand, and stability must be maintained against domestic as well as foreign threats.

2. As the dispute about the ESCB concentrates on what can be called the modern version of the question of the Standard, a series of other serious problems risks receiving little or no attention. They are problems related to the supervisory functions of the ESCB on the European financial system. It looks increasingly as if authorities and public opinion prefer to dicuss money, and pay no attention to credit. Once again the Currency School seems to prevail, a modernised but not radically different version of the XIXth century Currency School.

There are however good reasons to worry about the way the European financial space is coming into being. A contradiction can be detected between the philosophy underlying the Delors Report and that which permeates the documents introducing the European Financial Space. It is a contradiction which has to do with the concept of market freedom, and also with different views about the development of actual financial systems.

Since I began to study the mode of development of the financial systems of main western countries, I became convinced that the Anglo-American opinion according to which there is one development path along which all financial systems must develop is fundamentally incorrect. From the normative point of view this uniqueness is not theoretically warranted, nor is it borne out by the observation of reality.

Anglo-American financial theory wants financial systems to inevitably proceed from repression to liberalisation. As is often the case with economic theory, theorising proceeds from the idealisation of one particular real case. Even worse, some of the features of that particular real case which agree with the theorist's ideology are selected as representative, while other features which contradict that ideology are ignored, although they are present and important.

Like other students of the history of economic theory, I have also noticed that it is often the case that a system is recommended for the whole world and for the eternity of time if it suits the interests of important pressure groups in a hegemonic country at a particular time. It is not required that hegemony be political or economic. It might be only cultural hegemony, which often lingers on in a country after the other two have waned from it. Italians maintained cultural hegemony on financial matters long after they had ceased to be the most powerful bankers in Europe. The same has happened to the British in more recent times. The same seems to be happening today to the Americans. The institutional reforms the culturally hegemonic country introduces because of the successful pressure exercised by powerful groups are exported even to countries where they seem to fit very little to the local environment.

In the case of the theory of financial development, Anglo-American economists have since the XIXth century perfected a view according to which financial systems inevitably develop away from intermediaries and towards markets. Economic policy, to be appropriate and not to choke natural development must encourage the movement of the financial system along this path, removing obstacles which may impede the march of the financial system away form financial repression and towards financial liberalisation.

It seems however increasingly likely that what Anglo-American financial economists call financial repression is in reality another mode of financial development, which proceeds from institutions and intermediaries to more of those, with markets playing a distinctly minor role.

Anglo-American financial theory is a mid-nineteenth century child of laissez-faire and social Darwinism, coupled with what goes under the name of the "Whig interpretation of history". According to this complex product, economic systems, just like political systems, and like nature, develop from the simple to the complex. As they become complex, these systems develop a multiplicity of functions, and specialised organs come into being to perform them. The consoling political conclusion is that social development inevitably leads to pluralism and democracy. The economic conclusion is that economic development leads to the erosion of monopoly power and to the establishment of competitive markets. Economic authorities act correctly only if they behave like the midwives of history, helping natural trends to come successfully to light, and restraining those people, institutions and even countries who may want to put themselves in the way of the inevitable march of history.

Authorities ought therefore to encourage the creation of larger and more efficient financial markets, getting rid of regulations that were adopted in times of depression and even war and punishing instutions that derive rents from the existence of regulations.

This seems to have been the theoretical background to the strong and determined policy of financial deregulation inaugurated by English and American financial authorities in the the late seventies and pursued with great vigour in the eighties. That policy could of course be rationalised in very different terms, as a successful attempt to increase competition in the first phase of deregulation, to eventually raise the degree of concentration, and therefore of monopoly rent, present in the British and American financial systems. Likewise, in the air-transport system, deregulation experienced a first phase, when carriers multiplied and air fares decreased considerably under increased competition, followed by a second phase, when only the strongest, which not necessarily are the most efficient and safe, carriers survived and are now busy (but not necessarily successful) lifting prices and profits.

The analogy with air transport is appropriate to introduce a series of reflections that come to mind on the least talked about aspect of the ESCB, that of financial supervision. It has been repeatedly advanced, in the American debate on the effects of air transport deregulation, that excessive competition can reduce prices and put the safety of citizens at risk. In the case of the financial system, it is possible that an extension to the European financial space of securitisation as experienced in the US and Britain can seriously jeopardize the stability of the European financial and payments system.

The Anglo-American mode of financial development has seen in recent years a massive return to securitisation and a progressive prevalence of primary transactions over intermediated ones. Hard pressed banks have tended to save profit rates by devising more and more ways of taking transactions off their balance sheets. This has allowed them to keep ever decreasing prudential reserves. The total leverage of the US and British financial and economic systems has thus increased to a point considered dangerous by many analysts, as the illiquidity of financial institutions and generally speaking of markets increased as a result of the drive to greater profitability and cost efficiency by financial institutions. A system with minimum reserves is a flow system, running on the principle that either the flow will never stop, even only for a minute, or that a deus ex machina will always be present in the wings, a guardian angel who will provide the stock of reserves in case a liquidity crisis breaks out. A securitised financial system looks remarkably like a flow system, as securities are sold and bought as if they were commodities, free from problems of trustworthiness and creditworthiness which are usually attached to debt instruments. In a securitised world financial transactors behave as if the solvency of primary debtors is not a problem. The financial system, in fact, can become securitised only if all market participants are allowed to free ride on the central bank. The central bank is the guardian angel. It waits in the wings for a liquidity crisis to appear, solving it by injecting primary liquidity, which by definition it can produce at zero microeconomic cost, into the financial system by rediscounting and open market operations. An illiquid, totally securitised, financial system, has thus achieved efficiency and reasonable profits, in spite of fierce competition, if the lender of last resort function of the central bank has been guaranteed at all times. Only this guarantee can transform debt instruments into commodities that can be exchanged without any reference to the person or institution that has issued them.

In the case of a closed system this guarantee can be given without any conceptual difficulty. It is only a political problem that has to be solved, as the central bank, by performing the lender of last resort function routinely and without cost to financial institutions, eliminates the need financial institutions have of keeping prudential reserves. The country's economic authorities must calculate if the provision of lender of last resort functions is warranted by large savings on interest rates and other costs to borrowers and if enough citizens are lenders benefitting from this extension of state protection. It is however rather ironic that the propounders of deregulation, who are convinced believers in laissez faire and freedom from state interference in economic life, can ensure the success of a financial system totaly organised in markets only if the massive and continuous presence of the state as final guarantor of all debts can be assumed. Any even very momentary decline in this certainty is in fact capable of sparking off a first class financial crisis, which can destroy the efficient system created through deregulation and securitisation in a matter of hours.

The plot thickens however if the assumption of a closed financial system is removed. The securitised system may then be linked to other financial systems where securitisation has not prevailed because economic authorities do not believe in markets as inherently superior to institutions and also think that debts cannot seriously be separated from debtors, especially if the acts of lending and borrowing must be considered as repeated games and not as one-off transactions. In these other systems banks are likely to hold prudential reserves, to organise themselves an efficient and pervasive payments system and not to leave this function to the central bank. In this case the central bank has no obligation to perform routinely the role of lender of last resort. Debt instruments remain risky, and must be evaluated in connection with their issuers, and there is no publicization of private risk for the financial system as a whole.

Linking up two financial systems based on so divergent philosophies can be a source of great and frequent dangers. What is considered natural behaviour in one system not necessarily constitutes natural behaviour in the other one. Market participants in the securitised system, for instance, may assume that the central bank of the non securitised, bank-dominated other system sees its role as a lender of last resort exactly as their central bank does, and behave accordingly. With the result that in cases like that of the Herstatt bank, they may learn to their immense surprise and consternation that the other system's central bank considers itself in no way compelled to shore up its problem banks at all costs and in all cases, and can contemplate equanimously the prospect of their failure. Since all other banks have substantial reserves, this behaviour is perfectly rational and thoroughly responsible. But it might come as totally unexpected to the financial market participants in the other system, who work on the assumption that large institutions will not be allowed to fail. When they realize that they have been working under incorrect premises, financial market participants may scramble for reserves, and it is not at all certain that the reserves good for one system may be good for the other one too. If the rate of substitution between the two is low, the intervention of the other central bank (the one committed to routine lender of last resort functions) might not be enough to allay the outbreak of a destructive financial crisis.

Let us return to the ESCB as it seems to be emerging from the difficult negotiations now taking place. All signs seem to portend to the desire, on the part of Germany, to make sure that the exclusive role of the ESCB will be the preservation of monetary stability in the Community at a level acceptable by Germans. This means that the ESCB will be designed as a hands-off central bank, which is not supposed to be tied to a philosophy of routine performance of lender of last resort functions. Such philosophy would be grossly inconsistent with the primary function of warden of price stability, written in the first articles of the Draft Statute of the ESCB which has been circulated at the beginning of 1991.

While Europeans thus design an ESCB whose primary and almost exclusive role is the preservation of monetary stability in the Community, the European financial space is still constituted by a large securitised component, the British financial market, supplemented by the increasing degree of securitisation of other components, like the French , the Danish, the Dutch, the Italian. A serious contradiction thus emerges between the mode of European monetary unification and the mode of European financial integration. In the blueprint of the ESCB that has been circulated, financial supervision seems to be in practice delegated to national central banks and supervisory agencies, following the famous European "subsidiarity principle". It is then natural to ask how the central banks of the securitised systems will be able to be as austere as the draft statute of the ESCB demands with respect to the money supply if they are asked to perform the routine lender of last resort functions which their securitised, illiquid, financial systems, require.

This contradiction appears to be even more serious if we consider the fact that securitised systems have intense links with one another. This means that the financial markets of Britain, Holland, France, etc., are heavily influenced by events taking place in the US financial market, which is the most heavily securitised and the most illiquid in the world, routinely relying on the central bank to get it out of trouble. In view of these links one may reasonably ask how will the ESCB manage to be engaged in maintaining at the same time monetary and financial stability.

The contradiction we have detected stems from the different genesis of European monetary unification, which is a French initiative, and that of the Single European Market, which is a largely British initiative, and from the need to adjust these two philosophically divergent initiatives to the German imperative of agreeing only to an ESCB which would guarantee at least as much monetary stability as the Bundesbank. As in the case of the camel designed by a committee, the result seems to be a very strange animal. However, as it has been the case with many EC designs, in the end it may , like Galbraith's bumblebee, be perfectly able to fly.

Reflections on Central Bank Independence and Monetary Policy. The Case of Austria

Eduard Hochreiter *

Austrian National Bank

1 Introduction

In connection with the current discussion about the establishment of a European System of Central Banks and the reforms in the countries in transition in Central and Eastern Europe, there has been renewed interest in the institutional arrangements governing the central bank, the implementation of monetary policy and the relationship between the central bank and the government. The present paper attempts to capture major institutional features of the Austrian National Bank and looks at the question of independence. It further sketches the present policy approach and finally draws some conclusions.

2 Institutional aspects

Having the international discussion about the statutes of the European System of Central Banks[1] in mind, the following features of the Austrian National Bank Act appear relevant:

1. Prime target: price stability

According to the Austrian National Bank Act the prime task of the Austrian National Bank is to safeguard price stability. This task is extraordinarily clearly defined. Indeed, the formulation chosen in Article 2 paragraph 3 "....it shall ensure with all the means at its disposal that the value of the Austrian currency is maintained with regard both to its

---

* Enlarged version of a paper given at the conference "Adjustment to domestic and international shocks, and capital accumulation. Austria and Italy as case studies" at the University of Siena, November 8 and 9, 1991. Earlier versions were presented at workshops at the Institute for Advanced Studies, Vienna, December 1990, and at the University of Exeter in March 1992. Useful comments by participants of the seminars and by an anonymous referee are kindly acknowledged. The views expressed are those of the author and do not necessarily represent the position of the Austrian National Bank.

[1] For the official text see Amtsblatt der Europäischen Gemeinschaften (1992).

domestic purchasing power and to its relationship with stable foreign currencies" is more precise than that of any other Central Bank Act including that of the Deutsche Bundesbank and the Swiss National Bank.[2]

2. *Prohibition of fiscal financing*

Article 41 paragraph 1 explicitly prohibits the financing of public deficits at the federal, at the Länder as well as at the local authority levels.[3] Moreover, during the life of the Bank the Federal Republic must not issue paper currency.

3. *A high degree of independence*

In its decisions the Austrian National Bank commands a high degree of political, policy and financial independence.

3.1 *Political independence*

(a) Article 4 spells out the relationship between the Austrian National Bank and the Federal Government. The formulation employed in the Act "due regard shall be paid to the economic policy of the Federal Government" indicates that Article 4 is subordinated to Article 2 if a conflict of interest were to arise. This claim is also substantiated by the prohibition spelled out in Article 41 paragraph 2 that the Federal Republic must not adopt measures which are liable to hinder the Bank in the performance of the functions entrusted to it.

(b) The term of the members of the Governing Board is 5 years (renewable). Board members cannot be removed from office unless they no longer meet the requirements set for their appointment or election. The Governor is appointed by the President of the Federal Republic (on unanimous proposal by the Federal Government[4]), 7 members are appointed by the Federal Government and the remaining 6 are elected by the general meeting.

---

[2] For a comparison see Hochreiter (1990).

[3] Article 41 paragraph 1 Austrian National Bank Act also specifies the exception to the rule. At the request of the Federal Minister of Finance the Bank has to discount short-term Federal Treasury certificates up to an amount that must not exceed 5 percent of the Federal Republic's gross annual receipts from taxation.

[4] According to the Austrian Constitution, Article 67(1), the Governor is appointed by the Federal President "at the suggestion of the Federal Government or the Federal Minister authorized by it".

(c) The clause that Board members must not be active civil servants[5], neither at the Federal nor at the State (Länder) level, fosters the political independence of the Bank.

(d) In contrast to many other central bank laws, the National Bank Act also includes an explicit mechanism to solve conflicts. In case there is an infringement of Article 41 paragraph 1 and 2 (see point 2 above), an Arbitration Tribunal may be appealed to, which then has to arrive at a final decision within three days[6].

(e) The State Commissioners' task is to examine the Bank's business with regard to adherence to the law.

3.2 Policy independence

There is no explicit provision in Austria as to which institution sets the exchange rate regime[7]. In practice, the Bank, at least, has a significant voice in its selection. Moreover, the Bank is, free to decide on the instruments to implement the selected exchange rate regime. The Austrian National Bank Act stipulates which body, i.e., the Governing Board or the Board of Executive Directors, decides about the use of monetary instruments. Generally it can be said that traditional instruments (discount, lombard, minimum reserves)[8] are the domain of the Governing Board, whereas the utilization of the new, market-related instruments (open market operations) is decided upon by the Executive Board[9].

3.3. Financial independence[10]

Price stability is a public good, whose provision is entrusted to the central bank. Its efficient provision on the one hand and the appropriate information of the public concerning its provision on the other hand are decisive tasks of any central bank. This is all the more so as it is the public at large to whom the central bank ultimately is

---

[5] With the exception of university professors in law and economics (Article 22 paragraph 4 Austrian National Bank Act).

[6] Article 41 paragraphs 3 and 4 Austrian National Bank Act. The Tribunal consists of the president of the Supreme Court, and four members, two of whom shall be appointed by the Federal government and two by the Bank.

[7] Under the terms of the Foreign Exchange Act, the Austrian National Bank Acts on behalf of the Federal Republic as Austria's foreign exchange authority.

[8] Article 21 paragraphs 2 and 4 Austrian National Bank Act.

[9] Note, however, that the decision concerning the overall limit for open market operations is reserved for the Governing Board (Article 21 paragraph 3 Austrian National Bank Act).

[10] This point was also made in Hochreiter (1991).

accountable. Moreover, in the end, the public is the only dependable lobby of a stability-oriented central bank because of its vested interest in price stability for at least two reasons: First, stable prices tend to promote long-term growth and to prevent boom-bust cycles. Second, the public has more and more to lose through inflation because of its rising financial wealth.

The delicate task of running monetary policy efficiently and the difficulties to reach the very heterogeneous population requires a highly trained, specialized workforce and an elaborate information policy. To complement the institution's own expertise, outside knowledge from, e.g., university professors, journalists etc. has to be acquired.

All the tasks to be performed and mentioned above require substantial funds, which are to be provided by the Bank itself.

As far as the Austrian National Bank is concerned, the Bank commands a high degree of financial autonomy. Article 21 paragraph 10 stipulates that the Governing Board approves the cost estimates for the next financial year and approves the annual statement of account for submission to the general meeting. According to paragraph 12 of the same Article, it also authorizes expenditure not provided for in the cost estimates for the current year. Moreover, Article 69 paragraph 1 stipulates that certain income (profits from exchange rate changes, earnings from assets invested for the pension reserve etc.) is *not* entered in the profit and loss account. Finally, Article 69 paragraph 2 also stipulates that 10 percent of the net profit has to be allocated to the general reserve fund *before* profit distribution[11].

4. *Legitimation and accountability*

The Austrian National Bank derives its democratic legitimacy from Parliament and is ruled by statutes passed by Parliament. The Bank is therefore directly accountable to the law (strengthened by a State Commissioner who oversees the adherence to the law) and to the general public. Since the legislator may always change the law governing the ac-

[11] Of the remaining profit, the Federal Republic shall first receive one third which can be seen as seignorage distribution, the shareholders up to 10 percent dividend and any remaining portion shall be divided equally between the Federal Republic and other bodies as decided by the general meeting (Article 69 paragraph 3 Austrian National Bank Act).

tivities of the Bank, sufficient democratic accountability appears to be ensured. There are no reporting requirements to Parliament or other entities.

3 Central Bank independence and the political process in Austria

The Austrian National Bank Act entrusts the Bank with a high degree of independence and also spells out its functions in detail. This, however, does not imply that the Bank acts in a political vacuum. In fact, the opposite holds true. Moreover, as will be argued below, the Austrian system of social partnership in conjunction with an independent central bank greatly facilitates monetary management.

On a formal level the Austrian National Bank is a joint stock company. 50 % of the shares are held by the Federal Government, while the other 50 % are held by institutions close to the social partners[12]. Moreover, the Austrian National Bank Act stipulates that the Governing Board shall include representatives of banks, industry, trade and small business, agriculture as well as of salaried employees and wage-earners (Article 22 paragraph 3).

On an informal level close contacts among top policy-makers are maintained as a matter of course. In this context it has to be underlined that all major policy decisions are discussed in advance and a consensus is aimed at. To give but one example: The present monetary regime - the "hard currency option" - has been actively supported by all social partners. In the early 1970s, the policy was jointly designed by the Austrian National Bank, the Ministry of Finance and the trade unions, while at first the employers' organisations were somewhat reluctant[13]. All major policy makers, however, saw the advantages of a strict monetary regime. Thereby the adjustment cost (in terms of output lost) was minimized, productivity (by promoting innovation) fostered and the adjustment path (for example, by phasing of real wage changes) smoothed.

---

[12] These 50 % of the shares encompass 14 % held by banks and insurance companies, which, in a wider sense, may also be subsumed under the term "social partners". Note that the Federal Government decides who is permitted to subscribe the Bank's capital.

[13] See Hochreiter and Winckler (1991).

4 Some theoretical aspects

As has been noted above and analysed elsewhere in some detail[14], the Austrian National Bank Act allows the Bank to follow different strategies to achieve the prime goal. In principle it could also pursue a monetary targeting approach **and** flexible exchange rates. The Austrian National Bank, however, has since World War II consistently opted for a pegged exchange rate system[15], which - over time - was applied in different ways. In addition there have also been instances in the 1970s where the schilling was slightly de- or revalued against the peg currency (-ies).

The fact that Austria has been a pioneer in the application of novel exchange rate concepts is not widely known. Austria was the first country to put the nominal exchange rate concept into practice in 1971, it was the first country to explicitly employ (temporary) real effective appreciation to get to a lower inflation path in 1974 and in 1979 and Austria stuck to the single currency peg during the 1980s in the wake of massive foreign and domestic real shocks.

Prima-facie evidence suggests that Austria - over time - has been rather successful in achieving balanced low inflation growth or in rectifying external disequilibria with a relatively small loss in output. Why is Austria's experience different from that of other small countries and what may have been the contribution of the Austrian National Bank?

The theoretical model underlying Austria's monetary policy is straightforward. It is of the monetary approach type for a small open economy with fixed exchange rates and high capital mobility. It assumes long-term neutrality of money, long-term purchasing power parity, given terms of trade[16], demand determination of the money supply and the equilibrium interest rate differential with regard to the center country determined by exchange rate expectations and country-related risk factors.

The Bank has followed this approach closely, helped by the fact that the Act does not require the Bank to target nominal and real variables at the same time[17]. The

---

[14] Hochreiter (1990).
[15] For an analysis of the reasons see Hochreiter and Knöbl (1991).
[16] Note that the terms of trade and thus the equilibrium real exchange rate can be changed by supply side policy.
[17] Note that central bank legislation in other countries such as the US requires the central bank to achieve nominal and real targets. See e.g. Burdekin, Wihlborg and Willett (1992), p. 235.

Austrian National Bank Act makes it quite clear that the prime task of the Bank is to control nominal variables (for example, the domestic source component) and to pursue nominal targets (such as prices). The real side of the economy is left to fiscal policy (and supply side policy)[18].

The long-term success of the peg policy (minimized output and employment variations from trend) depends on the capability of the domestic economy to adjust to international developments[19] as well as domestic shocks; the smoother the adjustment the more successful the policy. This is a simple truth, which, as experience has shown, has often been forgotten.

If we now assume, e.g., that the price of oil rises (foreign real shock) or that the foreign demand for domestic products ceteris paribus falls (changes in tastes and preferences away from domestic products; domestic real shock), the real exchange rate and real wages have to fall. This can either be achieved via a devaluation-induced price rise or via a reduction in nominal wage (increases). A high degree of real wage flexibility is one prerequisite for smooth adjustment.

If, as is likely, money illusion on the part of workers has all but vanished, they are more likely to accept lower nominal wage increases if they can be reasonably sure that price rises do not get out of hand.

An example of this kind of reasoning is the attempted agreement among trade unions, employers and government in Finland, reached in October 1991 to offset the collapse of trade with the USSR (accounting for a 3 percent fall in real GDP), the recession in the UK (accounting for a 1 1/2 loss in real GDP) and the domestic recession (accounting for another 1 1/2 percent of GDP) by a cut in nominal wages by 7 percent and NOT by a devaluation of the markka. In the end the agreement collapsed and the markka was devalued by 12 %.

The second condition for smooth domestic adjustment relates to the credibility of monetary policy. It is trivial to say but hard to implement that building credibility takes time and requires steadfastness in difficult times, i.e., when the market tests the resolve of the central bank. In such a case it *must not* deviate from the path chosen (i.e.,

---

18 Insofar as price stability fosters long-term growth, the central bank can influence the real economy.

19 Note, however, that the peg policy does not necessarily imply the import of real growth from the center country. The growth part of the domestic economy is determined by domestic factors, in particular supply side policy.

devalue) but rather endure the comparatively short-term negative consequences of high short-term interest rates. The long-term gains of credibility are reflected in smaller risk premia and hence in a *lower* interest rate differential with regard to the center country than otherwise.

The third condition for smooth adjustment is a fiscal policy which does not unduly strain domestic savings, especially compared to the center country.

If we now pose the question of how these three conditions have been met in Austria, the following conclusions emerge: It is useful to go over statements and meeting records of Austrian prime policy-makers between 1978 and 1982. It is striking to see how early the Central Bank Governor, the Minister of Finance, the President of the Trade Union Federation and - somewhat later - the employers side understood the implications of a peg policy. The agreement to keep inflation down was universal, the unions were interested in the real wage and knew that it depended on productivity, the employers were aware of the fact that innovation and rationalisation would provide such productivity, while the Minister of Finance understood the need for budget consolidation[20].

A recent study by Knöbl (1990) has indeed shown that the degree of real wage flexibility in Austria - along with that of Sweden - is significantly higher than in Belgium and the Netherlands. The track record of wage agreements during the 1980s clearly indicates that the negative real shocks Austria's economy was exposed to were more than fully taken into account.

The building of credibility of the hard currency option has not come costless to the Austrian National Bank. In April 1977, e.g., a high official of the OECD indicated in a speech in Vienna that the schilling ought to be devalued. In August of that year the Federal Chancellor, Mr. Kreisky, voiced the opinion that exchange rate policy should be handled more flexibly. These statements resulted in sizable capital outflows, which were reversed after the devaluation expectations did not materialize.

---

[20] For a more detailed analysis see Hochreiter and Winckler (1991).

5 Summary

The Austrian National Bank Act defines the tasks of the Bank, in particular the prime goal of maintaining price stability in a more precise way than most Central Bank Acts, in particular the Bundesbank Act. The Act further endows the Bank with a very high degree of political, policy and financial independence. Finally, it explicity prohibits direct financing of fiscal deficits.

Therefore the Austrian National Bank Act already today conforms to the future European System of Central Banks Act as agreed at Maastricht in Dec. 1991[21], with the exception that limited overdraft facilities for the Federal Government are provided for.

Independence of the central bank does not imply that the Bank acts in a political vacuum. The composition of the share-holders and the Governing Board on the one hand and the Austrian system of the social partnership on the other hand allow the Bank to convey its policy intentions both formally and informally to policy-makers.

The model underlying Austria`s monetary policy is of the monetary approach type for a small open economy with fixed exchange rates and high capital mobility. The sustainability of the peg depends on the ability of the domestic economy to adjust to the exchange-rate level with regard to the centre currency (DM) chosen. It is this flexibility of the Austrian economy which explains the success of Austria's hard currency option. The independent Austrian National Bank has played an important part in it.

Bibliography

Austrian National Bank Act (1984), Second Edition 1988.

Angeloni, I. and Passacantando, F. (1991): "Monetary Policy in Italy, Institutional and Economic Aspects", *BIS*, April 1991, pp. 87-111.

Burdekin, R.C.K. and Willett, T.D. (1991): "Central Bank Reform: The Federal Reserve in International Perspective", *Public Budgeting and Financial Management*, Vol. 3, No. 3, pp. 619-649.

Burdekin, R.C.K., Wihlborg, C, and Willett, T.D. (1992) "A Monetary Constitution Case for an Independent European Central Bank", *The World Economy*, March, pp. 231-249.

Europäische Gemeinschaften (1992): "Protokoll über die Satzung des Europäischen Systems der Zentralbanken und der Europäischen Zentralbank", *Amtsblatt* Nr. C 224/104, 28. August 1992.

---

[21] See Europäische Gemeinschaften (1992).

Frisch, H. (1983): "Stabilization Policy in Austria, 1970-80", in: De Cecco, M. (ed.), *International Economic Adjustment - Small Countries and the European Monetary System*, Basil Blackwell, Oxford, pp. 117-140.

Grilli, V., Masciandaro, D. and Tabellini, G. (1991): "Political and Monetary Institutions and Public Financial Policies in the Industrial Countries", forthcoming.

Hochreiter, E. (1988): "Währungspolitik kleiner offener Volkswirtschaften bei hoher Kapitalmobilität", *Wirtschaftspolitische Blätter*, Nr.1/1988, pp. 76-83.

Hochreiter, E. (1990): "The Austrian National Bank Act: What Does It Say About Monetary Policy ?", *Konjunkturpolitik*, Vol.36, No 4, pp. 245-256.

Hochreiter, E. and Knöbl, B. (1991): "Exchange Rate Policy of Austria and Finland - Two Examples of a Peg", *De Pecunia*, pp. 33-61.

Hochreiter, E. and Winckler, G. (1991): "Signaling a Hard Currency Strategy: The Case of Austria", forthcoming in *Kredit und Kapital*.

Hochreiter, E. (1991): "Comments on Monitoring European Integration: The Making of Monetary Union" by Begg, D. et al, CEPR, London.

Schaumayer, M. (1991): "Central Bank Policy in Austria", in: Downes, P. and Vaez-Zadeh, R., (ed.), International Monetary Fund, pp. 167-175.

Swinburne, M. and Castello-Bianco, M. (1991): "Central Bank Independence and Central Bank Functions", in Downers, P. and Vaez-Zadeh, R. (ed.), International Monetary Fund, pp. 414-444.

Reflections on the Papers by De Cecco and Hochreiter

Francesco Farina
University of Siena

The European Monetary System (EMS) can be characterised as a cooperative but non-symmetric agreement between Germany and the small economies of the Deutsche mark area on the one side and countries affected by divergent macroeconomic performances like France and Italy on the other side.

The reason for cooperative behaviour is mainly in the shared objective to exploit a Pareto improvement by means of the public means of the public goods made available by the fixed exchange rates agreement. In fact, Germany has benefited from the public good of growing exchange rate stability, which also worked as a shield against the dollar fluctuations *vis-à-vis* the Deutsche mark, and the divergent countries from the public good of low inflation, once the strategy to peg their currencies to the Deutsche mark as the nominal anchor of the EMS implied the commitment to pursue deflationary monetary policies. The non-symmetric setting of the EMS consists in the hegemonic status of Germany. As it is well-known, the Bundesbank has dictated the monetary stance for the whole area, while the burden of interventions and realignments has mainly been placed on the weak-currency countries.

The papers by Hochreiter and De Cecco stimulate concerns about the central banks' independence and the Deutsche mark's role during the EMU process. The question which I will then address is to what extent the unification shock which has hit the leader could jeopardise the non-symmetric cooperation in the process towards European Monetary Union (EMU). To answer this question, possible shifts in the convenience to cooperate, with a leader whose policy stance has drastically changed, have to be detected.

Let us analyse how the balance between costs and benefits stemming from the EMS has turned out during the Eighties for the initially divergent countries. First of all, these countries simply had no alternative to the participation into the fixed exchange rate agreement. It can be reckoned that during the Seventies in most of the European countries, central banks proved unable to resist domestic expansionary pressures put in place by rational forward-looking agents aimed at augmenting the activity level: monetary authorities accomodated wage and price rises, and pursued competitive devaluations which represented a major source of instability for Germany. Eventually, since the output-inflation trade off progressively disappeared and the Phillips curve became vertical, the mix of expansionary monetary stance and flexible exchange rate policy ended up in huge increases in the inflation rate.

This sub-optimal outcome made it clear that a managed foreign exchange policy no longer could be relied upon as an instrument to get a permanent improvement in the employed and real output levels. In the absence of the EMS agreement, a divergent country would probably have suffered from a welfare loss bigger than the one which would have affected Germany. Central banks then felt that a shift to tight monetary policy and to the nominal fixity of the exchange rate was needed in order to bring the internal inflationary game between firms and unions to an end. If inside the EMS cooperation most of the times has prevailed an on opportunistic behaviour, that was then just because all members have gained from the participation.

In order to assess the costs related to the EMS participation, the reason why the originally high-inflation countries were forced to accept the hegemonic status of Germany has to be explained.

The view is widely shared according to which, for the "inward" game between monetary authorities and the private sector to be cooperative, the "outward" game between Germany and the Deutsche mark area on the one side and France and Italy on the other side had to be played with the leader exerting a "bargaining power". In fact, the counterproductive outcome of international monetary cooperation pointed out by Rogoff (1985) was avoided: due to the nominal anchor role performed by the Deutsche mark, the central banks of the divergent countries could not rely upon the credibility of the German commitment to abide by the task to provide the nominal anchor of the EMS also worked in avoiding that in the divergent countries the time-inconsistency problem[1] might occur. As wage and price setters knew that any attempt to impose their preferred output-inflation trade off would have been frustrated, in the private sector it was rationally anticipated that monetary authorities were not prepared to renege on the current anti-inflationary stance.

---

[1]See Kydland and Prescott (1977) pp. 473-910

Provided that capital controls and interventions in foreign currencies helped in keeping changes in bilateral parties at rates lower than inflation differentials, the nominal convergence triggered by the fixed exchange rate regime was eventually successful in starting up the real adjustment of these economies In France and Italy - but also in a non-EMS country like Austria whose economy is highly integrated with Germany - inflation rates started converging towards the German rate because the leading role of the Bundesbank was effective in enhancing the central banks' credibility and the private sector was convinced to cooperate with monetary authorities, too. The paper by Hochreiter clearly underlines that the credibility of central banks' independence was decisive in Austria to the extent that the adjustment cost was minimised (how profound was the impact of the tight monetary policy and of the exchange rate constraint on wage and price movements is shown by the econometric estimates of the Hochreiter and Winckler (1991) paper). The similar convergence problem experienced by Italy, where the anti-inflationary monetary stance has brought about the elimination of the wage-price spiral and a deep restructuring inside the productive system, has been evaluated elsewhere[2].

Therefore, the success of the EMS as an anti-inflationary mechanism and an instrument for furthering exchange rate stability has been mainly guaranteed by the circumstance that for the divergent countries the balance has been positive between the cost stemming from Germany's higher "bargaining power" and the benefit due to externality represented by the strongly needed Bundesbank's anti-inflationary reputation. However, the welfare loss undergone by the divergent countries cannot be overlooked. The contradiction between the nominal rigidity of the bilateral parties and the inflation differentials with Germany brought about huge current account imbalances and devaluation expectations *vis-à-vis* the Deutsche mark. The exchange rate stability has been mainly achieved by the initially high-inflation weak-currency economies by means of wide interest differentials with Germany. The rise in interest rates made growth rates slow down in large economies like France and Italy. By reckoning the structural features of the EMS as previously sketched, it remains anyway true that the welfare cost paid by divergent countries to counteract trade imbalances and resist speculative attacks against their currencies could not have been avoided.

The complementarity between cooperation and hegemony has then made the EMS performance very similar to the non-symmetric interdependence described by the

---

[2]See Farina (1992).

Stackelberg game, where the dominant country is in the position to optimise its own utility function and at the same time take into account how its monetary policy affects the "followers". In fact, Germany has got the privilege to determine the level of activity and possibly income distribution inside the ERM member countries and has gained from the non-inflationary support to the level of its internal demand guaranteed by the growing competitiveness of exports towards its partners. Yet, during the Eighties, the functioning of the EMS as an anti-inflationary mechanism for divergent countries has more than offset the welfare loss due to the imposition of the German output-inflation trade off.

Let us now turn the attention to possible negative influences of the German re-unification on the EMU process that might worsen the balance between costs and benefits accruing to the "followers".

The asymmetric shock, which has hit the leader, has called for a real appreciation of its currency. A nominal revaluation of the Deutsche mark would have helped in distributing the German excess demand among the EMS countries, thus ameliorating their employment and output levels and keeping in check inflation. Instead, since the real appreciation has been obtained through the rising German inflation rate, the needed augmentation in interest rates brought about the unwelcome consequence of further depressing growth in Europe.

By now, although German long-term interest rates are the lowest in Europe, the Bundesbank has considerably raised its short-term rate. As their interest rate differentials with Germany have almost disappeared, the still divergent EMS countries, and even France - which has by now become the best-performing large economy - are obliged to keep pace with the German nominal interest rates, as devaluation expectations still maintain a forward premium in favour of the Deutsche mark. In fact, Germany is no longer the lowest inflation country, but its high short-term rates are attracting capital inflows and financial markets keep considering the Deutsche mark as a nominal anchor for the EMS. By consequence, the revenue curve of all the ERM countries shows the long-term rate at a lower level than the short-term rate. Since the former rate witnesses that inflation expectations are decreasing, short-term real rates imposed by Germany to EMS countries are certainly too high, thus hampering production and investment demand. The main problem the EMS is now facing is then the restrictive monetary stance pursued by Germany, which is probably harsher than that needed by the EMS to reach inflation convergence.

Therefore, the question concerning the impact of the German reunification on the EMU process can be answered by observing that the lack of symmetry of the cooperative agreement is aggravating the costs borne by the other partners. By way of example, the interest rates levels imposed by Germany are damaging a still divergent country like Italy twice. First, by impeding the real rates' cut needed to boost the economy, so that the nominal rate will be reduced only if the Italian inflation will resume its fall. Second, by diverting capital flows towards Germany, so that the Italian capital account positive balance - already made thinner by outflows following the complete liberalisation of capital movements - can no longer be relied upon as a compensation for huge current account deficits.

It might be maintained that German national interest is presently clashing with the general interest of the EMS due to the welfare loss caused in the other EMS countries by the Bundesbank's policy. Therefore, if Germany will be unable to keep providing - in exchange of hegemony - not only price stability but also growth, for the other countries the balance between costs and benefits from their participation in the EMU might lean towards costs.

The conflict of interests between Germany and the "followers" might even worsen after the slow-down in the setting up of common monetary institutions entrusted with authority recently decided by the European Community. I will just mention two possible sources of instability. First, Germany has joined the gradualist approach to EMU for the sake of its own objectives: the establishment of the European central bank has been delayed, and full convergence as a pre-condition to the EMU has been advocated., just in order to preserve its policy stance from the "followers". Yet, as De Cecco's insightful analysis has stressed, the possible linking-up between the Anglo-Saxon and the continental financial systems might dangerously convert the Bundesbank to the role of lender of last resort function, just at the very moment in which the forthcoming European monetary institutions should inherit its anti-inflationary reputation. Second, the mismatch between divergent interest rates' tendencies in Europe might aggravate in the near future. Germany's shortage of capitals and high interest rates will last for long, as they are due to structural problems like inflationary tensions and excess capital demand created by the reunification process. Yet, German financial institutions are operating more and more in the international financial markets - in order to skip internal constraints and transfer funds to the deregulated markets of the City, according to De Cecco - and this tendency seems at odds with the domestic need for net capital inflows.

However, the present situation - that is, the fact that German national interest seems now to be parting from the general interest once Bundesbank hinders growth in the whole EMS area with a monetary policy which is only tailored on its domestic objectives - is more a weakness of a cooperative but non-symmetric agreement than a case of opportunistic behaviour. In fact, had the asymmetric shock hit one of the "followers" instead of the leader, the welfare loss which now impinges on them would have been much smaller. In this latter case, the money supply restriction would have not propagated EMS-wide, as instead has happened after the German reunification with the Bundesbank's monetary policy, which was already setting the pace for the whole area.

The suggestion can then be made that more symmetry on the path towards EMU should not be limited only to the exchange rate stability achieved in the late Eighties. To foster symmetry, the rule should be introduced in the "monetary constitution" leading to EMU according to which every asymmetric shock has to be treated as an EMS-wide shock, and then measures aimed at evenly distributing the burden among all partners are to be devised. In the German reunification case, the announcement would have been made that, for the German excess demand to be matched EMS-wide, the last realignment among currencies would have taken place. If rules fostering complete symmetry in the management of shocks had been set, the asymmetric shock would have turned out as an opportunity to even out growth rates and cope with a backwardness situation by means of increased cooperation. Besides, realignment would have not disturbed the path to EMU, as fears of credibility loss would not have arisen. In fact, financial markets would have certainly believed in the following commitment to irrevocably fixed exchange rates, as a cooperative approach to the instability stemming from an asymmetric shock signals that speculation will be efficiently contrasted by all members.

However, the decision not to devaluate currencies with respect to the Deutsche mark has probably to be traced back to the dissatisfaction with the "bargaining power" that Germany still holds despite opportunities for Pareto improvements shared with the rest of the EMS have now vanished. In this perspective, the hegemonic status of the leader, which considerably helped in the pursuit of price and exchange rate stability, seems now an obstacle to whatever strategy aimed at furthering benefits from cooperation through reciprocal compliance among less unequal partners.

References

Farina, F., (1992): "Monetary Policy", in F. Francioni (ed.) (1992) *"Italy and EC Membership Evaluated"*, Pinter Publishers, London

Hochreiter, E., Winckler, G., (1991): "Signaling a Hard Currency Strategy: The Case of Austria", forthcoming in *Kredit and Kapital*

Kydland, F. E., Prescott, E. C. (1977): "Rules Rather Discretion: The Inconsistency of Optimal Plans", *Journal of Political Economy*, Vol. 85, pp. 473-910.

Rogoff, K. (1985): "Can International Monetary Cooperation Be Counterproductive?", *Journal of International Economics*, Vol. 18, pp. 199-217.

The Future of the European Monetary Union

Marcello de Cecco
University of Rome "La Sapienza"

The process of monetary unification in Europe was given a decisive boost, after many years of stagnation, by the revamping of the idea of total European integration, which coincides with the advent of Jacques Delors to the headship of the European Commission in Brussels. This is not the place to go over the series of events which led to his appointment. But we cannot forget that it was Delors who gave new life to the idea of a completely integrated Europe. That he was given the enthusiastic support of most European authorities was perhaps the result of several long years of stagnation in Europe in the early eighties, which coincided with more rapid growth of the U.S. and Japanese economies. European opinion makers coined the expression eurosclerosys to describe this state of affairs. In the years after its inception, the EMS had been living a life of isolation, as the one example, with the Common Agricultural Policy, of a further step on the road to European integration. The idea of the single European market, which Delors began to propagandise, linked up with the operation of the EMS, and gave satisfaction in particular to British and German political leaders, who represented vested interests which feared that European integration, under Delors' stewardship, would mean an excessive dose of Brussels-inspired dirigism. A decisive move to get rid of most trade barriers within the EEC was seen by German industry as a possibility to boost stagnating demand for its products, while British financial circles saw it as a possibility to acquire the leadership of the integrated European financial market. The agreement of so many groups on the concepts of the single market and of complete monetary integration induced a very intense flow of ideas and policy measures, which after a very short time gained so much momentum as to start influencing not only people within Europe, but even in its neighbouring countries and to worry traditional European competitors like the U.S. and Japan. It is not an exaggeration to consider the movement towards a single European market to have induced the disintegration of Socialist Europe. The prospect of a huge single market in Europe made people on the European periphery worry about what their future would be outside it. These were not only the members of the Latin periphery. They were also the leaders of the developed parts of Yugoslavia, Czechoslovakia, the Soviet Union. They thought that there was a last chance to jump on the European train while it was still slowly departing. But in order to do so the modern parts of European periphery had to find ways of shaking off and leaving to their destinies their more backward brethren. European solidarity played against national solidarity. It was a very acceptable excuse to foster the regional autonomy of the richest parts of Eastern Europe. It was essentially this reason that even countries that by all accounts could not afford to drop their barriers and join the single European market did so without many qualms. The most developed sectors within them reacted to the formation of the great European market in a rather unusual fashion. Normally they would have underlined the dangers coming from competition from such strong rivals. They would have normally sought protection. This time, however, the fear of being passed-by once and for all by a great wave of modernisation prevailed upon the natural resistance of peripheral industrial and financial elites. It was widely felt that in a geographical context as integrated as the European land mass, traditional protectionism would no longer work anyway. It was also felt that labour costs were in the periphery still so much lower than in the centre of Europe, that capital would have moved to the periphery to start labour intensive lines of production which the centre countries would abandon. This movement was getting more and more momentum when the dissolution of the Eastern Empire and the unification of Germany occurred. German unification must be considered as the starting point of a completely new game of politics and economics in Europe. The EEC was formed on the Yalta map of Europe, with four large countries of comparable size exercising an oligopoly of power which could be either collusive or competitive, but where no country could definitely prevail upon the others. The American government was the midwife of the EEC and remained over the years the honest broker of its internal disputes. The EEC's secret was, even after the inception of the EMS, that its constituent states were too even-powered to start, anyone of them, an old-fashioned movement to unite all the rest. The national model of unification by annexation was thus discarded, and this removed the fear from all participants in the game. Granted that none among the four large countries was able by itself to integrate the others, a lot of common ground could be covered by all members of the EEC, and the smaller countries could also find satisfactory roles to play in the long and slow integration process, which had the novel feature of being completely open-ended. The EEC was a journey, but a journey to a distant and *unknown* destination. German reunification immediately negated this Yalta European integration model. There was once again in the middle of Europe a country large enough to start a traditional national style unification process. The German magnet was powerful enough, especially from the economic point of view, to attract the large number of small countries which the new post-Yalta Europe had generated.

While this new phenomenon was becoming clear, traditional integration policy was, however, not stopping. The most fascinating example of blend between the old and the new context is the Maastricht Treaty. Its text is almost completely designed with the old geopolitical model of Europe in mind. But the reasons why it was approved have to do with French anxiety to prevent the new Germany from going and uniting Europe in its own way, according to a classical solar model. Delors' original plan had been to generate a series of large European infrastructural initiatives which would re-start the lagging European economy and produce a centripetal movement towards the core of Europe. This core, of course, included France, Great Britain and Germany, and perhaps Northern Italy and Northern Spain. It posed delicate problems to the new periphery, delicate enough to set the ball moving which detached Slovenia and Croatia from Yugoslavia, the Czechs from the Slovaks, and Ukraine and Bjelorussia from the Soviet Union. Reunification gave Germany the chance of doing something similar on its own, and the Yalta geopolitical and strategic- military balance of power was still strong enough for France to exploit it to prevent the solar model of germano-centric Europe from coming into being, relegating France (and of course, Britain, Italy, and Spain) to the periphery. In the case of Spain and Italy, the new germano-centric Europe could even loosen up the national tissue, and cause the northern regions of these countries to secede, and to join germano-centric Europe. It was therefore by exploiting their residual powers in the old order that France and the other large countries of Europe imposed the Maastricht Treaty on a reluctant Germany. A close examination of the Treaty itself will reveal the basic contradiction on which it is founded: that it is the last attempt to bring to the ultimate conclusions the old European integration process, by forcing a quantum jump only possible because of the new geopolitical reality which has prevailed in Europe. Being a sort of political blackmail played by France on Germany, it is very unlikely that the German leadership, once the unification process has become irretrievable in Germany, will stand by the Maastricht Treaty. It is almost inevitable that the centripetal force of the German economy will start to integrate with it the economic structures of the smaller neighbours of Germany. This is a movement which, after only three years, is already quite easy to detect. The cost of German reunification has been imposed on all European countries, under the form of a capital flow to Germany induced by high interest rates in that country. But the small German neighbours in particular, but also its larger ones, have benefited from a strong demand for imports into Germany which has transformed the German trade accounts from structural surplus into structural balance or even deficit. While Japan and the U.S. went into recession, Europe enjoyed two years of further boom spurred by German excess demand. It is of the utmost importance to ascertain whether the Latin countries will be able to participate in the new solar model of germano-centric integration which is rapidly prevailing in Europe. If France were still an economy strong enough and independent enough to constitute a Latin pole of economic attraction, we could envisage a repetition of the Latin Economic and Monetary Union of the XIXth century. A close scrutiny will however reveal that the French economy has in the last seven to ten years become extremely closely integrated with the German one. Demand shocks generated in Germany now influence the French economy with the same force as they influence the economies of countries like Holland, Belgium or Switzerland. this did not use to be the case previously, and it is still not the case to anything like the same extent for countries like Italy, Britain, and Spain. It has therefore become very doubtful that France may lead an alternative group of EEC countries into a soft-currency bloc, which might be more interested than the German centred bloc in preserving the welfare state and local manufacturing activities at the expense of, perhaps, strict price and exchange rate stability. On the contrary, the new French government seems bent on reinforcing economic ties with Germany even further, presumably for the good reason that it would be now very costly for the French economy to re-acquire its autonomy from the German one. The decade of exchange rate stability in Europe which ended in 1992 had therefore the momentous effect of terminating, from the economic point of view, the centuries-old Franco-German polarisation. The degree of integration between the two countries is now, as said above, so high to make a split very expensive. It is, however, not impossible. But it will require a huge political quarrel between the two countries to make it happen.

Balance of Payments Constraints in the Italian Economy

Carluccio Bianchi
University of Parma

Introduction[1]

In Italy the beginning of the 1990's has been characterized by a few relevant institutional changes in the field of international monetary relations. The lira has finally joined the other main currencies in the narrow band of the European Monetary System, confirming the policy option of a stable exchange rate adopted by the Central Bank earlier in the 1980's. Administrative controls over capital movements have been completely removed, so as to guarantee complete financial integration with major world markets. Finally the Maastricht Treaty has envisaged the creation, within the end of the century, of a European Economic and Monetary Union (EMU), to be realized progressively in a series of rigidly predetermined phases.

The most recent political and economic debate in this country, then, has mainly centred around the implications of the Maastricht requirements for a full Italian participation to the future EMU. In this perspective, the main problems, submitted to extensive discussions and scrutiny, have been those connected with the too high (relative) inflation rate and the huge values of the public sector deficit and debt. Concern over these issues has led politicians and economists to devise convergence programs and paths implying substantial sacrifices in order to meet the required European standards. In his May 1992 Annual Report, for instance, the Governor of the Bank of Italy estimated that a reduction in public expenditure of 4 points (as a percentage of GDP) and an increase in taxation of 2 points, accompanied by a rigid incomes policy, were necessary to insure full participation to the EMU from its start. This set of measures, to be implemented immediately, would however imply obvious repercussions in terms of economic development: indeed, according to the econometric model of the Research Department of the Bank, the growth rate would be limited to a

[1] This article was written before the beginning of the crisis of the European Monetary System in the summer of 1992; thus the most recent events, and their consequences, are not considered in the paper. The main conclusions, however, turn out to be strengthened by the most up-to-date empirical evidence. In a certain way, then, the paper analysis has been foreshadowing.

figure just above 1% for at least three years, rising only slightly to a value around 2% towards the half of the current decade.

In the changed institutional context of the 1990's (but also in the late 1980's), therefore, it would seem that the true limits to the growth process of the Italian economy are those implied by the deplorable state of public finances and, to a minor extent, by the too high inflation rate. On the other hand, earlier problems and concerns, such as those connected with a balance of payments equilibrium, do not seem to worry or even matter too much. While from time to time lip service is paid to the opportunity of achieving a balanced *current account*, it is widely believed that a stable exchange rate, a high capital mobility and a favourable interest rate differential can easily secure the capital inflows necessary to guarantee a global external equilibrium, and perhaps even increase foreign reserves. From a theoretical stand-point, furthermore, it is generally agreed that a financially integrated small open economy ought to care about *the overall balance of payments*, rather than about current transactions only. In the changed institutional context, then, the external constraint to growth, that so many worries had generated in the past, would be virtually removed.

This paper purports to show that this widespread wave of optimism is largely unjustified. The external position of the Italian economy has deteriorated markedly in the past few years. Foreign debt has swollen, trade performance has worsened and interest rate payments have grown dramatically. The current account has shown a structural deterioration, partly disguised by the favourable terms of trade evolution. Unlike previous experience, moreover, the recent slow-down in the real growth process, triggered by the Persian Gulf crisis, has not allowed any substantial improvement in the trade balance. The financial fragility implied by the new exchange rate regime has been clearly revealed towards the end of 1991, when monetary policies on the two sides of the Atlantic have followed opposite trends. While in the USA interest rates have gone down, to stimulate recovery, in Europe a contrary stance has been pursued, following the lead of German authorities, worried by the resurgence of internal inflation. The Continental interest rate rise has exacerbated the debt service burden of the Italian balance of payments, originating a vicious circle quite well known in the experience of less developed countries. Furthermore, recurrent threats or fears of a devaluation have compelled the Bank of Italy to raise internal rates above normal standards, at least temporarily, in order to avoid or prevent capital flights.

Thus, despite the theoretical background and the commonly shared optimism, the actual situation of the Italian balance of payments is manifestly unsound. To ensure long-run financial sustainability and to avoid short-run exchange-rate instability, a current account equilibrium, or even a surplus, has to be recovered in the shortest possible time and be maintained thereafter. It is symptomatic, in this perspective, to notice that the same econometric exercise of the consequences of full adherence to the EMU, cited above, yields the result of a balanced current account, to be achieved through a compression of internal demand and thus a substantial improvement in the trade performance. Despite appearances, then, the balance of payments constraint, today as in the past, and perhaps even more, seems to be the major determinant of the growth rate achievable by the Italian economy in the future, at least in a medium term horizon.

The rest of the paper is organized as follows. The next section reviews the past empirical evidence with the purpose of outlining the role played by the balance of payments dynamics in the development of the Italian economy. The issue of the appropriate definition of the relevant external constraint is also addressed with reference to a theoretical framework within the Sargent-Wallace tradition. Section three, then, develops and generalises a constrained-growth model following Johnson's and Thirlwall's seminal contributions. The growth rates implied by the model are compared with actual outcomes and the Italian experience is contrasted with that one of other main industrial countries. Section four investigates the reasons behind the historical record of a slow-down in the growth performance and singles out the likely implications of the present situation for future developments. A final paragraph summarises the basic results of the paper and draws some conclusions from previous discussions.

1 The growth process and the balance of payments evolution

The average growth rate of the Italian economy has shown a marked decline over the last three decades. A similar experience has been shared by other industrialized countries; the relative slow-down, however, has been less pronounced[2] in the the OECD area.

---

[2] The ratio between Italian and OECD countries real growth, where calculated from OECD national accounts statistics, was equal to 1.5 in the 1950's. It has then steadily fallen in subsequent periods, passing to 1.2 in both time spans 1960-1974 and 1974-1980 and finally to 0.8 in the most recent interval 1980-91. Thus, the latest experience is characterized by a reversal of historical trends, whereby the average growth rate in Italy becomes lower than in other industrialised countries. The record appears

The empirical evidence available for the Italian economy is reported in figure 1. The whole sample period, starting from the 1960's, has been divided into three parts, using the two oil crises (actually the year following each one) as separating points. It can be easily checked that the average annual rate of change of GDP falls steadily in time; ultimately the growth rate of the most recent years appears to be less than half the value of the first subperiod. The performance of the Italian economy is even less satisfactory if one considers the fact that since 1970 the national accounts statistics have been substantially revaluated in order to include estimates of the so called "irregular economy"[3]. Indeed if comparable figures were used to evaluate the growth performance of the Italian economy, the overall 1980's record would appear rather poor, amounting to one third only of the average rate experienced in the period of higher development.

Traditional explanations of growth performances fall into two categories. On the one hand neoclassical theory emphasizes the role of supply factors such as population rise, capital accumulation and technical progress (which ultimately influences the gains in productivity). On the other hand Keynesian analysis prefers to underline the importance of aggregate demand dynamics, on the basis of the presumption that economic systems normally exhibit a wide underutilization of available resources, so that actual growth can be explained by effective demand behaviour (and related policy measures). The so-called neoclassical synthesis of the 1960's claims to have reached a consensus over the view that in the long run only supply factors matter, since free market economies tend to gravitate around full employment or equivalent natural levels of output. The role of aggregate demand is limited to explain cyclical fluctuations, so that, with reference to time periods measured in decades or so, there seem to be no limits to achievable growth other than factors availability[4].

---

only slightly better if the Italian performance is compared with that one of developed European nations. In this case it should be acknowledged that the growth ratio widens from 1.2 to 1.5 between the two oil shocks. It remains true, however, that in the most recent years the pace of economic development in Italy reduces substantially, so that the same ratio falls down to 1.0.

[3] The average growth rate of the 1970's has been raised by the National Statistical Office (ISTAT) from 3.1% to 3.8% as a consequence of the national accounts revision. The revaluation has been however more substantial in the 1980's, whence the average growth rate of the first half of the decade has risen from 0.9% to 1.7%. If the old data were used to quantify the growth performance of the 1980's, the average rate would be half a point less than the new official figure of 2.2%.

[4] It is interesting to notice, for instance, that a supply-based explanation has been used by Kaldor in trying to account for the slow-down in the rate of growth of the British economy (Kaldor, 1966).

While the internal consistency of the previous argument may be disputed even in the case of closed economies[5], its logical validity becomes altogether doubtful when open economies are considered. In such a context, in fact, domestic income cannot generally grow without limits, being rather constrained by the necessity to maintain an adequate level of foreign reserves. This target ultimately implies that on average the balance of payments must be in a substantial equilibrium over the medium-long run. Demand expansion, therefore, may be limited by the existence of an external constraint.

The evolution of the Italian balance of payments in the last thirty years is reported in figure 2. It can be easily seen that throughout the 1960's, with the only exception of 1963, and up to the eve of the first oil crisis, the current account balance shows a structural surplus. Despite private capital outflows, the overall balance is also generally positive, so that foreign reserves increase. In the subsequent period between the two oil shocks the current account undergoes an initial heavy deterioration[6], which however appears to be recovered towards the end of the decade. In the same period capital movements are mainly positive, as a consequence of the introduction of administrative controls and credit restrictions. The overall balance of payments, then, shows a more favourable dynamics than current transactions, even though it follows the same ultimate behaviour. The picture changes substantially in the most recent period after the second oil crisis. The current account registers persistent deficits, only partially relieved by the prolonged recession of the early 1980's, at first, and by the oil countershock, later on. Just after 1986, moreover, the current account performance worsens continuously; a structural deficit appears and then gets wider and wider, resulting even insensitive to the slow-down of economic activity. The overall balance, on the other hand, does not show a similar negative trend. Thanks to capital controls, earlier, and to a positive interest rate differential, later, foreign reserves tend to oscillate around an increasing level. Again, starting from 1986, a distinct development occurs between the evolution of the current account and that one of the general balance. While the former worsens progressively, the latter denotes an initial improvement, weakening with the inception of the new decade.

The reassuring picture of the most recent experience is however somehow obscured if one considers the role played by commercial banks in attracting foreign reserves through an ever increasing external indebtedness. It should be recalled that

[5] If the tendency towards full employment is not granted, the presumption to explain actual growth through potential output enlargement is logically flawed. The existence of hysteresis phenomena provides an additional argument against the validity of the neoclassical theory of growth.

[6] As the reader can easily check, its relative value is the worst in the whole historical record.

before the 1990's financial institutions' capital movements were registered "below the line", together with Central Bank operations, so that the official overall balance consisted of current account transactions and private "autonomous" asset flows only. As figure 3 clearly discloses, the relevance of a growing foreign indebtedness of commercial banks has been fundamental in the process of financing the wide current deficits of the 1980's. Furthermore, in the most recent years, only banks' behaviour has enabled reserves to increase, partly as a consequence of the stimulus coming from policy measures taken by the central monetary authorities. It is interesting to remark that without the commercial banks' contribution in 1991 the "autonomous" balance of payments deficit would have been the worst in the whole history of this country.

Looking at figures 2 and 3 from a longer term perspective, the influence of the so-called external constraint on the growth process of the Italian economy appears clearly defined. Current account transactions yield a substantial surplus in the period of higher development, when foreign reserves also increase at a steady pace. The first oil shock brings the current account and the overall balance into deficit, but the initial erosion is subsequently recovered towards the end of the decade. The second oil crisis, instead, implies a structural deterioration of current flows that appears to worsen progressively. Financial integration on world markets, also, seems to imply a net outflow of private non-bank capital movements checked by high interest rate differentials and countervailed by an increased foreign debt of financial institutions.

The more precise nature of the alleged balance of payments constraint can be discussed with reference to the evidence provided by figure 4. The chart plots the annual growth rate of the Italian economy against the current account-GDP ratio of the previous year. The correlation existing between the two variables is rather impressive, and is confirmed by elementary econometric analysis. Furthermore, the correlation becomes stronger if only the most recent experience after the two oil shocks is considered[7]. Even though correlation does not imply causation, and other explanations

[7] Regressing the annual growth rate (GR) on the lagged current account-GDP ratio (LR) for the whole sample period 1960-1991, one gets the following relationship (figures in parentheses report the t-Student statistics):

$$\underset{}{GR = \underset{(12.4)}{3.6} + \underset{(6.4)}{0.99}\,LR} \qquad R^2 = .58$$

If the analysis were limited to the most recent 1980-1991 period the same relationship would become:

$$GR = \underset{(13.4)}{3.0} + \underset{(5.8)}{1.02}\,LR \qquad R^2 = .77$$

are in principle possible, it is rather tempting to interpret the lead shown by the external balance variable as giving support to the idea that the relationship reflects the behaviour of policy makers who, monitoring the current account performance, adapt monetary policy to the desired external goal. The reaction function of monetary authorities is clearly revealed in the case of sharp sudden deteriorations in the current balance, leading to tight credit conditions, motivated by the need to curtail aggregate demand. Considering the time lags in the operation of monetary policy, and the consequences of systemic inertia, these measures would probably exert their influence on the growth of the economy in a subsequent period. Thus the supposed relationship could be interpreted as a part of the reaction function of policy makers, relating the use of available instruments to alternative goals; the strong correlation found would imply that the external constraint has played a fundamental role in influencing economic policy decisions[8].

Available evidence also shows that the correlation between the real growth rate and the (lagged) *current account balance* is much stronger than the alternative one between the growth rate and the (lagged) *overall balance of payments*[9]. This further result might be interpreted to mean that in a long term perspective current transactions only represent the true "fundamental" determinants of foreign exchange dynamics, while private capital movements are either too volatile or not too easily manageable, so that they are on the whole unreliable from the stand-point of maintaining a steady external equilibrium. On the other hand capital movements coming from loans or other official financial operations may be used just as a *temporary* device for facing *permanent* balance of payments deficits[10].

---

showing an even stronger correlation between the two variables. Furthermore, if 1988 were excluded from the sample, since its experience (and econometric analysis) classify it as an outlier, the coefficient of determination in the latest subperiod would rise to .86. Perhaps it is worth reminding that the previous econometric exercises have no pretension to "explain" actual events (the single-equation framework would be manifestly inadequate); rather they are just meant to measure the strength of the correlations found.

8 Indeed the importance of preserving an external equilibrium through time has always been emphasized in the Annual Reports of the Bank of Italy, especially by Governor Carli, who used to warn, ever since the 1960's, that "a country cannot live beyond its own means".

9 In fact regressing the annual growth rate on the lagged overall balance-GDP ratio would yield a much smaller coefficient of determination, amounting to .07 only. This value would increase only slightly if the foreign exchange variable were defined net of banks' capital movements (as in the official statistics until 1990). In this case the coefficient would be equal to .26 in the whole sample period, and to .19 in the years 1980-91, thus showing an even looser correlation in the most recent experience.

10 An indirect confirmation of the greater importance attached by Italian authorities to the current account dynamics, rather than to the overall balance of payments evolution, might be found in the choice of the "total domestic credit" as the most appropriate intermediate target of monetary policy against the alternative variable represented by domestic credit expansion. A discussion of the

More recently economic theory has given further support to the idea that current account flows rather than total foreign reserves change should be regarded as the true constraint to the real growth process. The point is that a steady current account deficit financed through compensating capital inflows may raise problems of sustainability when the real rate of interest is greater than, or equal to, the real growth rate, through a process of a continuous increase in external debt. To clarify the point at issue suppose a country pursues the goal of maintaining an external equilibrium by offsetting a deficit in the current account through a surplus in private capital movements. This situation would be described by the following equation

(1) $NM + i F = \Delta F$

where NM stands for net imports, i for the internal nominal interest rate, and F for the stock of outstanding financial assets owned by foreign residents[11]. If, for ease of computation, we choose to operate in continuous time, so that ΔF is replaced by dF/dt, and deflate all previous variables dividing them by nominal GDP, we get the new relation

(2) $nm + i f = \dot{f} + G f$

where lower-case letters indicate the derived ratios (so that, for instance, f measures the debt-income quotient), G stands for nominal GDP growth and, as usual, a dot over a given variable expresses its derivative with respect to time. Rearranging the terms of the previous expression we may also write

(3) $\dot{f} = nm + (i-G) f = nm + (r-g) f$

where *g* indicates GDP growth at constant prices and *r* the real rate of interest. It is easy to check that when $r \geq g$ the ratio between foreign owned financial assets and GDP tends to grow without limits if there is a deficit in the goods and services transactions of the current account[12]. And even if no explicit boundary may in principle be envisaged to

theoretical schemes behind the choice of different intermediate targets of monetary policy can be found in Vaciago (1983).

[11] For simplicity, thus, it is assumed that all external debt consists of national assets sold abroad. Actually foreign debt also comprises loans to residents denominated in some international currency, so that conversion in national units would require multiplying its face value times the exchange rate.

[12] In fact, assuming structural parameters to remain constant, the steady-state solution of equation (3) is given by

$$f^* = nm/(g-r),$$

thus making clear that a positive stationary value of f exists only when $r \leq g$. The hypothesis of constant coefficients is obviously a raw approximation of reality; its purpose, however, is merely to show the possible dynamics of the debt-income ratio implied by the structural assumptions outlined. Ultimately this ratio (as in the case of the similar analysis of public debt dynamics[13]), it seems however likely that a growing external debt, as a fraction of domestic income, may give rise to financial instability, if the Government's ability to refund debt is somehow questioned or a devaluation is expected. Any change in foreign investors' expectations may have dramatic consequences upon the level of foreign reserves (or the exchange rate) under the policy regime we are considering. In fact a retrieval of capital investments from abroad would generate a large external deficit since both the current and the capital account balance would share the same negative outcome. In a longer term perspective a vicious circle might also be generated by the necessity to increase the real rate of interest in order to attract a larger proportion of foreign financial wealth; in fact this need would directly and indirectly widen the gap between r and g and thus worsen the current situation and its future prospects. The possible existence of a risk-premium on the internally issued financial activities would imply a further stimulus to a high, and possibly increasing, interest rate.

The correct target of monetary authorities therefore seems to be that one of achieving and maintaining a current account equilibrium. Considering the historical legacy of the Italian economy, this policy may imply either a temporary surplus in the goods and services balance, to finance interest payments and refund cumulated debt, or even a permanent one if policy makers pursue the strategy of creating the conditions for generating a symmetric virtuous circle.

Hence there are both theoretical and practical (economic and political) reasons behind the claim that a current account equilibrium should be preserved by an open economy through time. Given this policy stance, the existence of an external constraint to achievable growth appears unignorable. In this perspective, the previously considered relationship between the growth rate and the lagged current account-GDP ratio would probably have to be interpreted as something more than a simple correlation, so that the true nature of the alleged constraint deserves further investigation. We turn to this subject in the next section. Before proceeding further, however, it is interesting to notice that the same growth rate-lagged current account ratio correlation provides an undeniable evidence of a progressive reduction in the real growth rate compatible with

---

variable coefficients would only alter the quantitative dimension of the phenomenon but not its fundamental features.

13 With regards to this topic, the obvious reference is to the pathbreaking analysis of Sargent and Wallace (1981). In the context we are discussing it might be observed that the foreign debt-domestic income ratio should be interpreted as a proxy for the more appropriate foreign debt-foreign income (or rather foreign wealth) ratio.

external equilibrium: that value falls steadily from 4.7% to 3.8% and then to 3% in the three subperiods previously specified.

2 External equilibrium and the constrained growth rate

In order to describe the maximum growth rate compatible with a current account equilibrium, we shall follow the approach outlined by Johnson and Thirlwall[14]. Even though in the past some criticisms have been raised against this approach, in our opinion they do not apply to the fundamental relationships we derive, since, under the assumptions made, they have the nature of ultimate identities[15]. Let us assume for simplicity, at least at an initial stage, that current account flows consist of goods and services transactions only, which we require to be in a continuous equilibrium, so that

$$(4) \qquad PX - P_m M = 0$$

where X are real exports, P their unit price, M real imports and P_m their price in national currency[16]. Using small-case letters to indicate the logarithms of the previously defined variables, we have

$$(5) \qquad p + x = p_m + m$$

so that, differentiating with respect to time, we may write

$$(6) \qquad \dot{p} + \dot{x} = \dot{p}_m + \dot{m}$$

---

14 Cf. Johnson (1958) and Thirlwall (1979), (1983).

15 An example of this type of criticism may be found in Onida (1983), Vicarelli (1985) and Castaldo-Palmisani-Rossi (1986). Some authors have questioned the heuristic nature of the proposed formulae, arguing that the true factors behind a country's growth performance remain unexplained. Others have raised objections to the use of export and import elasticities made by Thirlwall, alleging the problem of computing correct figures. Also the utilization of historical elasticities, as the ones reported in the text, has been criticized. In our scheme, however, the expressions for the constrained growth rate have the nature of sheer identities derived from the basic assumption that a current account equilibrium (or even a relative disequilibrium) is maintained in time. The formulae may then prove useful to ascertain whether an external constraint has effectively influenced the growth process of any country and how it has evolved over time. In this perspective the use of historical elasticities is justified, even though it must be admitted that some caution should be employed in the procedure of utilizing past figures to forecast the future.

16 Throughout the paper we shall follow the national accounting convention of expressing the value of traded commodities as the product of a quantity and a price index, as if they consisted of single homogeneous goods. This simplifying assumption enables to eschew problems of aggregation.

where, for instance, $\dot{p} = dp/dt$[17]. Next we let σ stand for the terms of trade $(p - p_m)$, and ε for the income elasticity of imports[18].

By proper substitution in (6) we can get an expression for the maximum rate of growth compatible with external balance (g*), given by[19,20]

$$(7) \qquad g^* = \frac{\dot{x} + \dot{\sigma}}{\varepsilon}$$

which, in the case of constant terms of trade, reduces to the simpler expression[21]

$$(8) \qquad g\sigma = \frac{\dot{x}}{\varepsilon}$$

The constrained growth rates implied by the previously derived formulae may then be used to evaluate the actual Italian experience as in table 1[22].

---

[17] The same expression might be used in discrete time if one chose to approximate the rate of change of every variable with its logarithmic difference. In this case one would have, for instance,

$$\dot{p} = p_t - p_{t-1}$$

recalling that, thanks to the log properties, $p \sim \log(1+\pi)$, where π is the "true" proportional change of the price level (or of any other variable involved).

[18] Thus, it will be $\varepsilon = \dot{m} / \dot{y}$.

[19] If discrete time were considered, expression (7) would have to include at the numerator an additional term given by the joint product of the rate of change of exports and that one of the terms of trade. As we explain further in the text, the same formula would hold true if the economy started from a position of initial disequilibrium under the hypothesis that the deficit, defined as a given fraction of exports, be maintained over time.

[20] If exports and imports could be written as a function of a demand variable (world trade, w, for exports and domestic income, y, for imports) and of the terms of trade, their rates of change would be given by the twin expressions

$$\dot{x} = \varepsilon_x \dot{w} - \eta_x \dot{\sigma}$$
$$\dot{m} = \varepsilon_m \dot{y} + \eta_m \dot{\sigma}$$

where η_x and η_m are the "classical" price elasticities of exports and imports respectively. Expression (7) in this case would reduce to the same formula proposed by Thirlwall (1983), whereby

$$g^* = \frac{\dot{\sigma}(1 - \eta_x - \eta_m) + \varepsilon_x \dot{w}}{\varepsilon_m}$$

In the case of Italy, however, and thus in a more general way, it is doubtful whether the export function can meaningfully include the terms of trade as an explanatory variable, while at the same time the dependence of imports upon the terms of trade is rather weak.

[21] It is interesting to notice that on some occasions even the Bank of Italy has made use of the approach we have just outlined; cf., for instance, Banca d'Italia, Relazione Annuale per il 1984, p. 299.

[22] The income elasticity of imports ε has been computed from the historical record.

Table 1: Actual and constrained growth rates: Italy, 1960-1991.

	60-74(*)	74-80(*)	74-80	80-91	83-91
dx/dt	10.9	6.2	4.9	4.3	5.0
dσ/dt	-1.6	0.3	-0.7	1.3	1.8
∈	1.9	2.2	1.0	2.1	2.4
g*	4.9	2.9	4.2	2.7	2.8
gσ	5.7	2.8	4.9	2.0	2.1
g	5.2	2.6	3.5	2.2	2.7

Data source: Istat. (*) Old national accounts data.

Recalling the temporal subdivision previously introduced, the table presents two additional columns. This is due to the fact that the left-hand side of the schedule reports data based on national accounts statistics prior to the revaluation, while the right-hand side considers the "new" figures. Obviously any meaningful time comparison must be based upon homogeneous data[23]. Last column, finally, concentrates upon the most recent cyclical phase, comparing its rather satisfactory growth record with previous experience.

The empirical evidence summarized in the table indicates that the actual and the constrained growth rates have been rather close in all periods considered, thus suggesting that the external balance has always exerted a dominant influence on the growth performance of the Italian economy. The historical decline in the average annual growth rate may then be ultimately related to the slow-down in export dynamics and to the increase in imports elasticity. The terms of trade have played a role that is rather difficult to evaluate: in fact they have remained substantially stable for long periods of time, then undergoing drastic changes on some occasions (actually the two oil crises and the more recent countershock). Owing to this behaviour, it may be incorrect to attribute to a whole subperiod a terms of trade change that should be more properly referred to a different time span. This consideration seems to fit the 1960-74 experience, wherein $g\sigma$ probably represents a better indicator of the really binding external constraint. In the latest subperiod, then, the higher value of the constrained growth rate g^* may be partly explained with the circumstance that the terms of trade

[23] On the other hand, a comparison between the second and the third column enables to appreciate the rather substantial changes attributable to the national accounts revision.

improvement has taken place only after 1985[24]. As the fifth column makes clear, the favourable contingency seems to have been exploited fully in the most recent cyclical phase[25].

The Italian experience summarized in table 1 can be usefully compared with that one of the other main industrialized countries, as in table 2.

Table 2: Actual and constrained growth rates: Industrial countries, 1960-1991.

	1960-1974			1974-1980			1980-1991		
	g^*	$g\sigma$	g	g^*	$g\sigma$	g	g^*	$g\sigma$	g
U.S.A.	2.9	3.5	3.6	2.0	5.0	2.5	2.6	2.5	2.6
Japan	8.7	9.9	8.8	5.0	26.3	4.5	5.9	4.5	4.2
Germany	4.2	4.0	4.1	1.0	1.4	2.5	3.0	2.7	2.2
France	4.4	4.8	5.2	2.5	3.5	2.6	2.4	2.1	2.1
U.K.	2.4	3.1	2.8	5.6	2.8	1.4	1.6	1.5	2.2
Italy	4.8	5.4	5.3	4.6	5.3	3.5	2.9	2.0	2.2

Data source: OECD (National accounts statistics).

The following remarks seem to be justified by the available evidence. Generally, in all countries and in all periods, actual and constrained growth rates are very similar, thus confirming the overall ability of the proposed model to explain reality[26]. Differences between theory and evidence are smaller in the first time span (again choosing to compare, for the earlier mentioned reason, $g\sigma$ to g); they become greater in the second subperiod, as a priori intuition suggests, since the considered interval is shorter and is characterized by greater turmoil. Between the two oil shocks all countries, with the exception of the USA, tend to grow less than allowed; this is

24 Actually, as we shall see later, even the stabilization policy implied by the second oil shock, resulting in a prolonged deflation in the early 1980's, has caused a sensible reduction of the average growth rate of the decade.

25 It is significant to notice, in this perspective, that the positive growth performance of the latest years has been made possible to a great extent by the terms of trade improvement triggered by the oil countershock and the dollar devaluation; together they have implied a relative price change amounting to more than one third of export increase.

26 The figures reported for Japan in the intermediate period, however, deserve some additional comments. All industrialized countries, with the notable exception of Germany, have reacted to the first oil shock, and the subsequent terms of trade deterioration, by reducing the average import propensity. This process has been particularly strong in Japan, where the value of the income elasticity of imports has fallen down to 0.3, from the former level of 1.5. This extremely low level of the denominator, coupled with the fact that the Japanese economy has experienced the sharpest terms of trade worsening among industrialized countries, explain the exceptionally high value of $g\sigma$ (26.3) reported in table 2.

particularly true for the UK, Germany, Japan and Italy (even though, as we have previously seen, Italy's record is largely influenced by the national accounts data revision). On the whole, the USA and France are the two countries for which theoretical and empirical figures are closest. In the USA, however, the result is mainly the consequence of the severe recession of the latest two years, without which the actual growth figure would have been higher than the constrained one, as in the second subperiod. The USA, in fact, have exploited their hegemonic position in the international monetary system to increase the pace of economic development. The opposite has been true for Japan, whose growth rates, even though higher than average, are always below potential (at least from the external equilibrium stand-point), thus yielding the well-known phenomenon of repeated and increasing current surpluses. The Japanese experience has been shared in the 1980's by Germany, despite the recent process of reunification has contributed to raise internal demand and reduce the structural surplus inherited from the past. Table 2, however, shows that an opposite strategy has been pursued in Germany in the period between the two oil crises, when the economy has achieved a higher than allowed increase in GDP. The United Kingdom, on the other hand, has followed a completely different growth path, with a definitely low income rise in the second subperiod and a better record in the third one. Finally, with reference to Italy, we can remark that on the whole, after the first oil price upsurge, economic development has generally proceeded at a lower pace than suggested by theory.

The increased discrepancies between actual and constrained growth rates observed in the most recent experience call for a generalization of the simplified model earlier proposed. In fact, as we noticed in the previous section, when discussing the issue of the sustainability of an increasing foreign debt, current account flows include not only goods and services transactions, but also income transfers of all kinds, such as net receipts from tourism and work abroad, other Government and private transfers, and, most of all, net interest remunerations on financial assets and liabilities. If we let T stand for the global value of these income transfers, we can write the following definition of the current account balance of payments

(9) $$P X + T - P_m M = S$$

where S is the eventual surplus. Let us express then net transfers as a fraction of the value of exports and, similarly, the surplus (or deficit) as a percentage of nominal imports; we can thus transform the previous definition in the new identity

(10) $P\,X\,(1+t) = P_m M\,(1+s)$

where lower-case letters indicate the derived ratios. Passing to logs, as beforehand, yields

(11) $p + x + t = p_m + m + s$

where, again, we have assumed t=log(1+t) and d=log(1+d). Differentiating with respect to time, we get

(12) $\dot{p} + \dot{x} + \delta t = \dot{p}_m + \dot{m} + \delta s$

where we have chosen to use δt and δs to indicate the change in the ratios of transfers to exports and of the surplus level to imports[27]. Using the previously introduced symbols, the actual growth rate could be defined by the expression

(13) $g = \dfrac{\dot{x} + \dot{s} + \delta t - \delta s}{\varepsilon} = \dfrac{\dot{x} + \dot{s} + \delta t + \delta d}{\varepsilon}$

where d (d =-s) is the ratio between the current account *deficit* and the value of imports.

On the basis of the methodology used to derive it, (13) is just a sheer definition. It can, however, be transformed into a generalized expression of a constrained growth rate, as equ. (7), if a priori assumptions about the *desired* surplus or deficit ratios are made. In the more general framework we have developed, it can be seen that a country may experience a higher growth performance if it can rely upon steady and increasing net income transfers from abroad or if she is available to accept a reduction in the surplus, or an expansion in the deficit, of the current account balance[28]. On the other hand, the growth rate will be eventually lower if a country experiences a structural

---

27 If discrete time were used, one could use *t* and *s* to refer to an initial situation, and then *t'* and *s'* to describe a final one, so that, using logs to approximate actual rates of change, δt and δs would indicate the variations in the ratios during the chosen time span.

28 The reader can easily check that if it were assumed, as until now, that $\delta t = \delta d = 0$, the expression for the constrained growth rate would again be equal to that one found in eq. (7). The generalized model, however, shows that the same value of g^* can be derived not only if it is assumed that the current account be in continuous equilibrium, but also if the monetary authorities of a country choose to maintain the same ratio of surplus (or deficit) through time. This remark may explain why we can speak of a constrained growth rate even with reference to countries like Germany or Japan, characterized by structural surpluses in the current account position.

decline in transfers or pursues the goal of eliminating a current imbalance inherited from the past.

The new formulae allow a few additional comments about the evidence reported in table 2. Net income transfers have been on the whole mostly unimportant in the main industrialized countries until the first oil shock, with the exception of Italy, and partly France, where they have always represented a relevant contribution to current account transactions. After 1973, however, these flows have assumed almost everywhere a greater and greater importance, so that on average they now account for about 3/10 of a point of the annual growth rate of the OECD area. In the most recent subperiod, net transfers dynamics has negatively contributed to GDP change in Italy (0.7% per year), in the USA (0.4%), in France (0.3%) and even in Germany (0.2%); on the other hand positive influences have been exerted on Japan (0.3%) and, to a limited extent, on the United Kingdom (0.1%). It comes out, therefore, that during the 1980's, in the USA, the actual growth rate has been even higher than warranted, while the opposite result has been true for Japan. Net transfers dynamics, instead, can explain perfectly well the reduced growth performance of Italy in the most recent experience[29]. Thus, in this country, the development prospects seem to be hindered by a further factor beyond the traditional ones commonly studied and outlined by applied international economists. The discussion of these topics is the subject of the next section.

3 Exports, imports, invisibles and the Italian growth prospects

As we have seen in table 1, one of the causes behind the historical decrease recorded by the Italian constrained growth rate is the reduction in export dynamics. As in the case of real GDP, a similar experience has been shared by other industrialized countries, but again the relative slow-down has been more pronounced in the Italian economy. The available evidence is reported in table 3[30].

It can be easily checked that the ratio between Italian and OECD export growth has shown a continuous reduction. While in the sixties Italian sales abroad tended to

[29] The residual differences between the actual and the constrained growth rate have therefore to be explained by a changed attitude of the Government authorities towards current account equilibrium. Thus, for instance, the higher growth performance of Germany in the second subperiod, followed by an opposite strategy in the third one, can be traced to the policy makers willingness to accept a deficit at first, and to convert it into a structural surplus lately. The opposite experience of the United Kingdom can be rationalized, mutatis mutandis, in the same way.

[30] For computational ease OECD exports are taken to include Italian data.

increase more than foreign competitors', in the most recent period an opposite trend has been experienced[31]. From the stand-point of economic theory, as well known, export volumes are made dependent upon world demand, the relative cyclical situation, the geographical and product structure of goods, international competitiveness and other non-price factors such as product quality, payment and credit conditions, and so on. In a long run perspective, as that one followed in this paper, cyclical mismatches may be disregarded, so that a country's export performance has to be ultimately related to the remaining factors just specified.

Table 3: The growth of Italian and OECD exports: 1960-91.

	60-74(*)	74-80(*)	74-80	80-91	83-91
Italian exports	10.9	6.2	4.9	4.3	4.8
OECD exports	7.9	4.7	4.7	4.7	5.7
Elasticity	1.4	1.3	1.0	0.9	0.8

Data source: Istat, OECD. (*) Old national accounts data

In the case of Italy, a large number of studies have emphasized the peculiar structure of foreign sales. According to the product life-cycle classification, exported goods (the so called "made in Italy") are of a mature type, incorporate little technology and are increasingly subject to a stronger competition coming from the newly industrialized countries (NIC's). These factors, in the end, would be the true responsible for the tendency of Italian exports to grow less than world demand, as shown by historical experience. In the latest cyclical phase, furthermore, the most dynamic component of aggregate demand has been represented by fixed investment; in this sector the Italian presence in international markets is definitely weak.

It should be admitted, however, that the characteristics of Italian exports often make the label of "traditional" products a caricature of its true features (quality and design). Thus, while "normal" traditional goods are generally distinguished by a low income elasticity of demand, Italian manufactures may not be hindered by such a limitation, thanks to their high standards. Other studies have analyzed the consequences of the peculiar geographical structure of Italian exports and of its evolution[32]. The main

[31] Furthermore, while OECD export growth has lately exceeded the low figures of the 1974-1980 interval, in Italy this recovery has not taken place.
[32] Cf. Credito Italiano (1983) and Vona (1987).

conclusion suggested by these analyses has been that through market diversification (i.e. switching to the most dynamic national outlets) Italian exporters have succeeded, at least until 1983, in compensating the relatively slower growth of the specific world demand[33]. After such a date, however, the evidence seems rather unfavourable; in the most recent period, indeed, Italian exports have increased at a rate steadily below that one of specific world demand: the difference can be estimated, according to OECD data, in a value around 2% per year[34].

The traditional explanation of a country's export performance, especially in the case of low-tech products, emphasizes the role of international price competitiveness, whose behaviour is reported in figure 5[35]. It can be easily checked that relative export prices show a steady improvement up to the first oil shock, at an average annual rate of about 0.6%. After the inception of floating exchange rates, competitiveness denotes an alternate short-run dynamics, within a long term pattern of a continuous deterioration, particularly relevant after adherence to the European Monetary System (EMS) in 1979. Indeed relative export prices worsen at an annual rate of about 0.9% in the 1974-1980 period and of 0.7% thereafter[36].

The role played by price competitiveness in influencing Italian export dynamics can be more precisely ascertained through a formal econometric analysis. Following Thursby and Thursby's suggestion[37], a general first order model yields the following function

(14) $x = a + b\,w + c\,Lw + d\,p + e\,Lp + f\,Lx + u$

---

[33] Cf. Vona (1987). The specific world demand is measured by weighing each foreign country's import change with the share of Italian exports directed to that market.

[34] Cf. OECD, Economic Outlook, various issues. Again, a similar experience has been shared by all industrialized countries; in the OECD area, however, the potential loss of export growth is estimated in an average annual value of 0.9%. Part of the explanation to this generalized phenomenon has to be searched in the successful performance of NIC's and NEC's.

[35] Competitiveness is measured in terms of relative export prices, using IMF (International Financial Statistics) data. An alternative expression, currently adopted by the Bank of Italy, refers to relative (wholesale) manufactured prices; this indicator, indeed, would be able to capture the effects of changes in firms' profitability as well, thus yielding a better estimate of export convenience. Using these alternative data, while the overall evolution of competitiveness would remain unvaried, there would be significant changes in the measure of relative price performance, with no substantial alteration in the 1974-80 period, and a lighter decline in the most recent experience, at an annual rate of 0.6%.

[36] According to the figures released by Bank of Italy, however, the relative export price worsening is only equal to 0.5% between 1974 and 1980. On the other hand, the overall decline since the birth of the EMS in 1979 amounts to 1.3% per year.

[37] Cf. Thursby and Thursby (1984).

where x stands for exports, w world demand, and p relative prices; L is the lag operator (so that $Lw = w_{t-1}$), all variables are expressed in logarithmic terms and u is the error term with the usual properties. The sample period used for estimation is the time span following the adoption of flexible exchange rates, i.e. 1973.1-1991.4.

The main result of the exercise is the confirmation of a relative stability in the value of the export elasticity to world demand (approximated by OECD exports) around 1.0[38]. If the sample period were limited to the most recent experience, this coefficient would only show a limited reduction, passing to 0.9. It is interesting to notice, instead, that the same econometric analysis indicates the existence of a structural change in the role played by competitiveness: in fact while in the whole sample period the price elasticity is around 1.2, in the 1980's it falls to 0.4![39]. The main parameters of the export function are confirmed if recourse is made to an alternative estimation technique, such as an error correction procedure[40].

Econometric evidence, therefore, suggests that the theoretical and the historical values of the demand elasticity of exports are quite close to each other. This result, in

[38] It should be noticed, however, that the estimated values of income and price elasticities are not independent of the choice of the variables used to proxy world demand. If, as in the text, OECD exports are chosen, instead of, for instance, GDP figures, then the income elasticity appears lower and the price elasticity higher (cf. Bianchi 1988).

[39] This result, however, cannot be interpreted as an evidence of a strengthened position of Italian exports upon world markets, being rather a consequence of the strong currency option adopted after the inception of the EMS. A stable exchange rate and a positive inflation differential have implied, as figure 5 shows, competitive losses, despite which foreign sales have continued to grow substantially in line with world demand. This combined behaviour of prices and quantities has produced the empirical result of a steadily decreasing price elasticity of exports, as the sample period is shifted towards the most recent years.

The Italian export function peculiarities can be usefully compared with those of the other main industrialized countries, using a common econometric procedure. The results of this exercise are reported in table A1. It can be easily checked that the demand elasticity of Italian exports is slightly lower than average (even though roughly in line with European records), thus implying growth prospects not higher than world trade expansion. The price elasticity is about double than average for the whole period, but, as we have just seen, with a marked reduction in the most recent years.

Tab. A1. Demand and price elasticities of exports in the main industrialized countries: 1973-1990.

	Demand Elasticity	Price Elasticity
USA	1.2	1.4
Japan	1.8	0.7
Germany	0.9	0.4
France	0.7	0.4
United Kingdom	0.8	0.3
Average of countries above	1.2	0.6
Italy	1.0	1.2

Data source: OECD.

[40] Cf. Mosconi-Prosperetti (1987).

turn, yields support to the claim that the evolution of Italian exports has been influenced by price competitiveness only to a minor extent. Indeed strict adherence to a dynamic purchasing power parity rule would have implied just a slightly lower growth in the sixties (around 0.7% per year) and a very modest higher increase in the 1980's (around 0.2%). It can be inferred, therefore, that the worsened performance of the most recent years must be attributed to other, more fundamental, structural factors. The weakened position of Italy in the international division of labour is superficially disguised by price behaviour: if the annual market share is reckoned in nominal terms, one gets the lulling picture of an ever growing figure; but if the same computation is made in the more appropriate context of constant prices, then the underlying tendency towards a steadily falling share is fully revealed.

The structural deterioration of Italian external trade, however, concerns not only foreign sales, but also purchases. We have already seen, in table 1, that the income elasticity of imports has shown a systematic historical increase. Some scholars have suggested that the closer and closer integration of international markets, the globalization of output and the renewed tendency within industrialized nations to specialize in the production of some finished goods should lead to a general increase in the average propensity to import everywhere. It must be admitted, however, that this statement is only partially true. OECD nations, on the whole, have drastically reduced their import elasticity in the period between the two oil shocks, as a part of their reaction strategy aimed at correcting current account imbalances[41]. In the most recent experience, then, import growth has accelerated again, but their demand elasticity has not exceeded that one of the 1960's. In Italy, instead, the reduction of the 1974-1980 period has been mainly a consequence of the national accounts statistics revision, while anyway in the 1980's, but especially in later years, the elasticity has risen to values greater than in the past. Hence, the Italian experience differs from that one of other industrialized countries both because the income elasticity of imports is higher and because it is growing. As in the case of export performance, only a small part of the explanation to this phenomenon is to be found in the historical deterioration of price competitiveness; furthermore, a great share of Italian imports (about half) consists of primary and intermediate goods, that do not seem very sensible to price behaviour. Table 4, with reference to goods transactions only, presents a structural decomposition of aggregate outcomes, thus allowing a more detailed analysis of on-going trends.

---

41 As already noticed (cf. footnote 26), this process has been particularly strong in Japan, where the income elasticity of imports has fallen from the 1.5 value of the sixties to 0.3.

It can be seen that with reference to energy goods only the specific elasticity in the 1980's is lower. The sectorial increase is rather marked in the case of intermediate products, final consumption goods and, mostly, investment goods, whose specific elasticity, in the most recent cyclical phase, is about twice the value of the sixties. Thus we can conclude that the historical increase in the average elasticity of imports in the Italian economy is due to the combined effects of a generalized rise in sector values, mainly relevant for consumption and investment goods, to the ever growing weight of this kind of products in the total import bill[42] and finally to the sustained process of capital accumulation that has characterized the most recent business cycle. On the basis of available data, one can infer that the diffused import penetration recorded by this country is attributable to a structural incapacity of internal supply to adapt to the needs of a changing demand, reflecting a deterioration of the industrial potential.

Table 4: Income elasticity of imports by sectors: Italy, 1960-1991.

	60-74(*)	74-80(*)	74-80	80-91	83-91
Energy	1.7	-0.6	-0.4	0	0.6
Raw materials	0.8	1.2	0.9	0.5	1.3
Intermediate goods	1.7	2.6	1.9	2.3	2.8
Final consumption	2.0	2.5	1.9	2.5	2.8
Investment goods	1.9	1.8	1.3	2.6	3.9
TOTAL	1.7	1.3	0.9	1.7	2.3

Data source: Istat. (*) Old national accounts

The increasing weakness of Italian trade patterns can be further disclosed by the evidence reported in figure 6, plotting the behaviour of the trade balance (as a fraction of GDP) at current and constant prices. It can be checked that the apparent improvement of the 1980's and the substantial stabilization of the ratio in the most recent years is completely attributable to the terms of trade improvement that has taken place after 1985. Without this favourable event the record would have been rather poor: at constant prices the trade balance shows a continuous deterioration since 1983. A similar phenomenon has concerned the overall current account dynamics, so that it can be claimed, again, that the structural decline of the Italian position upon world markets is superficially disguised by the favourable terms of trade behaviour and by the lighter

---

42 In 1991 final consumption, investment and intermediate goods accounted for 29.2%, 23.2% and 27.4% of total merchandise imports respectively. It should be remarked that, with regards to services, their specific income elasticity has shown a structural increase as well; this result can be deduced from a comparison between the figures reported in table 1, referring to national accounts statistics, and those in table 4, concerning commodity trade only.

energy disbursements implied by the oil countershock and the dollar devaluation of the second half of the 1980's.

In evaluating the future growth prospects of the Italian economy, according to the scheme developed in eq. (13), a few comments seem worthwhile with regards to invisibles, whose relevance has already been discussed at the end of the previous section. Figure 7 can help to outline the major issues involved. Again it may be noticed that income transfers, on the whole, have shown an unfavourable long term evolution, passing from a structural surplus, in the sixties, to a significant, and increasing, deficit in the most recent years[43]. Only in the period between the two oil crises this historical trend has been temporarily reversed, so that these items have positively contributed to the growth process. In every phase all components of aggregate flows have moved in the same direction, even though the relative importance of each one has changed in time. Thus, in the sixties, tourism and residual income transfers (including net receipts from work abroad and public unilateral transfers) have recorded the worst negative performance, while interest payments have denoted a light deterioration only[44]. In the eighties, while net revenues from tourists have continued to decline, interest payments and Government transfers have swollen[45]. The policy stance of financing current account deficits through compensating capital inflows, in particular, has generated a steady increase in foreign debt, whose value, approximately nil in 1980, has totalled 10.5% of GDP in 1991. Coupled with the generalized upsurge in interest rates, the growth in liabilities has increased the burden of foreign debt service beyond any reasonable amount, so that, today, the existing current account deficit is almost completely explained by interest payments[46]. On the other hand, receipts from work have continued to slide, while contributions to the EEC budget have risen, especially after the Spanish and Portuguese adhesion.

---

43 Figure 7 concentrates on the behaviour of some specific net income transfers. With reference to marketable service transactions (transport, insurance, finance, etc.), the record is not so unfavourable: while their particular balance is negative, its value, however (about 0.4% of GDP), does not show any substantial change in time.

44 The average annual change in the ratio between each specific balance and the value of exports has been equal to 0.6%, 0.5% and 0.1%, respectively, for tourism, residual transfers and capital incomes.

45 The relevant figures are now 0.4%, 0.5% and 0.7% for tourism, residual transfers and interest payments.

46 As the Bank of Italy has recently revealed, furthermore, the interest rate earned by Italian residents on foreign assets is definitely lower than the one paid on liabilities (for about 2 percentage point). This differential, due to the debtor situation of the country and to the weak position of the national banking system upon world financial markets, implies that an equal expansion of capital inflows and outflows leads to worsened net interest disbursements.

The results of all earlier discussions and trends can now be utilized to appraise the development prospects of the Italian economy, according to the constrained growth model outlined in the previous section. If we assume world trade to expand in the next few years substantially in line with the most recent patterns (i.e. between 5 and 6 per cent), we may estimate a likely increase of national exports around an annual average value of 5%. Positing terms of trade to remain constant, the historical income elasticity of imports would imply, according to eq. (7), a constrained growth rate of 2.5%. However, even in the favourable hypothesis of a Government policy stance aiming at a stable current account deficit (as a fraction of exports), the negative trend recently shown by net income transfers would reduce, according to eq. (13), the previous figure to 1.8%. Finally, a more ambitious goal of a gradual elimination of the inherited deficit would further bring down the theoretical growth rate to a value around 1%, if the plan is to be completed within a five-years period. It is interesting to notice that this latter figure is not far from that one envisaged by the Governor of the Bank of Italy in his analysis of the consequences of a full convergence towards the EMU requirements.

4 Conclusions

The average annual growth rate of the Italian economy has shown a marked slow-down in the most recent experience, both absolutely and relatively to other countries. Available empirical evidence seems to indicate a rather close historical correlation between the current account dynamics and the growth performance, so that the development process has been somehow externally constrained.

The maximum growth rate compatible with equilibrium in the current account balance has been shown to depend upon export increase, the terms of trade dynamics, the income elasticity of imports and, lately, the behaviour of net income transfers. In the Italian experience the recorded reduction in actual and constrained growth rates is fundamentally attributable to the effects of a decrease in export dynamics and of a rise in the income elasticity of imports. In the most recent years the terms of trade improvement has allowed a satisfactory growth performance, hindered, however, by a structural decline in net income transfers.

The export slow-down has been caused not only by a correspondent reduction in world trade dynamics, but also by a worsened position in the international division of labour. Price competitiveness has also deteriorated in a substantial way, and the process has been aggravated after adhesion to the EMS. Imports, on the other hand, have witnessed an increased penetration of foreign producers, especially in the final goods compartments, thus reflecting a structural incapacity of internal supply to adapt to the characteristics of a changing demand. The Italian weakness has been exacerbated by the strong process of capital accumulation in the second half of the 1980's, that has led to heavy purchases of capital goods abroad. Finally, the growing foreign indebtedness, coupled with a generalized interest rate upsurge in world financial markets, has determined a huge increase in interest payments, in a context where incomes from work and tourism have been steadily declining.

Unless the recent trends are somehow reversed, the growth prospects of the Italian economy appear rather gloomy. Given an expansion of world trade largely in line with the most recent experience, the high income elasticity of imports, together with the evolution of foreign transfers, constrains the achievable growth rate to a value around 2% at most, which is definitely lower than the average rate of older years. This rate, furthermore, is surely not adequate to promote a process of a substantial reduction in the unemployment rate, which remains too high, both at the national level and (most of all) in its regional dimensions.

References

Banca d'Italia: Relazione Annuale, Rome, Various years

Bianchi, C. (1988): "Cambio del dollaro, competitività e disavanzo estero degli Stati Uniti: le prospettive a medio termine", *Economia e Politica Industriale*, n. 57

Biasco, S. (1986): "Temi analitici su vincolo estero e struttura produttiva dell'Italia", in VV. AA., *Oltre la crisi, Ente Einaudi*, Roma

Caselli, P., L.F. Signorini (1987): "Interscambio con l'estero e struttura produttiva", *Temi di discussione*, Banca d'Italia, February

Castaldo, P., F. Palmisani, S. Rossi (1986): "Il vincolo esterno in Italia, Germania e Francia: elementi per un'analisi empirica comparativa", *Rivista di Politica Economica*, May

Cipolletta, I., S. Calabresi (1984): "Scambi con l'estero e internazionalizzazione dell'economia italiana", *Economia italiana*, September

Conti, G. (1984): "Internazionalizzazione dell'economia italiana e vincolo estero: note introduttive", *Economia italiana*, September

Conti, G. (1987): "L'integrazione internazionale dell'economia italiana: opportunità e vincoli", in Graziani, A. (Ed.): *Il dollaro e l'economia italiana*, Il Mulino, Bologna

Conti, G., M. Silvani (1987): "Struttura del commercio estero, equilibrio esterno e crescita economica: un confronto internazionale", *L'industria*, September

Conti, G., A. Massari, P. Modiano (1989): "Le determinanti dell'"Export Performance" dell'Italia: un'analisi quantitativa delle tendenze recenti", *Note Economiche*, June

Credito Italiano (1983): *Rapporto sulle esportazioni italiane*, Milano

Goldstein, M., M.S. Khan (1983): "Income and Price Effects in Foreign Trade", in Kenen, P.B., R.W. Jones (Eds.): *Handbook of International Economics*, North Holland, Amsterdam

Houthakker, G.S., S.P. Magee (1969): "Income and Price Elasticities in World Trade", *Review of Economics and Statistics*, May

Imbriani, C. (Ed.) (1991): *Commercio estero, competitività e specializzazione dell'Italia*, Franco Angeli, Milano

Johnson, H.G. (1958): *International Trade and Growth*, Allen and Unwin, London

Kaldor, N. (1966): *Causes of the Slow Rate of Economic Growth in the United Kingdom*, Inaugural Lecture, Cambridge University Press

Leamer, E.E., R.M. Stern (1970): *Quantitative International Economics*, Allyn and Bacon, Boston

Modiano P., F. Onida (1983): "Un'analisi disaggregata delle funzioni di domanda di esportazioni dell'Italia e dei principali paesi industriali", *Giornale degli Economisti*, Jan.-February

Mosconi, R., L. Prosperetti (1987): "Modelli econometrici della funzione di esportazione: il caso del settore meccanico italiano", Dipartimento di Elettronica, Politecnico di Milano, Rapporto Interno n. 87-026

Onida, F. (1983): "Bilancia dei pagamenti e crescita: il caso italiano - Un commento", in VV.AA., *Bilancia dei pagamenti, importazioni e crescita industriale: "il caso italiano"*, Franco Angeli, Milano

Onida, F. (1986): "Vincolo estero, competitività, fattori di forza e di debolezza strutturale: uno sguardo di sintesi", in ONIDA F. (Ed.), *Vincolo estero, struttura industriale e credito all'esportazione*, Il Mulino, Bologna

Perrucci, A. (1986): *Vincolo esterno e specializzazione internazionale*, Franco Angeli, Milano

Pierelli, F. (1983): "I mutamenti nella struttura degli scambi mondiali e la "posizione italiana"", *Contributi alla ricerca economica*, Banca d'Italia, March

Rolet, P. (1983): "Il vincolo esterno e l'elasticità prezzo e reddito nel commercio estero dei paesi della Comunità europea, degli Stati Uniti e del Giappone", *Economia Europea*, July

Sargent, T.J., N. Wallace (1981): "Some Unpleasant Monetarist Arithmetic", *Federal Reserve Bank of Minneapolis Quarterly Review*, Fall

Silvani, M. (1985): "Dipendenza energetica, struttura produttiva e composizione del commercio estero", in F. Onida (Ed.), *Vincolo estero, struttura industriale e credito all'esportazione*, Il Mulino, Bologna

Silvani, M. (1985): "Il vincolo estero dell'economia italiana: un "falso" problema?", in VV. AA., *Oltre la crisi*, Ente Einaudi, Roma

Thirlwall, A.P. (1979): "The Balance of Payments Constraint as an Explanation of International Growth Rates Differences", *Banca Nazionale del Lavoro Quarterly Review*, March

Thirlwall, A.P. (1980): *Balance of Payments Theory and the United Kingdom Experience*, Macmillan, London

Thirlwall, A.P. (1983): "The Balance of Payments and Growth: the Italian Case", in VV. AA., *Bilancia dei pagamenti, importazioni e crescita industriale: "il caso italiano"*, Franco Angeli, Milano

Thursby, J., M. Thursby (1984): "How Reliable are Simple, Single Equation Specifications of Import Demand?", *Review of Economics and Statistics*, February

Vaciago, G. (1983): "Politica monetaria e credito totale interno", in VV. AA., *La programmazione dei flussi finanziari*, Il Mulino, Bologna

Valcamonici, R., S. Vona (1982): "Indicatori di competitività per l'Italia e per i principali paesi industriali: metodologia e criteri di calcolo", *Bollettino*, Banca d'Italia, Jan.-June

Vicarelli, F. (1985): "L'equilibrio esterno: un vincolo allo sviluppo?", in VV.AA., *Moneta ed economia internazionale*, Cassa di Risparmio di Torino, Piemonte Vivo Ricerche, Torino

Vona, S. (1982): "Il commercio estero dell'Italia nell'ultimo decennio", *Politica ed Economia*, December

Vona S. (1983): "Cambi, competitività di prezzo ed esportazioni di manufatti: l'esperienza dei principali paesi industriali", in VV. AA, *Ricerche sui modelli per la politica economica*, Banca d'Italia, Roma

Vona, S. (1987): "Il commercio estero dell'Italia: un vincolo che non si allenta", *Rivista Internazionale di Scienze Sociali*, July- December.

VV. AA. (1983): *Bilancia dei pagamenti, importazioni e crescita industriale: "il caso italiano"*, Franco Angeli, Milano

Figure 1: The Italian growth performance, 1960-1991

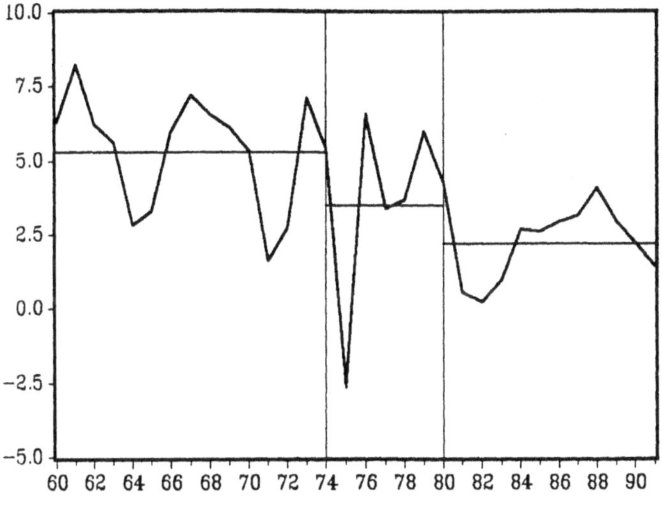

Source: Istat

Figure 2: The Italian balance of payments, 1960 - 1991 (deficits or surpluses as a percentage of GDP)

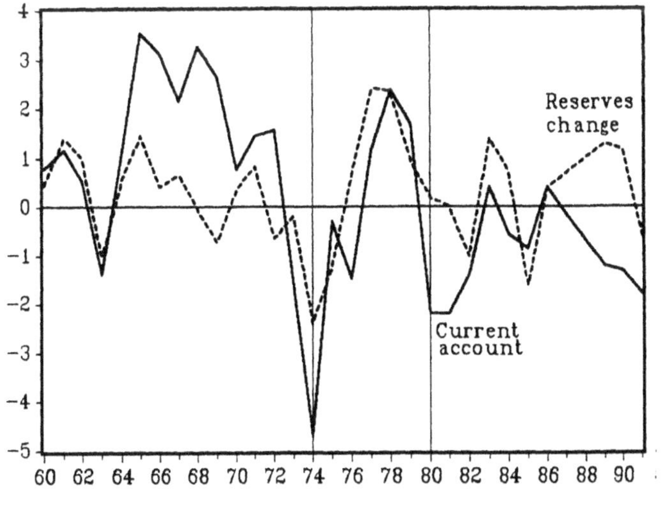

Source: Bank of Italy

Figure 3: The relevance of banks' capital flows, 1960 - 1991 (deficits or surpluses as a percentage of GDP)

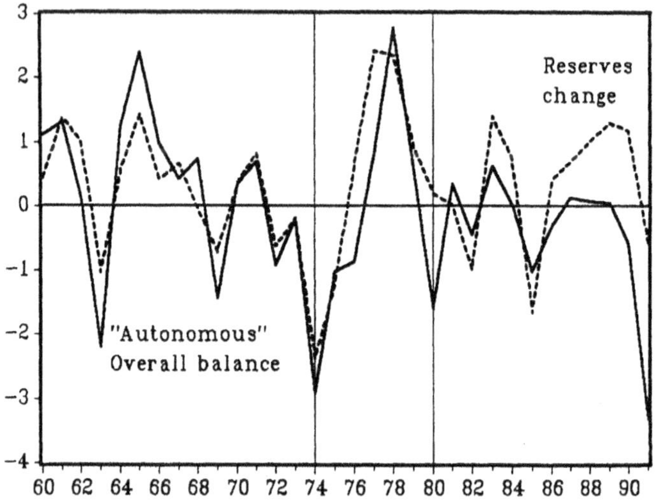

Source: Bank of Italy

Figure 4: The external constraint and the growth process, 1960 - 1991

GR = Growth rate
LR = Lagged current account/GDP ratio
Source: Istat, Bank of Italy

Figure 5: The behaviour of price competitiveness, 1960 - 1991
(relative export prices; index 1980 = 100)

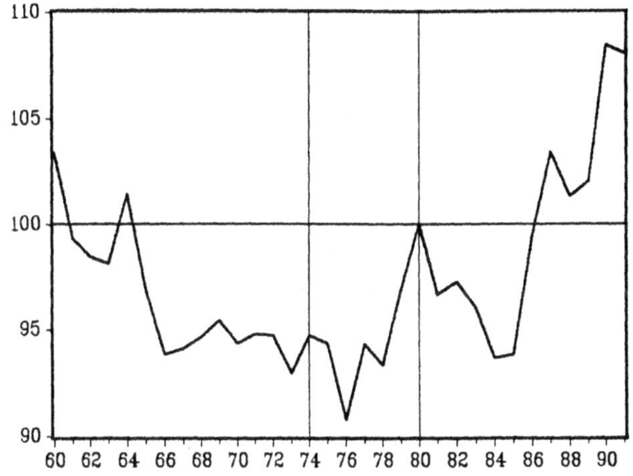

Source: IMF

Figure 6: The Italian trade balance, 1960 - 1991 (balances as a percentage of GDP)

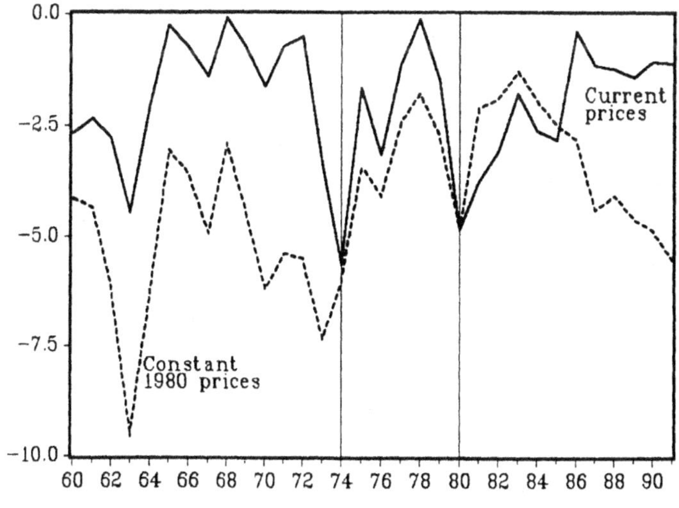

Source: Istat, Bank of Italy

Figure 7: The behaviour of income transfers, 1960 - 1991
(balances as a percentage of nominal exports)

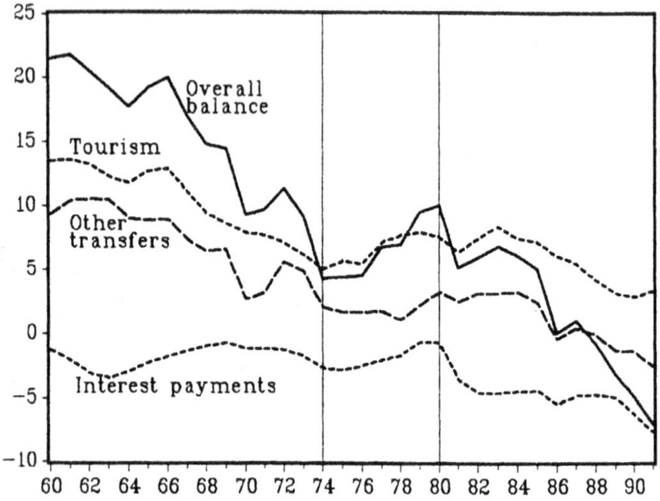

Source: Istat, Bank of Italy

Austria's Balance of Payments under Changing Domestic and External Conditions

Dieter Proske[1]

Austrian National Bank

1 Introduction

The Austrian balance of payments has experienced major changes during the eighties as compared to the seventies, the most striking being the switch from large current account deficits to a more or less balanced current account from 1982 on. More precisely: After yearly deficits of nearly 2% of GDP on average in the period 1974 to 1981 the current account showed an average surplus of somewhat less than 0,2% of GDP in the period 1982 to 1989. From 1990 to 93, a period which was much influenced by special events like the German unification and the opening of former Communist countries, the current account remained more or less unchanged on average.

In conformity with current account developments, net capital transactions changed, according to available statistics, from high capital imports in the seventies and early eighties to a nearly balanced capital account in the rest of the eighties. More precisely: Net capital imports of around 20 billion AS per year in the period 1974-1981 were followed by capital imports of around 5 billion net on average per year in the period 1982-1989. In the period 1990-1993, however, yearly net capital imports amounted again - mainly due to developments in the last two years - to 16 billion AS on average and monetary reserves rose considerably despite a slight deterioration in the current account especially in the last year.

The sudden improvement of the Austrian current account in the eighties and the comparatively good performance during the rest of the decade has been officially interpreted as the result of structural improvements in the supply side of the Austrian economy and a considerable increase in international competitiveness of Austrian enterprises.

[1] The paper represents the personal views of the author.

Table 1: Balance of payments results - averages per year in bill. AS

period	current account	long-term capital	short-term capital	total capital	err. and om. plus val. changes	change in off. mon. res.
1974-81	-16,6	8,7	11,0	19,7	5,1	8,3
1982-89	1,4	1,0	4,4	5,3	-3,0	2,3
1990-93	0,6	12,3	3,6	15,9	1,3	17,7

Source: Austrian National Bank, Balance of Payments Statistics

The following analysis provides evidence for a conflicting view. It shows that the turnaround of the current account in the early eighties and the balanced current account situation thereafter were actually due to weak domestic demand growth as compared with the seventies and with other countries. In particular they were due to a slowdown of investment activity. Given the significant improvement in international price competitiveness of Austrian goods, as represented by labour unit costs, the current account should have shown a surplus rather than a balanced result, if the supply structure had really improved. In view of this evidence, the generally highly praised current account performance in the eighties may rather be interpreted as an indicator for prevailing structural weaknesses in the Austrian economy at that time.

The change in the capital account in turn has, at several occasions, been interpreted as the result of Austria's increasing wealth in the eighties. A rich country tends to become a net capital exporter. In particular the strong increase of Austrian direct investment abroad was seen as a consequence of the increasing strength and dynamics of the Austrian economy. In the light of theoretical and empirical evidence these arguments do not seem very convincing either. As long as current account transactions are leading capital transactions, which is very likely the case for a country with an exchange rate peg like Austria, the capital account in its wider definition (including changes in official monetary reserves) does not only represent the opposite side of the current account by definition, but also results from current account developments. With a fixed exchange rate and in the absence of capital restrictions, the central bank is neither in a position to influence the total monetary base nor the total money supply. It can, however, through its domestic money creation, influence the breakdown of the monetary base into a domestic and a foreign component. As the Austrian central bank has apparently been aiming most of the time for a continuous, smooth and moderate increase in its monetary reserves and has used its instruments appropriately, net capital imports (excluding changes in monetary reserves) had to decrease as soon as the current account improved. These causal relationships, based on the monetary approach to the balance of payments, have been described in detail and estimated for Austria by Proske (1982) and shall not be dealt with in this paper. This paper raises the hypothesis that both, the ceasing of current account deficits and the reduction of net capital imports respectively may have been influenced by the same determinant, namely the development of capital productivity in Austria as compared with other countries.

Chapter 2 describes the development of the Austrian current account in the seventies and in the eighties. In chapter 3 the current account development is interpreted on the basis of a decomposed absorption approach. Weak domestic demand in general and a weak investment activity in particular are singled out as the main reasons for the current account improvement. Chapter 4 deals with the possible influence of the development of capital productivity on the current account and the capital account respectively. Chapter 5 tries to identify the common determinants of current account developments on the basis of an elasticity approach. It arrives at the same conclusions as the absorption based analysis. The current account improvement in the eighties was mainly due to comparatively weak domestic demand developments. Chapter 6 eventually discusses current account developments in the last 4 years on the basis of special factors at work at this time. Finally, the paper closes with a resume.

2 Austria's current account developments in the seventies and eighties

It is generally held that the Austrian balance of payments was in disequilibrium in the seventies and has been in equilibrium since the early eighties.[2]

The underlying Austrian current account had started to weaken at the beginning of the seventies. This tendency was interrupted by the recession of 1975, but it was clearly discernible in the second half of the decade, when the average current account

---

[2] Frequently such statements do not rest on solid economic grounds. It is not as simple to make positive statements about balance of payments equilibria or disequilibria since the beginning of the seventies, when the focus turned from the change in official monetary reserves to the current account as the main balance of payments result. External equilibrium or disequilibrium as represented by the current account situation can essentially be evaluated on the basis of two criteria: *sustainability* and *optimality*. The external situation is sustainable as long as enough foreign credits are available. Decreases in maturity and increases in interest rates of such credits can be viewed as early signs of an external situation which will not be sustainable. The criterium of optimality on the other hand is fulfilled when a country maximises welfare. Generally speaking a current account deficit, even if it is large and persistent, does not signal an external imbalance, as long as the domestic return on imported capital is higher than interest paid abroad for these funds.

deficit amounted to 2 % of GDP as compared to 1 % in the first half. Deficits were fluctuating, however, from year to year depending on the cyclical situation and oil price developments. Chart 1 shows the development of the current account and the respective reverse swings of the capital account for the years 1974 to 1993.

Chart 1:

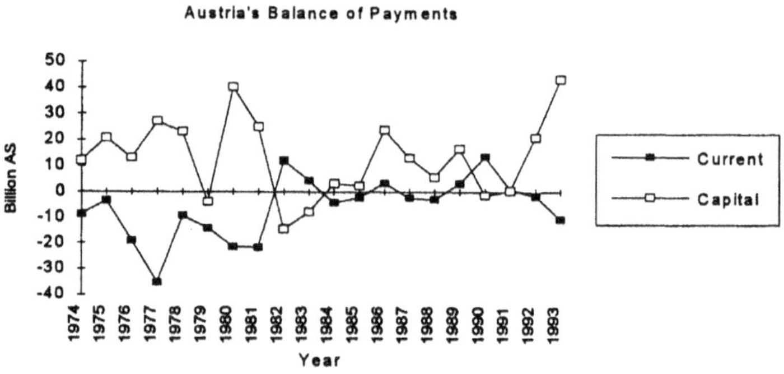

Four reasons for the "weak current account situation" in Austria were singled out in the discussions in the seventies:

a) The positive difference in demand growth in Austria as compared to other countries.[3]

b) The considerable appreciation of the real exchange rate of the Austrian schilling until 1978.

c) The effects of the "Free Trade Agreements" between EC and EFTA countries (integration effect). Within this agreement, tariffs for so called "non-sensitive goods" (i.e. the majority of traded goods) were abolished in a step-by-step process between 1972 and 1982. It was held that in the course of such a liberalisation process, the smaller partner loses in the early phase and catches up only later in terms of an effect on the trade balance. In fact, Austrian exports to EC countries were stimulated considerably by this agreement, thus fostering economic growth,

---

[3] Underlying this development was an economic policy mix which assigned to monetary policy the task of reducing the domestic inflation rate via an appreciating nominal (and temporarily also real) exchange rate. Fiscal policy in turn had to prevent, via increasing budget deficits, unemployment from rising. High employment was considered by far the most important economic policy goal until 1977. In the following years, however, the view was gradually adopted by Austrian policy-makers that high employment could only be reached as the (automatic) result of an increase in international competitiveness.

but imports were stimulated even more, thus increasing the trade and current account deficit.

d) Weaknesses in the supply structure of the Austrian economy, especially in the finished goods sector.

In the second half of the seventies, the view that prevailing current account deficits were not sustainable became widely accepted in Austria. The current account balance was considered a constraint on the continuation of full-employment policy based on budget deficits. The principal task of economic policy became maintaining a comfortable distance from a genuine balance of payments crisis. Therefore early reaction was recommended, despite the fact that the usual signs of a lack of sustainability did not show up yet. Austria was not even in danger of losing its triple-A status in foreign credit markets at this point. However, after 1976 it became a net debtor to the rest of the world.

Economic policy thus became current-account oriented. A package of "defensive" and "offensive" measures was designed to improve the external situation of the economy. The defensive (restrictive) measures were supposed to dampen domestic demand growth, while the offensive ones should increase the share of Austrian goods in total domestic and foreign demand.

The increase of the value-added tax on luxury goods in 1977 was probably the most prominent measure in this package. It was supposed to help dampen "excessive" consumption demand and increase the share of domestic goods in consumption at the same time. Luxury goods were especially qualified for this purpose, first because they were not necessities and second because they were mostly imported. Furthermore, the budget deficit was to be reduced step by step in the medium run and the international competitiveness of the Austrian economy was to be increased by a change in the mix of incomes and exchange rate policy (incomes policy was hardened and nominal exchange rate policy softened). In addition, various kinds of incentives to improve Austrian supply and the marketing of Austrian goods were set with the same goal.

While the real exchange rate actually showed a slightly decreasing trend from 1976 to the middle of the eighties, it was widely believed that the supply structure did not improve much until the early eighties. From this time on, however, the improvement of the current account was taken as a sign that the desired restructioning of the Austrian economy had eventually taken place. (See for example Lachs 1984).

3 Interpreting the current account improvement on the basis of a decomposed absorption approach

As is well known, from the identities Y = C + I + X - M and S = Y - C, it can be derived that the current account is per definition the difference between total saving and total investment in the economy (X - M = CA = S - I).[4] Taking GDP-growth into consideration the conclusions based on *the absorption approach will read as follows: A current account deficit can be reduced only if - at constant GDP - domestic expenses for consumption and investment are reduced* or if they remain constant while GDP is growing or if a combination of both occurs.

Total saving and investment (the difference of both being denoted as F in this context) can further be decomposed into sector savings and investments so that the contribution of government, private households and the private corporate sector to the current account results can be shown ($CA = F_G + F_H + F_C$).

As an identity, the figures as such do not tell us anything about causal relationships at first sight. If the three determinants of the current account are more or less independent of each other and if they are interpreted carefully, they nevertheless provide interesting information. Regression results show that the independence criteria is more or less fulfilled in our particular case. No statistical relationship could be detected between F_H and F_C and only a weak (R2 = 0.37) correlation could be found between F_H and F_G. Moreover the relationship between F_C and F_G proved to be statistically insignificant.

From the table below, it can thus be concluded that *the marked improvement of the current account in the period 1982 - 1989* as compared to 1974 - 1981, or even 1970 - 1981, *was due to a large decrease in investment.* This was true for the eighties as a whole as well as for any relevant sub period. Even in the years 1988/89, when investment activity had recovered somewhat, the average private investment rate was considerably lower than in the seventies. It was not accompanied by an increase in the total savings rate, in particular not by an increase of government saving, as one would have expected in view of the discussions in the seventies. Private household saving alone contributed somewhat, to the current account improvement in the eighties, when

[4] Y = gross domestic product, C=total domestic consumption (incl. gov. cons.), I = total domestic investment (incl. gov. inv.), X=exports and M= imports of goods and services, S=total domestic saving, CA=current account balance. F_G, F_H and F_C denote net non-financial sources of funds of general government, private households and private business (corporations) respectively.

the period as a whole is considered. It showed diverging trends however throughout the period. The private household savings ratio decreased from an average 6 % of GPD in 1974/81 to 5,5 % in 1982/85 but rose to 7,6 % in 1986/89.

Table 2: Saving, investment and the current account. Yearly averages in percent of GDP

	Period 1974/81	Period 1982/89
Total savings	14.2	11.5
of which:		
private households	6.0	6.6
private corporations	4.5	3.5
public sector	3.8	1.4
Total investment	15.9	11.4
of which:		
private corporations	12.0	8.6
public sector	3.9	2.7
Current account balance	- 1.6	0.2 *)

*) With a peak of 1.1 percent of GDP in 1982

This result is hardly compatible with the assumed increase of international competitiveness due to an improvement of the production structure in the eighties. It rather suggests that the current account improved because (excessive?) domestic demand growth slowed down considerably. The slowdown did not only show up in domestic demand but also in GDP figures and it did not only take place relative to the seventies but also relative to other countries. And above all it mainly manifested itself in a decrease in investment activity.

The following table and charts show to which extent not only real demand growth and investment demand in particular but also GDP-growth fell short in Austria in the late seventies and in the eighties when compared to respective growth rates in other European countries. Only real exports of goods and services continued to grow faster than the European average, but nevertheless could not mach export growth of total OECD.

Table 3: Rates of change of major economic variables in Austria and in European OECD-countries (yearly averages)

	(1) Austria	(2) OECD Europe	(3) Difference (1 - 2)	(4) Accumulated (Sum of diff. per period)
Real GDP				
1972 - 1977	3.95	3.13	+ 0.82	+ 4.92
1978 - 1981	1.85	2.15	- 0.30	-1.20
1982 - 1989	2.20	2.53	- 0.33	-2.64
Real Domestic Demand				
1972 - 1977	4.38	2.90	+ 1.48	+ 8.88
1978 - 1981	1.00	1.72	- 0.72	-2.88
1982 - 1989	2.28	2.77	- 0.49	- 3.92
Real Private Gross Fixed Investment				
1972 - 1977	4.53	1.88	+ 2.64	+ 15.90
1978 - 1981	0.52	1.47	-0.95	- 3.80
1982 - 1989	3.27	4.27	-1.00	- 8.00
Real Exports (goods and services)				
1972 - 1977	6.51	6.21	+ 0.30	+1.80
1978 - 1981	7.27	4.62	+ 2.65	+10.60
1982 - 1989	4.71	4.50	+ 0.21	+1.68
Real Imports (goods and services)				
1972 - 1977	7.93	5.08	+ 2.85	+ 17.10
1978 - 1981	4.30	3.10	+ 1.20	+4.80
1982 - 1989	4.97	5.41	-0.44	-3.52

Source: OECD-Economic Outlook No 54 / Dec. 1993

While real GDP-growth on average was nearly 1%-point higher in Austria than in OECD-Europe in the period 1972 - 1977 it was about one third of a percentage point per year lower thereafter, up to the end of the eighties. Between 1978 and 1989 the accumulated negative growth differential to OECD-Europe amounted to nearly 4 percentage points. Most of the relative output gains achieved in the early seventies were thus reversed in the following decade.

When real domestic demand is considered, the growth differential was even more pronounced. It was plus 1½ percentage points per year in the period 1972 - 1977 and minus half a percentage point per year in the period afterwards.

Chart 2

Cumulative growth differential; real domestic demand (Austria - weighted average of trading partners)

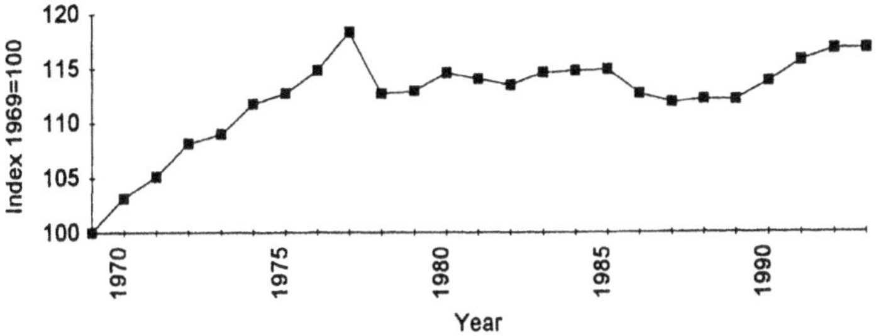

Source: OECD-Economic Outlook and regional Austrian trade statistics. Export weights.

Even more impressive than the development of total domestic demand was the development of real private gross fixed investment. In the period 1972 - 1978 this important demand component grew about 2½ percentage points faster per year in Austria than in other European countries, while it grew one percentage point per year slower in the period thereafter.

Chart 3

Private non-residential fixed investment; accumulated growth differences (Austria - OECD-Europe)

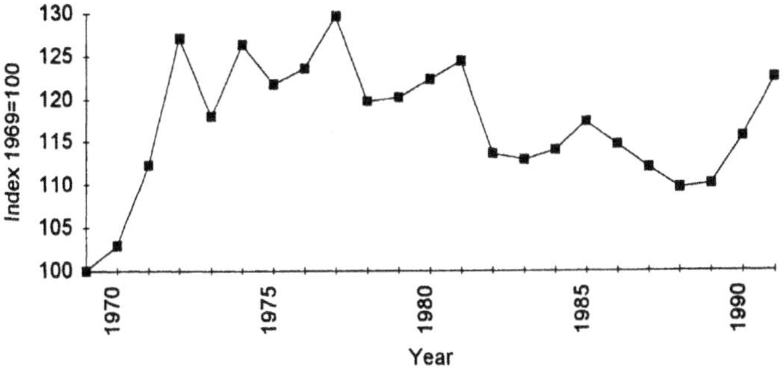

Source: OECD-Economic Outlook No. 54, Dec. 1993.

The average figures cover different developments throughout the period, however. Investment activity strengthened in the late eighties and real total domestic demand has been growing at rates which significantly exceeded the European average since 1988. Similarly, real GDP-growth in Austria has been exceeding the European average since 1988. Despite this acceleration of economic activity the current account remained in balance. The following factors may account for this phenomenon:

1) Despite more rapid growth during recent years the backlog in domestic demand accumulated between 1978 and 1987 vis-à-vis European countries[5] could not be fully compensated for until now.
2) An external shock, consisting mainly of sudden preference changes in European tourism, led to a turnaround in the development of the Austrian tourism balance. While this balance had deteriorated during most of the eighties, it has shown considerable improvements in the years after 1988.
3) An external demand shock, due to German unification and the opening of the East, led ceteris paribus to an improvement in the Austrian current account in 1990/93. At the same time it contributed to economic growth in Austria.
4) International price competitiveness as measured by unit labor costs has been improving again in the years after 1988 , following significant deterioration in the years 1985 to 1987. Trend wise unit labor costs have been improving since the mid seventies.

Chart 4 shows the development of unit labor cost in manufacturing industry in Austria as compared with Germany[6] and Austria's current account performance. It is consistent with the view that price competitiveness had some influence on current account developments. When labor unit costs in Austria rose less than in Germany the current account tended to improve and vice versa.

---

[5] OECD-Europe serves as a proxy for Austrian trading partners as three quarters of Austria's foreign trade is transacted with this group of countries.

[6] A negative value indicates that labor unit costs in Austria, expressed in a single currency, rose less than in Germany.

Chart 4:

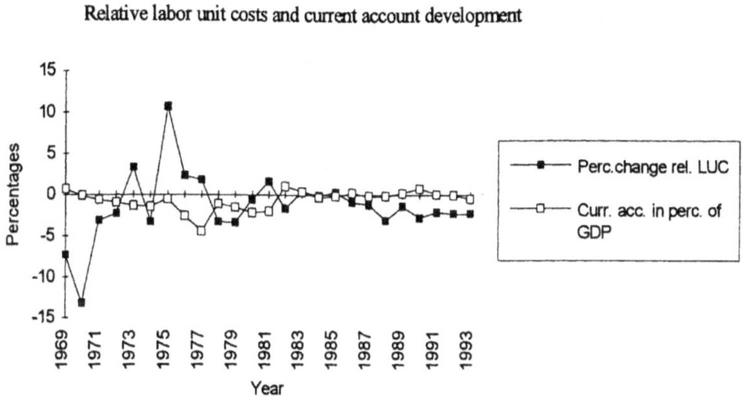

All of these factors tended to make up for the fact that the growth backlog to abroad accumulated since 1978 has been continuously used up, especially since 1988. *Thus the conclusion can be drawn that as soon as some or all of them would disappear* (without being replaced by other favourable ones) *the weakness of the Austrian external position would show up again.* Recent current account developments seem to support this hypothesis, which has been raised several years ago. As soon as preference changes in European tourism came to a still stand and did not cause further improvements in the tourism balance, and as soon as relative unit labor costs as compared with the average of trading partners deteriorated in 1992/93(although those with Germany were still favorable), the current account deteriorated accordingly.

4 The role of capital productivity as a common determinant of capital and current account developments

In the preceding chapter it has been pointed out that the current account improvement in the eighties was due to a slowdown in private investment activity and - to a lesser degree - an increase in private household saving. It can thus be explained by the (inter temporal) optimisation behaviour of these two sectors.

As far as *private household saving* is concerned its contribution to the current account improvement was restricted to the years 1986/89 (as well as 1990/91, which is not taken into consideration here). Its has been mentioned before, that the private household savings ratio was lower on average in the years 1982/85 than in the seventies. This was by and large in line with developments in other countries, where the saving propensity also decreased. As Wüger (1992) points out it was also in line with conventional theory. Private household saving up to 1985 could be very well explained by permanent income developments and error correction models. The increase in the savings quota in 1986 was caused by the drop in raw oil prices and the resulting current income gain which was initially considered as temporary. While this was also roughly in line with household savings behaviour in other countries, the further increase in the savings quota in Austria in 1989 was rather unique. It continued in 1990 and cannot easily be explained on theoretical grounds. The Austrian Institute for Economic Research therefore assumes that it was to a large part due to deficiencies in the respective statistics (Wüger, 1992, p.586).

Because of these peculiarities and because of its comparatively little contribution to current account improvements even on average, private household saving behaviour does not serve very well as an explanation for the balancing of the current in the eighties.

Argumentation has therefore to rely on investment behaviour. Investment in a highly open economy with free capital movements is usually considered as being independent of the consumption profile. As discussed by Cooper and Sachs (1985) for example, *in a small open economy investment is undertaken until the marginal product of capital equals the world interest rate.*

Other things being equal countries will therefore show a current account deficit when productivity of new investments is higher than abroad and they will show a current account surplus when it is lower.

On these grounds it could be concluded that the *slowdown in Austrian investment* as compared to other countries *and* with it the *improvement in the current account may have been caused by a relative decline in capital productivity in Austria.*

Unofficial, though nevertheless very useful estimates of the OECD-Secretariat with respect to capital productivity developments in member countries tend to support this view.

While in the earlier part of the seventies capital productivity (of the economy as a whole) was on average about the same in Austria as in other European countries, it was about 20 basis points lower in the later seventies and 40 basis points lower in the eighties. In the period 1978 - 1981 it decreased twice as fast per year in Austria than in other European countries. In this period the growth rate of real private fixed capital outlays fell back to not more than one fourth of the European average. Parallel to this development a considerable improvement of the real current account balance was already under way since 1978, though it did not manifest itself in nominal terms before the early eighties.

Lower marginal productivity of capital in Austria as compared to other countries could also have been a driving force behind a variety of phenomena concerning the capital balance which showed up during the eighties and which are commonly explained by other determinants: In particular long-term capital exports by private non-banks, including not only portfolio investment but also a dramatic increase in direct investments abroad, as well as a remarkable increase in the repatriation of profits accrued by foreign direct investors in Austria.

Using this interpretation it has to be taken into account, however, that capital productivity of the whole economy might not be the ideal measure in this case and that capital productivity measures generally are not very reliable statistics. The latter being true, however, for other statistics as well, such as labor unit cost or even balance of payments statistics.

5 Interpreting the current account improvement in accordance with the elasticity approach

The scheme used below follows the principle of the Lundberg-decomposition of GDP and was developed independently in the Austrian Institute for Economic Research and the Austrian National Bank on the basis of an article published by Walterskirchen and Smeral in 1981. The following analysis follows the WIFO-version (Walterskirchen 1991) which, in contrast to the OeNB-version, is based on national account data.

It breaks down the current account development into three analytically important elements, namely:

a) the difference in real demand growth

b) the change in international competitiveness as measured by market shares at home and abroad

c) the terms-of-trade effect adjusted for real recycling effects

The equation, underlying the tables below, reads for country i:

$$qn_i = d_i + x_i + m_i + q_o + t_i$$

All variables in the equation are defined as logarithmic growth rates vis-à-vis the year before.[7]

qn_i = nominal export/import ratio of country i

d_i = real domestic demand of country i as a share of domestic demand of OECD

x_i = real exports of country i as a share of OECD-exports

m_i = real import intensity of country i (i.e. imports in percent of total domestic demand) as a share of OECD import-intensity

q_o = real export/import quota of OECD as an indicator for real recycling in the wake of terms-of-trade changes

t_i = terms of trade of country i

In words: The logarithmic rate of change of the export/import quota (and thus, with some modifications, the change of the current account) is identical to the sum of the real growth differential, the logarithmic changes of real export and import shares and the terms of trade. The introduction of the real export/import quota of total OECD serves to correct terms-of-trade changes for real recycling effects. When oil prices rise, the terms of trade of most industrial countries will deteriorate. The current account of these countries, however, will only deteriorate to the extent to which oil exporters do not spend their income increments for imports of goods and services. The same holds - with a reverse sign - for oil price decreases.

The following table fills up the above mentioned identity with figures and thus shows the contribution of determinants to rate of change of the export/import quota in percentage points.

[7] Expressed in levels, the equation would read:

$$XN/MN = (Y^{-1}/Y_0)*(X/X_0)*(M*M_0^{-1} / Y*Yo)*(P_x /P_m)*(X_0/M_0)$$

XN denotes Austria's nominal and X Austria's real exports of goods and services. Correspondingly X_0 represents real exports of goods and services of all OECD countries. The same connotation is used for imports (M) and GDP (Y). P_x and P_m represent Austria's export and import prices respectively. For the derivation of this identity see Walterskirchen 1991.

Table 4: (Average percentage change per year)

Period	Export/ Import Ratio	Real Growth Differential	Market Share Exports	Relative Import Intensity	Recycling	Terms of Trade
1974/77	- 2.3	- 1.0	1.2	- 2.5	2.0	- 2.0
1974/78	- 0.2	0	1.2	- 2.0	1.9	- 1.4
1974/81	- 0.6	0.1	1.5	- 2.5	2.4	- 1.8
1978/81	1.2	0.7	1.8	- 2.5	2.8	- 1.7
1982/89	0.6	0.9	- 0.4	0.3	- 1.1	0.9

These figures tell us the following story: The export/import ratio (and the current account of Austria) deteriorated considerably between 1974 and 1977 because of a high growth differential in real domestic demand vis-à-vis abroad and a rising relative propensity to import. The first oil price increase, which fell into this period, had practically no direct influence in the medium term, when real recycling is taken into account. The negative effect of the terms of trade deterioration was compensated by a positive effect of about the same magnitude, due to higher import demand of non-OECD country, in particular OPEC countries.

From 1978 until 1981, after the shift to a more restrictive demand policy, the current account improved on average during the period, due to a negative demand differential to abroad and higher absorption of the oil countries in the course of the second oil price shock. Figures also show, however, that the import propensity was still rising quickly. Though market shares -expressed in terms of the Austrian share in total OECD-exports- increased at a somewhat faster rate than in previous years, competitiveness, as measured in this way, continued to decrease.

The situation changed considerably in the period 1982/89. The current account improved further and thus balanced because demand growth lagged further behind the OECD growth rate than it had in the years before. The loss in competitiveness slowed down, not because of gains in export market shares, but because of a reduction in the relative propensity to import. The market share of exports actually fell.

It can be concluded, therefore, that the current account in the eighties became balanced by and large because of an absolute and relative slowdown of the growth rate of the Austrian economy and because of a marked reduction in the relative import elasticity in Austria.

The loss of relative market shares in export markets in the eighties was apparently due to an unfavourable regional structure of Austrian exports. The countries Austria has been traditionally exporting to (especially OECD Europe and Germany in particular) showed slower economic growth than the OECD average. Ţhe gain in market shares on the domestic market could, in our present example, not fully compensate for the loss on the export side, so that total competitiveness as measured by relative market shares showed a slight decrease in the eighties. This represents already an improvement vis-à-vis previous periods, when competitiveness, as represented by this indicator, deteriorated considerably.

Measured by the share of Austrian exports in the export-weighted total demand abroad and by the share of Austrian imports in total demand (instead of domestic demand) in Austria, competitiveness shows a slight increase in the period 1982/89. This has commonly been interpreted as an indicator for the improvement in the supply structure of the Austrian economy. Empirical evidence, however, points to another direction. Apparently, competitiveness in domestic markets was not the dominant determinant of the decrease in relative and absolute import intensity in Austria. Regression results show that there exists a strong positive relationship between domestic demand and import elasticity, they also show that this relationship was not much different in the eighties from previous periods.

1966 - 1990	1966 - 1979	1980 - 1990
$mq = -1.28 + 0.89n$	$mq = -2.0 + 0.97n$	$mq = -0.94 + 0.93n$
(-2.1) (7.3)	(-2.2) (6.1)	(-1.1) (3.9)
$R2 = 0.70$	$R2 = 0.76$	$R2 = 0.63$

mq = logarithmic growth rate of real import quota (real imports of goods and services divided by real domestic demand)

n = logarithmic growth rate of real domestic demand

Figures in brackets = t-values for the coefficients shown above.

These regression results are in concurrence with the view prevailing in Austria that weak domestic demand growth leads to a change in the demand structure in Austria from items with high import content to items with lower import content, the reverse being true for strong demand growth. They also show that the respective behaviour patterns have hardly changed over time and that this generally accepted relationships was thus to a large part responsible for the decrease in import elasticity in the eighties.

Though there remains some room for other determinants, it is very unlikely that an improved supply structure of the Austrian economy was one of them. Too many other influences have worked in the direction of a reduction in import elasticity, one of the most important among them being the improvement of price competitiveness, as measured by unit labor costs. Furthermore, due to the completion of tariff-reductions within the Free Trade Agreement between EFTA and EC countries these agreements stopped to exert pressure in the direction of an increase in income elasticity as they did in the early eighties. An additional role was played by a technical factor, incorporated in the above calculations. We measured income elasticity as the relationship between total imports and total domestic demand. Exports, which also have a noticeable import content, were excluded. As exports of goods and services grew slower in Austria in the eighties than in the OED area as a whole (as can be seen from the decreasing market share) relative import elasticity had to decrease, other things being equal. Given all these influences on income elasticity it seems very unlikely that supply factors have played an additional, noteworthy role.

6 Current account developments in 1990/93: The item by item approach

Since the study was mainly concerned with the medium-term perspective and underlying macroeconomic relationships, it did not cover the last four years, which were influenced by at least three special factors. Preference changes in European tourism, German unification and the opening of the East.

In 1988 started a preference shift in European tourism away from the Southern, Mediterranean countries to the North. This change in preferences turned out to be very favourable for Austria. The tourism surplus showed considerable yearly increments from year to year, reversing the trend of decreasing surpluses, which had been experienced in the years before. 1992 the improvements in tourism came to a halt, however. 1992 and 93 Austria posted decreasing net receipts from foreign tourism which had reached a peak of more than 90 billion AS in 1991. Though the emerging world recession might have influenced this turnaround, changes in fashion and personal preferences will have played their role as well.

As far as German unification was concerned it led to a demand spur for foreign goods especially in the first two years 1990 and 1991. At the beginning mainly those countries having traditional trading ties with Germany, could benefit. Later on other countries intensified their efforts in this market and competition - aggravated by the recession - increased. In 1991 Austria lost market shares in Germany but nevertheless could benefit from the turnaround in the German current account. The German current account surplus was reduced from more than 100 billion DM in 1989 to somewhat less than 80 billion DM in 1990. In the years 1991 to 1993 Germany posted deficits between 30 and 40 billion DM per year. This dramatic deterioration in the German current account had to show up by definition in correspondent current account improvements in the rest of the world.

The opening of the East, which dates back to 1989 or even earlier has proved favourable so far for Austria from a balance of payments perspective and will probably do so for some more time. The trade balance with Eastern (Central) European countries has been improving year by year. In 1989 Austria's surplus with these countries was by not less than 15 billion AS higher than in the middle of the eighties.

Due to these influences, which worked together in 1990 and were supplemented by an improvement of price competitiveness not only vis a vis Germany but also vis a vis the average of trading partners, Austria posted a current account surplus of more than 10 billion AS in the said year. The tourism balance improved by not less than 6 billion AS, the traditional trade deficit with Germany decreased by 3 billion AS and the traditional surplus with Eastern and Central European countries rose by 3 billion AS.

In 1991 more or less the same trend prevailed. The current account closed with a surplus of about 1 billion AS and would have shown a much higher surplus if the traditional investment income deficit had not experienced an unusually strong increase.

1992 was already somewhat different. The trade balance with Germany and Eastern and Central European Countries continued to improve, but tourism could not provide positive contributions any more. In addition price competitiveness vis a vis the average of trading partners decreased somewhat. The current account posted a small deficit of close to 2 billion AS.

In 1993 the development of spacial factors was not so much different from that experienced in 1992. Consequently the current account deteriorated further and closed with a deficit of a bit more than 10 billion AS.

7 Summary

The current account balance is subject to a variety of influences. Simply identifying current account developments with changes in international competitiveness can therefore lead to a wrong perception of reality. The present study tries to demonstrate this, using the Austrian experience in the eighties as an example and applying three alternative approaches to current account analyses: An absorption approach, an elasticity-like approach and an item to item approach.

In contrast to frequently expressed alternative interpretations the study comes to the conclusion that, notwithstanding a clear trend to higher price competitiveness of Austrian goods, the dramatic improvement of the current account in the eighties was mainly due to slow demand growth, in particular slow investment growth. Despite possible weaknesses of capital-productivity data it should not be ruled out completely that a faster decrease in capital productivity in Austria as compared with abroad could have been a driving force behind the investment behavior and the improvement in the current account. This view is not necessarily inconsistent with the opinion that structural change might be on their way. In times of structural change capital productivity often decreases. Although this might eventually increase Austria's non-price competitiveness in the future, the present paper makes clear that it was not an important determinant of the dramatic current account improvement in the eighties.

Slow domestic demand growth worked mainly through two channels. Firstly, due to the negative demand differential vis-à-vis abroad, imports tended to grow more slowly than exports. Secondly, import elasticity decreased as a result of the demand slack.The paper shows that weak domestic demand would have improved the current account through its dampening effect on import elasticity, even in the absence of a negative growth differential to abroad.

In the last three to four years domestic demand development has lost in importance as a factor explaining the permanently balanced external position of the country. Instead, other - though temporary - influences came into play. They include the disappearance of the high German current account surplus, the opening of the East (given the comparative advantages Austrian firms still have in this region) and preference changes in European tourism. Each one of these three factors tended to improve the Austrian current account at least for some time during the last years. When they disappear and are not replaced by other favourable influences, the current account may deteriorate again.

References

Beirat für Wirtschafts- und Sozialfragen (1978): *Kurz- und mittelfristige Fragen der Zahlungsbilanzentwicklung*, Wien.

Beirat für Wirtschafts- und Sozialfragen (1980): *Bericht zur Zahlungsbilanzentwicklung*, Wien.

Cooper, R., Sachs, J. (1985): "Borrowing Abroad: the Debtors Perspective", in: *International Dept and Developing Countries*, J. Cuddington and G.W. Smith (Eds.), World Bank.

Lachs, Th. G. (1984): "Probleme der Zahlungsbilanz", *Geld und Kredit*, Gemeinwirtschaft No. 2, 35-39.

Proske, D. (1982): "Monetary Policy in Austria and its Interaction with the Balance of Payments", paper presented at the International Conference on Monetary Policy, held in August at the University of Witwatersrand, South Africa.

Salop, J., Spittäler, E. (1980): "Why does the Current Account Matter?" *IMF Staff Papers* (March), pp. 101-134

Seidel, H. (1986): "Der österreichische Weg in der Wirtschaftspolitik", in: *Österreichs Wirtschaftspolitik 1970-1985*, Beiträge zur Wirtschafts- und Gesellschaftspolitik Band 1, Wien, pp.11-40.

Smeral, E., Walterskirchen E. (1981): "Der Einfluß von Wirtschaftswachstum und Wettbewerbsfähigkeit auf die Leistungsbilanz", *WIFO Monatsberichte* No. 7, pp. 373-383.

Tichy, G. (1977): "Einige absorptionstheoretische Überlegungen zum österreichischen Leistungsbilanzdefizit", *Empirica*, No. 2, pp. 209-221

Tichy, G. (1986): "Finanzpolitik im Dienste der Zahlungsbilanz" in: *Handbuch der österr. Finanzpolitik*, Weisel/Leithner/Windisch (Hrsg.), Manz Verlag Wien, pp. 451-468

Walterskirchen E. (1991): "Leistungsbilanz und Wettbewerbsfähigkeit", *WIFO Monatsberichte* No. 3, pp. 134-141.

Wüger, M. (1992): "Günstige Konsumentwicklung bei rückläufiger Sparneigung", *WIFO Monatsberichte* No. 11, pp. 584-589.

IV. Cross Country Mobility Issues

Labour Supply Trends and the Worsening Dualism in the Italian Labour Market

Giuseppina Baffi[1)] and Paolo Piacentini[2)]

1) KPMG Peat Marwick consultant s.r.l., Rome
2) University of Rome "La Sapienza"

1 Introduction

There is no homogeneous economic and social environment called Italy. Growth theorists have sometimes considered this country as an exemplary case of a "dual" economy; but even dualistic models cannot sufficiently capture the complexity of territorial diversification and local specification throughout the country [1]. It is therefore difficult, and perhaps incorrect, to represent even in a brief outline, an "Italian" situation as an average or wholly aggregate one. This is particularly true of the labour market .

In the traditional interpretations of economic growth, the origin of dualism has often been attributed to demand or endowment factors: i.e. availability of material and entrepreneurial resources, and other local elements which benefit certain areas with respect to others.

Within such a framework, instead, labour supply and demographic trends have not received adequate attention; supply being considered as an "accommodating" variable in the longer run, due to adjust to availability and localization of demand through induced mobility. It would be pointed out that such adjustments do not happen without frictions and costs, and dualism may persist if sections of the population chose to subsist in forms of underemployment at the lower end of the dual economy.

But even a brief outline of demand and supply trends in the 1980's will immediately reveal that a more thorough look at "supply side factors" is required. The role of purely demographic factors appears almost dominant and likewise the evolution

[1] The classical reference on this point is Vera Lutz, "Italy. A Study in Economic Development", Oxford University Press, London 1962.

of the participation rate does not appear to be reducible to "demand pull" mechanisms, in terms either of activation or discouragement.

Demographic dynamics, at the beginning, were not homogeneous in terms of territory but did, however, appear to have contributed significantly in determining an increasing imbalance in the labour potential relative to the available job openings in different areas.

Table 1 below reports specific rates of unemployment based on sex and three broad territorial partitions of the country as per 1990 averages. This is meant only as an illustration of the width of the inter-regional imbalances in the Italian labour market[2]. Apart from further considerations of measurement and structure of total unemployment, the actual range went from a situation of virtual "full employment" of males in Northern Italy to rates of unemployment typical of a "Mediterranean" underdeveloped country in the South.

Table 1 - Unemployment rates (1990 averages)

Age group	Sex	North	Center	South
14-29				
	males	7,4	18,2	34,7
	females	14,7	32,3	57,4
	total	10,8	24,7	44,0
30-over				
	males	1,3	2,3	5,3
	females	4,9	7,6	15,6
	total	2,5	4,2	8,4

Source: Istat

The central question at stake becomes at this point the evaluation of the likely developments of the situation given actual trends in labour supply and demand. An exercise of extrapolation to the year 2000 is in fact outlined in the following section ,

2 The standard definition of unemployment overestimates the rate with respect to criteria adopted in other countries (e.g.USA), mainly because the inclusion of a person into the stock of unemployment as from the Quarterly Sample Surveys is not conditional to an "active" search for a job in the period of reference. This point, causes difficulties for comparisons and evaluations of international differences, but not of regional differentials within the country. For details on methodology, see ISTAT, "Rilevazioni campionarie sulle forze di lavoro", Metodi e Norme, Serie A, n.15, Roma 1978.

and the implications for future developments and consequences on "dualism" will be briefly discussed.

2 Future prospects of the labour force

It is appropriate at this point to formulate explicit hypotheses on the future evolution of the labour force, divided into age groups, sex and territorial distribution.

The profound changes in demographic and participation behaviour allow the prediction of further transformations; it is important therefore to outline clearly a scenario for the next decade, which might give direction to a policy action aimed at a better matching of requirements and availability of the labour force.

Labour Force , needless to say, is the result of the multiplication of the activity rate by the population of working age. Accounting for the demographical evolution of the working age population, and formulating hypotheses about the activity rates, it is possible to outline the trends in labour supply potential for the coming years.

The developments of population for age groups, sex and North/South geographical partition have been quoted here from the latest demographic projections carried out by Istituto di Ricerche sulla Popolazione (I.R.P.)[3]. The IRP projection chosen for this occasion, gives national and regional populations upon a fifty-years horizon, under the hypotheses of zero net migration and of a standstill in the decline of the birth rate (i.e. birth rates equal to their regional levels in 1987). However, given the short-term nature of our extrapolation (ten years) we do not suffer from the consequences or realism of alternative hypotheses on demographic trends still to come.

In Table 2 the predicted population is presented for the year 2000 horizon: it is important to note the dramatic decline in the number of younger persons aged between 14 and 24, in the northern and central regions.

In Southern Italy, given the high fertility rate still throughout the 1970's and a more moderate decline of it in the 1980's, the fall in the same age groups will not be so remarkable.

---

[3] See CNR-Istituto di Ricerche sulla Popolazione: "Tre scenari per il possibile sviluppo della popolazione delle regioni italiane al 2038(base 1988)", a cura di A. Golini, A. De Simoni e f. Heins, Roma 1989.

Table 2 - Population in working age ('000s)

North-Center

	1990			2000		
Age group	Males	Females	Total	Males	Females	Total
14-19	1547	1448	2995	988	939	1927
20-24	1397	1306	2703	1040	995	2036
25-29	1290	1308	2598	1283	1233	2516
30-39	2379	2407	4786	2847	2758	5605
40-49	2484	2582	5066	2527	2511	5038
50-59	2448	2590	5038	2360	2466	4825
60-64	1136	1259	2395	1081	1201	2283
65-70	992	1211	2203	1077	1281	2359
Total	13673	14111	27784	13204	13385	26589

South

	1990			2000		
Age group	Males	Females	Total	Males	Females	Total
14-19	1040	1011	2051	888	840	1728
20-24	791	840	1631	827	785	1612
25-29	770	844	1614	913	874	1787
30-39	1467	1532	2999	1851	1818	3669
40-49	1271	1247	2518	1451	1477	2928
50-59	1110	1163	2273	1145	1203	2348
60-64	509	560	1069	490	550	1040
65-70	434	496	930	506	606	1112
Total	7392	7693	15085	8071	8155	16226

Italy

	1990			2000		
Age group	Males	Females	Total	Males	Females	Total
14-19	2587	2459	5046	1876	1780	3655
20-24	2188	2146	4334	1868	1781	3648
25-29	2060	2152	4212	2196	2107	4303
30-39	3846	3939	7785	4698	4576	9274
40-49	3755	3829	7584	3978	3988	7966
50-59	3558	3753	7311	3505	3669	7173
60-64	1645	1819	3464	1571	1752	3323
65-70	1426	1707	3133	1583	1888	3471
Total	21065	21804	42869	21275	21540	42815

Source: Istat and IRP

In both areas only the age group 30-39 -- the generation of the 1960's "baby-boom" -- turns out to be on a significant increase. We do not report here year by year estimates: however, exactly the current year 1992 should mark the dividing line between net increase and decrease over the year of the total working age population. It is evident that the demographic weight of the southern regions will always be increasing.

As far as activity rates are concerned, we have performed specific extrapolations of the more recent trends, obtaining extrapolations up to 2000 for 32 series as combinations of 8 age groups, two sex and territorial partitions. The extrapolations are based on 1978-1990 data, and the criteria for interpolation are reported in the prospectus in the Appendix 1.

Table 3 presents the figures for the rates of activity so derived, and Table 4 the implied numbers in terms of labour force potential, with a comparison with 1990.

Table 3: Activity rates (% values)

North-Center

	1990			2000		
Age group	Males	Females	Total	Males	Females	Total
14-19	24,6	22,9	23,8	16,9	15,4	16,2
20-24	70,8	70,0	70,4	69,5	72,6	71,0
25-29	90,9	75,0	82,9	88,8	77,9	83,5
30-39	97,4	68,1	82,6	96,6	74,2	85,6
40-49	96,6	52,9	74,3	95,8	55,4	75,7
50-59	76,8	28,3	51,9	70,8	32,9	51,4
60-64	33,4	9,5	20,8	30,4	9,3	19,3
65-70	13,0	3,9	8,0	11,0	3,0	6,7
Total	70,5	43,5	56,8	70,6	46,5	58,5

South

	1990			2000		
Age group	Males	Females	Total	Males	Females	Total
14-19	25,1	19,2	22,2	21,2	11,0	16,2
20-24	69,0	51,4	60,0	70,2	62,6	66,5
25-29	89,5	50,2	69,0	86,5	58,8	73,0
30-39	96,7	48,6	72,1	95,3	61,0	78,3
40-49	95,9	41,1	68,7	95,0	48,4	71,5
50-59	81,1	26,2	53,0	77,6	25,1	50,7
60-64	41,5	11,3	25,6	38,9	11,2	24,2
65-70	13,6	3,6	8,3	11,0	3,5	6,9
Total	71,8	35,0	53,0	72,3	40,6	56,3

Italy

Age group	1990 Males	1990 Females	1990 Total	2000 Males	2000 Females	2000 Total
14-19	24,8	21,4	23,1	18,9	13,3	16,2
20-24	70,2	62,7	66,5	69,8	68,2	69,0
25-29	90,4	65,3	77,6	87,8	70,0	79,1
30-39	97,1	60,5	78,6	96,1	69,0	82,7
40-49	96,4	49,1	72,5	95,5	52,8	74,1
50-59	78,1	27,7	52,2	73,0	30,3	51,2
60-64	35,9	10,1	22,3	33,1	9,9	20,8
65-70	13,2	3,8	8,1	11,0	3,2	6,7
Total	71,0	40,5	55,5	71,2	44,3	57,7

Source: Istat

Table 4: Labour force ('000s)

North-Center

Age group	1990 Males	1990 Females	1990 Total	2000 Males	2000 Females	2000 Total
14-19	380	332	712	167	145	312
20-24	989	914	1903	723	723	1446
25-29	1173	981	2154	1140	960	2100
30-39	2316	1639	3955	2750	2046	4797
40-49	2399	1367	3766	2421	1391	3812
50-59	1880	734	2614	1671	811	2482
60-64	379	120	499	329	112	440
65-69	129	47	176	119	38	157
Total	9645	6134	15779	9318	6227	15545

South

Age group	1990 Males	1990 Females	1990 Total	2000 Males	2000 Females	2000 Total
14-19	261	194	455	188	92	281
20-24	546	432	978	581	491	1072
25-29	689	424	1113	790	514	1304
30-39	1419	744	2163	1764	1109	2873
40-49	1219	512	1731	1378	715	2094
50-59	900	305	1205	889	302	1191
60-64	211	63	274	191	62	252
65-69	59	18	77	56	21	77
Total	5304	2692	7996	5836	3307	9143

Italy

Age group	1990 Males	1990 Females	1990 Total	2000 Males	2000 Females	2000 Total
14-19	641	526	1167	355	237	592
20-24	1535	1346	2881	1304	1214	2518
25-29	1862	1405	3267	1929	1475	3404
30-39	3735	2383	6118	4514	3155	7670
40-49	3618	1879	5497	3799	2106	5905
50-59	2780	1039	3819	2559	1113	3672
60-64	590	183	773	519	173	693
65-69	188	65	253	174	60	234
Total	14949	8826	23775	15154	9534	24688

Source: Istat and Irp

According to the results of the exercise, it can be deduced that in the decade 1991-2000 total labour force should marginally increase by 3.8 % ; however, in the North-central part of the country the male labour force will mark a significant decline of 3,4 %, matched only partially by an increase of females of 1,5 % ; on the contrary, in the South, both male and female labour supply should still be on the increase. As a whole, labour force should increase by 14.3 % in the South (10.0 % males, 22.8 % females). The share of the southern labour force on the national total should in this way increase from 33.6 to 37.0.

It is evident that such dynamics, without some counteracting mobility, would determine a significant increase of the regional imbalances on the labour markets, with a worsening dualism as consequence. Potential situations of a labour shortage in the North would go hand-in-hand with a further worsening of unemployment rates in the South.

The projections on supply as assumed above are now put together with two simple hypotheses on the evolution of demand, in order to derive the outline of potential Italian unemployment for the year 2000. The figures on Table 5 are derived from two alternative hypotheses for the number of employment positions: zero growth, i.e. the same number of jobs as the 1990 values, and 0.65 % growth, i.e. the average yearly growth of total employment experienced over the period 1981-1989 in the country as a whole.[4]

[4] See ISTAT, "Occupazione e redditi di lavoro dipendente anni 1980-89", Collana d'informazione, n.22, 1990, for details. Italian national accounts now give total employment in terms of full time equivalents ("posizioni lavorative a tempo pieno"). Increase in the incidence of part time work might mean that total job positions have increased by more.

Table 5: Potential labour force and employment at year 2000 ('000s and % values)

North-Center	1990			2000 (*)			2000 (**)		
	Males	Females	Total	Males	Females	Total	Males	Females	Total
Labour force	9720	6167	15887	9318	6227	15545	9318	6227	15545
Employment	9342	5509	14851	9342	5509	14851	9967	5878	15845
Unemployment	378	658	1036	-24	718	694	-649	349	-300
Rate of unemployment	3,89	10,67	6,52	-0,26	11,53	4,46	-6,97	5,60	-1,93
South	1990			2000 (*)			2000 (**)		
	Males	Females	Total	Males	Females	Total	Males	Females	Total
Labour force	5334	2705	8039	5836	3307	9143	5836	3307	9143
Employment	4610	1844	6454	4610	1844	6454	4919	1967	6886
Unemployment	724	861	1585	1226	1463	2689	917	1340	2257
Rate of unemployment	13,57	31,83	19,72	21,01	44,24	29,41	15,71	40,52	24,69
Italy	1990			2000 (*)			2000 (**)		
	Males	Females	Total	Males	Females	Total	Males	Females	Total
Labour force	15054	8872	23926	15154	9534	24688	15154	9534	24688
Employment	13952	7353	21305	13952	7353	21305	14886	7845	22731
Unemployment	1102	1519	2621	1202	2181	3383	268	1689	1957
Rate of unemployment	7,32	17,12	10,95	7,93	22,88	13,70	1,77	17,72	7,93

Source: Istat and IRP. (*) Employment is kept constant at 1990 values. (**) Employment grows yearly at a rate of 0.65%.

With the first assumption of zero growth of net job openings, the determinant feature would consist in a further sharp increase of unemployment rates in the southern regions, where the persistent growth of the labour supply was already noted. The dynamics of a female labour force, in particular, which has been characterized by strong stimuli towards increase, could now face a dramatic perspective whereby half of the women are likely to remain unemployed. Of course, this result is dependent on the strong assumptions made, i.e. no employment growth, the continuation of a tendential increase of female participation rates, and no internal or external migration. In the North, on the contrary, even with constant job positions, the number of available male labour force would fall, in the year 2000, slightly short of demand, while female unemployment rate would only marginally increase.

We do not mean here that these results are necessarily a realistic prospect: they are rather indicative that "something should happen", that the mere continuation of past trends is likely to produce an unsustainable situation. Discouragement effects, resumption of internal migration, inflow of "foreign" labour force , further growth of "informal" or even "illegal" employment, social unrest and increasing crime, are all possible consequences which might be encouraged by a "natural" evolution which, ceteris paribus, will likely lead to a deepening of labour market imbalances.

In the column at the right of Table 5, a different scenario of growth of overall demand for labour has been introduced: the number of job openings at year 2000 result from the application of a compound yearly growth rate of 0.65 %. The value is not casual, since this approximately represents the effective average growth of total employment for the whole Italian economy in the period 1981-1989. However, the figure averages over quite different values of the single years, and we have not distinguished among different values of growth for sex or territorial partition.[5] Anyway, the figure is broadly indicative of the consequences on labour demand and supply balances if the 1990's followed the same pattern of the 1980's. Under these hypotheses, the imbalances would become even more striking: in Northern and Central Italy, the demand for labour for males would exceed "local" availability by about 649,000 units (i.e. a 7 % excess demand); such a gap could not be compensated by females even if perfect substitutability were supposed. While in South Italy excess supply and consequent unemployment rates would remain relevant, and still higher than its 1990 levels.

3 Concluding remarks

It is clear that a purely quantitative analysis cannot provide sufficient information on the likely evolution of the labour market dualism within the Italian economy. We have already said that "something should happen", since the continuation of the present trend would lead to an unsustainable situation. Adjustments in the behaviour of both the demand and the supply may be predicted, although an in depth analysis of these factors would go beyond the scope of this survey. Discouragement effects may reduce the figures of "explicit" unemployment in the South but would not change the essential reality of an excess ofsupply potential in front of a stagnating demand.

---

[5] Actually, the relationship between output and employment variations has been rather unstable over the 1980's: the evaluation of an elasticity coefficient between yearly changes in GDP and total or dependent employment for forecast or exptrapolation exercises is therefore hazardous.

On the other hand, demographic decline in the North would soon determine a situation of shortage of staff, unless a fall in labour demand, because of cyclical or technological factors, is assumed. Higher factor mobility, i.e. of labour from South to North and/or investments from North to South, remains an essential condition for avoiding a widening of the gap. As far as labour mobility is concerned, actual trends are clearly insufficient in determining a significant change in the basic situation.

Table 6: Net immigration rate (0/00 inhabitants)

	North Center	South
1982	2,0	1,9
1984	1,4	1,9
1986	1,8	0,3
1988	2,1	-0,5
1990	3,7	-0,3

Source: Istat and Svimez

Although immigration rates have been positive and slightly increasing in the North/Centre over the 1980's, they will not avoid tight labour market conditions in the coming years, ceteris paribus. Moreover, immigration flows there appear to have mainly come from other areas rather than from Southern Italy : notwithstanding the huge number of unemployed, the net migratory rate in the South was positive at the beginning of the decade, becoming only marginally negative towards the end. The "blockaded mobility" appears thus as the central problem in the bad performance of the Italian labour market. Its causes have often been brought about by a lack of sufficient incentives on the income side and by high penalties from the cost side, in particular on house availability and prices.

As for incentives to mobility allowing a way out from dualism, a wider survey would be necessary, including the analysis of policy and social factors contributing to a change in the "reservation level" of income for encouraging mobility. We will mention briefly only one argument here, referring to North/South wage differentials. In fact, from a "neoclassical" point of view, the existence of a differential in wage incomes (and costs, from the employers'point of view) is the most effective key to adjustment of imbalances, with the incentive to labour mobility out of and capital mobility into the lower wage segment. Trade Union action on this point, and in particular their opposition since the 1960's to any form of wage differentiation, through the imposition of nation-wide contractual agreements on wage standards for most sectors, has been sited as one of the institutional barriers towards the working of market forces. On this central point we think it necessary to propose some evidence, in order to warn against oversimplified interpretations.

In Table 7 we have summarized, from an extensive survey[6], the indices of the values for South (given North-Centre = 100) for labour cost and value added per employee in the industrial transformation.

Table 7: Cost of labour and value added per employee in the industry in the south (indexes: North-Centre = 100)

	Labour cost per employee		Value added per employee		Cost of labour per unit of v.a.	
	1980	1987	1980	1987	1980	1987
Total Industry	79,0	80,4	76,0	80,9	103,9	99,4
Chemicals	92,9	84,7	79,6	83,3	104,7	95,0
Engineering	73,7	76,7	73,0	75,8	101,0	101,1
Vehicles	90,5	91,5	82,5	83,5	109,6	109,7
Textile and clothing	62,5	63,8	61,8	63,9	101,2	99,8
Food and beverages	74,8	75,8	85,5	83,2	87,5	91,1

Source: see note n.6

It is evident that, notwithstanding the unification throughout the country of contractual wage norms, a de-facto difference in labour costs exists between the two areas: these are due to the differential entity of the wage drift, i.e. the surplus of actual over contractual wages, to the effect of policy measures, such as the partial relief of social insurance contributions in the less favoured area, and composition effects, such as the higher percentage of workers being presumably classified in the lower segments of the qualification ladder.[7] From the point of view of pro-capita wage costs, therefore, a differential encouraging factor mobility should already exist, and further differentiation of the minimum contractual wage standards may have presumably only a marginal effect. However, from the data on pro-capita value added, we see that cost differentials are being matched almost in an equivalent measure by productivity differentials, so as to make cost of labour per unit of value added more or less equal between the two areas. Dualism does not appear as the effect of applying equal wages to industrial sectors with different productivity and thus reducing labour demand potential in the backward area; but intrinsically originating from a structural and technological gap.

[6] Ditta, L., R.Padovani: "Regioni meridionali e sviluppo industriale degli anni ottanta", in "Rivista economica del Mezzogiorno", forthcoming.

[7] A "shift and share" exercise is performed in the work in footnote 6, for separating sectoral composition and differential dynamics' effects in the evolution of North/South gap in revenues and productivity.

This gap has remained at almost the same level over the period considered here. Wage differentials, given costs of mobility, are not sufficient to encourage labour mobility out of, and given productivity differentials, are not sufficient to encourage capital mobility into the Mezzogiorno. This deadlock is, we believe, at the heart of the Italian regional problem.

Appendix

The functional form for extrapolation has been chosen after trials over the following alternatives:

Straight Line	$Y = a + b*t$
Quadratic Curve	$Y = a + b*t + c*t^2$
Exponential Curve	$Y = e^{(a + b*t)}$
Logarithmic Curve	$Y = a * \log(b*t)$
Hyperbolic Curve A	$Y = a + b/t$
Hyperbolic Curve B	$Y = 1 / (a + b*t)$
Hyperbolic Curve C	$Y = t / (a + b*t)$
Power of t	$Y = a * t^b$

Several criteria for the quality of fit of estimated to effective values have been considered and the plausibility of extrapolations for activity rates, in particular for females, has also been qualitatively evaluated.

The chosen function are as from the following tables 8, 9, and 9a.

Table 8: Extrapolation functions - Functional forms

	Extrapolation functions			
Age Group	Males		Females	
	North-Center	South	North-Center	South
14 -19	$Y = a + bt$	$Y = a + bt$	$Y = a + bt$	Constant at average values
20 - 24	Constant at average values	Constant at average values	$Y = at$	$Y = a + bt$
25 - 29	$Y = a + bt + ct$	$Y = a + bt$	$Y = a + bt + ct$	$Y = a + bt$
30 - 39	$Y = a + bt$	$Y = a + bt$	$Y = at$	$Y = a + bt$
40 - 49	$Y = 1 / (a + bt)$	$Y = a + bt$	$Y = at$	$Y = 1 / (a + bt)$
50 - 59	$Y = 1 / (a + bt)$	$Y = 1 / (a + bt)$	$Y = a + bt + ct$	$Y = a + bt$
60 - 64	$Y = a + bt$	$Y = a + bt$	$Y = at$	Constant at end of period values
65 - 70	$Y = a\log(bt)$	$Y = 1 / (a + bt)$	$Y = a\log(bt)$	$Y = at^b$

Table 9: Extrapolation functions - Estimation results

Males - North Center				
Age Group	Function	Adjusted R-square	Standard deviation	Standard error of forecast
14 -19	Y = 36,4 - 0,84X	0.88	3.47	1.16
20 - 24	Constant at average values	-	-	-
25 - 29	$Y = 95{,}2 - 0{,}5X + 0{,}01X^2$	0.96	1.32	0.26
30 - 39	Y = 98,6 - 0,14X	0.86	0.43	0.16
40 - 49	Y = 1 / (0,01 + 0,000009X)	0.87	0.35	0.12
50 - 59	Y = 1 / (0,01 + 0,000104X)	0.95	2.65	0.56
60 - 64	Y = 37,2 - 0,29X	0.50	1.51	1.02
65 - 70	Y = 0,0013log(-3,12713X)	0.90	2.50	0.70

Males - South				
Age Group	Function	Adjusted R-square	Standard deviation	Standard error of forecast
14 -19	Y = 32,26 - 0,48X	0.75	2.10	1.02
20 - 24	Constant at average values	-	-	-
25 - 29	Y = 92,79 - 0,27X	0.73	1.21	0.61
30 - 39	Y = 98,56 - 0,14X	0.96	0.56	0.11
40 - 49	Y = 96,6 - 0,07X	0.40	0.37	0.28
50 - 59	Y = 1 / (0,012 + 0,00005X)	0.85	1.30	0.48
60 - 64	Y = 45,21 - 0,27X	0.40	1.58	1.23
65 - 70	Y = 1 / (0,05 + 0,0018X)	0.89	1.92	0.61

Table 9a: Extrapolation functions - Estimation results

Females - North Center				
Age Group	Function	Adjusted R-square	Standard deviation	Standard error of forecast
14 -19	Y = 36,19 - 0,81X	0.87	3.30	1.17
20 - 24	Y = 65,03X	0.87	1.94	0.66
25 - 29	Y = 56,58 + 2,0X - 0,05X	0.98	5.31	0.66
30 - 39	Y = 42,26X	0.96	7.50	1.47
40 - 49	Y = 42,26X	0.88	5.04	1.67
50 - 59	Y = 26,64 + 0,05X + 0,01X	0.89	0.61	0.19
60 - 64	Y = 10,69X	0.35	0.50	0.39
65 - 70	Y = 0,0019log(-0,97X)	0.81	0.80	0.33

Females - South				
Age Group	Function	Adjusted R-square	Standard deviation	Standard error of forecast
14 -19	Y = 37,76 + 1,08X	0.90	4.38	1.31
20 - 24	Constant at average values	-	-	-
25 - 29	Y = 38,7 + 0,87X	0.82	3.69	1.49
30 - 39	Y = 34,51 + 1,15X	0.97	4.50	0.70
40 - 49	Y = 1 / (0,03 + 0,0004X)	0.89	2.23	0.71
50 - 59	Y = 27,4 - 0,1X	0.30	0.62	0.50
60 - 64	Constant at end of period values			
65 - 70	Y = 5,61X	0.61	0.64	0.38

Macroeconomic Consequences of a Labour Supply Shock. A Simulation Study of the Austrian Experience in 1990 and 1991

Karl Pichelmann and Michaela Schamschule*

Institute for Advanced Studies, Vienna

1 Introduction

In recent years issues of international migration have been pushed to the forefront of economic policy agenda in many European countries. After stagnating during the first half of the Eighties, migrant flows into Western Europe have increased substantially in the second part of the decade. Even Southern European countries like Italy, Spain and Portugal, which used to be traditional sending countries of migrant workers, have now become net immigration countries. Additionally, the already apparent rise in migration pressures from developing countries is likely to be strongly accerbated by the emergence of new sending countries in Eastern Europe.

The increased flow of immigration into Western Europe has met with growing efforts to limit the number of immigrants by establishing more effective entry controls. To some extent, these policies have been motivated by increasing difficulties regarding the social and cultural integration of migrants in the receiving countries; but the mounting migration pressures have also raised serious concerns about the effects of immigration on the earnings and employment opportunities of the destination countries' resident population.

Against this background this chapter tries to adress some of the macroeconomic implications of a rapid increase in foreign labour supply for the receiving country's economy using the Austrian experience in 1990/1991 as a potentially illuminating example. The chapter is organized as follows: In section 2 we sketch the basic economic reasoning with respect to the effects of immigration on native well-being and review briefly some of the available empirical evidence most of which refers to the U.S. In section 3 we focus on the rapid inflow of foreign labour into Austria in 1990 and

* Revised version of a paper presented at the University of Siena, November 1991. We are indebted to Franz Hof and several other conference participants for helpful comments and suggestions. Of course, the usual disclaimer applies.

1991. We characterise the institutional and legal setting of foreign employment in Austria and, then, proceed to analyse the impact effects of a labour supply shock on aggregate output, productivity, earnings and employment using ex-post simulation of a large-scale econometric model of the Austrian economy. Finally, section 4 offers some tentative conclusions.

2 A brief background discussion

A common approach of the immigration-welfare literature models immigration flows as exogenous shifts in the supply of labour to geographically defined labour markets. Under standard neoclassical assumptions, the following propositions regarding the economic consequences of such labour supply shocks in the receiving country can be derived (Berry and Soligo 1969; Greenwood and McDowell 1986; Meier and Wenig 1992):

- the wage rate declines: Immigrant workers enlarge the existing labour force in the receiving country and, therefore, exert downward pressure on real wages. The magnitude of the decline of the wage rate depends upon the elasticities of domestic labour supply and labour demand and may also be affected by the existence of immigration quotas.

- total employment rises: Lower real wages lead to higher overall employment in the receiving country.

- native employment declines: Assuming that immigrants are willing to work at lower wages, they will partly displace the native labour force. The displacement effects will tend to be greater the more elastic the domestic labour supply and the less elastic the labour demand.

- total native labour earnings decline: As a result of the lower wage rate and non-negative displacement effects, the natives' total income from labour declines. However, depending on capital endowments some of the natives will be more than compensated by increased interest income, while other wage earners will suffer because their decline in labour earnings is not offset by an increase in capital income.

- total returns on capital rise: The increase in the labour force changes the capital-labour ratio inducing a shift in the wage-interest ratio.

- total output increases: Inflows of labour (and capital) into the country of immigration result in increased economic activity and, therefore, higher total output.

- earlier immigrants' income may decline: Given that their skills are similar to those of the new immigrants or that they compete for the same jobs, earlier immigrants are likely to experience declining wage rates as a result of inflows of new migrant labour into their local labour market.

The basic message from this literature is that immigration, in general, raises native well-being. Clearly, there may be winners and losers and the average income of the whole economy may fall, but the change in total native income is predicted to be positive. In principle, therefore, compensation mechanisms could be designed that make everybody better-off. Thus, there exists a complete analogy with free trade arguments; indeed, under standard assumptions trade in goods and factors are perfect substitutes, producing the same outcomes. It should be noted, though, that standard economic analysis may fail to take account of the full costs of immigration given that an increased inflow of foreigners may give rise to negative consumption and production externalities or may meet with resistance by the resident population because of differences in social and cultural norms (Freeman 1993).

Yet, labour supply shocks do not only put pressure on real wages, they also result in a restructuring of employment. In general, the overall level of employment will be rising. However, unless all additional labour is fully absorbed by the economy, the receiving country is likely to experience rising unemployment rates, at least in the short run. Unemployment induced by substitution processes between different groups of workers may affect both natives and early immigrants. In particular, since today most Western European countries experience inflows of rather unskilled labour the most pronounced labour market effects should be observed at the lower end of the wage (and productivity) distribution. Therefore, many recent studies concentrate on the welfare effects of immigration on the less-skilled and the less-experienced resident population.

Most of the empirical literature investigates the welfare effects of immigration in the United States where immigration has always been an important component of demographic changes and where plenty of data is available. Although immigrant inflows accounted for only five percent of the growth in the US labour supply in the last two decades, they were heavily concentrated in certain areas and skill groups. This fact can be exploited in empirical analyses.

The effects of immigration on the wage rate have recently been studied by LaLonde and Topel. The hypothesis tested was that "the largest impact of immigration on wages and employment must be for individuals who are good substitutes for new immigrants in terms of both location and skills" (LaLonde and Topel 1991, p. 301). Empirical estimates were performed for the immigration effects on wages and employment of three groups of the native population that were regarded as substitution-prone, namely young blacks, Hispanic natives and recent immigrants. However, contrary to their expectations, the estimates revealed that the increased inflows of migrant labour had only minor negative effects on the wage rate of the less-skilled native population. Butcher and Card (1991) investigated the wage effects of labour supply shocks on various percentiles of the wage distribution. Their calculations confirm by and large the above mentioned results.

Even if the effects of immigration on the receiving country's wage rates turn out to be small, the per capita income of the resident population may decline as a result of increased unemployment. If the immigration of labour reduces the annual weeks of employment of natives and earlier immigrants, the empirical analyses should reveal a decline in the annual per capita income of those groups of the population that are most easily substituted for by migrant labour.

Altonji and Card (1991) investigated the employment effects of immigration on less-skilled natives in the United States. In a comparison of high- and low-immigrant cities they found evidence for significant displacement effects between immigrants and less-skilled natives. In particular, the estimates showed very strong displacement effects for black females without college education. For less-skilled white women and white men the displacement effects were less pronounced. With respect to industry composition, adverse effects on labour force participation rates and employment rates of the less-skilled native population were found particularly in the low-wage service industry, in agriculture and manufacturing.

Thus, the overall picture emerging from cross-sectional analyses of high- and low-immigration areas in the US seems to be that some groups of unskilled natives may well have been subjected to significant displacement processes, but, in general, that immigrant flows have had only modest adverse effects on native wages and employment. It should be noted, however, that city comparisons may tend to underestimate the effects of immigration in case that local labour supply shocks are quickly transmitted to other areas via a high degree of induced factor mobility flows.

3 Immigration and the Austrian labour market in 1990/1991

3.1 The institutional framework for the employment of foreigners

Until recently, Austria did not have a separate immigration law. This may seem surprising as migration has always played an important role in the Austrian economy. However, within the general framework of international and constitutional law there exist several Austrian laws and decrees that regulate specific aspects of migration.

The "Passgesetz" and the "Grenzkontollgesetz" regulate the process of entry and exit of the Austrian territory. It applies to citizens and aliens likewise. The "Niederlassungsgesetz" specifies the requirements for obtaining a residence permit and defines the rights and obligations in connection with the permit. The "Fremdenpolizeigesetz" regulates the rights and duties of aliens residing within the Austrian territory. The "Ausländerbeschäftigungsgesetz" determines the central aspects of the employment of foreigners on the Austrian labour market. Finally, the "Staatsbürgerschaftsgesetz" regulates the granting of the Austrian citizenship to foreigners.

The Austrian authorities issue several types of labour market permits which allow foreigners to take up gainful activities within the Austrian territory. In general, the issuing of permits is conditional upon the fulfillment of some general and individual requirements, and the validity of the permits is limited to a certain period of time, a restricted territory or a particular occupation.

Employment permits with a maximum duration of one year are issued to employers and, thereby, restrict the foreign worker's employment to a particular job. In case of short-time work or layoffs employment permits are to be cancelled with priority, which enables the authorities to react quickly to changes in labour market conditions. Employment permits are renewable before the expiry. If the foreign worker wants to engage in a new employment relation or if an employment spell was interrupted for more than six months, a new employment permit has to be applied for (Coulon 1991; BMAS 1991).

Exemption certificates ("Befreiungsschein") facilitate the integration of foreigners who have been employed in Austria for a period of five or more years. Exemption certificates put the foreign workers on an equal footing with Austrian citizens in the sense that they are entitled to choose freely their occupation, employment, place of work and employer. The validity of the exemption certificate is limited to five years; extensions are possible. Special regulations for "second generation" foreign workers give them easier access to exemption certificates. However,certain reqirements regarding length of stay in Austria and/or schooling in Austria have to be fulfilled.

Work permits ("Arbeitserlaubnis") introduced in 1990 have an intermediate status between the traditional forms of employment permit and exemption certificate. Designed to facilitate the process of integration, this instrument creates greater job mobility insofar that work permits allow for job mobility within the federal state where the previous job was located. Work permits are granted for a maximum period of two years and may be renewed before expiry.

The 1990 amendment to the Law on the Employment of Foreigners introduced the concept of a national quota ("Bundeshöchstzahl") setting an upper limit to foreign labour force participation in Austria. The amendment rules that the nation-wide share of foreign labour supply must not exceed 10 per cent of (last year's) total labour supply.

For 1991, the national quota for foreign labour force participation - based on the estimated 1991 overall potential labour force - was set at 308,000 permits. If this absolute national limit is reached, no additional permits are to be issued. By the end of December 1990, 289,095 permits had already been issued. Therefore, 93.8 percent of the national quota for foreign labour force participation were already used (Nowotny 1991).

In addition, a specific quota-system allocates 92 per cent of the nation-wide upper limit among the nine Austrian federal states by decree of the Minister for Labour and Social Affairs. With the exception of Vienna, all federal quotas were fully exhausted in October 1991.

In the so-called regular procedure ("Normalverfahren") the local labour market office decides about applications for permits conditional on the local labour market situation and after consultation with representatives of the social partners. The 1990 amendment to the Law on the Employment of Foreigners introduced a concept of priority ("Prioritätenkatalog") determining that new employment permits should not be issued unless vacant jobs could not be filled with other job seekers according to the following ranking: natives, recognized asylants, foreigners holding exemption certificates, foreigners entitled to social security benefits, foreigners subject to special considerations (for example, family members of guestworkers that have been working in Austria for a long time), refugees that have applied for asylum (Nowotny 1991; Coulon 1991). Thus, the concept of priority tries to protect the resident work-force from the competition of newly arrived immigrant labour and puts a brake on the inflow of foreign workers (Nowotny 1991).

The flexibility of the system is enhanced by the regulation that by decree of the Minister for Labour and Social Affairs special quotas may be set for limited periods and specific sectors ("Kontingentverfahren", procedure using contingents). Within these quotas, no special consideration of the local labour market situation is necessary unless the federal quota is surpassed.

Finally, the differences between the sum of the federal quotas (284,000 in 1991) and the nation-wide quota (308,000 in 1991) serve as an overdraft facility for all federal states ("Überziehungsreserve"). When a federal quota is already exhausted, employment permits may nonetheless be granted upon approval of the labour market agency and after consultation with representatives of the social partners ("Kontingent-Überziehungsverfahren"). Indeed, by the end of October 1991, 20,832 employment permits of a total overdraft facility of 24,000 had been issued.

3.2 The effects of a labour supply shock: A simulation analysis

After a period of sluggish growth in 1986/87, the Austrian economy entered into a boom phase in 1988. Fuelled by both foreign and domestic demand real GDP growth attained rates of 4 to 4 1/2 per cent in the period 1988-1990 and showed only a modest decline to 3 per cent in 1991. With the usual lag due to pro-cyclical productivity developments, the strong expansion of output was accompanied by a sharp rise in the demand for labour. Growth of total dependent employment was 1.8 per cent in 1989, accelerating to 2.3 per cent both in 1990 and 1991. However, while the rate of unemployment had fallen to 5 per cent in 1989, it rose by almost one percentage point in the course of the two subsequent years. Obviously, in a mechanical accounting sense the rapid employment growth in 1990/1991 had been outpaced by an unusually fast expansion of the labour force, mainly due to massive inflows of foreign workers.

Several economic and institutional factors may have combined to account for the sharp increase in foreign labour supply at the turn of the decade. The rapid expansion of output and employment gave rise to tighter labour market conditions, confronting firms with increasing difficulties to fill vacant jobs at given wages; indeed, econometric estimates seem to indicate that the Austrian unemployment rate was already close to the NAIRU in 1989 (Pichelmann 1993). Thus, demand-pull elements attracting migrant labour have certainly played a major role in the rapid build-up of the foreign labour supply. However, several institutional regulations facilitating immigration and foreign employment, e.g. efforts to integrate the growing number of refugees and asylum-seekers, more generous procedures regarding family unification, and, in particular, the introduction of a new nation-wide quota system (see section 3.1.), seem to have been important contributing factors as well.

Anyway, as a result foreign labour supply in Austria increased sharply by some 100 000 workers in the period 1990/1991 pushing the share of foreign labour in the total labour force from about 6 per cent to more than 9 per cent within two years. It may be interesting to note that, contrary to widespread public perceiptions about the major source countries, two thirds of the additional foreign workers originated from the traditional guestworker countries Yugoslavia and Turkey. Immigrants from the CSFR, Hungary and Poland, on the other hand, accounted for only about 10 per cent of the inflow of migrant labour.

The following assessment of the macroeconomic effects of the sketched inflow of foreign workers is based upon simulation analysis of a large-scale macroeconometric model of the Austrian economy. The model has been built at the Institute for Advanced Studies and is in regular use to produce the Institute`s quarterly forecasts for the Austrian economy. The model consists of approximately 400 equations and may well be characterized as a fairly conventional Keynesian macro model incorporating some neoclassical elements, in particular with respect to the detrmination of potential output and the derivation of factor demand relations. Another important feature of the model is the sluggish adjustment of wages and prices to output gaps and/or to deviations of actual unemployment from its equilibrium level.

The scenario for the simulation anlysis has been designed as follows. As a starting point a reference model solution was produced for the period 1990-1995 using realized values for 1990 and 1991 and forecast values thereafter. In the simulation exercise foreign labour supply was reduced by 50 000 in 1990 and another 60 000 in 1991. For the convenience of the reader we then simply use the simulation solution of the model as a baseline which is compared with the reference model solution over the entire period of analysis.

The results of our simulation exercise clearly demonstrate the transmission mechanisms of a labour supply shock affecting both the demand side and the supply side of the economy. The sharp rise in labour supply puts downward pressure on wages and, despite some moderating impact on price inflation as well, results in a reduction of real wages compared to the baseline. The negative impact upon wages is mitigated to some extent by a reduction in domestic labour supply induced by the deterioration of employment prospects, but this effect turns out to be quantitatively of minor importance. The reduction in wages, however, does not fully translate into a decrease in unit labour costs in the medium run because of induced productivity effects with labour productivity falling below the baseline. The potential output of the economy, however, has unambigously increased. The demand side effects turn out to be favourable as well. While private consumption remains nearly unaffected, both investment and net exports respond positively to the labour supply shock due to an increase in profitability and improvements in relative competitiveness. In summary, according to our estimates GDP was raised by one quarter of a percentage point in the short-run and by about three quarters of a percentage point in the medium run. However, these positive outcomes have to be weighed against a significant increase in unemployment and, last not least, against a reduction in per capita GDP.

Table 1: Macroeconomic implications of the labour supply shock 1990/91

	Deviation from the Baseline Short-Run	Medium-Run
	in per cent	
Gross Wages per Employee	- 0.7	- 3.7
Unit Labour Costs	- 0.7	- 2.7
Labour Productivity	-	- 0.7
Capital Productivity	+ 0.2	+ 0.6
GDP	+ 0.2	+ 0.8
GDP per capita	- 0.8	- 1.3
	in 1000s	
Domestic Labour Supply	- 5	- 15
Employment	+ 5	+ 49
Unemployment	+ 39	+ 45

4 Concluding remarks

This paper has discussed some of the macroeconomic consequences of a rapid increase in labour supply using the Austrian experience in 1990 and 1991 as a potentially illuminating example. We conclude from our analysis that the rapid increase in foreign labour while definitely stimulating aggregate growth of the Austrian economy has been associated with mounting distributional pressures reflected inter alia in a significant increase of unemployment. These effects of immigration on the distribution of income may be part of an explanation for the wide-spread resistance of the resident population against rapid increases of foreign labour. In our view, any sustainable immigration policy must therefore be complemented by a reasonable redistribution of the overall gains from immigration.

References

Altonji J.G. and Card D. (1991): The Effects of Immigration on the Labor Market Outcomes of Less-Skilled Natives, in: Abowd J.M. and Freeman R.B., *Immigration, Trade, and the Labor Market*, The University of Chicago Press, Chicago, pp. 201-234.

Bundesministerium für Arbeit und Soziales (1991): *Ausländerbeschäftigung 1990*, Wien.

Butcher K.F.and Card D. (1991): Immigration and Wages: Evidence from the 1980's, in: *American Economic Review, Papers and Proceedings*, vol. 81, no. 2, pp. 292-296.

Coulon J. (1991): *Ausländer im Österreichischen Recht*, Verlag Orac, Wien.

Freeman, R.B. (1993): Immigration from poor to wealthy countries. Experience of the United States, in: *European Economic Review* 37, pp. 443-451.

Greenwood M.and McDowell J. (1986): The Factor Market Consequences of US Immigration, in: *Journal of Economic Literature*, vol. 24, December 1986, pp. 1738-1772.

Lalonde R.J. and Topel R.H. (1991a): Immigrants in the American Labor Market: Quality, Assimilation, and Distributional Effects, in: *American Economic Review, Papers and Proceedings*, vol. 81, no. 2, pp. 297-302.

Lalonde R.J. and Topel R.H. (1991b): Labor Market Adjustments to Increased Immigration, in: Abowd J.M. and Freeman R.B., *Immigration, Trade, and the Labor Market*, The University of Chicago Press, Chicago, pp. 167-199.

Meier V. and Wenig A. (1992): Welfare Implications of International Labor Migration, Paper presented at the Vienna conference on Migration, March 1992.

Nowotny I. (1991): Ausländerbeschäftigung in Österreich, Die Gesamtproblematik und aktuelle Situation, in: *WISO* 14/1, pp. 37-63.

Pichelmann K. (1993): *Die Bekämpfung der Arbeitslosigkeit in den OECD Staaten aus der Sicht Österreichs*. Studie im Auftrag des BM für Finanzen, Paris-Wien, mimeo.

V. Macroeconomic Theory

Imported Material Price Shocks under Alternative Wage Regimes

HELMUT FRISCH * - FRANZ X. HOF *

1. *Introduction*

The effects of a foreign raw material price shock on a small open economy depend in a critical way on the reaction of domestic real producer wages. The recent oil price shock (1990) stimulates a renewed interest in the question how wage policy should react to such an external supply shock. In response to the first and second oil shock the OECD countries pursued a wide diversity of wage policies. In two studies, Marston and Turnovsky (1983, 1985) shed light on this issue by developing a model that distinguishes between three targets of wage policy, namely, stabilizing real consumer wages, stabilizing the level of employment, and stabilizing the level of real income. They find that the effects of a foreign material price shock on the domestic economy differ according to these three wage policies.

Their results suggest the following ranking: gross output falls most when real consumer wages are stabilized. When employment is stabilized, gross output falls, but less so than in the former case. When the level of real income is stabilized, gross output actually rises. Under each target of wage policy the responses of the *real* variables are the same whether the exchange rate is fixed or allowed to float.

Noticeably missing from Marston and Turnovsky's list of wage policy targets is the case of nominal wage rigidity. This omission may be important because the applied literature suggests that although rigid real wages may be appropriate for European economies, nominal wage rigidity may be more appropriate for the US[1].

In the present paper we examine the case of nominal wage rigidity within the context of the Marston - Turnovsky model. We find

* University of Technology Vienna, Institute of Economics, Karlsplatz 13, A-1040 Vienna (Austria).

[1] Studies examining this issue include Branson and Rotemberg (1980), Bruno and Sachs (1981, 1985).

Originally published in Economic Notes by Monte dei Paschi di Siena
Vol. 20, n. 2-1991.

that the case of nominal wage rigidity gives rise to complications not found in the Marston - Turnovsky analysis. This is because the results are no longer independent of the exchange rate regime and because they depend fundamentally on the elasticity of substitution between imported materials and the domestic factors of production as well as upon the parameters of the money demand function. These complications lead us to consider the following six cases:

1) Stabilizing real income

2) Stabilizing employment

3) Rigid nominal wages and flexible exchange rates (low interest elasticity of money demand)

4) Stabilizing real consumer wages

5) Rigid nominal wages and flexible exchange rates (high interest elasticity of the demand for money)

6) Rigid nominal wages and fixed exchange rates.

The main finding of this paper is that we are able to rank these six cases according to the magnitude of the output response due to the foreign raw material price shock. We find that in case 1), where real income is stabilized, a foreign price shock has a positive effect on domestic output. In the other cases domestic output falls, where the magnitude of change becomes greater as we move from case 2) to case 6). As such, the strongest negative output effect occurs in the case of rigid nominal wages and fixed exchange rates. In ranking the cases 1), 2), 4), and 6) we make use of a simple AS - AD diagram. However, the case of "rigid nominal wages under flexible exchange rates" cannot be ranked without examining the reduced form equations. It is this result that leads us to distinguish cases 3) and 5).

The rest of this paper is organized as follows: the framework of the model is outlined in section 2; for each wage policy the corresponding aggregate supply function is derived. In section 3 we discuss the effects of a foreign material price shock on the domestic economy using a simple diagram. In section 4 we consider the complete ranking of the six cases analyzed in this paper by means of the reduced form equations. The main conclusions are summarized in section 5.

2. *The Model*

2.1 *The Production Sector*

Domestic gross output Z_t is produced with labor L_t, fixed capital K_t, and imported raw material N_t. The production function is assumed to take a separable form. Capital and labor combine to produce the domestic value added V_t, by means of a Cobb - Douglas production function. Final domestic output Z_t is produced according to a CES-production function in which V_t and N_t serve as its arguments:

$$V_t = L_t^{(1-a)} \cdot K_t^a \tag{1}$$

$$Z_t = [\beta N_t^{-\rho} + (1-\beta) V_t^{-\rho}]^{-(1/\rho)} \tag{2}$$

The constant elasticity of substitution between N_t and V_t, denoted by $\sigma = 1/(1+\rho)$ is typically less than unity. Bruno and Sachs (1981) report 0.2 as a plausible approximation. Throughout our discussion we shall assume σ to be less than or equal to one ($\sigma \leqslant 1$).

In addition to V_t, two further concepts of real value added have to be distinguished:

$$V'_t = (P_t Z_t - P_t^n N_t) / P_t \tag{3}$$

$$Y_t = (P_t Z_t - P_t^n N_t) / P_t^I = V'_t P_t / P_t^I, \tag{4}$$

where V'_t = value added in terms of the domestic final good, P_t = domestic price of the domestic final good, P_t^n = price of imported raw materials in domestic currency, Y_t = real income defined as value added measured in units of the consumer basket, and P_t^I = domestic consumer price index.

The following analysis is conducted by using log-linear approximations for all functions and equations. Lower case letters will denote the logarithms of the variables. The production functions (1) and (2) then become

$$v_t = (1-a)\, l_t + a k_t \tag{1'}$$

$$z_t = c_1 n_t + c_2 v_t + g_z \tag{2'}$$

where g_z is a constant, $c_1 = \beta (Z_0 / N_0)^\rho$, $c_2 = (1-\beta)(Z_0 / V_0)^\rho$, and hence $0 < c_1 < 1$, $0 < c_2 < 1$, and $c_1 + c_2 = 1$.

The subscript 0 denotes the values of the corresponding variables in the initial equilibrium. Since capital is treated as fixed input, k_t will be ignored for the rest of this paper.

Domestic producers are assumed to maximize profit $P_t Z_t - W_t L_t - P^n_t N_t$ by choosing the variable inputs L_t and N_t; W_t denotes the nominal wage rate. The profit maximizing quantities of labor, imported materials, domestic gross output, and value added are functions of the real producer wage $(w_t - p_t)$ and the domestic real price of imported materials $(p^n_t - p_t)$:

$$(5) \qquad l_t = -\frac{1}{\alpha}(w_t - p_t) - \frac{c_1}{\alpha c_2}(p^n_t - p_t) + h_l$$

$$(6) \qquad n_t = -\frac{(1-\alpha)}{\alpha}(w_t - p_t) - \frac{c_1(1-\alpha) + \sigma\alpha}{\alpha c_2}(p^n_t - p_t) + h_n$$

$$(7) \qquad z_t = -\frac{(1-\alpha)}{\alpha}(w_t - p_t) - \frac{c_1(1-\alpha + \sigma\alpha)}{\alpha c_2}(p^n_t - p_t) + h_z$$

$$(8) \qquad v'_t = -\frac{(1-\alpha)}{\alpha}(w_t - p_t) - \frac{c_1}{\alpha c_2}(p^n_t - p_t) + h_v$$

where h_l, h_n, h_z and h_v are constants. These equations show that all quantities depend negatively upon the real factor costs. It can be further shown that

$$c_1 = (P^n_0 N_0)/(P_0 Z_0) \text{ and } c_2 = (P_0 Z_0 - P^n_0 N_0)/(P_0 Z_0)$$

so that c_1 and c_2 represent the shares of imported raw materials and value added in gross output.

The domestic price of imported materials, p^n_t, can be written as

$$(9) \qquad p^n_t = q^f_t + e_t,$$

where q^f_t is the price of imported materials in foreign currency, and e_t the nominal exchange rate.

The real exchange rate, i.e. the relative price of foreign to domestic final goods, is defined as

(10) $$s_t = (p^f_t + e_t - p_t),$$

p^f_t being the price of the foreign final good in foreign currency.

Denoting the real foreign price of imported materials by

(11) $$\theta_t = q^f_t - p^f_t$$

the domestic real price of imported materials can be written as

(12) $$(p^n_t - p_t) = \theta_t + s_t$$

According to (12) an increase in θ_t is attenuated by a real appreciation of the domestic currency and reinforced by a real depreciation, i.e. by a rise in the real exchange rate, s_t.

Next we consider the definition of the domestic consumer price index CPI given by

(13) $$p^I_t = \delta p_t + (1 - \delta)(p^f_t + e_t), \qquad 0 < \delta < 1,$$

where δ denotes the share of the domestic final good in the consumption basket.

From equations (10) and (13) it is evident that the relative price $(p_t - p^I_t)$ can be expressed as

(14) $$(p_t - p^I_t) = -(1 - \delta)s_t.$$

2.2 *The Asset Markets and the Demand for Domestic Goods*

We complete the description of the model by specifying the financial asset markets and by introducing the demand for domestic final goods. Domestic residents allocate their financial wealth between domestic money, domestic bonds and foreign bonds. The asset markets are in equilibrium if

(15) $$(m_t - p^I_t) = \gamma_0 + \gamma_1 y_t - \gamma_2 r_t, \qquad 1 \geqslant \gamma_1 > 0, \quad \gamma_2 > 0; \text{ and}$$

(16) $$r_t = r^f_t + (E_t e_{t+1} - e_t),$$

where m_t = domestic nominal money supply, r_t = domestic nominal rate of interest, r_t^f = foreign nominal rate of interest, $E_t e_{t+1}$ = rational expectation of e_{t+1} formed at time t. All the variables are in logarithms, except interest rates.

Equation (15) is the money market equilibrium condition with nominal money supply deflated by the consumer price index and the demand for real balances depending positively upon real income and negatively on the domestic nominal interest rate. The income elasticity of the demand for money is assumed to be less than or equal to one ($\gamma_1 \leqslant 1$). The uncovered interest parity condition (16) expresses the assumption that domestic and foreign bonds are treated as perfect substitutes.

The real demand for the domestic product $(z_t + p_t - p_t^I)$ depends on real domestic income y_t, the expected real rate of interest $[r_t - (E_t p_{t+1}^I - p_t^I)]$ and the real exchange rate s_t:

$$(17) \quad (z_t + p_t - p_t^I) = d_0 + d_1 y_t - d_2 [r_t - (E_t p_{t+1}^I - p_t^I)] + d_3 s_t$$

$$0 < d_1 < 1, \qquad d_2 > 0, \qquad d_3 > 0;$$

where $E_t p_{t+1}^I$ is the rational expectation of p_{t+1}^I formed at time t.

Substituting (10), (12), (13), (14), (16), and

(18)

$$y_t = v'_t + (p_t - p_t^I) = z_t - (c_1/c_2)(1-\sigma)(p_t^n - p_t) + (p_t - p_t^I) + h_y$$

where h_y is a constant, into equation (17), ignoring constant terms and rearranging yields:

$$(19) \qquad z_t = d_5 s_t - \frac{d_1 c_1 (1-\sigma)}{(1-d_1) c_2} \theta_t - \frac{d_2 [r_t^f - (E_t p_{t+1}^f - p_t^f)] + d_2 \delta E_t s_{t+1}}{(1-d_1)},$$

where

$$d_5 := [(1-d_1)(1-\delta) + d_2 \delta + d_3 - d_1 (c_1/c_2)(1-\sigma)] / (1-d_1)$$

is assumed to be positive. Equation (19) is an IS-curve where the domestic nominal rate of interest r_t has been eliminated by taking into account the uncovered interest parity equation; subsequently it will be called aggregate demand curve. (19) states that the demand for the domestic final good z_t depends positively upon the real exchange rate s_t and negatively on the foreign real price of imported raw material θ_t, provided that the elasticity of substitution between N_t and V_t is less than unity (i.e. $\sigma < 1$).

The negative dependence of z_t on θ_t can be explained as follows: in case that $\sigma < 1$ a rise in θ_t leads to a reduction in real income y_t by raising the real value of imported material

$$(20) \qquad n_t + (p_t^n - p_t) = z_t + (1 - \sigma)(p_t^n - p_t) + g_n = \\ = z_t + (1 - \sigma)(s_t + \theta_t) + g_n$$

for any given z_t. The resulting excess supply in the goods market is eliminated by a reduction in z_t.

2.3 *Alternative Wage Policies*

We will now consider four alternative targets of wage policy. Three of them were suggested by Marston and Turnovsky (1983, 1985), namely the stabilization of

1) real consumer wages $(w_t - p_t^I)$,
2) employment l_t,
3) real income y_t,

at their corresponding initial equilibrium values $(w_0 - p_0^I)$, l_0, and y_0. To this list we add the case of

4) nominal wage rigidity (defined by $w_t = w_0$).

2.3.1 *Stabilizing Real Consumer Wages*

If the target of wage policy is to keep the real consumer wage constant so that $(w_t - p_t^I) = (w_0 - p_0^I)$, the real producer wage must be adjusted in accordance with

$$(21) \qquad (w_t - p_t) = (1 - \delta)\, s_t + (w_0 - p_0^I) \qquad \text{(wage rule 1)}$$

Wage rule 1 states that the real consumer wage is kept constant if any variation in the real exchange rate is accompanied by a less than proportionate change in the real producer wage.

By substituting equation (21) into (7) and ignoring constant terms we obtain the aggregate supply function corresponding to wage rule 1:

(7.1)

$$z_t^{s,1} = -\frac{c_2(1-a)(1-\delta) + c_1(1-a+a\sigma)}{ac_2} s_t - \frac{c_1(1-a+a\sigma)}{ac_2}\theta_t$$

An increase in θ_t or s_t raises the real price of imported material $(p_t^n - p_t) = (s_t + \theta_t)$ thereby reducing the firms' demand for labor and raw material as well as their supply of gross output z_t in accordance with (5), (6), and (7).

Note that an increase in s_t leads to a larger reduction in the supply of z_t than a rise in θ_t since under wàge rule 1 any real depreciation of the domestic currency is accompanied by an increase in the real producer wage. This rise in the real price of labor causes an additional reduction in gross output z_t.

2.3.2 *Stabilizing Employment*

Stabilizing employment (defined by $l_t = l_0$) involves setting the real producer wage in accordance with

$$(w_t - p_t) = -(c_1/c_2)(s_t + \theta_t) + a(h_1 - l_0) \quad \text{(wage rule 2)} \tag{22}$$

Employment is maintained if any decrease in the demand for labor caused by an increase in $(s_t + \theta_t) = (p_t^n - p_t)$ is perfectly compensated by an appropriate fall in the real producer wage. The results of section 2 imply that (c_1/c_2) is substantially smaller than unity. Substituting (22) into (7) and ignoring constant terms yields the aggregate supply curve

$$z_t^{s,2} = -\sigma(c_1/c_2)s_t - \sigma(c_1/c_2)\theta_t \tag{7.2}$$

An increase in s_t or θ_t leads to a fall in the domestic gross output z_t, since the reduction in the real producer wage required for stabilizing employment can only partially offset the fall in the demand for imported raw materials.

2.3.3 *Stabilizing Real Income*

It can be shown that both wage rule 1 and wage rule 2 imply a decline in domestic real income if the foreign price of imported materials rises in real terms. Thus as a third target of wage policy we consider the stabilization of real income (defined by $y_t = y_0$). The corresponding wage rule is (ignoring constant terms):

$$(23) \qquad (w_t - p_t) = -\frac{c_1 + c_2 a(1-\delta)}{c_2(1-a)} s_t - \frac{c_1}{c_2(1-a)} \theta_t \qquad \text{(wage rule 3)}$$

A comparison of (22) and (23) shows that under wage rule 3 the required fall in the real producer wage in response to a rise in θ_t (or in s_t) is larger than that implied by wage rule 2.

By substituting (23) into (7) we obtain the corresponding aggregate supply function

$$(7.3) \quad z_t^{s,3} = [(c_1/c_2)(1-\sigma) + (1-\delta)] s_t + (c_1/c_2)(1-\sigma)\theta_t$$

Equation (7.3) shows that the dependence of z_t on s_t and θ_t is reversed. A rise in s_t or θ_t raises the supply of real output z_t. This expansive effect is due to the "extreme" fall in the real producer wage implied by wage rule 3. The resulting rise in employment is large enough to guarantee an increase in gross output regardless of the (ambiguous) reaction of the demand for raw materials[2].

2.3.4 *Constant Nominal Wages*

Constant nominal wages, i.e. $w_t = w_0$, imply that

$$(24) \qquad (w_t - p_t) = (w_0 - p_t)$$

It will be useful for the graphical analysis in the next section to rewrite (24) as

$$(25) \qquad (w_t - p_t) = w_0 + s_t - (p_t^f + e_t) \quad \text{(wage rule 4)}$$

[2] Under wage rule 3 the demand functions for labor and raw materials are given by

$$l_t^{d,3} = \frac{1 - c_2\delta}{c_2(1-a)} s_t + \frac{c_2}{c_2(1-a)} \theta_t, \qquad n_t^{d,3} = \frac{(1-\sigma) - c_2\delta}{c_2} s_t + \frac{c_1 - \sigma}{c_2} \theta_t$$

An increase in s_t leads ceteris paribus to a proportionate increase in the real producer wage. Note that a real depreciation for given values of p_t^f and e_t implies a fall in the domestic price level p_t. Substituting (25) into equation (7) yields the following aggregate supply function

$$(7.4) \qquad z_t^{s,4} = -\frac{(1-\alpha)+c_1\alpha\sigma}{\alpha c_2} s_t - \frac{c_1(1-\alpha+\alpha\sigma)}{\alpha c_2}\theta_t + + \frac{(1-\alpha)}{\alpha}(p_t^f + e_t - w_0)$$

A rise in s_t due to a fall in p_t (as mentioned above) implies an increase in $(w_t - p_t)$ and $(p_t^n - p_t)$. Both effects work into the same direction and lead to a decrease in gross output z_t.

An increase in θ_t raises the real price of imported material $(p_t^n - p_t) = (s_t + \theta_t)$ thereby reducing the supply of z_t.

The last term of (7.4) shows that a nominal depreciation generates ceteris paribus a positive output effect: for a given level of the real exchange rate s_t a rise in e_t implies that the nominal depreciation is perfectly matched by an increase in p_t. This rise in the price of the domestic good has no influence on $(p_t^n - p_t) = (s_t + \theta_t)$ but causes the real producer wage $(w_t - p_t)$ to fall thereby boosting domestic production.

3. *Comparative Statics*

Now we proceed to analyze the effects of an increase in the real foreign price of imported materials, θ_t, on the small open economy under the four different wage rules discussed in the preceding section. In accordance with Marston and Turnovsky (1983, 1985) the following simplifying assumptions are made:

i) The foreign nominal rate of interest, r_t^f, and the price of foreign final goods in foreign currency, p_t^f, are constant. An increase in the real foreign price of imported material, $\theta_t = q_t^f - p_t^f$, thus is due to a rise in the nominal foreign price of imported materials, q_t^f.

ii) Any increase in θ_t is expected to be *transitory* (i.e. it is expected to disappear in the next period). For the model analysed in this paper it can be shown that transitory disturbances do not affect the rational expectations $E_t e_{t+1}$, $E_t p^I_{t+1}$, and $E_t s_{t+1}$ in (16), (17) and (19)[3]. These expectations can be treated as constants and ignored for the further analysis.

The model of section 2 can now be reduced to three equations: the aggregate supply equation (7.i) corresponding to wage rule i, the aggregate demand equation (19′) and the money market equilibrium condition (26)[4].

$$(7.i) \qquad z_t^{s,i} = -\lambda_1^i s_t - \lambda_2^i \theta_t, \qquad i = 1, 2, 3$$

(7.4)

$$z_t^{s,4} = -\frac{(1-a) + c_1 a\sigma}{ac_2} s_t - \frac{c_1(1-a+a\sigma)}{ac_2}\theta_t + \frac{(1-a)}{a}(e_t - w_0)$$

$$(19') \qquad z_t = d_5 s_t - \frac{d_1 c_1 (1-\sigma)}{(1-d_1)c_2}\theta_t$$

$$(26) \quad z_t = [\frac{\delta}{\gamma_1} + \frac{c_1}{c_2}(1-\sigma) + (1+\delta)] s_t - \frac{(1+\gamma_2)}{\gamma_1} e_t + $$
$$+ \frac{1}{\gamma_1} m_t + \frac{c_1}{c_2}(1-\sigma)\theta_t .$$

The results of the comparative statics will be derived by means

[3] Under each wage rule analyzed by Marston and Turnovsky there exists a unique forward looking solution for any endogenous variable x_t. The general form of these solutions is given by

$$x_t = \psi_0^{x,j}\theta_t + \sum_{i=1}^{\infty} \psi_i^{x,j} E_t \theta_{t+i} + \ldots \qquad j = 1, 2, 3$$

where j denotes the number of the wage rule. Leading this solution one period and taking expectations E_t yields

$$E_t x_{t+1} = \sum_{i=0}^{\infty} \psi_i^{x,j} E_t \theta_{t+1+i} + \ldots \qquad j = 1, 2, 3$$

Transitory disturbances in θ_t which are expected to disappear in the next period leave the projections of the future path of the exogenous variable θ (denoted by $E_t \theta_{t+1+i}$; $i \geq 0$) unchanged. Thus they do not affect the rational expectations of the endogenous variables, $E_t x_{t+1}$.

[4] The LM-curve (26) is derived by substituting (10), (12)-(14), and (18) into (15) and ignoring the variables p_t^f, r_t^f, and $E_t e_{t+1}$, which are assumed to remain unchanged.

of graphical representations. For this purpose the equations (7.i), (19′) and (26) are presented in the (z_t, s_t) - plane.

First, we consider the response of the domestic economy to a θ_t – shock under wage rules 1, 2 and 3 by using Fig. 1. Note that the model dichotomizes under each of these wage rules. The aggregate supply function (7.i), where $i = 1, 2$ or 3, and the aggregate demand schedule (19′) determine the equilibrium values of the real variables z_t and s_t independently of the LM-curve (26). The LM-curve determines the nominal exchange rate e_t under a regime of flexible exchange rates or the level of the nominal money supply m_t in the case of fixed exchange rates.

Since we are mainly interested in the reactions of the real variables, which are identical under fixed and flexible exchange rates because of the model's dichotomy, we can ignore the LM-curve in Fig. 1.

A rise in θ_t shifts the positively sloped aggregate demand curve z_0^d to the left to z_1^d provided that $\sigma < 1$. This leftward shift is the same in each of the three cases analyzed in Fig. 1 since the z^d-schedule does not depend on the different wage rules.

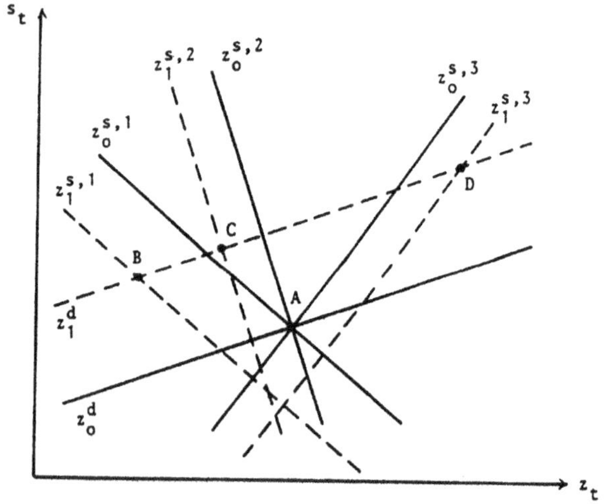

Figure 1

The aggregate supply curves $z^{s,1}$, $z^{s,2}$, and $z^{s,3}$ can be characterized by the following properties:

a) $z^{s,1}$ and $z^{s,2}$ corresponding to wage rule 1 and 2 are negatively sloped; $z^{s,2}$ is steeper (in absolute value) than $z^{s,1}$.

b) An increase in θ_t causes $z^{s,1}$ and $z^{s,2}$ to shift to the left, the leftward shift of $z^{s,2}$ being smaller than that of $z^{s,1}$.

c) $z^{s,3}$ corresponding to the real income target (wage rule 3) is positively sloped. In addition a rise in θ_t causes $z^{s,3}$ to move to the right.

Consider first the case that the objective of wage policy is to stabilize *real consumer wages* (wage rule 1). Since both curves, the z_0^d-schedule and the $z_0^{s,1}$-curve, move to the left to z_1^d and $z_1^{s,1}$ in Fig. 1, z_t necessarily fall while s_t may rise or fall. If σ is "small" so that $\Phi_3 := (\alpha(1-\sigma) - (1-d_1)) > 0$, the new equilibrium depicted by point B is characterized by an increase in s_t. In this case the leftward shift of z^d exceeds that of z^s. The real depreciation implies an increase in the real producer wage according to wage rule 1 $[\Delta(w_t - p_t) = (1-\delta)\Delta s_t]$ and an unambiguous increase in the real price of raw material $[\Delta(p_t^n - p_t) = (\Delta\theta_t + \Delta s_t)]$. As the real prices of both factors of production rise, employment l_t and the input of raw material n_t fall.

Consider next the case where the objective of wage policy is to stabilize *employment* (wage rule 2). If $\sigma < d_1$, the leftward shift of the z^d-curve exceeds that of the $z^{s,2}$-schedule. The decline in output z_t is accompanied by a rise in s_t similarly to the previous case. Note that $\Phi_3 > 0$ is sufficient for $\sigma < d_1$.

The new equilibrium point C lies to the north-east of B indicating that domestic production z_t declines less than under wage rule 1. In addition the real exchange rate s_t will be higher than in the previous case implying that the real price of raw materials $(p_t^n - p_t) = (\theta_t + s_t)$ will be higher too.

The real producer wage $(w_t - p_t)$ is adjusted downwards in accordance with wage rule 2 to keep the level of employment constant. The decline in domestic production z_t results from a reduced input of raw materials n_t.

What are the effects of a raw material price shock if the target of wage policy is to stabilize *real income* (wage rule 3)? A rise in θ_t shifts the (positively sloped) supply curve $z_0^{s,3}$ to the right to $z_1^{s,3}$. The new equilibrium D is characterized by an increase (!) in domestic production z_t and a rise in s_t reinforcing the increase in the domestic real price of raw material $(p_t^n - p_t) = (\theta_t + s_t)$. It can be seen from Fig. 1 that the variables z_t, s_t and $(p_t^n - p_t)$ reach their highest levels under wage rule 3, since D lies to the north-east of both B and C.

Moreover, the decline in the real producer-wage $(w_t - p_t)$ implied by wage rule 3 is stronger than that under wage rule 2. This "extreme" fall in the real wage causes employment l_t and domestic production z_t to rise unambiguously.

To conclude the discussion we analyze the case of *rigid nominal wages* by means of equations (7.4), (19') and (26). In contrast to the former cases (wage rules 1, 2, and 3) the effects of a rise in θ_t on the *real* variables differ depending on whether the domestic economy has fixed or flexible exchange rates.

We begin with a regime of *fixed* exchange rates. It should be noted that the model is again block recursive. The aggregate supply function (7.4) and the aggregate demand function (19') determine the equilibrium values of the real variables z_t and s_t. The LM-curve (26) determines the domestic money supply m_t.

The analysis can be carried out as shown by Fig. 2. An increase in θ_t shifts both the supply curve $z_0^{s,4}$ as well as the aggregate demand curve z_0^d to the left to $z_1^{s,4}$ and z_1^d. The new equilibrium point is E_{fix}. Output falls while the effect on s_t is uncertain. A necessary and sufficient condition for a real depreciation of the domestic currency is $\Phi_3 > 0$. In this case the leftward shift of the z^d-curve exceeds that of the $z^{s,4}$-curve.

In addition Fig. 2 provides a ranking of the effects of a θ_t-shock in the cases of stabilizing real consumer wages (wage rule 1) and rigid nominal wages with fixed exchange rates. To make a comparison possible we have to draw the supply surve $z^{s,1}$ into Fig. 2. An inspection of equations (7.1) and (7.4) shows that

i) the slope of $z^{s,1}$ (in absolute value) exceeds that of the $z^{s,4}$-schedule

ii) the increase in θ_t shifts both $z^{s,1}$ and $z^{s,4}$ to the same extent to the left.

Thus, the new equilibrium E_{fix} lies always to the left of point B provided that $\Phi_3 > 0$. Moreover, Fig. 1 implies that E_{fix} must also lie to the left of C and D.

To sum up the graphical results for $\Phi_3 > 0$, a rise in θ_t causes the strongest negative effect on domestic output and employment in the case of rigid nominal wages under a regime of fixed exchange rates.

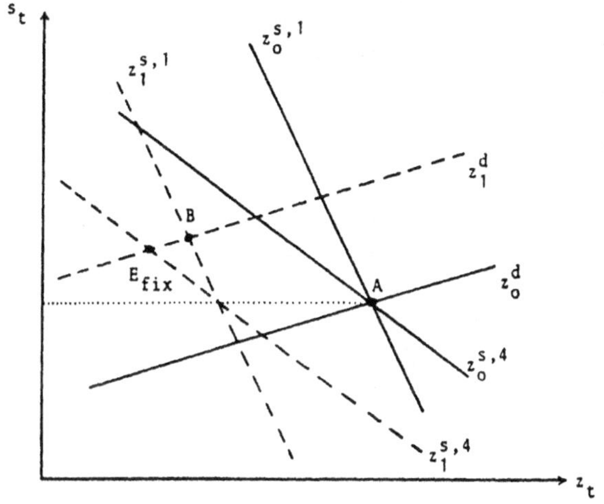

Figure 2

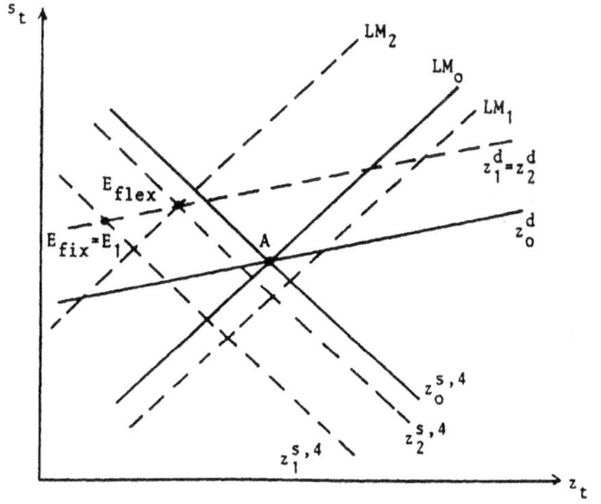

Figure 3

If we consider *flexible* exchange rates the model does not dichotomize. In this case the three equations (7.4), (19') and (26) determine simultaneously z_t, s_t and e_t. In the graphical analysis carried out in Fig. 3 the LM-curve (26) must explicitly be taken into consideration[5]. The impact effect of an increase in θ_t shifts the $z_0^{s,4}$-curve and the z_0^d-schedule to the left to $z_1^{s,4}$ and z_1^d as well as the LM_0-curve downwards to LM_1. The new equilibrium in the goods market E_1 which is identical with E_{fix} lies above the LM_1-curve in a zone of excess supply in the money market. To eliminate the disequilibrium the interest rate has to fall and the nominal exchange rate e_t to rise. This depreciation of the domestic currency shifts the LM_1-curve upwards and to the left to LM_2. In contrast to the former cases also the supply curve $z_1^{s,4}$ moves upwards to $z_2^{s,4}$. The new equilibrium is found on an unchanged z_1^d-curve at E_{flex}.

The new equilibrium with flexible exchange rates lies to the right of the point $E_1 = E_{fix}$. The nominal depreciation dampens the negative output effect, but the overall effect of a rise in θ_t will remain negative.

4. *Comparison of the Effects*

From Fig. 1 and 2 an unambiguous ranking of the equilibrium points E_{fix}, B, C, and D corresponding to rigid nominal wages under *fixed* exchange rates and to the cases of stabilizing real consumer wages, employment and real income has been derived. However, this graphical analysis does not provide an unambiguous ranking of E_{flex} (the case of rigid nominal wages under *flexible* exchange rates) in relation to B and C. The remainder of this paper will concentrate on this problem.

For this purpose we will start with the reduced form equations for the case of rigid nominal wages and flexible exchange rates. It can be shown that there exists a unique forward looking solution for any

[5] In Fig. 3 the slope of the z^d-schedule is smaller than that of the LM-curve. This situation arises if

$$d_2 \delta + d_3 > (c_1 / c_2)(1 - \sigma) + (\delta / \gamma_1)(1 - d_1)$$

This inequality holds if d_3 is sufficiently large implying that domestic and foreign final goods are near substitutes.

endogenous variable x_t. The general form of these solutions is given by

$$x_t = a_0^x w_t + \sum_{i=1}^{\infty} a_i^x E_t w_{t+i} + b_0^x \theta_t + \sum_{i=1}^{\infty} b_i^x E_t \theta_{t+i} \tag{27}$$

As in this paper only transitory changes in w_t and θ_t are considered the expectations $E_t w_{t+i}$ and $E_t \theta_{t+i}$ (for $i \geqslant 1$) can be regarded as constants and ignored for the further analysis. For the following discussion we will use the simplified representation

$$x_t = a^x w_t + b^x \theta_t \tag{27'}$$

The coefficients a^x and b^x of the reduced form (27') are summarized in Appendix I.

Under the assumptions of this analysis (described in Appendix II) one can derive the following signs for the reduced form coefficients ("multipliers") a^x:

$$a^x > 0 \quad \text{for} \quad x = (w - p),\ (w - p^I),\ e,\ p,\ \text{and}\ p^I \tag{28}$$

$$a^x < 0 \quad \text{for} \quad x = l,\ n,\ z,\ v',\ y,\ (p^n - p),\ \text{and}\ s \tag{29}$$

(28) indicates that a rise in the nominal wage w_t leads to a rise in the producer- and consumer real wage and to an increase in nominal variables as the nominal exchange rate, the domestic price level and the consumer price index. From (29) follows that employment, the input of raw material, domestic gross output, and real income fall as a consequence of a rise in nominal wages. It also implies a decline in the domestic real price of imported materials and in the real exchange rate.

In addition equation (27') can be used to derive the reduced form equations under wage rules 1, 2, and 3 (in the case of flexible exchange rates): stabilizing the target variable $T_t\,[T = (w - p^I),\ l,\ y]$ implies that according to (27')

$$\Delta T_t = a^T \Delta w_t + b^T \Delta\theta_t = 0\,, \tag{30}$$

where: $\Delta T_t := T_t - T_0$, $\Delta w_t := w_t - w_0$, and $\Delta\theta_t := \theta_t - \theta_0$.

From (30) it is obvious that this policy involves adjusting the nominal wage w_t to changes in θ_t in accordance with

$$\left.\frac{\Delta w_t}{\Delta\theta_t}\right|_{\Delta T = 0} = -\,(b^T / a^T) \tag{31}$$

Inserting (31) into (27′) yields the reaction of any endogenous variable x_t in case that the target variable T_t is stabilized:

$$(32) \qquad \left.\frac{\Delta x_t}{\Delta \theta_t}\right|_{\Delta T = 0} = -(b^T / a^T)\, a^x + b^x,$$

where $\Delta x_t := x_t - x_0$. The adjustments of the nominal wage w_t to variations in θ_t under wage rules 1, 2, and 3 are described in Appendix III. The rest of this analysis will be based on a ranking of these nominal wage reactions.

If $(\gamma_1 \Phi_1 - \gamma_2 \delta \Phi_3) := \gamma_1[d_2 \delta + d_3 + (1 - \delta)(1 - \sigma)] - \gamma_2 \delta [\alpha(1 - \sigma) - (1 - d_1)] > 0$ the ranking

$$(33) \qquad \left.\frac{\Delta w_t}{\Delta \theta_t}\right|_3 < \left.\frac{\Delta w_t}{\Delta \theta_t}\right|_2 < \left.\frac{\Delta w_t}{\Delta \theta_t}\right|_4 = 0 < \left.\frac{\Delta w_t}{\Delta \theta_t}\right|_1$$

is obtained, where the subscripts denote the wage rule.

A rise in θ_t leads to a rise in nominal wages under policy rule 1 and to a decline under policy rule 2 and 3. The decline is largest when real income is stabilized (rule 3). For rigid nominal wages $(\Delta w_t / \Delta \theta_t)$ is zero and lies between the two cases of rule 1 and 2.

Note that $\Phi_3 < 0$ (arising for instance if σ is close to unity) is sufficient for $(\gamma_1 \Phi_1 - \gamma_2 \delta \Phi_3) > 0$.

If, on the other hand, $\Phi_3 > 0$, the sign of $(\gamma_1 \Phi_1 - \gamma_2 \delta \Phi_3)$ is still positive as long as γ_2, measuring the responsiveness of the demand for real balances to the interest rate, is not "too high". If γ_2 becomes sufficiently large, the expression $(\gamma_1 \Phi_1 - \gamma_2 \delta \Phi_3)$ becomes negative. This changes the ranking of the effects of a variation in θ_t on the nominal wage by reversing only the results generated under policy 1 and policy 4 so that

$$(34) \qquad \left.\frac{\Delta w_t}{\Delta \theta_t}\right|_3 < \left.\frac{\Delta w_t}{\Delta \theta_t}\right|_2 < \left.\frac{\Delta w_t}{\Delta \theta_t}\right|_1 < 0 = \left.\frac{\Delta w_t}{\Delta \theta_t}\right|_4$$

In this situation a rise in θ_t causes the nominal wage to fall not only under wage rule 2 and 3 but also under wage rule 1.

Subsequently we will assume that $(\gamma_1 \Phi_1 - \gamma_2 \delta \Phi_3) > 0$ and $\Phi_3 > 0$ (in accordance with Figures 1, 2, and 3). In this case we can use the ranking of the nominal wages given by (33) to derive the ranking for the main endogenous variables. Equation (27') implies that the endogenous variables x_t which depend positively upon the nominal wage w_t (i.e. $a^x > 0$) show the same ranking as w_t:

$$(35) \qquad \left.\frac{\Delta x_t}{\Delta\theta_t}\right|_3 < \left.\frac{\Delta x_t}{\Delta\theta_t}\right|_2 < \left.\frac{\Delta x_t}{\Delta\theta_t}\right|_4 < \left.\frac{\Delta x_t}{\Delta\theta_t}\right|_1$$

for $x = (w - p)$, $(w - p^I)$, e, p, and p^I.

Note that the reaction of these endogenous variables in the case of nominal wage rigidity lies between that generated under policy rule 1 and policy rule 2. From the discussion in section 3 we know that real producer wages $(w_t - p_t)$ fall in the case of wage rule 3 and 2 and will rise under wage rule 1. For the case of rigid nominal wages the direction of change is ambiguous.

Real consumer wages $(w_t - p_t^I)$ are stabilized under policy 1 and decline under either policy.

For the endogenous variables x_t depending negatively upon the nominal wage w_t (i.e. $a^x < 0$) the ranking is reversed so that in equation (35) any "$<$" sign has to be replaced by a "$>$" sign:

$$(36) \qquad \left.\frac{\Delta x_t}{\Delta\theta_t}\right|_3 > \left.\frac{\Delta x_t}{\Delta\theta_t}\right|_2 > \left.\frac{\Delta x_t}{\Delta\theta_t}\right|_4 > \left.\frac{\Delta x_t}{\Delta\theta_t}\right|_1$$

for $x = l$, n, y, v', z, s, and $(p^n - p)$.

Under wage rule 1 the restrictive effects of a θ_t-shock on employment l_t, imported raw materials n_t, real value added v'_t, real income y_t, and domestic gross output z_t are aggravated by a rise in the nominal wage w_t required for stabilizing the real consumer wage $(w_t - p_t^I)$. Under wage rule 2 these effects are attenuated by the fall in the nominal wage necessary for keeping employment constant. Thus in the case of constant nominal wages (wage rule 4) the new equilibrium values of the variables listed in (36) will be lower than under wage rule 2 but higher than under wage rule 1.

In terms of the graphical analysis carried out in section 3 these results imply that E_{flex} lies

a) between B and C provided that $(\gamma_1 \Phi_1 - \gamma_2 \delta\Phi_3) > 0$

b) to the left of B if $(\gamma_1 \Phi_1 - \gamma_2 \delta\Phi_3) < 0$.

5. *Conclusions*

This paper has examined the effects of an increase in the real foreign price of imported materials on a small open economy. For this purpose we have generalized a model by Marston and Turnovsky (1983, 1985) which analyzes the implications of three different targets of wage policy (stabilization of real consumer wages or employment or real income) by adding the case of rigid nominal wages.

The following conclusions emerge from the analysis:

Under the three targets of wage policy investigated by Marston and Turnovsky the responses of real variables to a foreign material price shock are completely independent of the exchange rate regime. Under nominal wage rigidity, on the other hand, the economy's response depends on whether the exchange rate is fixed or flexible.

A rise in the foreign price of raw materials has its most restrictive effect on output and employment when nominal wages are rigid, exchange rates are fixed and the elasticity of substitution between imported materials and domestic value added is low.

When nominal wages are rigid but exchange rates are flexible, domestic output falls, but by less than under fixed rates. The output decline is, however, more pronounced than under a policy that stabilizes employment.

Comparing nominal wage stickiness under flexible exchange rates with a policy of stabilizing real consumer wages does not show clear results as long as the elasticity of substitution between imported materials and domestic value added is significantly smaller than unity. In this situation the ranking of the two cases depends on the parameters of the money demand function. If the interest elasticity of the demand for money is not "too high", domestic output and real income will decline less than under a wage policy of stabilizing real consumer wages, but more than under a policy of stabilizing employment.

APPENDIX I

The coefficients a^x of the reduced form (27') are:

x	a^x
$(w-p)$	$(1+\gamma_2)(ac_2 d_4 - c_1 \Phi_3)/D_4$
$(w-p^I)$	$(1+\gamma_2)\{c_2[a(d_2\delta + d_3) + (1-\delta)(1-d_1)] - c_1\Phi_3\}/D_4$
$(p^n - p)$	$-(1+\gamma_2)(1-a)c_2(1-d_1)/D_4$
l	$-(1+\gamma_2)[c_2 d_4 - c_1(d_1 - \sigma)]/D_4$
n	$-(1+\gamma_2)(1-a)[c_2 d_4 - d_1(c_1-\sigma) - c_2\sigma]/D_4$
z	$-(1+\gamma_2)(1-a)[c_2 d_4 - d_1 c_1(1-\sigma)]/D_4$
v'	$-(1+\gamma_2)(1-a)[c_2 d_4 - c_1(1-\sigma)]/D_4$
y	$-(1+\gamma_2)(1-a)[c_2(d_2\delta + d_3) - c_1(1-\sigma)]/D_4$
s	$-(1+\gamma_2)(1-a)c_2(1-d_1)/D_4$
e	$(1-a)c_2\{\gamma_1[d_2\delta + d_3 - (c_1/c_2)(1-\sigma)] - \delta(1-d_1)\}/D_4$
p	$(1-a)c_2\{\gamma_1[d_2\delta + d_3 - (c_1/c_2)(1-\sigma)] + (1-\delta)(1-d_1) + \gamma_2(1-d_1)\}/D_4$
p^I	$(1-a)c_2\{\gamma_1[d_2\delta + d_3 - (c_1/c_2)(1-\sigma)] + \gamma_2\delta(1-d_1)\}/D_4$

where $d_4 = (1-\delta)(1-d_1) + d_2\delta + d_3 > 0, \quad \Phi_3 = a(1-\sigma) - (1-d_1),$

$$D_4 = c_2[a(d_2\delta + d_3) + (1-d_1)(1-\delta)] - c_1\Phi_3 + \\ + (1-a)c_2\gamma_1[d_2\delta + d_3 - (c_1/c_2)(1-\sigma)] + \\ + \gamma_2\{c_2[a(d_2\delta + d_3) + (1-d_1)(1-a\delta)] - c_1\Phi_3\}$$

The coefficients b^x of the reduced form (27') are:

x	b^x
(w − p)	$-c_1\{\gamma_1[d_2\delta + d_3 + a(1-\delta)(1-\sigma)] - (1-\delta+\gamma_2)\Phi_3\}/D_4$
$(w - p^l)$	$-c_1(\gamma_1\Phi_1 - \gamma_2\delta\Phi_3)/D_4$
$(p^n - p)$	$c_2\{d_4 - (1-\gamma_1)(1-a)(d_2\delta + d_3) + \gamma_2[a(d_2\delta+d_3) + (1-d_1)(1-a\delta)]\}/D_4$
l	$-c_1\{(1-\gamma_1)\Phi_1 + \gamma_2[\Phi_1 + \delta(d_1 - \sigma)]\}/D_4$
n	$-\{\sigma d_4 + (1-\gamma_1)(1-a)[(d_2\delta+d_3)(c_1-\sigma) + c_1(1-\sigma)(1-\delta)] + \gamma_2\{d_4[c_1(1-a)+\sigma a] + (1-a)[d_1(c_1-\sigma) + c_2\sigma]\}\}/D_4$
z	$-c_1\{\sigma d_4 + (1-\gamma_1)(1-\sigma)(1-a)[(1-\delta) + d_2\delta + d_3] + \gamma_2[(1-a+a\sigma)d_4 + (1-a)d_1(1-\sigma)]\}/D_4$
v'	$-c_1\{d_4 + (1-\gamma_1)(1-a)(1-\delta)(1-\sigma) + \gamma_2[d_4 + (1-a)(1-\sigma)]\}/D_4$
y	$-c_1\{\Phi_1 + \gamma_2[d_2\delta + d_3 + (1-\sigma)(1-a\delta)]\}/D_4$
s	$c_1[(1+\gamma_2)\Phi_3 + \gamma_1(1-a)(1-\sigma)]/D_4$
e	$c_1\{\delta\Phi_3 + \gamma_1[d_2\delta + d_3 + (1-\sigma)(1-a\delta)]\}/D_4$
p	$-c_1\{(1-\delta)\Phi_3 - \gamma_1[d_2\delta + d_3 + a(1-\delta)(1-\sigma)] + \gamma_2\Phi_3\}/D_4$
p^l	$c_1(\gamma_1\Phi_1 - \delta\gamma_2\Phi_3)/D_4$

where $\Phi_1 = (1-\delta)(1-\sigma) + d_2\delta + d_3 > 0$

APPENDIX II

It is easily verified that

$$a^x < 0 \quad \text{for} \quad x = (p^n - p) \text{ and } s$$

The condition

$$\text{(AII.1)} \qquad (d_2 \delta + d_3) > (c_1 / c_2)(1 - \sigma)$$

which is equivalent to the assumption made in Table II of Marston and Turnovsky (1983) that $D_3 > 0$ is sufficient for

$$a^x > 0 \quad \text{for} \quad x = (w - p), \ (w - p^I), \ p, \text{ and } p^I$$

and

$$a^x < 0 \quad \text{for} \quad x = v', \ y, \ l, \text{ and } z$$

$a^n < 0$ if and only if

$$\text{(AII.2)} \quad (d_2 \delta + d_3) > (c_1 / c_2)(1 - \sigma) + (1 - d_1)[c_2 \delta - (1 - \sigma)] / c_2$$

$a^e > 0$ if and only if

$$\text{(AII.3)} \qquad (d_2 \delta + d_3) > (c_1 / c_2)(1 - \sigma) + (\delta / \gamma_1)(1 - d_1)$$

(AII.3) is equivalent to the assumption that the slope of the aggregate demand curve z^d is smaller than that of the LM-curve in Fig. 3. Note that the conditions (AII.3) and $\gamma_1 \leqslant 1$ are sufficient for the validity of (AII.2).

APPENDIX III

The reaction of the nominal wage w_t to a transitory θ_t-shock under wage rule i (i = 1, 2, 3) is given by

$$\left. \frac{\Delta w_t}{\Delta \theta_t} \right|_1 = \frac{c_1 (\gamma_1 \Phi_1 - \gamma_2 \delta \Phi_3)}{(1 + \gamma_2)\{c_2 [\alpha (d_2 \delta + d_3) + (1 - \delta)(1 - d_1)] - c_1 \Phi_3\}}$$

$$\left.\frac{\Delta w_t}{\Delta \theta_t}\right|_2 = - \frac{c_1 \{(1-\gamma_1)\Phi_1 + \gamma_2 [\Phi_1 + \delta (d_1 - \sigma)]\}}{(1+\gamma_2)[c_2 d_4 - c_1 (d_1 - \sigma)]} < 0$$

$$\left.\frac{\Delta w_t}{\Delta \theta_t}\right|_3 = - \frac{c_1 \{\Phi_1 + \gamma_2 [d_2 \delta + d_3 + (1-\sigma)(1-\alpha\delta)]\}}{(1+\gamma_2)(1-\alpha)[c_2 (d_2 \delta + d_3) - c_1 (1-\sigma)]} < 0$$

It can be shown that $(\Delta w_t / \Delta \theta_t)|_3 < (\Delta w_t / \Delta \theta_t)|_2 < (\Delta w_t / \Delta \theta_t)|_1$.

REFERENCES

W. BRANSON - J. ROTEMBERG (1980), "International Adjustment with Wage Rigidities", *European Economic Review*, 13 (3), pp. 309-332.

K. BRUNNER - A. CUKIERMAN - A.H. MELTZER (1980), "Stagflation, Persistent Unemployment, and the Permanence of Economic Shocks", *Journal of Monetary Economics*, 6 (4), pp. 467-492.

E.R. BERNDT - D.O. WOOD (1979), "Engineering and Econometric Interpretations of Energy-Capital Complementarity", *American Economic Review*, 69, pp. 342-355.

M. BRUNO - J. SACHS (1981), "Supply versus Demand Approaches to the Problem of Stagflation", in H. Giersch (ed.), *Macroeconomic Policy for Growth and Stability*, Institut für Weltwirtschaft, Universität Kiel.

M. BRUNO - J. SACHS (1985), *Economics of Worldwide Stagflation*, Harvard University Press, Cambridge, Massachusetts.

J. DREZE - F. MODIGLIANI (1981), "The Trade-Off between Real Wages and Employment in an Open Economy (Belgium)", *European Economic Review*, 15 (1), pp. 1-40.

R.P. FLOOD - N.P. MARION (1982), "The Transmission of Disturbances under Alternative Exchange Rate Regimes with Optimal Indexing", *Quarterly Journal of Economics*, 97, pp. 43-66.

H. FRISCH (1985), "Real and Nominal Shocks in an Open Economy Model with Wage Contracts", *Giornale degli Economisti e Annali di Economia*, 7-8, pp. 347-373.

J.A. GRAY (1976), "Wage Indexation: A Macroeconomic Approach", *Journal of Monetary Economics*, 2, pp. 221-235.

R.C. MARSTON (1984), "Real Wages and the Terms of Trade: Alternative Indexation Rules for an Open Economy", *Journal of Money, Credit, and Banking*, 16, pp. 285-301.

R.C. MARSTON (1985), "Stabilization Policies in Open Economy", in R.W. Jones - P.B. Kenen (eds.), *Handbook of International Economics* - Vol. II, North-Holland, Amsterdam, chapter 17, pp. 859-916.

R.C. MARSTON - S.J. TURNOVSKY (1983), "Imported Materials Prices, Wage Policy, and Macroeconomic Stabilization", *NBER Working Paper* No. 1254.

R.C. MARSTON - S.J. TURNOVSKY (1985), "Imported Materials Prices, Wage Policy, and Macroeconomic Stabilization", *Canadian Journal of Economics*, 18, pp. 273-284.

R.A. MUNDELL (1963), "Capital Mobility and Stabilization Policy under Fixed and Flexible Exchange Rates", *Canadian Journal of Economics and Political Science*, 29, pp. 475-485.

J. NIEHANS (1984), "International Monetary Economics", The Johns Hopkins University Press, Baltimore, chapter 12, pp. 245-265.

E.S. PHELPS (1978), "Commodity-Supply Shock and Full-Employment Monetary Policy", *Journal of Money, Credit, and Banking*, 16, pp. 285-301.

J. SACHS (1980), "Wages, Flexible Exchange Rates, and Macroeconomic Policy", *The Quarterly Journal of Economics*, pp. 731-746.

T.J. SARGENT (1979), *Macroeconomic Theory*, Academic Press, New York.

S.J. TURNOVSKY (1981), "Monetary Policy and Foreign Price Disturbances under Flexible Exchange Rates", *Journal of Money, Credit, and Banking*, 13, pp. 156-176.

S.J. TURNOVSKY (1983), "Wage Indexation and Exchange Market Intervention in a Small Open Economy", *Canadian Journal of Economics*, 16, pp. 574-592.

GPSR Compliance

The European Union's (EU) General Product Safety Regulation (GPSR) is a set of rules that requires consumer products to be safe and our obligations to ensure this.

If you have any concerns about our products, you can contact us on ProductSafety@springernature.com

In case Publisher is established outside the EU, the EU authorized representative is:

Springer Nature Customer Service Center GmbH
Europaplatz 3
69115 Heidelberg, Germany

Batch number: 10726013

Printed by Printforce, the Netherlands